AMERICAN POLICY IN SOUTHERN AFRICA:

The Stakes and the Stance

Edited by René Lemarchand
Contributors:

Gerald J. Bender
Larry Bowman
R. Hunt Davis, Jr.
Jennifer Davis
William J. Foltz
Allen Isaacman
René Lemarchand

Edgar Lockwood
Tilden J. Lemelle
Winston P. Nagan
Ntajala Nzongola
Stephen R. Weissman
Martin Weil

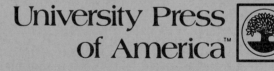

University Press of America

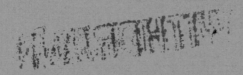

AMERICAN POLICY IN SOUTHERN AFRICA:

The Stakes and the Stance

Edited by Rene Lemarchand

Contributors:

Gerald J. Bender
Larry Bowman
R. Hunt Davis, Jr.
Jennifer Davis
William J. Foltz
Allen Isaacman
Rene Lemarchand

Edgar Lockwood
Tilden J. Lemelle
Winston P. Nagan
Ntajala Nzongola
Stephen R. Weissman
Martin Weil

University Press
of America™

Copyright © 1978 by

University Press of America, Inc.™

4710 Auth Place, S.E., Washington, D.C. 20023

ISBN: 0-8191-0401-9

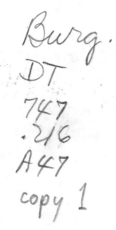

Library of Congress Catalog Card Number: 77-18582

TABLE OF CONTENTS

iii

PART THREE: THE POTENTIAL SIGNIFICANCE OF U.S. BLACK CONSTITUENCIES

PART FOUR: THE USE AND MISUSE OF SECRECY

CONCLUSION

NOTES ON CONTRIBUTORS

1. LARRY BOWMAN:
   Associate Professor of Political Science at the University of
   Connecticut. Author of Politics in Rhodesia: White Power in an
   African State (1973). Has contributed articles to International
   Affairs, The Jornal of Commonwealth Political Studies, International
   Studies Quarterly Africa Report.

2. R. HUNT DAVIS, JR.:
   Associate Professor of History at the University of Florida.
   His most recent articles include "John L. Dube: A South African
   Exponent of Booker T. Washington," Journal of African Studies (Winter,
   1975/76), and "Charles T. Loram and an American Model for African
   Education in South Africa," African Studies Review (September, 1976).
   Author of Bantu Education and the Education of Africans in South Africa
   (1972).

3. JENNIFER DAVIS:
   Research Director for the American Committee on Africa and the
   African Fund.

4. WILLIAM J. FOLTZ:
   Associate Professor of Political Science and Chairman of the
   Council on African Studies at Yale University. His publications include From French West Africa to the Mali Federation (1964) and
   various shorter studies of international and communal conflict.

5. ALLEN ISAACMAN:
   Professor of History and Afro-American Studies at the University
   of Minnesota, and Associate of the Centro de Estudos Africanos at the
   Universidade Eduardo Mondlane of Maputo, Mozambique. Publications
   include Africanization of a Portuguese Institution: The Zambesi
   Prazos 1750-1902 (1972), and The Tradition of Resistance in Mozambique
   (1976). Recipient of the Herskovits Award in 1973.

6. RENÉ LEMARCHAND:
   Professor of Political Science at the University of Florida
   (Gainesville). Publications include Political Awakening in the Former
   Belgian Congo (1964) and Rwanda and Burundi (1970). Editor and Co-
   author of African Kingships in Perspectives (1977). Recipient of
   the Herskovits Award in 1971.

7. EDGAR LOCKWOOD:
   Director of the Washington Office on Africa, which is jointly
   sponsored by several Protestant denominations and the American Committee
   on Africa to report on and influence U.S. policy toward Southern
   Africa. He has written articles for Issue and Christianity and
   Crisis and a preface to the Kissinger Study of Africa. He and Christine
   Root write and edit the quarterly Washington Notes on Africa and
   contribute a monthly column to Southern Africa.

GERALD J. BENDER

Lecturer in the Department of Political Science, UCLA. Has published several chapters in books and contributed articles to various journals including Foreign Policy, International Security, Comparative Politics, Western Political Quarterly, Issue, Revue francaise d'etudes politiques africaines, Africa Today. Author of Angola Under the Portuguese: The Myth and the Reality (1978).

8. TILDEN J. LEMELLE:
    Chairman of the Department of Black and Puerto Rican Studies at Hunter College of the City University of New York. Publications include "The Future of Race in International Relations", Journal of International Affairs (Fall 1971), "Race, International Relations, US Foreign Policy and the African Liberation Struggle", Journal of Black Studies (September 1972). Co-editor of Race Among Nations (1970), editor of Studies in Race and Nations from 1969 to 1972, and currently one of the Senior Editors of Africa To-Day.

9. WINSTON P. NAGAN:
    Associate Professor of Law at the University of Florida. Born in South Africa. Publications include "The Black American Reaction to Apartheid" Issue (Fall 1974); "Notes on the Statutory Definition of Terrorism", in Law in American Society: Journal of the National Center for Law-Focussed Education (1973). He has contributed articles to the Rutgers Law Review, the DePaul Law Review, the Valparaiso Law Review, and The New African.

10. NZONGOLA-NTALAJA:
    Associate Professor of Political Science at Atlanta University. He is the author of "The Bourgeoisie and the Revolution in the Congo", Journal of Modern African Studies, VIII, 4 (1970).

11. STEPHEN R. WEISSMAN:
    Associate Professor of Political Science at the University of Texas at Dallas. Author of American Foreign Policy in the Congo 1960-1964 (1974). Has contributed articles on Zaire and International Politics to The Journal of Modern African Studies and Nation, and articles on urban social policy and inter-governmental relations in the US to Polity, the Western Political Quarterly and Impact. Has served as urban policy consultant for Stanford Research Institute and Marshall Kaplan, Gans and Kahn Inc.

12 MARTIN WEIL:
    Professor of Political Science, University of California at Los Angeles.

INTRODUCTION

The current crisis in Southern Africa is more than just another test
case for American foreign policy; it signals a change of historic significance
in the overall balance of forces in the African Continent, and because of the
moral and racial issues involved -- not to mention the economic interests at
stake -- it is bound to engage the emotional commitments of a large number of
Americans. The impending choices confronting American policy-makers are between
expedience and morality, between our interests as a nation and the interests
of others as nations and nationalities, between the claims of oppressed majorities and the counterclaims of oppressive minorities. As we seek to attune
our commitments and responsibilities to the regnant theme of human rights we
are made all the more aware of the moral implications of these choices -- and
of the fact that they may be informed by ethical principles that are not
universally shared.

In Africa more than anywhere else in the world the pathways to racial justice
and propriety are tortuous and strewn with countless obstacles. The end is
not yet in sight. Seen through the fog of guerilla warfare and racial strife, the

last bastions of white supremacy may seem about to cave in, ripped apart
by bullets and explosives but also by other missiles -- by the determination
of black Africans to control their own destinies and by the cumulative pressures emanating from East and West. Nonetheless, the ultimate outcome of
the struggle is anyone's guess. Whether this rending process will bring any
hope of redemption for the white minorities of Rhodesia and South Africa,
and any hope of compromise between moderate and extremists at both ends of
the racial spectrum, is an open question. And so, also, is the shape of
the polities that will eventually emerge from the drastic restructuring of
race relations. If the ultimate consequences of the widening white-black
confrontations are impossible to predict this is in part because the responses
of the superpowers and their allies to the evolving shape of racial conflict
are equally hard to ascertain. While everyone seems to agree that Americans
are currently being faced with "critical choices", how these choices will be
perceived by US decision-makers, through what policies they will be implemented,
and with what degree of consistency these will be pursued are questions about
which one can only speculate.

This book represents a collective effort to come to grips with these
questions. By offering a critical assessment of past US policies towards
specific territories, and through analytical discussions of the forces which
impinge on the shaping of our African policies, it seeks to enhance our comprehension of current developments and at the same time sharpen our awareness of the economic, social and political parameters within which our foreign
policy choices are made. Above all, it seeks to convey to the reader a sense
of moral concern about the immediate and long range implications of our policies
toward Southern Africa.

The contributions to this volume originated from a conference on Southern

Africa organized at the University of Florida in the Spring of 1976, under
the joint auspices of the Social Science Research Council, the Center for
African Studies and the Institute of Black Culture of the University of
Florida. To this First Florida Regional Seminar on Africa were invited
a number of scholars, mostly political scientists, who had already established their names as authorities on Southern and Central Africa. As the Conference got under way it soon became apparent that the participants had a
great deal more to say to one another than was allowed by the format of the
Seminar, and that in spite of my effort to ensure a fairly broad coverage
of issues and areas there remained many gaps to be filled. These lacunae
became all the more evident in the light of the subsequent procession of
events in Rhodesia (Zimbabwe), South-West Africa (Namibia) and South Africa.
I therefore decided to solicit further contributions from qualified scholars
to deal with some of the issues that had been left out of our discussions.
The papers by Professors Weissman, Davis, Nagan and Bowman fall into this
category.

Although some of the papers which make up this book were written at
different points in time, and with different publics in mind, the end product
is not altogether lacking in coherence, unity and timeliness. The main
focus is on US-African relations, and more particularly on the significance
of recent events in Southern Africa for a comprehension of the foreign policy
options of the United States. The contributions have been selected with an
eye to the specific problems and issues that have arisen in individual states
as well as to the more global dimensions of our Africa policy. The first
of these concerns is made plain in the chapters included in Part One ("The
Regional Context: Issues and Alternatives"); the second is the subject of
Parts Two, Three and Four, dealing respectively with "The Incidence of
Strategic and Corporate Interests", "The Use and Misuses of Secrecy", and
"The Potential Significance of American Black Constituencies".

Predictably, the choice of themes and countries around which this book is contructed reveals a certain measure of arbitrariness. Some readers may wonder, for example, why neither Namibia nor the former High Commission Territories (Swaziland, Lesotho and Botswana) were included in the list of countries discussed in Part One. Others will question the wisdom of putting together a reader on the Africa policy of the United States which does not even deal with the mechanics and politics of decision-making in Washington. These omissions are in part due to limitations of space and pressures of time, but they also reflect a deliberate choice of priorities. What ultimately happens in Zimbabwe, Mozambique and South Africa is clearly of greater significance from the standpoint of US foreign policy, and in terms of the future of the people of Southern Africa, than developments in Swaziland and Namibia. Similarly, changing perceptions of the role of US corporate and strategic interests in Southern Africa are liable to have a far more decisive impact on the content and direction of US policies than in internal divisions and rivalries that have occasionally plagued the State Department, however significant these may have been in specific instances. These, at any rate, are the assumptions that have dictated our choice of topics and contributors.

In spite of obvious differences of ideological orientation, constitutional norms and social organization among the states that make up the geopolitical map of Southern Africa, they all share some elements of unity. Virtually all of the states discussed in this book, with the qualified exception of Zaire, have or continue to experience the worst form of white supremacy -- that which is associated with the presence of white settler communities fully committed to the principle of minority rule. The result has been everywhere to encourage the rise of radical militancy among African nationalists, even where nationalism has yet to acquire cohesiveness and organizational unity. And this in turn has produced an environment highly

congenial to the intrusion of East-West rivalries. The reason for this is
not simply that the structure of conflict in Southern Africa has created
the objective conditions that make it possible and desirable for Communist
states to establish effective links with the forces of African nationalism;
far more significant is the fact that African nationalism has consistently
been perceived by the spokesmen of white supremacy as a Trojan horse for the
penetration of international communism (whether of the Russian, Chinese or
Cuban variety), thus in effect triggering a self-fulfilling prophecy: as
long as all expressions of African nationalism are perceived as a Communist
threat in disguise, and treated as such, African nationalists are left with
no other alternative but to seek support from Communist states, or from
independent African states already gravitating in the orbit of Marxist influences.

Out of this situation have emerged some very complex processes of
interaction involving the spill-over of anti-regime forces across national
boundaries as well as various forms of alliances between insurrectionary
movements or factions and external powers. This multiplicity of political
actors and arenas, together with the intricacy of tactical linkages arising
therefrom, forms the basic common denominator of the case-studies included
in this book. At no other point in the history of decolonization has the
influence of political, military and economic forces external to Africa
assumed greater potential significance in shaping the future of Africans.
And never before has there been a wider range of opportunities for Americans
to demonstrate their collective commitment to racial justice.

There is hardly any need to stress the timeliness of the issues raised
in this volume; nor is there any point in emphasizing the advantage of a
broader perspective on current issues than is usually afforded through the
press. Suffice it to note that our main purpose here is to present the

reader with analyses in depth of the central issues confronting US policy-
makers, and in so doing contribute to a more dispassionate judgement of the
dilemmas that have been forced upon us by the current crisis. This is obviously not the only source to which the intelligent reader may turn for
up-to-date information on Southern Africa; nor is it the most exhaustive from
the standpoint of its subject matter.* My chief concern in preparing this
volume has been to pose what seemed to me to be the right questions, and while
some may disagree with me as to what constitutes the "right questions" I would
like to think that the answers have contributed in a meaningful way to a deli-
neation of the basic choices facing American foreign policy in Southern Africa.

As one reflects on the mixture of equivocation, indifference and sheer
wrongheadedness that have characterized our policies in Southern Africa, one is
impelled to look for explanations at different levels: How far have our policy
choices, or non-choices, been conditioned by our inability to reconcile our
conflicting African and European interests? How far should they be attributed
to Secretary Kissinger's peculiarly Manichaean vision of Africa as an arena for
East-West rivalries in which the forces of African nationalism are reduced to the
status of mere epiphenomena? Or does the root of our troubles lie in a gross
exaggeration of the staying power of white minorities, and if so, how can we
explain this appalling misreading of the African situation?

Again, further questions come to mind: Should the protection of our
economic and strategic interests in Southern Africa take precedence over the

---

*For additional information on the issues discussed in this volume, see in
particular US Policy Towards Southern Africa (Hearings before the Subcommittee
on African Affairs of the Committee on Foreign Relations of the US Senate,
Washington: 1976); Gwendolyn Carter and Patrick O'Meara, eds., Southern
Africa in Crisis (Bloomington and London: 1977); Frederick S. Arkhurst,
US Policy Toward Africa (New York, 1975); Chester A. Crocker, ed., The International Relations of Southern Africa (Washington, DC, 1974).

overriding moral and political imperatives of racial justice and majority rule? What role, if any, can American black constituencies play in giving a new direction to our Africa policy? How should one assess the significance of covert CIA activities in the formulation and implementation of our policies in Zaire and Angola? To what extent are current developments in Southern Africa once again susceptible to this form of US interventionism?

For most white South Africans and Rhodesians today these questions are of secondary significance compared to what they perceive as the central problem posed by the current thrust of US policies. The problem, in essence, is that the United States has no right to impose majority rule in Southern Africa unless it is willing and able to protect the rights of white minorities in conditions of majority rule. Though by no means academic, the question can only be settled once the larger issues have been resolved -- issues of racial justice and political equality -- and then not so much by unilateral American action as by a concerted effort between African whites and blacks. Ultimately the sheer recalcitrance of the white minorities to come to grips with the larger issues may well turn out to be a major liability if and when they decide to reach a tolerable modus vivendi with African majorities. How to convert this potential liability into a source of credibility and mutual trust ought to be the immediate concern of the white regimes in Rhodesia and South Africa. Only in a context of genuine depolarization can the United States make a meaningful contribution to the institutionalization of democratic pluralism in Southern Africa. And the initial step in this direction, if it ever materializes, will come not from Washington but from Pretoria.

* * * *

Two of the papers presented at the conference have since been published elsewhere: Professor William Foltz's ("Economic and Strategic Influences on

US policies in Southern Africa") and my own ("The CIA in Africa: How Central? How Intelligent?"), which have appeared respectively in The Journal of Politics, No. 1 (1977) and The Journal of Modern African Studies, No. 3 (1976). Professor Weil's piece ("Can American Blacks do for Africa what the Jews did for Israel?") is here reproduced with permission of the editors of Foreign Policy.

Neither the conference nor the book would have materialized without the generous financial support of the Social Science Research Council, The African Studies Center of the University of Florida, and the Institute of Black Culture of this same university. As Editor I wish to thank the participants to the First Florida Regional Seminar for their communications and kind cooperation in preparing this volume. Thanks are also due to Marilyn Gordon and Sharon Hill for their exemplary patience in transforming into legible typescript countless sheets of hieroglyphic notes and annotations. Finally I want to express my sense of gratitude to the Truman Institute of Hebrew University of Jerusalem for offering me a much needed leave of absence from the University of Florida in the fall of 1976, when I first began editing the materials presented here. It would be difficult to think of a more pleasant environment in which to undertake such a task. Needless to say, neither the Truman Institute nor the Social Science Research Council are responsible for the views expressed in this book.

PART ONE

THE REGIONAL CONTEXT: ISSUES AND ALTERNATIVES

Editor's Note

"That twisting line is the moving edge of history": A line that ran along Angola's northern border, down to the Zambeze river and eastward between Mozambique and Tanzania: A line which, thirteen years ago, Waldemar Nielsen described as a "symbolic battleline" drawn around eight countries or territories under white control "but under siege by all the revolutionary ideas and influences in the contemporary world". By the fall of 1975, a year and a half after the Portuguese coup, the defense perimeter of the white minorities had receded dramatically, leaving only Namibia, Rhodesia and South Africa as the last remaining enclaves of white supremacy. The suddenness of this transformation also marked the lowest ebb of our Africa policy. Never before had the chasm been more painfully evident between our proclaimed moral commitments and the actual conduct of our policy in Southern Africa.

The familiar flaws in our Africa policy emerge in full light from the discussions that follow: A continuing disposition to reduce the shifting balance of forces in Africa to the idiom of detente; a baffling misunderstanding of the revolutionary implications of African nationalism; a corresponding tendency to overestimate the staying power of white oligarchies; and, particularly in the case of the former Portuguese territories, a persistent inability to adjust our European interests to the exigencies of our presumptive African allies.

It is perhaps not a matter of coincidence that these defects became most glaringly evident during Secretary Kissinger's tenure in office: Few other Secretaries have displayed a crasser ignorance of African realities, a greater unconcern for the claims of African nationalists, and, one might add, a more impressive talent for radically shifting his ground once his previous policies proved unworkable -- for posing as the champion of "the struggle for (African) independence and racial equality" (to quote from his 1976 Lusaka speech) once it became clear that the previously held assumption that "the whites are here to stay" was no longer tenable.

As several of the contributors to this volume emphasize, there can be little doubt that the Kissinger era coincides with a decisive shift in US policy towards Africa, a shift in the direction of a far closer military, economic and political rapprochement with the racist regimes of Southern Africa than had been the case in previous years. This is amply borne out by the language of Option 2 of the much-quoted NSSM 39. Nor can there be any question that Kissinger bears full personal responsibility for the disastrous involvement of the CIA in the Angolan civil war -- a fact which helps to explain why the subsequent "Kissinger Agreement" on Rhodesia, aiming at a "rapid negotiated settlement leading to majority rule", was received with understandable skepticism by black African nationalists. If one can argue that Kissinger did more in six months to bring a Rhodesian settlement than the British were able to do in eleven years, it is equally pertinent to note that he probably did more than any other American Secretary to cast discredit upon American policy in Southern Africa, to the point of removing all credibility from his own subsequent policy moves, no matter how well-meaning these may have been.

"Foreign policy" Kissinger wrote in 1956, "is the art of weighing probabilities; mastery of it lies in grasping the nuances of possibilities." At the root of Kissinger's setbacks lies not only his failure to properly weigh the probability of African rule in Angola and Mozambique, but, even more importantly, his inability "to grasp the nuances of possibilities" offered by the emergence of the forces of African nationalism.

As the chapters on Angola and Mozambique demonstrate, the style and substance of Kissinger's African policy -- the first characterized by a heavy reliance on centralization and secrecy, the second by an almost pathological tendency to reduce all forms of African nationalism to some kind of adversary relationship between East and West -- were woefully inadequate to deal effectively with the rapidly changing context of African politics. Yet American policy in Southern Africa has also been conditioned by structural factors which in effect considerably narrowed the range of options available to Kissinger. As Nzongola points out, the coincidence of "class" interests between the Mobutu regime and the Holden faction in Angola, together with the leverage made available to Mobutu through American investments in Zaire, goes far in explaining Mobutu's decision to cast his lot with Holden Roberto as well as the American decision to actively support Mobutu's Angolan client. Again, as Isaacman and Davis show, American policy in Mozambique can hardly be dissociated from the expansion of American capitalism in the area, and the pressures originating from American business interests in Rhodesia and South Africa have been equally instrumental in shaping American policy towards the white minority regimes of Southern Africa. The perceived economic stakes were a fundamental element in the background of our diplomatic stance.

Under the Carter administration a decisive change is occuring in both the stakes and the stance. No longer is Communism seen as the ubiquitous menace behind the smokescreen of African nationalism; white racism is now perceived as the more serious threat posed to American interests in Southern Africa. What is at stake is no longer the preservation of a regional balance of power compatible with the postulate of detente, but the preservation of peace through racial justice. American opposition to apartheid thus implies a deliberate and concerted effort to effectively counter and ultimately help liquidate all traces of white supremacy in Southern Africa.

How to translate our commitment to peaceful change into reality is one of the most arduous tasks currently facing the Carter administration. That this may turn out to be an immensely more problematic undertaking than had been imagined even by our most optimistic policy-makers is made abundantly clear in Nagan's discussion. The struggle against white power, at any rate, will be the acid test of American diplomacy in Southern Africa. Although it would be premature to form as much as an interim judgement of the performance of the Carter administration on that score, it is not too early to convey to the reader a sense of perspective on the critical issues and alternatives confronting American policy-makers in Southern Africa.

CHAPTER I

US Policy Towards Mozambique, 1946-1976: "The Defense of
Colonialism and Regional Stability"

by

Allen Isaacman & Jennifer Davis

On June 25, 1975, Mozambique achieved full independence after a decade
of armed struggle and a long tradition of resistance dating back to the six-
teenth century. Since World War II the United States had actively supported
the repressive Salazar and Caetano regimes despite Washington's ostensible and
often articulated commitment to majority rule. This paper examines the broad
sweep of U.S. policy as well as the factors which placed the U.S. in direct
opposition to the aspirations of the Mozambican people. Although it focuses primarily on the period prior to Mozambican independence, we have attempted to
identify the subtle changes in U.S. policy which have occurred since the April
1974 coup in Portugal and how they are part of a larger American strategy to
contain radical change in Southern Africa.

I. U.S. Foreign Policy Toward Mozambique 1945-1974

Although the Atlantic Charter enshrined the principle of self-determination
the United States consistently ignored this fact when formulating policy on
Southern Africa, in general, and the Portuguese colonies, in particular. The
perceived strategic value of the Azores, and the militantly anti-communist
posture of the Salazar regime initially underlay both America's close relationship
with Lisbon and its willingness to accept uncritically Portugal's claim to the
"backwater" colonies of Mozambique, Angola, and Guinea-Bissau. Growing American
investment in the colonies and neighboring Zimbabwe, South Africa, and Namibia subsequently reinforced U.S. ties to the fascist government in Portugal.

The links between the Salazar regime and the United States were formalized
in 1943 despite Portugal's sympathies for the Axis powers. As part of this

agreement which enabled the United States to establish a temporary military base on the Azores, the American negotiators acknowledged Portuguese sovereignty over all her colonies.[1] The use of the Azores as leverage against any American deviation from this principle was a recurring theme in Portuguese-U.S. relations during the subsequent decades.

Under the tutelage of the Cold War warrior George Kennan, the United States embraced Portugal as a member of the free world and defined the Azores as critical to our national survival. Wrote one high level official, the "air defense of the United States is impossible unless the United States is in some sort of international arrangement giving the Air Force ready use at least of the geography needed for air bases and interception systems" which, he concluded, stretched from Kansas to Iceland, the Azores and Western Europe.[2] The logical extension of this convergence of strategic interests was Portugal's admission into NATO in 1949. Two years later United States-Portuguese relations were cemented in the Azores agreement which provided Washington with a military base in the South Atlantic.[3] Portugal's NATO affiliation and the diplomatic leverage which she acquired in exchange for an American base on the Azores carried profound implications for the subsequent liberation struggle.

As a NATO ally, Portugal benefited from a progressively expanding package of United States economic and military aid which strengthened the position of the repressive regime both at home and in the African colonies. United States military assistance jumped from 11 million escudos in 1951 to one billion 484 million escudos in 1955, an increase of more than 100 fold. Even more significant then the size of the increments was the fact that the aid constituted more than 40 percent of Portugal's total military budget.[4] For the entire period from 1949 until the outbreak of the Angolan revolution, the United States provided aid of more than $370 million, all but $90 million of which was for military assistance.[5]

By the eve of the liberation struggles which began in Angola in 1961, Portugal's antiquated military machine had been revamped and modernized with the United States and her NATO allies serving as principal suppliers. During this period, Washington provided more than 250 planes which formed the core of the Portuguese air force. The shipments included between 100 and 140 F-84 thunderjets and F-86 Sabre jets, many of which were deployed in the colonies throughout the early phase of the conflict. In addition, Washington contributed two warships, a large though indeterminant number of jeeps and a variety of light weapons.[6]

The Salazar regime also benefited from the unyielding diplomatic support of the United States throughout the Truman and Eisenhower administrations. Such senior policy-makers as Ambassador George Kennan and Secretaries of States Dean Acheson and John Foster Dulles publicly defended the totalitarian regime and on numerous occasions reiterated Portugal's right, indeed her obligation, to retain control of her colonies euphemistically known as "overseas provinces.' In the preface to a book written by the Portuguese Foreign Minister Franco Nogueira defending Portuguese colonialism, Dean Acheson enthusiastically endorsed Lisbon's efforts to "create a multi-racial society."[7] George Kennan was even more blunt in his defense of Portugal, a position which he reiterated as late as 1971.

> The situation in the great Portuguese territories of Angola and
> Mozambique differs fundamentally from that prevailing in South
> and South West Africa in that the central issue is not that of .
> race. . . . Neither the personal observations of a detached visitor
> nor the literature of unbiased scholars who addressed themselves
> to Portuguese-African affairs afford much confirmation for such
> allegations.[8]

The "objective" scholars to whom Kennan referred represented a small but influential group of academics who helped to popularize the myth of lusotropicalism.[9]

Lisbon's academic allies in this country claimed that the unique absence of racism among the Portuguese people enabled them to create a harmonious relationship with Africans living in Mozambique, Angola and Guinea-Bissau.[10] Among the most prominent academics who promoted this discredited concept was D. M. Abshire, director of Georgetown University's Center for Strategic and International Affairs. His "objectivity," however, is particularly suspect in light of the racial and cultural arrogance which is manifest throughout his writings,[11] as well as the Center's close relationship with the Department of State.

The rationale for United States policy provided by these scholars, as well as their Brazilian and Portuguese counterparts, was premised upon the interlocking proposition of racial egalitarianism and Lisbon's self-legitimating claim that Mozambique, Angola and Guinea-Bissau were not colonies but "overseas provinces." This legal fiction, which Lisbon first advanced in 1951, was clearly designed to thwart United Nation investigations of oppressive conditions within the colonies. By adopting such a posture, moreover, Portugal was able to claim that these regions did not fall within the definition of Article #73 of the U.N. Charter and that she was, therefore, not obliged to take measures which would facilitate their ultimate independence.[12]

Between 1955 and 1960, as the movement for self-determination and independence spread across Africa, a number of Third World and Socialist nations at the U.N. challenged Portugal's claim that Mozambique and the other Portuguese territories in Africa were overseas provinces. They argued that Mozambicans lacked full Portuguese citizenship, and were simply an oppressed majority whose social and economic position was considerably inferior to that of the white settlers. Throughout the debates, the United States abstained or opposed every measure which challenged the prevailing Portuguese interpretations or implied any criticism of

Lisbon's policy in Africa. As late as 1959 Washington refused to endorse the
principle that Portugal had an obligation to provide relevant agencies of the
United Nations with information about the colonies--a resolution which won overwhelming approval.[13]

Even the outbreak of the Angolan revolution in March 1961 brought only
a slight and temporary shift in United States policy--despite the hopes raised by
Kennedy's accession to the White House. Adlai Stevenson, U.S. Ambassador to the
U.N., speaking at the first Security Council meeting after the March 1961 rising,
said that he felt sure that "Portugal recognizes that it has a solemn obligation
to undertake the systematic and rapid improvement of the people of its territories."
He also spoke of the need to avoid a Congo situation by "step-by-step planning"
of change.[14]

The following month the U.S., stepping slightly ahead of the United Kingdom
and France, its normal policy allies, voted for General Assembly Resolution 1605
which called on the Portuguese government to introduce reforms leading to the
"transfer of all powers to the people of these territories . . . without any
conditions . . . or distinctions . . . in order to enable them to enjoy complete
independence and freedom." And in January 1962 the U.S. voted for Resolution
1742 which affirmed the right to "self-determination and independence" and condemned
Portuguese "repressive measures" in Angola. But even then the U.S. delegation
spent much energy attempting to water down the resolutions, raising arguments
against the use of "repressive" as "too strong" and "unwarranted," despite strong
evidence of Portuguese violence. Further, the U.S. was unhappy about the inclusion of "independence," arguing that possibly the peoples of the territories
would choose to continue a close association with Portugal, thus the United States
should not prejudge the situation.[15] This semantic obfuscation indicated that

the United States' public commitment to majority rule, tenuous at best, was already in the process of reevaluation. In light of the expiration of the Azores agreement in December of that year and Portugal's militantly anti-communist posture, Pentagon officials urged a rapprochement with Lisbon.[16] Powerful Southern Senators such as Ellender of Louisiana urged a similar tactic arguing that the "natives" were "incapable of self-government."[17] Their position ultimately prevailed.

At the United Nations American officials warned against "destructive criticism of Portugal" and urged that Lisbon be given more time to peruse the reforms which it had purportedly initiated in the aftermath of the 1961 Angolan uprising. This theme of Portuguese reform was echoed by Ambassador Adlai Stevenson at the Security Council Debates on the Portuguese territories. Having stressed his belief in peaceful change, he continued:

> The core of the problem is the acceptance and the application of the right of self-dtermination . . . Mr. Nogueira, the Foreign Minister of Portugal, has contended that the criteria and procedure defined by the United Nations cannot . . . be considered the only criteria for a valid and real self-determination. I hope that he does not fear that any of us are seeking to deprive Portugal of its proper place in Africa. . . . Portugal's role in Africa will be ended only if it refuses to collaborate in the great and inevitable changes which are taking place. If it does collaborate, its continuing role is assured, and I for one, sitting here, on my own behalf, would like to express with pride the gratitude of my Government for the progress that Portugal is attempting to make to improve the conditions of life among the inhabitants of its territories.[18]

Thus, by the end of 1962, it had become evident that Washington was prepared to make greater rhetorical commitments to the principle of self-determination, but there would be no substantial departure from earlier policy. From that year on the United States consistently refused to support any resolution which moved beyond declaratory language and attempted action to achieve a self-determination for the people of Mozambique or the other Portuguese colonies.

The U.S. voted "No" when the General Assembly called on all member states to "refrain forthwith from offering the Portuguese government any assistance that would enable it to continue its repression of the peoples of the territories under its administration and for this purpose to take all measures to prevent the sale and supply of arms and military equipment to the Portuguese government."[19] The U.S. voted "No" when the General Assembly asked the Security Council to take appropriate measures, including sanctions, to secure Portugal's compliance with the demand for the granting of freedom and independence to its colonies.[20] The U.S. voted "No" when the General Assembly condemned the role of foreign economic interests which act as "an impediment to the African people in the realization of their aspirations to freedom and independence" and called on all member states to "prevent such activities on the part of their nationals."[21]

American diplomatic efforts outside of the U.N. also reflected a growing rapprochement with Portugal. Although Undersecretary of State George Ball was ostensibly sent to Lisbon in 1963 to convince the Salazar regime of the need to initiate the process of self-determination, he returned to Washington having uncritically accepted the "tribal" nature of the insurrections and recommended that the United States adopt "a tough-minded but not unsympathetic understanding of her [Portugal's] problems and responsibilities."[22] Admiral Anderson, former U.S. Ambassador to Portugal, was unequivocal in his support for the Portuguese colonial regime. Upon returning from a trip to Mozambique and Angola early in 1964 he declared that he was "tremendously impressed" by the progress and racial harmony which he observed in Portugal's overseas territories.[23]

The Ambassador's statement clearly underscored the improved relations between Lisbon and Washington, and precipitated a sharp rebuttal from the Central Committee of FRELIMO. "The only conclusion which can be derived from these

official visits," noted the late FRELIMO President, Eduardo Mondlane, "is that
the United States of America cannot identify itself with our ideals for self-
determination and independence."[24] He concluded that the

> . . . activities of the United States of America are not only an
> obvious connivance with Portugal but also raise suspicisions of
> connivances with the imperialist government of the Republic of
> South Africa. . . . We can only believe that the United States of
> America wishes to reassure its ally, Portugal, of its sympathy
> and material support in sustaining Portuguese colonialism and im-
> perialism on the African continent. On the basis of the fact
> above, we are forced to conclude that when our people finally
> rise up to take arms against Portuguese imperialism, the United
> States of America, like the Republic of South Africa, will inter-
> vene against us in support of Portugal.[25]

His assessment would prove prophetic.

Throughout the remainder of the sixties, United States policy continued
to reflect an apparent contradiction between theory and practice. The rhetoric
spoke of a U.S. commitment to self-determination while simultaneously the
practice gave military, economic and diplomatic assistance to Portugal as a
NATO ally. In an effort to camouflage these obvious contradictions, United
States officials adopted the strategy of "communication and dialogue," stressing
the necessity for peaceful change and always assigning to Portugal itself the
central role in bringing about the desired changes.

Thus, in 1969, U.S. Ambassador Seymour M. Finger, speaking at a meeting
of the Preparatory Committee for the 10th Anniversary of the Declaration on the
Granting of Independence to Colonial Peoples and Countries, chided those who
attacked Portugal too fiercely:

> We recall that most of the members of the United Nations became in-
> dependent through peaceful means and, while such peaceful change
> remains possible--however slow it may be--we are convinced that
> such peaceful means are in the best interest of everyone concerned.
>
> Let us not proceed obstinately with tactics of the past--of
> repeating year after year resolutions which are known to be inef-
> fectual on the day they are adopted--of adopting resolutions based
> on myths such as the red herrings of foreign military bases and
> foreign economic investment. Such outworn shibbloeths cannot sub-

stitute for the hard thought we must all give to the solution of the remaining hard-core problems. Though it may appear elementary to say so, it would also be wise not to slander those countries whose cooperation is considered important in achieving the objectives of resolutions to be adopted. This does not mean that there cannot be legitimate and constructive criticism; indeed, there must be. But it does mean that we should keep our eye on the real problems and act responsibly in terms of the real interests of dependent peoples.[26]

A Department of State policy statement subsequently developed a similar theme:

> U.S. policy towards Portuguese Africa . . . supports the right of all peoples to self-determination. We believe Portugal's ability to accelerate the advancement of the peoples of its African territories both politically and economically ultimately will determine what role Portugal will continue to have in the African continent. Portugal's official policy of racial equality, in contrast to the institutionalized racial discrimination of South Africa, is an important factor which whill have a bearing in determining this future role, and hopefully will help ease tensions in the area.[27]

In fact, while the U.S. kept detecting signs of 'reform' and goodwill on the part of the Portuguese, oppression had been intensifying in all the colonies.

In 1964, under the leadership of FRELIMO, an armed struggle began in Mozambique--after long years of frustrating political protest which had been met only by implacable Portuguese repression. As the guerrilla war expanded, FRELIMO winning considerable support among the population and establishing increasing areas of control, Portuguese tactics grew increasingly harsh. Four hundred and forty thousand people were forcibly moved into aldeamentos (strategic hamlets) in an attempt to remove FRELIMO's base of support;[28] herbicides were used to destroy the food supplies;[29] villages were bombed or burned by troops who arrived in helicopters, destroyed everything in sight and flew out again;[30] serious attempts were made to discredit FRELIMO in the eyes of the people by the use of black troops, dressed in FRELIMO uniforms, who would descend on a village and wreak havoc.[31]

Not surprisingly, throughout this period Washington's lines of communications extended only as far as Lisbon. Tentative advances for assistance which FRELIMO is reported to have made in 1963 were quickly rebuffed.[32] As one expert noted, "insurgents requests for aid normally provoked defensive lectures about why the United States could not aid them without improperly interferring in another state's internal affairs but could aid their [incumbent] adversary without so interferring."[33] Moreover, United States officials in Mozambique privately accepted the official Salazar line that "FRELIMO was nothing but a bunch of communist-inspired terrorists who lacked a base of popular support."[34]

Nevertheless, the American government continued to adhere publicly to a position of "majority rule through peaceful change." In reality this commonly articulated cliche represented a betrayal of any theoretical commitment to the principles of self-determination because of its exclusion of any military form of struggle. It insured the perpetuation of the oppressive Salazar and Caetano regimes, which were unlikely to yield power voluntarily.

It is hard to reach any other conclusion in light of the military assistance Washington provided and the candid comments of such liberals as G. Mennon Williams, Undersecretary of State for African Affairs. At a meeting of newspaper officials in Chicago in 1963, he declared unabashedly that, "It is neither in our interest to see the Portuguese leave Africa, nor to curtail their influence out there."[35] The United States justified its military aid by arguing that it was merely satisfying its NATO commitments and that the material would only be used for the defense of Western Europe--a limitation which the Portuguese repeatedly rejected by advancing the fiction that the colonies were overseas provinces and vital to the defense of Western democracy.[36] In reality, United States officials made no effort to enforce the restrictions and in the face of indisputable evidence that

Lisbon used American war materials against the liberation forces,[37] the American representatives at the United Nations first denied the charges and then lamely attempted to assure all interested parties that the United States had received a promise from Lisbon that NATO weapons would not be employed in Angola.

Despite the partial arms embargo which the Kennedy administration imposed in 1961, the United States managed to provide a small but significant amount of military assistance as the colonial wars escalated. Among the weapons were thirty T-37C fighter planes which were particularly effective in counter-insurgency activity.[38] In 1963 Washington agreed to cover 50 percent of the funding for three Portuguese warships under an Export-Import Bank Loan agreement.[39] The United States also trained more than 2,000 military personnel in anti-guerrilla activities and the American military attaches stationed in Lisbon regularly visited Mozambique to advise Portuguese officials. In addition to this overt military assistance, the Central Intelligence Agency facilitated Lisbon's acquisition of twenty B-26 bombers for use against African liberation forces. At his Federal trial, John Hawke, an English mercenary, acknowledged that he "flew B-26 bombers to Portugal for use in their African colonies, and the operation was arranged through the State Department and the C.I.A."[41]

Throughout this period American capitalist interests, anxious to maintain stability throughout Southern Africa, staunchly supported the Salazar regime. Gulf's discovery of oil in Angola reinforced these links. Not only did the powerful corporation become an outspoken supporter of the colonial government, but the growing taxes and royalties paid to Lisbon (increasing from $61 million in 1972 to $392 million in 1974) eased the enormous strain on the Portuguese treasury which was allocating a substantial portion of the national budget to fight the colonial wars. Gulf's success also spurred a rash of exploratory investments by

American and multi-national petroleum corporations in Mozambique hoping to discover similar oil and natural gas deposits.[42]

The Nixon regime abandoned even the facade of sympathy for the aspirations of the Mozambican people in favor of an overt and staunchly pro-Salazar position. The most important indication of this shift came in 1971, when in a gesture of remarkable generosity, the U.S. made a series of unprecedented economic commitments totalling over $435 million to Portugal, as a quid pro quo for the formal extension of the Azores Pact until February 3, 1974. The U.S. had, in fact, continued to exercise its base rights on the island without any formal agreement for several years. Thus many observers saw the signing of the Pact as simply an excuse for offering massive new aid to Portugal, by this time heavily pressed on three war fronts in Africa.

Under the terms of the Azores Agreement, Washington made the following commitments:

-- $15 million in P.L. 480 agricultural commodities
-- the loan of a hydrographic vessel at no cost
-- $1 million for educational development programs
-- $5 million for drawing rights for non-military excess equipment
-- the waiver of MAAG support payments ($350,000 for the Military Assistance Advisory Group maintained by the U.S. in Lisbon)
-- $400 million of Import-Export (Exim) loans and guarantees for development projects.

The funds projected were out of all proportion to previous development commitments through the Exim Bank to either Portugal or Africa. The total of Exim loans to Africa in the whole period 1946-1970, for example, was less than $358 million.[43] From 1934 through 1971 Exim had only authorized loans of $105 million to Portugal, less than $50 million for the period from 1946-1970.[44]

This financial support came at a critical time for the Caetano regime faced with economic chaos and mounting internal opposition to the colonial wars.

The New York _Times_, hardly a champion of the liberation movements, commented in an editorial that this new pact will help Portugal meet the costs of its colonial wars to preserve the white minority in Angola, Mozambique, and Guinea-Bissau."[45]

In the face of FRELIMO's growing success,[46] Washington flagrantly violated its self-imposed arms embargo and provided critical military equipment to be used explicitly in Mozambique. Highest priority was placed on aircraft to ferry troops and supplies both from the metropole to Mozambique and within the besieged colony. Beginning in 1971, the United States government allowed direct sales of Boeing 727's, 737's and 707's to Lisbon. TAP and its Mozambican counterpart DETA were also allowed to purchase Boeing 707's and 737's. Initially, many of these sales were financed through loans from the Import-Export Bank.[47] The Portuguese privately acknowledged that its military chartered the TAP planes for transporting men and materials to Africa but the United States government, nevertheless, permitted the sales to continue. In June 1971 a Portuguese air force commander, Colonel Costa Maia, speaking in Angola, publicly confirmed the military role of these transports and declared that it would help to improve the morale of his troops.[48] Three months later, David Newsom, Undersecretary of State for African Affairs, refused to consider any ban on the sales of Boeing transports blithely noting, "Though these air and freight services can obviously carry military as well as civilian passengers, the sale of passenger transport planes to Portugal has not been deemed to come within the terms of our 1961 arms embargo."[49] In 1973 it was announced that TAP had purchased Boeing 747 jumbo jets to facilitate the redeployment of troops from the metropole to Mozambique and Angola.

The sale of jet transports directly to DETA was simply an extension of

Newsom's twisted logic and duplicity. Mozambican colonial officials could hardly

hide their glee. Shortly thereafter a contract was signed in which DETA and

another "commercial" airline agreed to perform military services for the occu-

pation army. Portuguese authorities hailed, "This wonderful example of cooper-

ation between civil and military elements."[50] Excerpts from an official report

capture the strategic significance of this arrangement.

> We cannot but stress the unusual event. The celebration of the
> contract by the DETA Mozambique Airlines and Empresa Mocambicana
> de Aviacao Commercial (EMAC), who will give the Military Region
> of Mozambique regular air transport on a charter basis.
>
> At the ceremony which took place in the Library of the Regional
> Military General, there were present the Commander-in-Chief of
> Armed Forces of Mozambique, Provincial Secretaries of Communications
> and Public Works, Directors of Railways, DETA and EMAC, many heads
> of services, Officers General and other high ranking armed forces
> officials.
>
> The Provincial Secretary of Communications and General Kaulza
> [Commander-in-Chief of the Portuguese army in Mozambique] spoke
> of the act, emphasizing the great importance of this coordination,
> expressed in the contract which they had signed.[51]

In addition to the jet transports, the United States exported light air-

craft and helicopters to Mozambique. These included a number of Rockwell Inter-

national Strike Commanders and a dozen Bell helicopters.[52] Washington defended

these sales, ostensibly to private firms, as purely commercial, despite evidence

that the Portuguese military was using such civilian aircraft against FRELIMO in

the north.[53] A mercenary pilot interviewed in the British Sunday _Times_ acknowl-

edged that, "At Nacala, a Portuguese military base, the [civilian] aircraft

registrations were removed by air force personnel. They put a washable paint over

the registration." After this camouflage, he continued, "we arrived at Nangololo,

we made a very steep approach to avoid being shot by the terrorists."[54] At that

time Nangololo was a newly established military base in the north which played a

central role in Lisbon's efforts to contain the liberation forces. Similarly, the Bell helicopters provided strategic support for the Cabora Bassa Dam project in Tete district.[55]

During the Nixon years United States exports of herbicides to Mozambique also increased dramatically. Between 1970 and 1972, for example, sales jumped from $28,000 to $413,000, an increase of 1500 percent.[56] The defoliants were ideally suited for spraying such broad-leafed plants as cassava, which is the primary crop in Mozambique. Despite the fact that U.S.-produced herbicides were discharged in northern Mozambique and that until 1970 these defoliants were on the State Department's munitions lists, American officials admitted that they exercised no licensing controls over the export of the lethal chemicals, except to Communist countries.[57]

During the Nixon administration the total American budget for training Portuguese military personnel doubled. Significant indications of the trend toward more direct support were provided by the tenfold increased in the number of Portuguese air force pilots trained by the United States in fiscal year 1971-72,[58] as well as the exchange of strategic tactical information between American and Portuguese commando experts at a Conference held in 1972.[59] This assistance was provided despite the Defense Department's admission that it had no control over where these Portuguese officers were ultimately deployed.[60]

As part of the Nixon-Kissinger "tilt," American corporations and their multi-national counterparts were encouraged to invest in Mozambique. The extent of official sympathy for the Portuguese colonial presence is clearly reflected in the annual assessments of economic opportunities in Mozambique for American investors published by the Department of Commerce. As late as 1973 they still saw Lisbon as the guardian of stability and security, gave complete credence to Portugal's claims about the nature of its rule, and saw the liberation movement only in terms of a disruptive force.

> Although it subscribes to racial equality and integration, Portugal
> continues under heavy criticism in the U.N. and elsewhere for ad-
> ministering Mozambique and her other African territories as overseas
> provinces permanently linked to Portugal, rather than granting them
> independence. Since 1964 Portuguese authority has been challenged
> by a relatively small but persistent nationalist guerrilla opposition
> in the frontier areas of the northern districts of Cabo Delgado and
> Niassa, and in the western districts of Tete--and more recently,
> adjacent areas of Beira and Vila Pery districts. Meanwhile, in ad-
> dition to military and social development activities in the war-
> affected areas, Portugal has fostered greater autonomy in Mozambique
> --which has been granted the designation of 'State of Mozambique'--
> and its First Legislative Assembly, elected in March 1973, had for
> the first time a non-white majority. Nevertheless, although security
> has been maintained in most of Mozambique, the costs of containing
> guerrilla warfare are considerable and continuing, with no immediate
> end in sight.[61]

At the vanguard of American capitalist expansion were the large oil

companies who received very generous concessions from Lisbon designed "to ex-

ploit the colonial economy of Mozambique."[62] Among the major petroleum firms

which engaged in exploratory operations were Hunt International, Sunray, Shell,

Skelly, Clark and Amoco, while Gulf Oil served as a distributing agent for

Sonarep--the principal Mozambican processor.[63] At the same time, Bethlehem

Steel received a mineral concession to operate in part of Tete district. United

States firms such as Caterpillar Tractor Company and General Electric provided

construction equipment and power grids, respectively, for the strategic Cabora

Bassa Dam.[64] Through the late '60's and early '70's, the United States ranked

on average as the seventh largest supplier to Mozambique and second largest im-

porter of Mozambican commodities.[65]

The increased political, military and economic assistance to the be-

leaguered Caetano regime taken together with growing United States investment

in South Africa estimated at over a billion dollars by 1972, our violation of

United Nation sanctions against Rhodesia through the Byrd Amendment, and our

adamant refusal to recognize, or even communicate with FRELIMO, constituted a

coherent Kissingerian policy outlined in Option Two of the leaked National
Security Council Study Memorandum #39 (NSSM 39).[66] This strategy was premised
upon the proposition that:

> The whites are here to stay and the only way that constructive
> change can come about is through them. There is no hope for the
> blacks to gain the political rights they seek through violence,
> which will only lead to chaos and increased opportunities for the
> communists. We can, by selective relaxation of our stance toward
> the white regimes, encourage some modification of their current
> racial and colonial policies and through more substantial economic
> assistance to the black states [a total of about $5 million
> annually in technical assistance to the black states] help to draw
> the two groups together and exert some influence on both for peace-
> ful change. Our tangible interests form a basis for our contacts
> in the region, and these can be maintained at acceptable political
> costs.[67]

This policy option, although not as overtly anti-Mozambican as others

that were advanced, including armed support for the minority regimes, was de-

signed to strengthen United States ties with anti-communist regional powers in

order to "stabilize Southern Africa"--a euphemism for continued United States

presence. Indeed, the overriding concern of Option Two was to encourage

"political arrangements short of majority rule." To this end, the plan called for

increased export of "dual purpose equipment"--which translated means war materials

which Washington could claim had a civilian function such as herbicides, defoliants,

helicopters, light airplanes and jet transports. Despite this covert policy

the United States periodically reaffirmed its public position in support of majority

rule through peaceful change. As late as September 1973, the Department of State

issued a report "supporting self-determination and the peaceful resolution of

political disputes." Toward this end, the position paper concluded, "we have

prohibited the export of U.S. arms for use in the Portuguese territories since

the outbreak of the first armed insurgency in Angola."[68]

II. The Portuguese Coup, Mozambican Independence and U.S. Foreign Policy: 1974
     to the Carter Administration

The April 1974 coup in Portugal, catalyzed by the collective success of
the liberation movements in the colonies, provided Washington with yet another
opportunity to redefine its policies toward Mozambique. Rather than unequivocally
supporting majority rule the United States adopted a low profile while covertly
supporting conservative elements during the five-month power struggle between
General Spinola and militant members of the Armed Forces Movement committed to
revolutionary change within Portugal and independence for the colonies.

In June, President Nixon and President Spinola met in the Azores--an
event given little publicity except by the South African press, which reported
from Lisbon: "President Antonio de Spinola jetted hom this week like a Caesar
triumphant. The moral and material support promised him by President Nixon can
now open the way to a more stable and prosperous Portugal which, in turn, should
enable the Portuguese leader to put an end to many of the doubts in the African
territories about a 'sell-out' to militant Black nationalism."[69] Throughout
the period from April to September, when Spinola was removed, U.S. officials
refrained from commenting on his transparent efforts to maintain a Portuguese
political and economic presence in Mozambique.[70]

Following the March 1974 congressional testimony of Paul O'Neil, Director
of the State Department Office on South African Affairs, in which he asserted
that "We do not, . . . feel that Portugal must be completely excluded from the
future of these areas."[71] Washington's silence can only be interpreted as reluctance to recognize the inevitability of Mozambican independence. As such,
American policy further alienated FRELIMO which felt compelled to reaffirm its
long-standing opposition to any neo-colonial arrangement.[72]

The objectives of FRELIMO are very clear: the total and complete independence of the Mozambican people and the liquidation of Portuguese colonialism. The Mozambican people are an entity quite distinct from the Portuguese people, and they have their own political, cultural and social personality which can only be realized through the independence of Mozambique.

We are not fighting to become Portuguese with black skins. We are fighting to affirm ourselves as Mozambicans without this meaning contempt for the Portuguese people or any other people. In this respect, FRELIMO reaffirms its wish to fully cooperate with all peoples in the world on a basis of independence, equality, respect and mutual interest.[73]

FRELIMO's concerns proved well founded. Although it had led the struggle against Portuguese colonial rule a number of splinter groups in exile as well as conservative Portuguese and Africans within Mozambique attempted to subvert the Mozambican revolution by presenting themselves as potential leaders on the eve of independence.[74] Reports circulated that the United States as well as other Western European countries were anxious to promote a moderate alternative to FRELIMO. According to Paulo Gumane, former president of COREMO, United States embassy officials in Zambia offered him financial assistance if he organized an anti-FRELIMO coalition within Mozambique.[75]

Within five months the National Coalition Party was founded as an alternative to FRELIMO. Its composition is revealing. Among its most prominent members were Gumane, Joanna Samiao, a coopted Mozambican member of the Portuguese parliament, and a number of prosperous European and African bureaucrats, traders and farmers.[76] Not surprisingly, the National Coalition Party maintained close ties to Spinola and the conservative elements who clearly sought to create a neo-colonial arrangement. The Party, however, lost whatever credibility it had after its association with reactionary white settlers who participated in the abortive coup in September-October 1974.[77] According to Gumane, this attempt to subvert FRELIMO had a long history, and he admitted that he had received funds from the

C.I.A. as early as 1962.[78]

The failure of the rightist coup in Mozambique and the removal of Spinola apparently convinced policy-makers in Washington that FRELIMO would prevail. It thus necessitated a shift in United States policy. Under the direction of the new Assistant Secretary for African Affairs, Donald Easum, Washington endorsed the process of decolonization and sought to open direct lines of communication with FRELIMO. His public statements that the United States would use its influence to precipitate change in Southern Africa were well received throughout the continent. In early November 1974, Easum met with FRELIMO President Samora Machel in Dar-es-Salaam. They discussed a number of issues including the possibilities of American aid to an independent Mozambique which would face severe economic problems.[79] After completing these discussions Easum flew to Maputo where he was the first foreign diplomat to meet with the newly formed transitional government. As a further indication of the United States' desire to normalize relations, the American Consul General in Lourenco Marques sent a telegram to Prime Minister Chissano reaffirming his government's purported commitment to majority rule.

> The policy of the United States toward the peoples of Africa has long been one of support for their self-determination, and thus the United States strongly supports the efforts of the Portuguese Government in the decolonization of its African territories. . . .
>
> The Government of the United States of America is hopeful that the friendship that has long existed between the people of the United States and the people of Mozambique will result in a relationship of increasing understanding and cooperation as Mozambique proceeds to independence.[80]

Such pronouncements notwithstanding, the United States took few concrete steps to improve relations with the transition government. Efforts to provide Mozambique with modest financial assistance failed to produce any tangible results. A five million dollar grant passed by the House Appropriations Committee, for example, was allowed to expire after FRELIMO officials indicated their reluctance to have an AID team visit their country.[81] Similarly, discussions to establish a scholarship fund to enable Mozambican students to study in the U.S. stalled as did negotiations to provide the former Portuguese colony with 16,000 metric tons of wheat.[82] Although the details of these negotiations are not public, it is clear that in the case of both the AID assistance and the fellowship program the transitional government felt that their potential for providing a base for subversion outweighed any short-term economic benefits.

The slight shift toward a more positive commitment to change in Southern Africa was short-lived. Forty-eight hours after returning from his African trip Easum was informed that Kissinger was removing him from his post. He had been too enthusiastic in his pledges of American support for majority rule.[83] In his place Kissinger selected Nathaniel Davis, a diplomat with no experience in Africa, who had recently been in the headlines for his role in the de-stabilization of the Allende government while he was Ambassador to Chile.[84]

The Davis appointment was universally condemned by African leaders. In an attempt to allay African hostility, Davis made a trip to Africa immediately after his confirmation in June 1975. He was in Dar-es-Salaam on the eve of Mozambican independence, reportedly anxious to attend the celebrations. In an unmistakable gesture FRELIMO invited neither Davis nor members of the U.S. consulate in Mozambique to the celebration. Indeed, the United States had isolated itself so badly from FRELIMO, that American officials in Mozambique tried unsuccessfully to persuade liberation support group members from the United States, who unlike their government had been invited to the ceremonies, to serve as "intermediaries" to the new government.[85]

The conspicuous absence of an official American delegation reflected FRELIMO's displeasure with the United States' unswerving support for the colonial regime. It also suggested a deterioration of the tenuous ties which had been established during Easum's discussions with President Machel and members of the transitional government. Several factors, including the United States' overtly hostile position toward the M.P.L.A. in Angola,[86] a growing anti-Mozambican propaganda campaign in the American press,[87] and the removal of Easum who represented a symbol of American moderation all contributed to this uneasy relationship.

Since independence the United States has done very little to improve the diplomatic climate. Official policy can best be described as low-keyed and distant. While Washington had no difficulty recognizing a variety of right-wing regimes overnight, it conspicuously deferred formal and diplomatic recognition of Mozambique for several months despite President Ford's independence day message to President Machel that "I am confident of a future in which our two people will work together in freedom, peace and security of all mankind."[88] Such lofty presidential proclamations notwithstanding, when Mozambique closed its border with Rhodesia in March 1976 in support of the United Nations' sanctions imposed on the Smith regime, the United States did not initially choose to join with Britain and the Commonwealth Nations in providing assistance to compensate her for the anticipated $50 million loss in revenue.[89] On the contrary, an extended and acrimonious debate occurred in the Congress when Senator Clarke and other liberals sought to include a $12.5 millian grant to Mozambique. Conservative Senators most notably James Allen of Alabama, took the opportunity to denounce the Mozambican government as a ruthless dictatorship and pawn of the Communists, while vehemently defending the Smith regime.[90] Allen threatened a filibuster and succeeded in getting the allocation withdrawn, although in the end a compromise was reached whereby the State Department was allowed to put the money together in piecemeal form.[91]   While Mozambique ultimately received the aid government leaders were very sensitive to the harsh attacks in Congress which certainly were not designed to improve relations between the two countries.[92]

Allen's outspoken criticism of Mozambique on the Senate floor was part of an orchestrated propaganda campaign designed to discredit the newly independent country. At the forefront were U.S. corporate interests anxious about investments in Southern Africa. Their sentiment was clearly articulated by the Executive Vice-President of the United States Industrial Council who vilified President Machel and demanded "that the United States employ its influence to sustain responsible orderly government and to oppose the expansion of revolutionary regimes." After all, he concluded, "Southern Africa is the mineral treasure house of the continent."[93] His words were echoed by a variety of reactionary organizations such as the Heritage Foundation. In a publication describing "the plight of Mozambique," the Foundation bemoaned the fact "neither the free enterprise system nor the basic philosophy of a free and open society has impressed Mozambique's FRELIMO leaders any more than they have those of Guine-Bissau, Angola, Tanzania, Somalia, Uganda, the Congo, and a score of other African states. The developments seem to indicate a dismal failure on the part of the leaders of the free world to make an adequate case for the political and economic system they claim to represent."[94]

The American public was also bombarded with these distorted images in the mass media. President Machel was continually depicted as a doctrinaire bearded radical, a poorly educated soldier obviously unqualified to govern a "modern" nation. In a lurid report, Time magazine claimed that to compensate for the lack of both leadership and popular support, "Thousands of people have been packed off to reeducation centers where Machel's brand of Marxism is taught with a heavy

and sometimes brutal hand."[95] The prestigious New York _Times_ News Service
carried repeated articles, many based on South African sources and unverified
claims, of political repression and incarceration.[96] In a similar vein, the
Los Angeles _Times_ noted that, "The legal system here has fallen apart in seven
months of independence, and citizens have been swept up by the thousands and
sent to prisons, jail and concentration camps."[97] The Washington _Post_ joined
the ill-informed chorus alleging that, "Mozambique's black Marxist rulers, avowedly
opposed to racism are reported to be stepping up a campaign of harassment and
humiliation against their new country's remaining white Portuguese residents."[98]

In addition to uncritically accepting and popularizing these fabrications,
the press continually depicted Mozambique as a "pawn" of either the Soviet Union
or China. American journalists frequently speculated on which Communist power
would ultimately triumph. Robin Wright, a Southern African specialist whose
columns appear regularly in the most influential American newspapers, reflected
this preoccupation of her colleagues:

> The Sino-Soviet race for influence in Africa has taken a dramatic
> turn with the Soviets gaining a new edge in Mozambique, a vital
> strategic base for operations in eastern and southern Africa.
> Mozambique's new ties with the Soviets, marking a major ideological
> shift for the newly independent nation, could have broad ramifi-
> cations for southern Africa, particularly with the Soviets, al-
> ready influential in Angola.
>
> Moscow obviously dreams of being first in Rhodesia when its
> white rulers give way to the black leaders of a new state of
> Zimbabwe.[99]

Coming on the aftermath of the Angolan debacle the specter of Soviet expansionism reinforced "Cold War" anxieties which lay deeply rooted in the American
psychic. Most Americans quickly internalized the image of Mozambique as a repressive, racist country which had become a Russian satellite. They were given
few chances to read anything different. Reports of a variety of American

observers, academic, church and political, which presented an alternative
picture of creative change and popular support were constantly ignored by the
press.

The propaganda campaign in the American and Western European press, dis-
turbed and alarmed the Mozambican government. Not only were the images projected
in the mass media identical to the stereotypes being propogated by the Salisbury
and Pretoria regimes, but more importantly they created a climate which would be
conducive to Western intervention in Southern Africa. On December 17, the Ministry
of Information issued a statement denouncing these distortions, which it observed
were designed to:

> 1. Persuade world public opinion that the liberation struggle
> in Southern Africa is not being carried out by the oppressed
> peoples of Southern Africa, and that the liberation combat is re-
> duced to rivalry between the United States and The Union of Soviet
> Socialist Republics. The present situation in Southern Africa
> will be the result of the Cold War, and the impetuous development
> of the combats in Zimbabwe, Namibia and The People's revolt in
> Southern Africa, would be reduced to 'manoeuvres' by the socialist
> countries.
>
> 2. Induce world public opinion to think that the government
> of The People's Republic of Mozambique is an aggressive govern-
> ment and that the racist and imperialist forces that invade us
> are doing so in self-defense.
>
> 3. Persuade world public opinion that a climate of insta-
> bility and people's revolt exists in Mozambique and that the
> imperialist lackeys that participate in the massacre and slaughter
> of our people are representatives of the will of the masses.[100]

The attacks on Mozambique in the Congress and in the press ultimately
reflect fundamental differences between Washington and Maputo over the direction
of political change in Southern Africa. Whereas United States' policy is
directed toward promoting moderate anti-communist black governments that will
create a stable environment for Western investments, policy-makers in Mozambique
are diametrically opposed to such a scenario. They contend that majority rule

must be accompanied by a restructuring of the society in order to avoid a "neo-colonial" arrangement. Based on their own experience, moreover, FRELIMO has concluded that armed struggle is generally an inevitable and integral part of the process of national liberation.

Events in Angola in the summer and fall of 1975 demonstrated the divergent positions and hardened relations between the United States and Mozambique. As Bender has noted elsewhere in this book, the United States provided diplomatic, economic and military assistance to UNITA and FNLA in order to prevent the preeminence of MPLA which Washington defined as Soviet dominated.[101] Mozambique, on the other hand, recognized MPLA as the only movement which enjoyed a national following and sought to restructure the society. It, therefore, enthusiastically supported MPLA and even sent a small contingent of troops to Angola.

By late 1976, the future of Zimbabwe had become a major source of tension between the United States and Mozambique. For Mozambique the conflict raised not only ideological issues, but questions of national survival. Under Kissinger's aegis the United States had sought to negotiate a peaceful transfer of power in Rhodesia which would essure the ascendancy of a moderate black government. The Americans were willing to invest over a billion dollars in a special fund to provide white settlers with "guarantees" that would encourage them to stay, thus "stabilizing" the economy. If implemented, such a solution would lead to the substitution of a black elite for a white elite, but it would not alter fundamental economic and social structures and relationships, and it would leave the position of most of Zimbabwe's six million people virtually unchanged.

Mozambique has remained staunchly opposed to such an "American" solution and has been the most outspoken of the front-line nations on this subject. More-

over, it has provided sanctuary and military assistance to ZIPA (Zimbabwean
Peoples Army) so that it could continue the struggle against the Smith regime
and has played a central role in forging the Patriotic Front--a political alliance of Zimbabwean nationalists.[102]

In reprisal Rhodesian forces have repeatedly attacked Mozambican territory.
According to official sources in Maputo, between March 3, 1976, when Mozambique
closed its border to Rhodesia and implemented the U.N.-sponsored boycott, and
March 1977, 143 different incursions have occurred.[103] Although most were of
relatively small scale, they included the massacre of more than 600 Zimbabwean
refugees at Nyazonia in August 1976 and a five-pronged invasion of Tete district
in November.[104] These aggressions are part of a broader strategy of the Smith
regime to demoralize the ZIPA troops and their Mozambican allies and to internationalize the widening conflict in Southern Africa by compelling Mozambique
to seek external assistance which would justify the Rhodesian claim of Communist
expansionism.

Although the United States has publicly deplored the violence American
citizens often participate in these attacks. By late 1976 there were at least
300-400 American mercenaries in the Rhodesian army.[105] The counter-insurgency
skills which they learned in Vietnam are ideally suited for the raids into Mozambique. While it is against the law to serve in a foreign army, the Justice
Department has refused to prosecute the mercenaries or to order that their citizenship be stripped. It has also ruled that magazines such as Soldier of Fortune
and Scare A Hawk, which regularly carry recruitment advertisements, are not violating any laws.

Whatever the exact nature of American involvement in the Rhodesian conflict it is clear that it can only lead to a further deterioration of relations

between the United States and Mozambique. Indeed, a substantial thawing depends on a major shift in America's Southern Africa policy. As long as Washington continues to perceive the struggles for majority rule in Zimbabwe, Namibia and South Africa in terms of global power politics, and as long as it supports overly or covertly white minority regimes in an effort to prevent the "radicalization" of the region, relations with Mozambique can hardly be expected to improve. Although the Carter administration has not yet outlined a position on Southern Africa as of March 1977, his belief that the United States should invest heavily in South Africa[106] as well as the announcement that Kissinger's aide, William Schaufele, has been initially reappointed Undersecretary of State for African Affairs, holds out little hope that such changes will be implemented. While the repeal of the Byrd Amendment and the March 1977 shipment of food supplies to ease the shortage in the aftermath of the southern Mozambican floods[107] are positive actions, such policies are dwarfed by Washington's multiple ties to the Vorstez regime--a regime which remains committed to the perpetuation of exploitative political and economic relations throughout Southern Africa.

III. Conclusion

Little in United States policy toward Mozambique appears to be unique or produced in response to peculiarly Mozambican conditions. Rather, policy was shaped by the general concerns that determined America's posture toward the whole of Southern Africa. Several such crucial determinants can be easily identified.

Firstly, there was the increasing desire after the Second World War to open areas in Africa for direct American economic penetration as a source of valuable raw materials, areas for investment and a promising market. This thrust sometimes created a conflict of interest between the United States and the old colonial powers, as in the Congo where the United States sought to establish a

direct relationship with the region's African leadership rather than relying on
Belgium to act as broker. Ironically, Portugal's underdeveloped economy forced
it to respond to the rise of militant nationalist movements in Angola, Guinea-
Bissau and Mozambique by opening up the colonies to foreign investment, thus
creating an alliance between the colonial authorities and American interests.

Secondly, there was the overriding United States' desire to maintain
stability throughout the region preferring the reactionary minority regimes
to liberation movements committed to the establishment of independent states
under African control. This decision flowed logically out of a set of Cold War
premises depicting profound societal change as leading inevitably toward communism
and the expansion of Soviet power.

Thus, even where the United States acknowledged the need for change, such
as in the Portuguese colonies and in South Africa, there has always been an overriding stress on the need for peaceful change. This has acted as a fundamental
constraint on America's willingness to give support to any effective liberation
movement. The perceived need for a United States' military base on the Azores,
moreover, reinforced Washington's links to the colonial regime. From the first
treaty signed in 1943 until the coup in Portugal, the American base on the
Azores provided Lisbon with leverage against any United States action which might
undercut her position in Africa. The Azores agreement of 1971 represented the
culmination of Portuguese efforts to link the two issues. In exchange for a new
lease the American government enthusiastically agreed to provide vast amounts
of economic assistance which not only eased Lisbon's financial crises but
bolstered her colonial resolve.

As important as any of the above is the key role assigned to South Africa
in the design of American policy. As the dominant national power with the most

complex and developed economy in Africa, accounting for some 22 percent of the
continent's GNP and 40 percent of its industrial production, South Africa has
always been regarded as crucial to maintaining regional stability. Direct
American investment in South Africa (over 1½ billion dollars by 1976) far
exceeds the level of United States economic involvement in any other Southern
Africa country. South Africa also possesses by far the greatest military capacity
in the area and maintains a major naval base in the Cape as well. Her economic
and military potential in conjunction with militantly anti-Communist posture provided an obvious attraction to Washington. Thus the preservation of South Africa
has obviously played a considerable role in defining American policy. Recent
diplomatic efforts under Kissinger's aegis which focused on Zimbabwe and Namibia
indicates that the United States would be willing to settle for moderate African
governments in the more peripheral countries of the region in order to preserve
the core state of South Africa.

Similar thinking was certainly involved in the formation of policy toward
the Portuguese colonies. Policy was made not only on the bases of American interests in Mozambique, where the direct level of involvement was very low, but
also in terms of Mozambique's place as a buffer region. The aim was the maintenance of a cordon sanitaire along South Africa's northern boundaries, while simultaneously supporting Portugal's colonial presence. Purported American aid to
anti-FRELIMO groups after the coup in Lisbon would be consistent with Washington's
efforts to promote moderate African governments not unlikely to provide sanctuary
and military assistance to South African liberation forces.

During this period growing American preoccupation with the Indian Ocean
as a strategic area also enhanced Mozambique's international importance. By
1971 Pentagon warnings of a Soviet threat to vital oil routes had generated

sufficient pressure for base construction to be initiated on the tiny island of

Diogo Garcia. Thereafter, Mozambique, with its long coastline, was viewed from

the perspective of Soviet-American balance of power policy in the Indian Ocean.

By 1973 the advances being made by FRELIMO were causing the United States and

its NATO allies so much concern that in June the Defense Planning Committee of

NATO issued a secret instruction to the Supreme Allied Atlantic Command (SACLANT)

to develop contingency plans for the defense of the South African region and

the Indian Ocean although this was outside the NATO area.[108] One year later,

immediately after the coup in Portugal, Admiral Hugo Biermann, Chief of Staff

of South Africa's armed forces, flew to Washington for an unprecedented meeting

with Admiral Thomas Moorer, Chairman of the United States Joint Chiefs of Staff,

and with acting secretary of the Navy, J. William Middendorf.[109]   American

officials attempted to dismiss the visit as private and unimportant but knowledge-

able observers indicated that the topics discussed focused on the strategic im-

plications of Mozambique's imminent independence. That the United States con-

tinues to attach great value to Mozambique's critical Indian Ocean position is

reflected in the Fall 1976 trip which the American Ambassador made to the

Bazarut Island to ascertain whether rumors of a Soviet naval presence were cor-

rect. They proved to be false.

While United States policy toward Mozambique has avoided the open hostility

exercised towards Angola it is highly unlikely that policy in the future will

be determined by criteria appreciably different from those that have operated

in the past. As long as Washington continues to perceive the struggles for

majority rule in Southern Africa in terms of global power policy, as long as it

feels its own interests dangerously threatened by the establishment of socialist

forms of society and as long as it supports minority regimes, it forfeits the possibility of markedly improved relations with Mozambique and other progressive African nations.

51

NOTES

1. William Minter, Portuguese Africa and the West (New York, 1972),
    p. 39.

2. Adolph Berle, Tides of Crises (Reynal, 1957), p. 8.

3. For the details of the Azores agreement see Department of State,
    Defense: Use of Facilities in the Azores. Agreement between
    the United States of America and Portugal (Washington, 1951).

4. Minter, Portuguese Africa, p. 46.

5. S. J. Bosgra and Chr. van Krimpen, Portugal and NATO (Amsterdam,
    1972), p. 59.

6. Ibid.

7. Cited in the preface to Franco Noguiera, The Third World (London,
    1967), pp. 11-17.

8. George F. Kennan, "Hazardous Course in Southern Africa," Foreign
    Affairs 49 (1971):230.

9. "The ideology of lusotropicalism maintains that because of the
    historically unique absence of racism among the Portuguese
    people, their colonization and governing of tropical, non-
    European territories, have been characterized by racially
    egalitarian, humane interaction and legislation." Quoted
    from "The Myth and Reality of Portuguese Rule in Angola:
    A Study in Racial Descrimination" (Ph.D. dissertation,
    University of California, Los Angeles, 1975), p. 26.

10. The concept of lusotropicalism was first advanced by the Brazilian
    scholar Gilberto Fryre (see Gilberto Fryre, Portuguese
    Intergration in the Tropics (Lisbon, 1961)). Among its
    strongest proponents in the United States were George Kennan,
    Francis Rogers, David Abshire, Lewis H. Gann and Peter
    Duignan. For a brilliant critique of lusotropicalism see
    Gerald Bender, The Myth and Reality of Portuguese Rule in
    Angola: A Study of Racial Domination (Berkeley and London,
    1977).

11. See, for example, David M. Abshire, "The Portuguese Racial Legacy,"
    Portuguese Africa: A Handbook, eds. David M. Abshire and
    Michael A. Samuels (New York, 1969). Buried in a footnote
    Abshire acknowledges that he basically concurs with the
    assessment that "the tribal society was probably the most
    unsuccessful, the most stagnant form of society that mankind

has ever known. African traditional history records migra-
tions, battles and conquests, but it never tells of any
mental tranformations or changes in social structures."
(Ibid., p. 105.)

12. For the official Portuguese legal position see Franco Noguiera,
    The United Nations and Portugal (London, 1963), pp. 139-69.

13. For an excellent discussion of this subject see Mohamad El-Khawas,
    "Mozambique and the United Nations," Issue 11:4 (1972): 30-
    35; Minter, Portuguese Africa, pp. 50-51.

14. Cited in Jennifer Davis, ACOA Background Paper: U.S. Policy and
    Portuguese Colonialism, The United Nations Facade (New York,
    1969), p. 3. Stevenson's statement was made at a meeting of
    the Security Council of March 15, 1961.

15. Davis, ACOA Background Paper, p. 4.

16. John Marcum, "The Politics of Indifference: Portugal and Africa,
    A Case Study in American Foreign Policy," Issue 11:3 (1972):10.

17. Cited in Ibid.

18. United Nations, Security Council Debate, S/PV. 1045, 26 July 1963.

19. See General Assembly Resolution 1807, 14 December 1962.

20. See General Assembly Resolution 1819, 18 December 1962.

21. See General Assembly Resolution 2107, 21 December 1965.

22. For a summary of Ball's negotiations see George Ball, The Disipline
    of Power: Essentials for a Modern World Structure (Boston,
    1968), pp. 245-52.

23. Minter, Portuguese Africa, p. 97.

24. Quoted from a press conference release by the Central Committee of
    FRELIMO in Dar-es-Salaam on 12 June 1964.

25. Ibid.

26. United States Mission to the United Nations, Press Relations USUN-41
    (69), Statement by Ambassador Seymour Finger, 17 April 1969.

27. Department of State, Background Notes: Angola (Washington, 1973),
    p. 6.

28. This is the official Portuguese figure. See J. De. Sidro, "Why and
    Wherefores of the War in Mozambique," Portugal: An Informative
    Review (Lisbon, 1972), p. 8.

29. Sunday _Times_ (United Kingdom), 9 July 1972.

30. See, for example, Eduardo Mondlane, _The Struggle for Mozambique_ (Baltimore, 1969); John Paul, _Mozambique, Memoirs of a Revolution_ (Middlesex, 1975); Adrian Hastings, _Wiriyamu_ (London, 1973); Jošé Amaro, ed., _Massacres na Guerra Colonial; Tete, um exemplo_ (Lisbon, 1976).

31. Many of these African collaborators fled to Rhodesia at the time of independence where they are now engaged in similar repressive actions against Zaimbabweans as well as Mozambican peasants living along the border.

32. Marcum, "The Politics of Indifference," p. 11.

33. _Ibid._

34. This sentiment was articulated by officials at the American Consulate in Lourenco Marques (now Maputo) in 1968 during conversations with Allen and Barbara Isaacman.

35. Quoted in Bosgra and van Krimpen, _Portugal and NATO_, p. 62.

36. Noguiera, _The United Nations_, pp. 139–68.

37. Cited in John Marcum, _Revolution in Angola_ (Cambridge, 1969), p. 275. See also United Nations, General Assembly A/5160, "Report of the Special Committee on Territories under Portuguese Adminis- tration," 15 August 1962, p. 142.

38. Bosgra and van Krimpen, _Portugal and NATO_, p. 60.

39. _Ibid._

40. For United States' training of Portuguese military and the number of visits by U.S. military attaches to Mozambique, see Department of State, _Implementation of the U.S. Arms Embargo (Against Portugal and South Africa and Related Issues)_ (Washington, 1973), pp. 89–90. This hearing was held before the Subcommittee on Africa of the House Committee on Foreign Affairs on 20, 22 March and 6 April 1973; Robert A. Diamond and David Fouquer, "Portugal and the United States," _Africa Report_ 15 (1970):17.

41. Quoted in David Welsh, "Flyboys of the CIA;" _Ramparts_ (December 1966):

42. For a carefully documented analysis of the increasing American and Western European investments in Mozambique see United Nations, General Assembly, A/9623, "Report of the Special Committee on the Situation with Regard to the Implementation of the Decla- ration on the Granting of Independence to Colonial Countries and Peoples," p. 50.

43. Minter, _Portuguese Africa_, p. 162.

44. Ibid.

45. New York Times, 9 December 1971. Ultimately, most of the credits were never used since Lisbon worked better financial arrangements with Western European countries. Nevertheless, the agreement provided important psychological support for the Caetano regime at the moment of its greatest crises.

46. For a good summary of FRELIMO's military success during this period see Richard Leonard, "FRELIMO's Victories in Mozambique," Issue 4:2 (1974):38-45.

47. For a detailed discussion of the sale of these planes see "Statement of Jennifer Davis," Implementation of the U.S. Arms Embargo (Against Portugal and South Africa, and Related Issues), Hearing before the Subcommittee on Africa of the House Committee on Foreign Affairs, 20, 22 March and 6 April 1973 (Washington, 1973), pp. 78-80.

48. Daily Telegraph, 21 June 1971; Johannesburg Star, 25 June 1971.

49. Ibid.

50. "Report on the Signing of a Contract between DETA and Another Mozambican Commercial Airline and the Military to Perform Services for the Army," Implementation of the U.S. Arms Embargo, p. 244.

51. Ibid.

52. "Statement of Bruce Oudes," Implementation of the U.S. Arms Embargo, pp. 7-8; "Statement of Jennifer Davis," Implementation of U.S. Arms Embargo, pp. 79-80.

53. Quoted in the Sunday Times (United Kingdom), 9 July 1972.

54. Ibid.

55. "Statement of Bruce Oudes," Implementation of the U.S. Arms Embargo, pp. 7-8.

56. The original source for these figures are the Bureau of Census, FT-410 Export Statistics. They were reprinted in Implementation of the U.S. Arms Embargo, p. 61.

57. This lack of control was acknowledged by Ruaer H. Meyer, Director, Office of Export Controls on 20 March 1973 before the House Subcommittee on African Affairs. See Implementation of the U.S. Arms Embargo, pp. 61-62.

58. In that year, eighty-three Portuguese airforce officers received training compared with an average of eight or nine in the previous seven years. "Statement of Bruce Oudes," Implementation of the U.S. Arms Embargo, pp. 8-9.

59. The strategic conference was held at the Portuguese airbase at Monsanto (Diario de Noticias, 3 October 1972).

60. George Bader, Regional Director for Africa, Office of the Assistant Secretary of Defense, candidly acknowledged that, "We would have no prohibition of U.S.-trained Portuguese officers going where their country sent them." Quoted in Implementation of the U.S. Arms Embargo, pp. 8-9.

61. U.S. Department of Commerce, ET 73-105, Foreign Economic Trends (Washington, 1973). This assessment was prepared by the American Consulate in Mozambique.

62. United Nations, General Assembly, A/9623, "Report of the Special Committee," pp. 50-57.

63. Ibid.

64. Ibid.

65. For import and export statistics during this period see Provincia de Mozambique, Boletim Mensal de Estatistica (Lourenco Marques,).

66. For a penetrating analysis of NSSM 39 see Edgar Lockwood, "National Security Memorandum 39 and the Future of United States Policy Toward South Africa," Issue 4:3 (1974):63-70.

67. Quoted from National Security Council Interdepartmental Group for Africa, "Study in Response to National Security Memorandum 39: Southern Africa," p. 27.

68. Department of State, Background Notes, Angola, p. 16.

69. The Star (International Airmail Edition), 22 June 1974.

70. For a detailed statement of Spinola's long-term, though somewhat vague, strategy see Antonio de Spinola, Portugal e o Futuro (Arcadia, 1974).

71. Testimony of Paul O'Neil, Director of the State Department Office on Southern African Affairs, before the House Committee on Foreign Affairs, 14 March 1974.

72. FRELIMO's opposition to any agreements which might lead to a neo-colonial arrangement were articulated at the Second Party Congress in 1968. For a detailed discussion of the Congress, see "II Congresso da FRELIMO--Importancia e Significado Historico," Tempo 303 (July 1976):54-61.

73. Statement of the Executive Committee of FRELIMO, issued on 27 April 1974.

74. One of the most prominent anti-FRELIMO groups was GUMO (Grupo Unido de Mozambique). For a thorough analysis of its program as well as its fundemental dificiencies see Expresso, 4 May 1974. Other groups included FRECOMO (Frente Comun de Mocambique), which called for a privileged Makua-Lomwe position in the new government and COREMO (Comite Revolucionario de Mocambique).

75. London Observer, 23 March 1975.

76. Ibid. For an important discussion of the politics of ethnicity and the efforts of anti-FRELIMO forces to exploit ethnics tensions, see Edward A. Alpers, "Ethnicity, Politics and History," Africa Today 4 (1974):63-70.

77. Ibid. Jorge Jardim, a prominent Portuguese businessman with links to the Portuguese and Malawian governments, has written an elaborate account of the efforts to coopt the Mozambican revolution. See Jorge Jardim, Mocambique Terra Queimada (Lisbon, 1976).

78. Expresso, 10 May 1974.

79. It was estimated that on the eve of independence Mozambique's external debt was estimated at one billion dollars and the economy was totally dependent on South Africa. Thus, FRELIMO inherited a classic underdeveloped economy--the legacy of 400 years of Portuguese colonial rule and economic exploitation. (See The Financial Times, 3 April 1975, for a comprehensive summary of the economy just prior to independence.)

80. Quoted from Department of State, "U.S. Congratulates Mozambique's Joint Transitional Government," Department of State Bulletin (Washington, 1974), p. 668.

81. Washington Post, 22 March 1975. Personal communications with Edgar Lockwood, Director of the Washington Office on Africa, 13 May 1975, based on his discussion with State Department officials.

82. Personal communications with Edgar Lockwood, Director of the Washington Office on Africa, 13 May 1975, based on his discussion with State Department officials.

83. For a statement of Easum's assessment of events in Southern Africa, see Donald B. Easum, "U.S. Policy Toward South Africa," Issue 5:3 (1975):66-72.

84. For the vehement opposition to Davis' appointment, see Nomination of Nathaniel Davis to be Assistant Secretary of State for African Affairs, Hearing before the Committee on Foreign Relations, United States Senate, 19 February 1975 (Washington, 1976).

85. Interview with Jim Weikert, member of the Committee for a Free Mozambique, New York, January 1977.

86. For an excellent discussion of U.S. involvement in Angola, see Gerald Bender, "Kissinger and Angola: Anatomy of Failure," in this volume.

87. Isaacman is currently preparing a study of the propaganda campaign against Mozambique to be published shortly.

88. Quoted from the weekly compilation of Presidential documents, dated 30 June 1975.

89. United Nations, Security Council S/PV 1880, 16 March 1976, pp. 18-20.

90. New York Times, 21 May 1976; The Baltimore Sun, 26 May 1976; The Washington Post, 28 May 1976.

91. Personal communications with Edgar Lockwood, Director Washington Office on Africa, on 25 March 1977.

92. A number of Mozambican high-level officials indicated to Isaacman that they found the attacks in Congress and in the American press reprehensible. They also indicated that such a U.S. reaction was detrimental to the improvement of U.S.-Mozambican relations.

93. Quoted in the New York Times, 11 August 1975.

94. William P. Yarborough, Trial in Africa: The Failure of U.S. Policy (Washington, 1976), p. 12.

95. Time, 23 August 1976, p. 26.

96. John Burns, for example, writing for both the New York Times and the International Herald Tribune, uncritically accepted accounts of life in Mozambique from departing Portuguese settlers, defectors from FRELIMO and businessmen who had spent some time in Mozambique. It is not unreasonable to assume that all three of these groups had vested interests in propagating a series of distortions and myths about independent Mozambique. Yet Burns reproduced their accounts verbatum without qualification to present an unflattering picture of life under FRELIMO which bore no relation to reality. See, for example, New York Times, 25 July 1976 and International Herald Tribune, 2 August 1976.

97. Los Angeles Times, 11 February 1976.

98. The Washington Post, 1 January 1976.

99. Ibid., 16 April 1976.

100. Communique from the Ministry of Information, Maputo, on 17 December 1976. It also appears as an Official United Nations' document of the Security Council, #S/12258.

101.   Bender, "Kissinger and Angola."

102.   The first news conference given by ZIPA, for example, was held in
        Maputo on 22 September 1976. It was subsequently distributed
        world-wide by the Mozambican Information Agency. In addition,
        the Mozambican weekly _Tempo_ has carried numerous articles
        lauding the revolutionary struggle of ZIPA.

103.   List of Mozambican locations attacked by the Rhodesian army:

Location	Number of Times Attacked
Chicualacuala	22
Mavue	6
Chitanga	6
Pafuri	5
Mapai	6
Massangena	2
Nwenetsi	1
Espungabera	9
Chazuca	1
Catandica	2
Goi-Goi	1
Manica	5
Chirara	5
Rotanda	4
Nyazonia	1
Gaerizi	1
Mussurize	1
Pungue	1
Guro	1
Mavonde	1
Zumbo	2
Mucumbura	8
Luia	4
Chioco	3
Mazoe	3
Changara	4
Cuchamano	3
Nura	8
Gento	5
Mafigo	4
Caponda	2
Base de Segruanca	1
Fingoe	1
Messenguezi	2
Kangodzi	1
Magoe	1
Chacombedzi	4

Initially, the Rhodesian incursions were limited to short raids along
        the Mozambican border. Small groups of Rhodesian commandos,
        often supported by foreign mercenaries, including Americans,

attacked frontier villages which they claimed were staging
areas for ZIPA. In response to the March decision of the
Mozambican government to enforce the U.N.-sponsored boycott
against Rhodesia and the increasing success of ZIPA, however,
the Smith regime began to escalate their military activity.

On 25 June 1976, a large Rhodesian force, supported by
helicopters and armored vehicles, attacked in and around the
town of Mapai, an important transportation center in Gaza
province. Included in the ranks of the invaders were a number
of Mozambican mercenaries who had previously served in elite
brigades of the Portuguese colonial army and had subsequently
fled to Rhodesia. The invaders, dressed in FRELIMO uniforms
and singing FRELIMO songs, caught the residents by surprise,
killing a number of civilians as well as FRELIMO soldiers and
virtually destroying the town. The incursions was clearly
meant to warn the Mozambican government that unless they cur-
tailed their support of ZIPA, other population centers would
be vulnerable, including Maputo, the capital located less than
250 miles from Mapai.

Mozambique and her Zimbabwean allies refused, however, to
be intimidated and the Smith regime intensified its military
offensive. In August, Rhodesian troops, again dressed in
FRELIMO uniforms, attacked Nyazonia, a refugee camp of 10,000
Zimbabweans who had fled from Rhodesia. According to the testimony of survivors, which was subsequently corroborated by a
U.N. commission, members of the camp were rounded up and indis-
criminately shot. The massacre lasted for more that two hours.
In the end, 600 people were killed, and many more were wounded.
Predictably, Smith and his ministers hailed this action against
"terrorists" as a great victory for "Western civilization," a
sentiment shared by most Rhodesians who were feeling increasingly
threatened.

During the subsequent two months, however, the Rhodesians
had little cause for cheer. Zimbabwean freedom fighters repeatedly penetrated deep into the heart of the Rhodesian state,
periodically disrupting vital sections of the transportation
system, attacking Rhodesian army posts and European plantations.
These actions dramatically intensified the level of anxiety within
the minority community.

In response, the Salisbury government launched its most
substained offensive against Mozambique. On 31 October 1976, more
that 800 ground forces and paratroopers, including mercernaries
from Western countries (it is estimated that there are between
200 and 300 Americans serving in the Rhodesian army), supported
by helicopters, armored cars, heavy artillery and jets, simultaneously assaulted five Mozambican military bases in Tete district.
At the same time, a smaller Rhodesian expedition moved south into
Gaza province and again attacked Mapai. For forty-eight hours
the invaders bombarded civilian and military positions, leaving

a large, though not yet determined, number of victims behind.
As an extension of this aggression, Rhodesia has intensified
its air raids against Mozambican territory, and during the
past three months Hunter fighter and Canberra light bombers
have repeatedly bombed locations in Tete, Manica, and Gaza
province.

The rash of attacks raises three important questions
which directly affect any analysis of the balance of power
within this vilatile region. Why has it been so difficult
for Mozambique to prevent these incursions? What does Smith
hope to gain through this policy of military escalation? To
what extent has the Rhodesian government achieved its Military
and political goals?

The heavily forested and rugged terrain along the 800-mile
Mozambican-Rhodesian border makes it particularly difficult to
prevent Rhodesian attacks. (Conversely, ZIPA forces enjoy a
similar tactical advantage when they penetrate the Rhodesian
frontier.) Access to captured FRELIMO uniforms and flags and
the use of defectors familiar with both the border terrain and
the indigenous languages also facilitate the Rhodesian penetra-
tions. As the attacks escalated, reports from field commanders
indicated that Mozambican border forces lacked sufficient
heavy artillery and anti-aircraft equipment to twart the intensive frontal assault. Untimately, the border troops regrouped
and, with the aid of reinforcements, were able to drive out
the invaders. The recent wave of air attacks further demonstrates
that without a functioning air force Mozambique will remain
vulnerable, a situation which is not likely to improve for
another two years until the first group of Mozambican jet pilots
complete their training.

The Rhodesian decision to escalate the conflict with
Mozambique was motivated by the government's deteriorating
internal position. The most immediate concern was the growing
lack of confidence within the European community. The emigration
of substantial numbers of settlers and the outflow of capital
were symptomatic of widespread demoralization. Smith's announcement of the impending negotiations in Geneva reinforced the
sense of despair. Thus, the attacks served to demonstrate the
continued prowess of the Rhodesian military and to appease the
right wing of the Rhodesian Front which had vehemently opposed
negotiations. The incursions also drove home a message to the
Africans living in Rhodesia by reassuring those who colloborated
that the government was not about to collapse and by demonstraging
to opponents of the regime that they would be vulnerable even if
they fled into neighboring Mozambique.

The military campaign had immediate strategic objectives
as well. The Rhodesian High Command believed that the preemptive
invasion of Tete province would enable the Rhodesian army to
capture a large supply of military equipment and inflict sub-

stantial losses on ZIPA and FRELIMO troops. These setbacks, in
turn, were supposed to thwart a ZIPA offensive planned for
November, the beginning of the rainy season. In addition, it
was assumed that as a result of the casualties inflicted, the
Mozambican civilian population would oppose continued sanctuary
and support for ZIPA and perhaps, in the long run, would even
turn against FRELIMO. Toward this end the Rhodesian government
initiated a radio propaganda campaign that emphasized the
irresponsibility and tyranny of FRELIMO and reportedly has
provided funds for an opposition party in exile called FUMO.

The long-term goal of Rhodesian military policy is to
internationalize the conflict in Southern Africa by drawing the
Western countries in as its allies. This strategy assumed
greater urgency after Western intelligence reports confirmed
that ZIPA was seriously jeopardizing the government's military
position. Pressure by Kissinger and Vorster to negotiate a
transition to majority rule intensified the quest for an alternative strategy.

At the heart of the government's plan are efforts to redefine the conflict with ZIPA in "Cold War" terms rather than
acknowledging it as a struggle for self-determination and majority
rule. Rhodesian propaganda seeks to convince the United States
and its NATO allies that it is legitimately defending Western
interests against communist-dominated ZIPA backed by Marxist
Mozambique. A victory for ZIPA, Salisbury contends, would
further increase the influence of the Soviet Union, who was
the recent beneficiary of the war in Angola. Aside from the
immediate strategic advantages, the escalating attacks on
Mozambique are designed to force it to seek military assistance
from socialist countries, especially Cuba, which would enhance
Smith's claim of communist aggression and compel South Africa
and her Western allies to intercede either covertly or overtly.
This assistance would rejuvenate the tottering regime and provide it with international legitimacy.

SOURCES: Tempo 319 (14 November 1976):48-63; Ibid., 322 (5 December
1976):52-54; New York Times, 14 August 1976; Washington Post, 2
November 1976; New York Times, 22 August 1976; Washington Post,
3 November 1976; New York Times, 2 November 1976; The Sunday
Times, 4 November 1976; 7 November 1976; Washington Post, 9
November 1976; New York Times, 25 February 1977; The Sunday
Times (London), 5 December 1976; Washington Post, 18 December
1976; 6 December 1976; Tempo 336 (13 March 1977:59.)

104. Tempo 307 (22 August 1976):2-11; Tempo 309 (5 August 1976):33-39.

105. Washington Post, 9 December 1976; The Sunday Times, 4 March 1977.
      For discussion of the role of mercenaries by proponents of
      the system see "SOF Interview Major Nick Maprecht," Soldier
      of Fortune (Spring 1977).

106. Financial Mail, 5 November 1976.

107. The United States sent seventy-six tons of rice, wheat and condensed milk to help in the aftermath of the floods. _Tempo_ 338 (27 March 1977):16.

108. Washington _Post_, 2 May 1974.

109. Christian Science _Monitor_, 10 May 1974.

CHAPTER II

KISSINGER IN ANGOLA: ANATOMY OF FAILURE

BY GERALD BENDER

*For more than a decade, basic Angolan realities have had little impact on the formulation of U.S. policies toward that large and potentially wealthy country. Prior to the Portuguese coup in April 1974, a desire to maintain amicable relations with Portugal, a NATO ally, dominated American policy. Following the coup American government officials were preoccupied with the maintenance of "some form of equilibrium between the great powers."[1] Since the Angolan civil war U.S. domestic politics have strongly influenced American policy toward Angola. This should not suggest that officials in the State Department, CIA, and other branches of government have been oblivious or unsympathetic to Angolan realities-- they have always been considered but ultimately eclipsed by domestic or larger global concerns. The neglect of Angolan realities has proved to be the fundamental flaw in U.S. policy, resulting in a commitment to losing sides (first Portugal, then the FNLA/UNITA coalition) and, ironically, in weakening rather than strengthening the "equilibrium" vis-à-vis the Soviet Union. The principal architect of U.S. policy before and after the Portuguese coup was Henry Kissinger whose realpolitik ignored basic political realities in at least four different spheres: global, Angolan, Portuguese, and domestic American.

---

*I would like to express my appreciation to the following people who provided valuable criticisms and comments: Richard L. Sklar, Tamara Bender, Samuel P. Huntington, Bernard Brodie, David Laitin, Shimshon Zelniker, and G. Harvey Summ.

This chapter was written in early 1976 and revised during the summer of 1976.

The Early Years

Beginning with his inaugural address in January 1960 and through-out most of the three years of his presidency, John F. Kennedy attempted to project an image of the United States as a "friend of all oppressed peoples." In order to cultivate this image the United States frequently supported anti-Portuguese measures in the United Nations, which provoked anti-American demonstrations in Lisbon and Luanda and threats from Salazar to expel the U.S. from the Azores. Arthur Schlesinger, historian and Kennedy advisor, proudly proclaimed that the President's anti-colonial posture in the U.N. left the New Frontier "free of automatic identification with colonialism." [2]

U.S. Angolan policy under Kennedy was not limited to verbal attacks on Portuguese colonialism. The CIA began to shift its support from generally reactionary clients to those who were more moderate. As part of this change in CIA operations, Holden Roberto's FNLA (then called UPA or GRAE) was extended several million dollars of military and financial support. [3] Although a number of contem-porary observers interpret this early support for Roberto as indic-ative of America's historically "reactionary" and anti-MPLA position in Angola, few in Washington shared this perspective at the time. In fact, by 1962   Roberto headed the only Angolan nationalist movement recognized by the OAU and enjoyed the support of most African leaders, including Kwame Nkrumah, Patrice Lumumba, and Sekou Toure. Few world leaders expected the Portuguese to be able to hold out against both the "wind of change" and a major armed insurrection; therefore,

Roberto appeared to be the most likely first president of an independent Angola. They were wrong for many reasons, including the important fact that the United States, like other major powers who assisted Angolan nationalists, never gave enough support to enable the nationalists to win a military victory.

As the Angolan war dragged on, the U.S. under President Johnson continued modest support for Roberto but also tried to normalize relations with Lisbon. Washington became more reluctant to support U.N. resolutions critical of Portugal when the Azores base was presumed to have an increased importance. While there was a rather strict adherence to the U.N. arms embargo against supplying weapons to Portugal for use in Africa during the 1960s, the CIA allegedly attempted to appease Salazar in 1965 with twenty B-26 bombers for Portugal's colonial wars. The operation was apparently uncovered by the Treasury Department and immediately halted after only seven of the planes had been delivered.[4] However, the continued support for Roberto enabled some to assert that, at worst, the United States supported "both sides" in the Angolan anti-colonial struggle.

The Nixon/Kissinger Metamorphosis

Less than three months after Richard Nixon became President, his Advisor on National Security Affairs, Henry Kissinger, undertook a major review of U.S. policy toward southern Africa. He directed the National Security Council's Interdepartmental Group for Africa (consisting primarily of employees from the State and Defense Departments as well as the CIA) to prepare a study including a brief background on each country, major problems in the area, U.S. interests (economic, political, strategic, and scientific), and six policy options based on differing projections of how the future could unfold in southern Africa. This study is known as the National Security Study Memorandum (NSSM) 39.[5]

Kissinger presented NSSM 39 to President Nixon in early January 1970 with the recommendation that the U.S. adopt a "general posture... along the lines of option two" which called for the United States to "maintain public opposition to racial repression, but relax political isolation and economic restrictions on the white states."[6] In order to better appreciate the perspective on the future of southern Africa held by Kissinger and the National Security Council in 1970, it is useful to quote the premise upon which "option two" was based:

> The whites are here to stay and the only way that constructive change can come about is through them. There is no hope for the blacks to gain the political rights they seek through violence, which will only lead to chaos and increased opportunities for the communists. We can, by selective relaxation of our stance toward the white regimes, encourage some modification of their current racial and colonial policies and through more substantial economic assistance to the black states (a total of about $5 million annually in technical assistance to the black states) help to draw the two groups together and exert some influence on both for peaceful change. Our tangible interests form a basis for our contacts in the region, and these can be maintained at acceptable political cost.

In addition, the African insurgent movements were considered ineffectual and not "realistic or supportable" alternatives to the white regimes. Kissinger questioned "the depth and permanence of

black resolve" and dismissed the possibility of "a black victory at
any stage." However, the depth and permanence of Portuguese resolve
was not questioned, an error which John Marcum has aptly described
as "a basic miscalculation stemming from faulty intelligence, in
both senses of the word."[7] (It is of interest to note that the
Soviet Union apparently made the same mistake. Following a visit
to Angola in February 1974--with Portuguese permission--by the ubiquitous Victor Lewin, the Soviets cut off all aid to the MPLA in March
1974 and did not resume until August or September of the same year.
Knowledgeable sources indicate that Lewin's pessimistic report on the
military effectiveness of the MPLA and deep political splits within
the party played an important role in the Soviet decision to halt
its aid to the MPLA.)

Clearly, from the late 1960s until the Portuguese coup, U.S.
policy demonstrated two mutually exclusive goals: (1) to express
sympathy with the aspirations of Angolans for self-determination;
(2) to assist Portugal, a NATO ally. In pursuit of the former goal
the U.S. adopted a stance of "communication" and "dialogue" (recommended in NSSM 39) which assumed that the most efficacious means for
realizing self-determination was communication, not violence. That
assumption was not only naive but hypocritical because no one honestly believed that Salazar or Caetano could be convinced through
"communication" of the need for self-determination in the colonies.
In fact, the United States never moved the Portuguese an inch closer
to granting independence to Angola, Mozambique, or Guinea-Bissau.
Furthermore, the policy of communication did not include relations
with the nationalist movements (aid to the FNLA was halted in 1969),
who were generally ignored so as not to offend the Portuguese. This

fear of offending Portugal actually prevented the American Consulate in Luanda from maintaining more than the most minimal communication with Africans.

Pursuit of the second goal, assistance to a NATO ally, was less hypocritical. The U.S. trained Portuguese officers in the United States and supplied Portugal with airplanes, equipment which could serve either civilian or military purposes, $400 million in credits and loans (little of which Portugal used), napalm, herbicides, and, most importantly, moral support. There was always a sophistic explanation of how each example of U.S. aid to Portugal could be interpreted in "two ways," but the sum total of American actions left no doubt about which side the U.S. actually supported in the wars for independence in the Portuguese colonies. The U.S. placed its bets on the tenacity of the Caetano regime and the white settlers--and lost.

The October 1973 war in the Middle East came very close to precipitating a major American shift toward open support of Portugal in her African wars. American use of the Azores to resupply Israel during the Yom Kippur war considerably strengthened Lisbon's bargaining position with the United States over the pending renewal of the Azores treaty. The treaty negotiations had been practically moribund by the time Henry Kissinger stopped in Lisbon in December 1973 (following a trip through the Middle East) in order to thank the Portuguese for use of the Azores and to discuss the treaty.[8] In light of the troublesome Arab boycott, Portugal raised the ante and demanded that the U.S. provide the Portuguese military with weapons for use in Africa. Kissinger--who is alleged to have been unaware of the fact that the United States supported a U.N. resolution prohibiting this kind of assistance agreed, much to the surprise of the Portuguese and to the horror of his closest aides. Fortunately for the United States, the Caetano government did not pursue the matter before it was overthrown five months later, thus sparing Kissinger and U.S. foreign policy considerable problems.

The Portuguese Coup: A Lost Opportunity for Change

The April 1974 coup in Lisbon gave the U.S. a new opportunity to adopt a fresh policy toward the Portuguese colonies in Africa. Only a month before the coup Kissinger had replaced his Assistant Secretary of State for African Affairs David Newsom--who had been cast in the difficult role of principal spokesman for the policy of communication with the white-ruled regimes in southern Africa--with Donald Easum, Ambassador to Upper Volta and a PhD in diplomatic history. Easum, as Kissinger's chief advisor on African affairs, lost little time in attempting to shift the focus of American policy in view of the imminent decolonization in Angola, Mozambique, and Guinea-Bissau. During a five-week tour of Africa in late 1974, Easum told a press conference in Dar-es-Salaam (November 2) that "we are using our influence to foster change in South Africa, not to preserve the status quo."[9]

Despite the long American record of neglect of the nationalists in the Portuguese colonies and ambivalence toward normalizing relations with the liberation movements in the months after the coup, Easum engineered a diplomatic breakthrough with Mozambique's FRELIMO in early November 1974. Following a frank and important meeting with FRELIMO President Samora Machel in Dar-es-Salaam, Mr. Easum visited Mozambique; he was the first foreign diplomat to hold a formal meeting with the transitional government in Maputo. While

many applauded Easum's efforts to change U.S. policy, the Secretary
of State clearly was not among them; less than forty-eight hours
after returning from his African trip, Easum was informed that he
would be replaced (after only nine months in office).

Secretary Kissinger selected Nathaniel Davis to succeed Easum.
Davis, who had no previous diplomatic experience in Africa, was best
known for his role as American Ambassador to Chile during the Allende
overthrow. In an unprecedented action, the Organization of African
Unity--led by Zaire's President Mobutu Sese Seko, known to be an ally
of the U.S.--strongly and unanimously condemned Mr. Davis's nomination.
Predictably, concern was immediately expressed in the United States
and Africa that the U.S. might attempt to implement a policy of
"destabilization" in Africa.

However, when the three Angolan nationalist parties moved from
the military to the political sphere in the latter part of 1974,
Washington showed little inclination to become involved in Angola.
The general perception in the State Department of the relative
balance of power among the three parties prior to the signing of the
Alvor Agreement (15 January 1975) was that the U.S. had little cause
for concern. This viewpoint may be summarized as follows: [10]

> The FNLA, thanks to considerable aid and training from China
> and Zaire, was assumed to have the largest and best trained and
> equipped army among the three movements. Certainly the FNLA's
> army would guarantee it a strong position, if not dominance, in
> any independent government.
> There was some question whether the MPLA's three-way factional

fight (among Neto, Chipenda, and the Andrade brothers) for leadership would leave the party as a formidable force. Intelligence sources reported that the split in the MPLA was so severe that they had absolutely no military presence in Angola at the time of the coup. With the defection of Chipenda's forces, considered to constitute the backbone of the MPLA army, the MPLA army was estimated to have about 3,000 soldiers. An MPLA recovery was thought to depend upon Soviet assistance, which was considered to be unlikely. Throughout most of 1974 it appeared that the Soviets had given up on the MPLA, possibly because of the party's debilitating internecine quarrels. The Soviets had cut all their support to the MPLA in early 1974 (before the Lisbon coup) and did not resume it until the late fall, and then only modestly.

UNITA, with its apparently widespread support in the populous central highlands, was thought to have the greatest popular appeal of the three parties. It was even believed that if elections were held, UNITA had a possibility of winning a majority, certainly a plurality. If elections were not held, however, UNITA was seen as extremely vulnerable with its small and poorly armed military forces. UNITA was estimated to have only 1,500 weapons at this time. Moreover, UNITA's cadres beneath the top echelon of leadership were considered weak.

The Decision to Intervene

The CIA first raised the possibility of resuming "program assistance" for the FNLA in mid-January 1975 at a meeting of the 40 Committee, a small group of officials chaired by Henry Kissinger which

approves or rejects all proposed covert activities.[11]   If the
40 Committee had restricted its consideration to Angola's internal
situation, a different course of action might possibly have been
followed. But the Angolan context was not perceived as the most
relevant factor; domestic politics and global considerations took
precedence.

The question of intervention in Angola was being considered
at the nadir of the first six years of the Nixon administration's
foreign and domestic policies. The NATO alliance was seriously
tested by Portugal's inclusion of communists in the government
and the dispute between Greece and Turkey which left both countries
in a position of questionable utility to the alliance. The situation was not improved for Nixon when Congress cut his aid request
for Turkey. Even worse was the disastrous state of affairs in
Southeast Asia only months before the end of the Vietnam war. In
the Middle East step-by-step diplomacy no longer held promise for
an all-inclusive settlement. In addition, the CIA was more on the
defensive than at any other time in its history with the revelations
of its "destabilization" activities in Chile and its illegal participation in the domestic spying on over 10,000 American citizens.
And then, of course, there was Watergate!

At his press conferences during these months, Henry Kissinger
asked whether it was possible to conduct foreign policy
while America engaged in "this orgy of self-destruction." To complicate matters for the Secretary of State, his policies of detente

and SALT (Strategic Arms Limitation Talks) were under strong attack from conservative critics in both political parties who were encouraged by none other than Nixon's Secretary of Defense--and Kissinger's principal rival in the Cabinet--James Schlesinger. Kissinger was almost desperate to demonstrate that it was still possible for the U.S. to carry out a decisive and coherent foreign policy in this "climate of recriminations." One source familiar with the January meeting of the 40 Committee asserts: "I think Kissinger saw this [situation in Angola] as the place to find out if you could still have covert operations."[12]

At this meeting, which occurred just before the Angolan transitional government was installed on 31 January 1975, the CIA requested approval of $300,000 in covert support to help the FNLA during the predicted scramble for power. It was asserted that the money would give the U.S. "some capital in the bank with one of the leaders of a government that was going to control a fairly sizeable country."[13] The CIA averred that aid to Roberto would provide the "most stable and reliable government."[14] In addition, the argument was advanced that this aid would signal to President Mobutu of Zaire, who had been strongly backing the FNLA for a decade and who viewed the MPLA as a mortal enemy, that Washington was sympathetic to his position. The U.S. has been more opposed to Soviet activities in Zaire than in any other African country and has roughly $800 million invested there (about three times more than in Angola). Therefore, Zaire was always a primary consideration in all American decisions concerning covert aid to the FNLA. One account of the meeting indicates that the Secretary of State used the word "compelling" to describe the CIA presentation on Angola; the request was therefore "routinely approved." [15]

While there appears to be little controversy over the factors which led to the decision, there has been considerable disagreement over the significance of the clandestine aid that was given in January 1975. Defenders have argued that $300,000 is really inconsequential within the context of American covert aid to factions in other foreign civil wars. Kissinger, in fact, argued that the money was given only to assist in political organizing, "to buy bicycles, paper clips, etc.," adding that it wasn't even given in a lump sum. Furthermore, it has been argued, the $300,000 was considerably less than the amount the Soviets had given the MPLA since resuming their support in October or November of 1974.

Critics, on the other hand, have pointed to a number of factors which they argue give the initial grant of $300,000 infinitely greater significance than the U.S. government has claimed. They maintain that it was not the magnitude of the aid which was important but what it signified. For example:

(1) While small, this covert aid to Roberto was thirty times more than the CIA had been supplying him in recent years.

(2) The CIA money should not be considered in isolation but combined with the military aid given Zaire which had been turned over to the FNLA.

(3) The aid indicated that the United States had decided to meddle in Angolan affairs even before the transitional government had an opportunity to prove whether or not it

could work.

(4)   Given the perceived relative strength of the FNLA and
      the weakness of the MPLA at the time, the aid gave rise
      to speculation that the U.S. was intent on helping to
      assure FNLA dominance.

(5)   The covert support hardened a commitment to the FNLA,
      thereby starting the U.S. down the road to support of a
      movement which virtually all officials in the State De-
      partment (below the Secretary) viewed as having the
      narrowest base, least popular support, and practically
      no political organization.

(6)   While the amount was not great, it did make a noticeable
      difference in the FNLA's spending which was clearly per-
      ceived by the Soviet Union, thus signaling to Moscow that
      the U.S. was back in the business of supplying the FNLA
      with "program assistance."[16]

(7)   The impact of the American aid had to be viewed in con-
      junction with the large amounts of support which China
      had been giving to the FNLA at the same time. The com-
      bination of American and Chinese aid, the critics
      charge, was a clear signal to the Soviet Union that if
      they failed to escalate their support for the MPLA,
      Holden Roberto might possibly acquire the means to
      carry out his frequent threats to crush the MPLA.

The last point lies at the heart of the debate over the impact of

the initial installment of U.S. covert aid. The question which has

yet to be adequately answered is: Was the large Soviet buildup of

the MPLA in March/April 1975--which so "alarmed" Secretary Kissinger--

(a) merely a response to the American and Chinese aid, i.e., an at-

tempt to bring the MPLA up to a level of military parity with the

FNLA,[17] or (b) a manifestation of Soviet aggressive and expansionist policies aimed at putting "the MPLA into power in Angola through stepped up shipments of arms?"[18] This difference in interpretation of Soviet motivation and actions permeates the American debate over Angola both within government and among the general public. The debate has been clouded further by conflicting "facts" presented by the interested parties in order to prove their contentions about Soviet actions at different stages of the Angolan conflict. In short, there is little agreement about which country or nationalist party did what, when, how, and why.

One fact which has not been disputed is the decision by the 40 Committee in January 1975 to reject the CIA's request for $100,000 for UNITA. This decision later came to haunt the Secretary of State and other officials. As the fighting continued throughout 1975, Roberto demonstrated daily why almost no U.S. official or any commentators in the mass media praised his leadership or organization beyond the acknowledgment that he represented the best means of stopping the MPLA. On the other hand, UNITA, and particularly its leader Jonas Savimbi, continued to impress favorably a growing number of Americans. Seven months passed, however, before the 40 Committee decided (on July 18th) to also send covert aid to UNITA. The January decision not to support UNITA was apparently based on "past connections [with the FNLA], and an irrepressible habit of thinking in terms of 'our team' and 'theirs,' [which] enticed the Administration into choosing one side."[19]

Following the military defeat of the FNLA and UNITA in early

1976, one of the leading American governmental experts on Angola offered an interesting analysis of why the initial refusal to assist
UNITA was a major error for those who believed in the course of intervention. His postmortem analysis can be paraphrased as follows:

> I will never understand why we backed the FNLA. Every-
> body knew that Roberto had little political organization nor did he
> have support outside the northwest corner of the country.
> Our biggest mistake was not to have supported UNITA back in
> January 1975. If we had I am sure that the entire course of
> the struggle would have been different. We were certain that
> it would be impossible to form a government in Angola without
> the MPLA and almost as certain that it would be impossible
> for the MPLA and FNLA to exist peacefully in the same govern-
> ment. On the other hand, there were numerous signs that UNITA
> and the MPLA could work together; they were really the natural
> allies in the struggle. I'm convinced that if UNITA had been
> well armed by the middle of 1975 (when our intelligence re-
> vealed that they still had only 3,000 weapons in their army),
> the MPLA would have formed a coalition with them rather than
> fight them. Moreover, since the arms we finally sent to UNITA
> did not arrive until almost September, we contributed to UNITA's
> decision to seek military aid from South Africa, which ultimately
> proved to be Savimbi's Achilles heel.

Background to the Major Escalation in July 1975

The occasional exchanges of gunfire and kidnapping which characterized relations between the MPLA and the FNLA at the time of the
installation of the transitional government (31 January 1975) had become open warfare by the time the 40 Committee met in mid-July to ap-
prove a major escalation of American covert support. During those six

months each of the three parties attempted to consolidate its influence and control within the region of the country considered to
be its "natural" stronghold: the FNLA in the northwest, the MPLA
in the west-central area including the capital Luanda, and the UNITA
in the central highlands. Because no clear demarcations existed among
these spheres of influence, there were frequent clashes. The only
party which seriously tried to penetrate another's bailiwick
was the FNLA which challenged the MPLA for control of Luanda and its
outlying areas.[20] The capital thus became the focal point of most
of the fighting during early 1975.

By late March the FNLA, reinforced with soldiers from Zaire's
army, had moved approximately 4,000 troops to within 35 miles (north)
of Luanda. In taking the town of Caxito (23 March 1975) the FNLA
killed and mutilated over sixty MPLA supporters which, according to
the MPLA, marked the beginning of the civil war, and, for Henry Kissinger, signified "the first of repeated military clashes." Clearly
it was a major turning point in the struggle.[21] The fighting
between the FNLA and the MPLA had taken on the proportions of a holy
war: each party viewed the other as the devil incarnate, incapable
of redemption, part of an international plot directed against itself.
Moreover, each party became convinced that the elimination of the
other was necessary for the peace and tranquility of the country.

At this time the Soviet Union greatly expanded its military
assistance to the MPLA. From March to July American officials
estimate that the Soviets delivered over 100 tons of arms (valued
at between $20 and $35 million) to the MPLA in Angola. This was

clearly an "escalation" from the previous levels of Soviet
support, but the crucial question for American policy makers
centered on whether this Soviet aid (especially in March and April)
was also a major escalation in the war. In other words, was this jump
in Soviet aid merely intended to bring the MPLA to a level of
military parity with the FNLA--the position held by most experts
in the State Department's Africa Bureau and a number in the CIA--
or was it intended to provide the MPLA with enough military equipment
to forceably seize power, as the Secretary of State believed? Kissinger's alarmist perception later provided the rationale for a
counter American escalation in July. [22]

Henry Kissinger was attuned to more than battle reports at the
time of the 40 Committee's June meeting when the CIA suggested that
the U.S. vastly increase its support in Angola in order to counter
Soviet aid. Following General Spinola's aborted coup attempt, Portugal was seen as having slipped deeper under Communist control, increasing a perceived threat to the security of the NATO alliance.
The ignominious end of the Vietnam war had raised questions about
American power and resolve which troubled the Secretary of State. He
was momentarily bolstered, however, by the strong backing he received
in Congress during the Mayaguez incident in mid-May and felt that
perhaps it was possible to win over the anti-war alliance in
Congress. [23]

Early in June reports began to appear which seemed to confirm

suspicions that Somalia had become a "Soviet satellite in Africa."
Defense Secretary James Schlesinger showed aerial photographs of
Soviet missile installations at Berbera to the Senate Armed Services
Committee, then proceeded to leak them to a mass circulation weekly--
just in case his point had been missed by the public. Schlesinger's
point, of course, was that the Soviets were taking advantage of
detente to expand their spheres of influence to the detriment of
the U.S.--and Somalia was only the latest example. His charges that
Kissinger was either naive about the Soviets or so intent on saving
detente that he was prepared to overlook almost any Soviet aggression struck a responsive chord in the Joint Chiefs of Staff and the
right wing of the Republican Party. "There was plainly an incentive,"
Morris maintains in the light of Schlesinger's attack, "for Kissinger
to prove that he could stand up to the Russians."[24]

Kissinger is reported to have been generally favorable to the
June CIA requests for Angola funding and to support for UNITA. First,
however, he wanted to have both the State Department and the National
Security Council conduct thorough studies of the situation before the
40 Committee's next meeting in mid-July.

In response the State Department's Bureau of African Affairs,
Policy Planning, and Intelligence and Research recommended that the
U.S. stay out of the Angolan conflict, attempt to seek a diplomatic
solution but play no active role in the war. Chief spokesperson for
this position was Assistant Secretary of State for African Affairs
Nathaniel Davis, who, reflecting the overwhelming majority in the

bureau, argued:[25]

(1) Neither the FNLA nor the UNITA troops are any match for the MPLA army and the U.S. would therefore be associated with the losing side.

(2) When the U.S. efforts ended in failure, the two African leaders with whom the United States had cooperated in this matter, Presidents Mobutu of Zaire and Kaunda of Zambia, would be jeopardized.

(3) The U.S. might ultimately have South Africa as its only ally which would prove to be a major diplomatic setback.

(4) To assist Savimbi and Roberto would be perceived as a major escalation by the Soviet Union and therefore lead to even greater Russian involvement.

Instead, Davis argued, the appropriate U.S. response should be to launch a diplomatic effort pointing to Soviet activities as a violation of the OAU's position against outside intervention in Angola (essentially the course China pursued during the latter half of 1975).

Kissinger rejected the State Department's case against intervention. Unexpectedly, Davis resigned in August. "He believed the policy was utterly wrong," one official stated, "and he was unable to carry out a policy he was inimically opposed to."[26] With his timely resignation after only five months in office, Davis altered his public image from the 'scoundrel in Chile' to the 'hero of Angola.' In both cases, however, the public gave too much credit to Davis and too little to the bureaucracy.

While the State Department overwhelmingly opposed U.S. intervention in Angola, it did not speak with a single voice.[27] The opposition

represented a wide variety of viewpoints whose common denominator
was the belief that the United States would lose regardless of the
war's outcome. At one extreme were the "optimists"--those who did not
perceive Soviet assistance to the MPLA (before Angolan independence)
as significantly more threatening than the total amount of aid
channeled to the FNLA and UNITA from the United States, Europe, and
Africa. Moreover, the majority of optimists did not see an MPLA
victory as representing a disaster for the U.S. On the contrary,
they were (and still are) convinced that the U.S. could maintain
relatively normal relations with a government in Luanda dominated
by the MPLA.

The "pessimists" tended to view soviet actions in Angola as
highly aggressive and expansionistic. They saw (and still see) the
MPLA as a threat to the United States because either they thought
that the Marxists in the Party would not take political stands independent of Moscow or, even if they believed the MPLA desired to be
independent, they were certain that the Soviet Union would not allow
any opposition to its "hegemonic aspirations" in Angola. The pessimists therefore concluded that an MPLA victory would create problems
for the U.S.; nevertheless they opposed intervention because they
were convinced it would result in even greater problems.

Practically all those who preferred diplomacy to military intervention pointed to the FNLA's incompetence and the kiss of death
which would result from any association with South Africa. This positi
is cogently expressed by one of the most "pessimistic" among high-level
officials at the State Department: "If the U.S. can be seduced to join
this ménage à trois, then the U.S. will be completely and publicly

screwed in Africa. There is no win for Uncle Sam in this unholy bed."

While the State Department and National Security Council were conducting their reviews of various options on Angola in June/July 1975, the Senate Foreign Relations Committee's Subcommittee on African Affairs held a series of public hearings on southern Africa. Considerable attention had been focused on Angola because of numerous charges in American and European newspapers that the United States was intervening in Angola through Zaire. The Angola hearings revealed that the Administration had little to fear from Congress at that time. Whereas the three academic witnesses who testified before the Subcommittee vigorously condemned any form of direct or indirect American involvement in Angola, only one Senator had enough time or interest to attend the hearings--the Subcommittee's chairman, Dick Clark, a freshman Senator from the midwest farming state of Iowa.[28]

Clark pressed Nathaniel Davis on U.S. intervention on July 14, 1975, only three days before the 40 Committee approved the CIA's request for Angola and one month before Davis's resignation. In response to Clark's inquiry as to whether the U.S. military aid to Zaire was being passed on to one or more Angolan factions, Davis responded that that would be possible only after specific agreements were signed and special procedures followed and added that he was "certain" this had not occurred. When Clark noted that those agreements were sometimes violated (e.g., Turkey), Davis responded, "I have no knowledge of violations of the agreement [between the U.S. and Zaire]."[29] For the time being the Senate was held in check; it would present no problems until the fall.

According to the House Select Committee on Intelligence report of January 1976, National Security Council aides blocked recommendations which called for diplomatic efforts rather than military intervention.[30] The NSC provided the justification for the 40 Committee's July 18th decision to increase the previous level of American covert aid to the FNLA roughly 100 times and to include UNITA as a recipient of CIA aid. Secretary of State Kissinger and others were convinced that it would be futile to attempt diplomacy with the Soviets on Angola without first building up the FNLA and UNITA forces.

In order to accomplish this buildup the 40 Committee authorized the following measures:[31]

> A direct shipment of arms to the forces led by Roberto and Savimbi and replacement of arms that had been supplied previously and would continue to be supplied by Zaire and Zambia. It was agreed to permit Zaire and Zambia to provide as much non-American equipment as possible at first in order to minimize the overt link with the United States.

> Exposure of Soviet military assistance to the MPLA through information programs and other means with special emphasis on possibly embarrasssing those African nations serving as conduits for Soviet aid to the MPLA.

> The launching of an information program designed to build up the abilities and integrity of the FNLA and UNITA.

> Dispatching $14 million in two stages ($6 and $8 million) to the FNLA and UNITA.

The $14 million which was approved in July was increased to $25 million in August and to about $32 million in November. However, the report of the House Select Committee on Intelligence cites rather convincing evidence that "CIA 'costing' procedures and the use of surplus equipment have resulted in a substantial understatement of the value of U.S. aid....staff advises that the CIA's ordnance figure should at least be doubled." [32]

If one were to adjust the underestimated value of American assistance and add to it the total cost of aid sent to the FNLA and UNITA from China, France, Great Britain, West Germany, Belgium, South Africa and others, it would appear to be more or less equal to the CIA estimate of Soviet aid to the MPLA of $80 million through October 1975 when the major foreign interventions occurred. Officials in the Ford Administration reported that French assistance to the FNLA was "substantial" although below the American level, whereas they characterized British support as "modest." [33] As noted earlier, there has been so much disagreement over the question of who gave how much to whom and when that it is doubtful whether the truth will ever be known.   Nevertheless, it is possible to declare that there was no significant difference in the amount of outside assistance to the two sides (MPLA vs FNLA/UNITA) between July and October 1975.

Pre-Independence Escalation and Foreign Intervention

Those four months (July-October 1975) were a crucial period in the Angolan conflict. It began in July when the MPLA expelled the

FNLA and UNITA from the capital and the transitional government
collapsed. This was followed by South Africa's first incursion
into Angola on August 9th. In mid-August Portugal reassumed power
in Luanda; finally, October 23rd marked the major invasion by South
Africa just prior to independence. During these four months the
MPLA destroyed the myth of the FNLA's military superiority by
expanding its presence throughout Angola; by mid-October the MPLA
controlled twelve of the sixteen district capitals. While it might
be correct to say that this four-month expansion by the MPLA could
not have been accomplished without Soviet aid, it was achieved--
contrary to assertions by the Secretary of State and other officials--
without (a) the use of foreign troops, (b) a significant advantage
in the number or quality of weapons over the FNLA, or (c) a larger
army than the forces of the FNLA and UNITA.[34]

During the three weeks prior to Angola's independence (11
November 1975), several important events occurred which dramatically
altered the course of the war and, ultimately, U.S. participation.
On October 23rd a column of approximately 1500 white soldiers, including
South African regular troops, a number of (former) Portuguese soldiers,
and a variety of European and American mercenaries, crossed into
southern Angola from Namibia and launched a major attack against the
MPLA. With minor support from the Chipenda faction of the FNLA and
UNITA troops, and backed by dozens of tanks, French Panhard armored
cars and helicopters, the column marched north for 400 miles in less
than three weeks, driving the MPLA and their Cuban allies from most
of the area they had won during the summer. Some Portuguese observers

in Angola thought that the South African-led attack, which eventually included over 5000 South African troops, would reach the capital before independence. [35]

At the same time, with the support of between 2000 and 3000 Zairien regular troops from the north, the FNLA launched a major armored attack. Just prior to November 11th, the FNLA and Zairien troops massed tanks, heavy artillery, and mortars at Quifangondo, only 12 miles north of Luanda, where FNLA President Holden Roberto proudly boasted that he would "flatten the capital." At the time of their departure, a number of Portuguese commanders predicted that a "bloody massacre" would occur in Luanda when (not "if") the FNLA troops arrived in the capital. On November 12th foreign diplomats in Luanda were quoted as fearing that the mercenary column from the south was about to "link up with troops north of Luanda and choke off the city." [36] There is very little question that if the MPLA had not received immediate and extensive outside assistance at this point, they would have been in grave danger of being defeated militarily by this north/south pincer movement, spearheaded by well over 5000 foreign troops. This is precisely when the Cuban soldiers arrived en masse.

The Cuban Dimension

The numerous versions and interpretations of the nature of Cuban involvement in Angola range from lauding it as a defensive response to attacks by a racist South Africa to portraying it as an act of aggression by a Soviet pawn. An accurate picture of Cuban involvement is necessary not only to comprehend what happened in Angola but also to understand and analyze the breakdown on this issue of U.S.-Soviet relations in 1975-76 and the performance of Henry Kissinger during his final two years as Secretary of State.

The Cuban operation during the Angolan war must be viewed in phases, rather than as part of some grand plot formulated at the outset. [37] At least four phases can be discerned and discussed in terms of the number of Cuban soldiers in Angola, the apparent goals of the Castro regime, the military exigencies resulting from the intervention of external forces against the MPLA, and the impact of Cuban assistance on the outcome of the war.

According to U.S. intelligence sources no more than 100 Cuban advisors were in Angola before the beginning of the summer of 1975 when approximately 200 more (advisors) arrived. [38] Their presence was neither initiated nor funded by the Soviet Union, rather it was part of Cuba's general military assistance program to a number of countries and liberation movements in Africa, Latin America, and the Middle East. In fact, this initial help raised few eyebrows since Cuba had been providing military assistance to the MPLA for over a decade. In addition, at this particular time, Angola was not one of Cuba's largest or most important military programs in the Third World (i.e., Guinea, Tanzania, Somalia, Equatorial Guinea, Syria, South Yemen). Nor was the Cuban assistance substantial enough to make any appreciable difference in the fighting between the MPLA and FNLA. Cubans were not even involved as combatants until after September. Thus, the Cuban assistance during this period can be characterized

as an attempt to help train and organize the green MPLA army which
American sources believed had almost no officers over the age of 30.

On September 7th troops embarked from Havana, arriving in
Angola at the end of September (27th), bringing the total number of
Cubans in Angola to approximately 1000. If this second phase of
Cuban involvement, spanning most of October, is viewed in isolation
or only in relation to the fact that it preceded the South African
and Zairien invasions by a few weeks--as the State Department and a
number of American and British journalists have portrayed it--
then it could be considered as the turning point when Cuba decided
to provide the assistance necessary for an MPLA victory.[39] But it
did not occur in isolation.

The decision to increase the number of Cubans in Angola came
in response to a request by the MPLA which had become gravely
concerned by a number of ominous developments in August. The first
invasion by South Africa on August 9th constituted a major escalation
of the war; in addition, no one in Angola (including the Portuguese)
knew if it was a single action or part of a larger plan to push
further into MPLA-controlled territory. Before the end of August,
the MPLA was convinced that a major South African invasion was imminent.
The party was also threatened in the north when the FNLA and Zairien
troops, along with hundreds of former Portuguese commandos, moved to
within thirty-five miles of the capital only days after the South
African thrust into the South. The massing of troops in Zaire on
the borders of Cabinda further threatened to challenge the MPLA's
hold over the oil-rich enclave. Moreover, the seizure of power by
the Portuguese in mid-August meant that the MPLA was forced to sur-

render some of its control in the capital to a Portuguese regime
which the party considered to be hostile. The fall of the Gonçalves
regime in Lisbon at this time merely confirmed the MPLA's worst
fears about the Portuguese. Finally, the millions of dollars worth
of American weapons to the FNLA and (for the first time) to UNITA,
approved by the 40 Committee in July, began to arrive in late August
and early September, signaling to the MPLA a major American escalation whose magnitude was as yet unknown.

In light of these developments it is highly unlikely that, when
the Cuban Government agreed to the MPLA request (in August) to
treble its presence in Angola, either the MPLA, Cuba, or the Soviet
Union believed the approximately one thousand Cubans could provide
the MPLA with a decisive edge for winning the war outright. If this
had been the intention, surely the new arrivals would have been
sent immediately on offensive missions instead of remaining in
the back lines instructing or being defensively deployed in Cabinda.
In fact, according to U.S. intelligence sources, Cubans were not
sent to the front until late October, after the South African
invasion. Thus the magnitude of the Cubans' second phase was not sufficient to measurably increase the MPLA's offensive power. At best,

the Cubans helped to consolidate control over those parts of the
country where the MPLA had already been dominant.

The third phase--which lasted only a few weeks--was initiated by
the October 23rd invasion by South African regular troops and a large
assortment of mercenaries. This escalation, along with the FNLA/Zair-
ien thrust in the north, not only threatened the MPLA but the Cubans
as well. Both were now clearly on the defensive; few familiar
with the situation in Angola at the time were prepared to wager against
the probability that the foreign invaders would reach the capital. [40]
It would have been difficult to dispute Fidel Castro's depiction of
the situation in early November when the leadership of the Cuban Communist Party decided to grant the MPLA's request for a substantial
increase in troops and weapons:

> [When the first Cuban troop unit arrived in Angola on Nov-
> ember 5th] the foreign interventionists were 25 kilometers
> from Luanda in the north, their 140 millimeter artillery was
> bombing the suburbs of the capital and the South African
> fascists had already penetrated more than 700 kilometers into
> the south from the Namibian border, while Cabinda was heroi-
> cally defended by MPLA fighters and a handful of Cuban in-
> structors. (41)

The only way to interpret the Cuban dispatch of an additional two to
three thousand troops by independence day (November 11) as an offen-
sive operation would be to ignore the role of the South African,
Zairien, and mercenary forces. In fact, Secretary of State Henry
Kissinger appears to have viewed the situation in precisely those
terms. With respect to those same events prior to independence,
Kissinger argued in testimony before the Senate Foreign Relations
Committee:

> The UNITA forces launched a successful counteroffensive
> which swept the MPLA out of the southern and most of the
> central part of Angola. In the north the FNLA also made
> significant advances. By Independence Day--November 11--the
> MPLA controlled only the former colonial capital of Luanda
> and a narrow belt across northcentral Angola.
> In October massive increases in Soviet and Cuban military
> assistance began to arrive.[42]

From this perspective the Secretary of State could conclude that Cuban actions during the third phase represented an effort "to take unilateral advantage of a turbulent local situation...."[43]

Whereas Kissinger overlooked the presence of foreign troops and assistance to the FNLA/UNITA forces, he greatly exaggerated the importance of the Soviet and Cuban assistance to the MPLA before independence. For example, on the night of Angolan independence the Secretary of State told the Pittsburgh World Affairs Council that "the forces of the MPLA achieved control of the capital with substantial Communist assistance," completely ignoring the vital fact that Luanda has always constituted the very core of MPLA strength in Angola.[44]

The fourth and final phase of the Cuban operation during the Angolan war commenced around independence day when, in Castro's words, "Cuba sent the men and weapons necessary to win that struggle."[45] By the end of 1975 an alleged 7000 Cubans were in Angola, and by late January, 1976, the number had risen to over 12,000. The war ended the following month. The FNLA, UNITA, and remnants of their foreign backers were no match for the MPLA and Cuban forces.

While this account of the phases of Cuban intervention fixes the decision to provide the material and manpower necessary for a quick and undisputed MPLA victory to the first weeks of November 1975, it does not answer the question of whose decision it was to meet the MPLA's request for help. The debate has focused on whether the Cuban government acted on its own or as a reluctant surrogate of the Soviet Union. Most U.S. officials, including the Secretary of State, and a host of journalists argued that the Cubans went to Angola to pay off their approximately five and one-half billion dollar "IOU" to the Soviet Union for military and economic assistance extended since 1960.[46] In other words, as "surrogates" of the Soviets. Both the MPLA and the Cubans have vociferously denied these charges. In a speech on 19 April 1976 marking the fifteenth anniversary of the Bay of Pigs invasion, Castro asserted that the Soviet Union "never requested" him to send soldiers--"Cuba's decision was made absolutely under its own responsibility."

While Americans are generally reluctant to accept Fidel Castro's word on most matters, The Washington Post confirmed Castro's version in a story, based on allegedly reliable leaks, which maintained that high "American officials familiar with the available evidence do not believe that the Cubans were 'pressured' by Moscow into furnishing men for the Angolan battlefields."[47] My own discussions with State Department officials in the African and Latin American bureaus convince me that Castro's (and The Washington Post's) interpretation is essentially correct. The decision to send troops was made by the Cubans themselves. They consulted with the Soviets over logistics and strategy but, in the words of a leading expert in the State Department, "the Cubans were never pushed by the Russians to do anything in Angola they didn't want to do." However, more important than whether or not the Soviet Union could command the use of Cuban troops in Angola is the fact that by early November there was a coalescence of interests among the MPLA, Cuba and the Soviet Union to have the Cuban Government send the men "necessary to win that struggle."

The Debate

At the peak of the pincer movement against the MPLA, just five days before Angola's independence, the Senate Foreign Relations Committee held a significant closed hearing on Angola. There had been charges daily that the U.S. was involved clandestinely in the Angolan war, yet no Administration official had publicly confirmed the allegations.[48] Some Committee members were determined to discover precisely what the U.S. was doing in Angola and why. Accordingly, they invited testimony from William Colby, Director of the CIA, and Secretary Kissinger who, because he was abroad at the time, was replaced by Undersecretary of State Joseph Sisco. The November 6th hearing was necessitated by the Senate's apparent failure to exercise its recently acquired power of oversight over covert operations. The Hughes-Ryan Amendment to the Foreign Assistance Act, passed in December 1974, had led most Congressmen to believe that it was no longer possible for the U.S. to become involved clandestinely in a foreign war without their approval. Angola proved that they were mistaken, as is illustrated by the experiences of one member of the Senate Committee, Dick Clark, Chairman of the Subcommittee on Africa.

Following his mid-1975 hearings on southern Africa, Clark asked for and received a CIA briefing in late July on U.S. covert activities in Angola.[49] A short time later Nathaniel Davis, Assistant Secretary of State for Africa, passed a note to Clark during a public hearing asking not to be pressed on certain points about Angola because "we both know" about these covert activities. Clark was frustrated by this experience because it indicated that "classified briefings actually become an impediment to effective oversight." In fact, he concluded that the oversight role provided "for nothing more than an ex-post-facto communication to Congress of decisions already reached ...[with] no provision for advice or consent."

Robert Ingersoll, Deputy Secretary of State, also briefed Clark's African Subcommittee at this time. Committee members protested that the Administration lacked any concept of what the FNLA could or would do with the increased American aid. They suggested that it would be much wiser to discuss the Angolan situation with the Soviets, whose level of escalation was still not great by July 1975. Ingersoll retorted that this would be futile because the Soviets simply would not respond. The U.S. would first have to send substantial material aid to Angola as "bargaining chips." This remained the Administration's posture until discussions with the Soviet Union on this matter were initiated in late October, 1975. Unfortunately for the architects of that strategy, by the time the U.S. chose to bargain with the Soviet Union, Uncle Sam's biggest "bargaining chip" (South Africa) had come up double zero--through ineffectiveness against the Cubans and bringing considerable condemnation to the American backed FNLA/UNITA side.

For a firsthand view of the situation, Senator Clark visited Angola in August where he met the leaders of the three contending factions. He returned further convinced that American involvement was a mistake and communicated this to the Director of the Central Intelligence Agency. But Colby disagreed. Frustrated, Clark reported on his trip to the full Foreign Relations Committee, explaining his objections to American policy in Angola, which resulted in the Committee deciding to call Kissinger and Colby for a complete review of Angolan and African policy. The stage was set for the first major confrontation between the Administration and the Senate over Angola.

On November 6th, behind the locked doors of the Senate chamber, Colby and Sisco admitted that the CIA was covertly supplying the FNLA and UNITA with money, rifles, machine guns, mortars, vehicles, ammunition, and logistical support. Many Senators expressed strong doubts about the/deepening American involvement. Clark argued that the U.S. course of military intervention was alienating most African leaders, to which Sisco responded that the U.S. had to deal with the immediate problem of Soviet influence. Colby added that the U.S. had a general interest in preventing a new country from falling under Soviet influence.

While the few interested Senators were generally attuned to the realities within the Angolan context, the Administration was clearly focused on the global balance of power between the Soviet Union and the United States. From this perspective Colby and Sisco defended American covert aid on the grounds that it provided the U.S. with "bargaining chips" with the Soviet Union. The Senators strongly disagreed but the only action they could take would be to pass an amendment prohibiting such aid. They were prevented from doing so only by the factor of secrecy which still cloaked America's intervention

Ironically, that cloak of secrecy fell the following day when The New York Times published the essence of Colby's and Sisco's testimony before the Foreign Relations Committee. The Washington Post published more details of the testimony the day after.[50] These stories began an unprecedented series of "leaks" to the press by various members of Congress and other opponents of U.S. intervention in government agencies, including the Department of State, Department of Defense, and the CIA. Over the next two months there were so many leaks about American covert activities in Angola that, according to one knowledgeable source in State Department intelligence, only minor details escaped the attention of the public; "all of the essential facts were published in the newspapers."[51]

However, it was only in early December that the Secretary of State acknowledged during a press conference that the U.S. was indirectly providing military assistance for use in Angola. This was the first public avowal of American intervention by any official in Washington. The admission of U.S. involvement not only ignited a major debate in the media and among the public but also lifted restrictions from Congressmen who had been unable to introduce legislation (to cut off U.S. participation) on the grounds that it was not a "public" matter.

Differing perceptions of the lessons of Vietnam were evidenced in the debate on Angola. On one side were those (including President Ford, Dr. Kissinger, Director Colby, and Secretary Schlesinger) who argued that it was imperative for the U.S. to reestablish its "resolve" and "will to resist" Soviet expansion throughout the world. On the other side it was argued that, after Vietnam, the U.S. should not become involved in more remote civil wars where it has no immediate interests.[52] The country's mood indicated that the American public, embittered and disillusioned by recent American losses in Southeast Asia, would not support even minor involvement in another remote and confusing civil conflict. This was confirmed in a nationwide poll conducted by Lou Harris (released on 21 November 1975) which showed that 72 percent of all Americans felt that the U.S. should avoid involvement in all guerrilla-type wars in the future when it appears the U.S. is participating in the civil war of another country.[53]

To a large majority of the Congress, media, and the general public, too many uncomfortable parallels existed between Angola in 1975 and Vietnam before the Gulf of Tonkin Resolution in 1964:

- both were remote civil wars in areas outside traditional spheres of American interest or influence;

- neither was vital to U.S. economic or security interests;

- American involvement in both places followed the departure of a European power from its colony;

- American allies needed vast amounts of equipment, training, and manpower to operate all but the most rudimentary weapons and equipment;

- it was not clear in either case that it would make a significant difference to the U.S. which side won the war;

- the U.S. backing a movement (FNLA) which, in comparison to its rivals, lacked leadership, organization, motivation, and military capabilities (U.S. support for UNITA came too late to be considered relevant); and

- there was no "light at the end of the tunnel" in either conflict--it was never clear when or how the wars would end.

(Actually, the Administration's decision to significantly increase its covert commitment in Angola four times within four months in late 1975 provided an ominous sign that the U.S. was locked into another endless spiral of escalation with the Soviet Union.)

The protestations by Kissinger, Colby, Moynihan, and Ford that Angola was not "another Vietnam" were doubted by many, including those who shared a deep concern over the alleged threat which Soviet activities in Angola portended for the ability of the superpowers to compete on a global scale without resort to war or other unacceptable means. By emphasizing only the global stakes in Angola, the Ford Administration indicated that it had failed to learn a vital lesson from the experience in Southeast Asia--a lesson which had not escaped the majority of the Congress or the public.

Both "global" and "local" circumstances must be carefully considered before the U.S. commits itself to a faction in a foreign civil conflict. After all, the U.S. did not withdraw from Vietnam and Cambodia because of a change in the perceptions of the "global" aims. The principal American aim was always to stop "Soviet expansion." The U.S. withdrew when it became clear that "locally" a victory required more than American aid. After spending over $150 billion, it became obvious that more than money and arms was needed to forge a winning combination or to effectuate a desired solution. This realization forced Americans to take a hard look at the Thieu and Lon Nol regimes and most concluded that their prospects for victory ranged from poor to nil. By the war's end, few Americans disagreed with the proposition that sending further arms or men to Vietnam or Cambodia would be a tragic waste.

Yet, in Angola the Administration was once again telling the public that global ramifications were more important than local realities. In fact, Secretary Kissinger underscored his preoccupation with the global dimension when he told Senator Clark, during the height of the debate, that his opposition to U.S. intervention may be right in the African context, but it was wrong in the global context. However, neither Clark nor a majority of his colleagues was ever persuaded that it was possible to ignore the Angolan context and still win globally. On the contrary, Clark was convinced that the U.S. was backing the only "sure loser," which guaranteed a loss globally. "Our task," the Senator observed, "was essentially to save the Secretary from himself."

The Angolan context had changed considerably by early December when the Senate Foreign Relations Committee strongly endorsed Senator Clark's proposed amendment to the Foreign Assistance Act to cut off all covert aid to Angola. The Committee firmly believed that the Angolan context indicated the U.S. could not win. Given the massive Cuban presence, an estimated $100 million in Soviet arms, and the poor quality of the FNLA/UNITA troops, it was concluded that the U.S. had no other choice than an immediate cessation of aid. Once the magnitude and sophistication of the Russian arms in the hands of thousands of Cuban troops were apparent, it was no longer a question of going "tit-for-tat" with the Soviet Union in arms supplies. It was also necessary to consider who would operate the increasingly sophisticated American arms being sent. Both Roberto and Savimbi had told _Time_ and _Newsweek_ that they didn't have Angolans trained to utilize much of the equipment they received.[54]

The Committee assumed that since neither the FNLA nor UNITA could absorb or utilize the $28 million in additional military aid proposed by the Administration, the U.S. was faced with some unpalatable options:

(1) increase South African participation (which would, in effect, amount to an American-South African alliance);

(2) hire mercenaries from around the world; and/or

(3) send American advisors and possibly some troops.

They concluded that these options were unacceptable and that the only alternative was to cut off all further aid. When the Clark amendment fell victim to President Ford's veto of the Foreign Assistance Act, Senator John Tunney introduced an amendment to the defense appropriations bill to prevent any American covert aid from going to Angola.

The day before the Senate voted on the Tunney Amendment (19 December 1975), Secretary Kissinger pushed for a "compromise" over the Administration's $28 million request during a private meeting with two dozen Senators. Kissinger admonished that the U.S. could not sit idly by while the Soviet Union was heavily involved 8000 miles from its shores. He persuaded many of the Senators that some type of compromise was necessary, but Tunney remained adamant. For him it was not a question of another $10, $28, or $100 million in arms but, like many of his colleagues, he was concerned about who would operate the equipment and fire the arms:

> The United States cannot save a losing cause with money alone. We would have to supply aircraft, tanks, antiaircraft guns and missiles, helicopters and other weapons. Who is to

> fly and operate them? There is no time for training programs,
> there are no allies ready to intervene with such equipment.
> We would have to send instructors and advisers and, in all
> probability, American troops in a pattern too reminiscent of
> Vietnam. (55)

On the 19th of December 1975, the Senate passed the Tunney Amendment
by 54 votes to 22. The following month (January 27, 1976) the House
of Representatives passed its version of the same amendment by an
even greater margin (323 votes to 99) which, for all practical purposes, brought an end to further American participation in the Angolan war. By this time the war was virtually over in any case. The
FNLA and UNITA were finally defeated militarily in early February
1976, thus ending the war but, given the tenacity of Ford and Kissinger and the challenge of Ronald Reagan in the presidential primaries, not the debate.

Overview

That American policy toward Angola from the mid-1960s through
the end of the civil war in early 1976 was dominated by domestic and
global considerations to the exclusion of Angolan realities was never
more evident than in the Ford Administration's decision to choose
sides in that civil war. Once the Administration's defense of its
decision to intervene is stripped of its rationalizations, rhetoric,
euphemisms, and moralizing, what remains is a single-minded determination to respond to the Soviet Union. That determination was not
the result of a conviction that one of the contending factions was
better for the U.S. or for Angola, but arose from the simple fact
that the Soviet Union was backing one of the factions.

Ironically, the CIA saw no real difference among the three nationalist groups. James Pott, CIA Director of African Affairs, told
Senator Tunney before the Senate vote on his amendment that it would
make "no difference" to the U.S. which of the three movements won.
When Tunney pressed him on the "no difference," Pott conceded "well,
perhaps 5 percent." Colby displayed a similar perspective before
the House Select Committee on Intelligence (in mid-December 1975)
when asked about the differences among the three contesting factions:
"They are all independents. They are all for black Africa. They are
all for some fuzzy kind of social system, you know, without really
much articulation, but some sort of let's not be exploited by the
capitalist nations." If they were all so similar in outlook, why,
the Committee tried to determine, were certain nations supporting
one group against another?

Congressman Les Aspin: "And why are the Chinese backing the
moderate group?"

Mr. Colby: "Because the Soviets are backing the MPLA is the
simplest answer."

Mr. Aspin: "It sounds like that is why we are doing it."

Mr. Colby: "It is." [56]

If Colby's answer did not sound as though it were straight out
of the cold war handbook, neither did it have the ring of detente.
In Kissinger's understanding of detente, the United States "must prevent the Soviet Union from translating its growing strength into
global or regional preponderance. But we must do so without escalating every crisis into a massive confrontation."[57] Detente
clearly did not rule out competition. In fact, if one carefully

considers Soviet and American competition throughout the Third World during the years immediately preceding the Angolan war, the Soviet Union does not appear to have faired very well. Soviet plans for increased influence in Latin America were partially thwarted by the overthrow of the Allende regime in Chile. In the Middle East the Soviets suffered a series of defeats in Egypt, Syria, Iraq, and South Yemen. In Cambodia, Soviet diplomats were rather unceremoniously sent home when the Khmer Rouge took power. Finally, at the time of the Portuguese coup, the Soviets had few close allies in black Africa besides Guinea, Congo-Brazzaville, and Somalia.

What then was so special or unique about Angola that prompted the U.S. to escalate the "crisis into a major confrontation?" Did the Administration see something unusual in Soviet behavior in Angola which necessitated an American military response? How does one determine when the Soviets have exceeded the boundaries of detente to the point that a military confrontation is worth risking? Kissinger's attitude was revealed in June 1975, when the U.S. position in Indochina began to crumble. When the Secretary of State was asked to reconcile Soviet behavior in Vietnam, Portugal, and the Middle East with detente, he responded that "Vietnam was not caused by the Russians," it had "its own dynamics," of which Soviet "actions were only a part." The trouble in Portugal "was not caused by the Soviets," but "by the internal dynamics of Portugal itself." On the Middle East: "I would not be surprised if in Moscow, they made the same argument and said that we have been using detente to improve our position."[58] Apparently Kissinger made an important distinction between

Soviet activity in a given country and the "internal dynamics" of that country. Yet, if Vietnam, Portugal, and the Middle East could be accommodated within detente because the Secretary of State believed that their problems were caused by internal dynamics, rather than by the Soviet Union, why not Angola? If ever there was a clear-cut example of the internal dynamics--as distinguished from the Soviet Union--causing a civil war, it was Angola.

Moreover, even if by some twist of the imagination it were possible to view Moscow as the cause of the Angolan war, why did the Administration decide that Angola was the place to oppose the Soviets militarily--especially when Washington saw no vital interests to protect nor perceived more than a slight difference to the U.S. no matter what the outcome of the war? Given the Soviets' long time support of the MPLA and the American record of support for Portuguese colonialism, the U.S. decided to compete militarily in an area where Moscow held a strong hand. Furthermore, why did the Administration choose in mid-July 1975 to make its military stand on the side of the FNLA and UNITA? By early June intelligence sources had revealed that China was giving up on the FNLA and had told Roberto not to expect more than $100,000 in aid by the end of 1975, at which time all help would cease. Apparently, the Chinese were very disappointed in the performance of the FNLA troops, a view which was shared by almost all American observers. Why, then, did Washington decide to inherit what the Chinese saw as a losing military cause?

The President and Secretary of State frequently castigated the Congress after passage of the Tunney Amendment for being naive about

Soviet intentions in Angola and for not understanding how to deal
with the Soviet Government in such a confrontation. However, after
Vietnam, the Administration's assumption that the Soviets would
choose to compromise in Angola when faced by U.S. military power also
appears to be exceedingly naive. What led the Administration to
assume that the Soviet Union would be more amenable to military
pressure on the ground in Angola than to diplomatic leverage involving grain sales, SALT, and other bilateral matters?

The Administration's path to intervention in Angola is strewn
with unanswered questions, false assumptions, and profound misunder-
standings. The policy failed both in Angola and the United States
because the Secretary of State misperceived:

- the strengths and weaknesses of America's so-called
  "allies" and "enemies" in Angola;

- the will of the Soviet Union not to give in to combined
  American and Chinese military pressure;

- the determination of Cuba to support the MPLA;

- the degree to which South African intervention
  would prejudice the American cause; and

- his own ability to convince the Congress and American
  public that Angola would not become "another Vietnam."

Thus it was Henry Kissinger's failure to grasp either the Angolan or
the American realities which led ultimately to the defeat of his
policy during the Angolan civil war.

A New Post-War Policy?

The Kissinger policy failed during the Angolan war because it
accomplished precisely the opposite of what was intended. Through

covert military intervention the Secretary of State sought to minimize or negate Soviet influence in an independent Angola. At the
time the American policy was implemented, relations between the
Soviets and the MPLA were still not cordial, having just been resumed
after almost a year of recriminations between the two. Yet during
the war the American, Chinese, South African, and other support for
the MPLA's rivals forced the Party to depend increasingly upon the
Soviet Union, which ultimately magnified Soviet influence far beyond
their most optimistic expectations.

Following the Angolan debacle the Secretary of State was anxious
to prevent the Soviet Union from extending its influence from Angola
to the rest of southern Africa. Attention immediately focused on
Rhodesia. How would Henry Kissinger play his weak hand in Rhodesia?
Would he repeat his Angola policy of trying military means, rather
than diplomatic, to curb Soviet influence, as urged by Ronald Reagan
and other American conservatives? The overriding problem with this
option (as Reagan discovered the week before the California primary
in June 1976) was that it left only one side to support against the
Soviets--that of Ian Smith, a thoroughly unpopular and unviable alternative.

Initially, Kissinger tried to prevent the spread of Soviet influence by adopting a dual approach toward southern Africa. On the
one hand, he vigorously endorsed majority rule in Rhodesia and Namibia; on the other hand he sought to prevent "further Angolas" by
threatening U.S. retaliation if the Soviets or Cubans became involved in either of the territories dominated by white minority regimes.

Despite the Secretary's endorsement of majority rule, however, the fact remained that U.S. policy did not appear to provide concrete support of that goal. On the contrary, the continued importation of Rhodesian chrome under the Byrd Amendment combined with the threats against the Soviets and Cubans appeared to give sustenance to the Smith regime at its darkest hour. The policy was widely attacked within the U.S. and abroad (even by most countries which had supported the U.S. position on Angola) because it lacked credibility and was, once again, out of step with African realities.

At this juncture, Secretary of State Kissinger decided to take a hard look at African realities prior to his two-week African trip in late April, 1976. His first surprise was to learn that practically all African countries, including some of the MPLA's strongest supporters, were opposed to using Cuban troops to liberate Rhodesia. In fact, the Zimbabwean guerrillas were in agreement with the four African Presidents designated by the Organization of African Unity to coordinate Rhodesian policy (Julius Nyerere of Tanzania, Samora Machel of Mozambique, Kenneth Kaunda of Zambia, and Seretse Khama of Botswana) that the actual fighting should be done by the Zimbabweans themselves. He was also surprised to learn that the Soviets had their own difficulties with Rhodesia. Their best "bargaining chip" was Joshua Nkomo, a controversial leader who had been discredited after the breakdown of his negotiations with Ian Smith. Moreover, the Chinese had the inside track on the Soviets in the area of training the Zimbabwean guerrillas. Finally, he discovered that with few exceptions African leaders were adamant about keeping the cold war out of Africa and to accomplish this they were determined to prevent the Americans and Soviets from backing opposite sides in Rhodesia.

Kissinger's advisors on Africa strongly urged him to consider these facts and to adopt a new policy which would include concrete assistance to Zimbabweans because

- it was "right" with regard to majority rule;
- not providing assistance would leave the field open to the Soviets; and
- U.S. pressure might succeed in encouraging the whites to negotiate in Rhodesia, thereby forestalling a bloody civil war.

In effect, the Secretary of State was encouraged to endorse means which would achieve the same goals supported by the Soviet Union. For the first time in over seven years, Henry Kissinger listened to his Africa experts.

On 27 April 1976 in Lusaka, Zambia, Kissinger spelled out his new African policy. It contained ten points which he pledged to carry out in order to help realize majority rule in Rhodesia and Namibia.[59] Many subsequently criticized the policy for offering too little, too late and especially the Administration for its feeble efforts to push Congress, in the face of Reagan's challenge prior to the Republican convention, to implement the policy. Yet, far more important than the scope or the implementation of the policy is the fact that it removed the U.S. from an almost certain collision course with the Soviet Union and/or Cuba over an issue (majority rule in Rhodesia) which could only have resulted in another ignominious setback for the United States. By adopting the recommendations of his former critics, Henry Kissinger had learned that, contrary to his conviction during the Angolan debate, his African policy would never succeed in the global context unless it were also relevant to African realities.

Ironically, however, that lesson was not applied to the problem of normalizing relations with post-war Angola. The Kissinger policy toward Angola after the war continued to be guided by domestic and global concerns. And once again, in pursuit of his goal to minimize Soviet and Cuban influence in Angola, Kissinger accomplished precisely the opposite.

After the war the general perception within the State Department of Angolan realities has been that the MPLA is an extremely heterogeneous movement containing a number of factions competing for power. Prominent among the factions is one commonly identified as "the moderates," those who support a multiracial government and who favor a policy of non-alignment. The moderates generally believe that Angola's independence can be better maintained by normalizing relations with the U.S. in order to reduce dependence on the Soviet Union. In fact, in early February 1976 an aide to Senator Tunney returned from Angola and reported to the Assistant Secretary of State for African Affairs that a number of MPLA cabinet ministers and other top officials "all took great pains to point out the danger of forcing the MPLA into a cycle of ever-greater reliance on the Soviets by refusing to deal with them."[60] He further indicated that the MPLA was interested in immediate discussions with the U.S. about normalizing relations.

The feeler was rejected by the State Department, whose attitude was "we will have to give them a diplomatic victory someday, but not now." It was announced that the MPLA would not be recognized until Cuba began to withdraw its forces. However, when the MPLA announced the beginning of the Cuban withdrawal four months later, the condition for U.S. recognition was raised from "substantial" to "complete" withdrawal of Cuban troops (and heavy weapons), signaling what one top Angolan expert in the Department described as "a harder U.S. line on Angola."[61] In late June, contrary to strong recommendations by U.N. Ambassador William Scranton, Kissinger vetoed Angola's application for membership in the United Nations.[62] The "line" hardened even more after the execution of the American mercenary, Daniel Gearhart, which Henry Kissinger stated "hurt any chance of American aid to Angola or any other improvement in relations."[63]

It was no coincidence that the hardening of the Administration's line on Angola coincided with the conservative challenge mounted by Ronald Reagan during the primaries. From Florida in February to California in June, Ford (with considerable help from Kissinger) tried to appeal to the right wing of the Republican Party through caustic attacks on Cuba and Angola.[64] The attacks won few Reagan supporters and did nothing to lessen Soviet or Cuban influence in Angola. On the contrary, the Administration's hardening line ensured that the Angolan moderates' fear of being forced "into a cycle of ever-greater reliance on the Soviets" would become reality. In a manner so reminiscent of the self-fulfilling prophesy which had pervaded American policy toward Cuba in the early 1960s, American attempts to curb Soviet influence in Angola have ultimately expanded it.

And Henry Kissinger inadvertently demonstrated for the fifth time in seven years that an American policy toward Angola based exclusively on U.S. domestic or global concerns, instead of on Angolan realities, is doomed to failure. [65]

Conclusions

The failure of Secretary of State Kissinger's Angolan policies raises important questions about recent American foreign policy in general and suggests some caveats for future policy makers. When Kissinger took his first serious look at Angola in early 1975, he not only ignored the internal dimension of the conflict but misperceived the nature of external involvement as well. Specifically, he stumbled into a Sino-Soviet dispute apparently without realizing it. The Secretary was not alone in this regard; most American analyses of the global ramifications of the Angolan conflict tended to downplay or ignore the Sino-Soviet dimension. The result was that many Soviet actions in response to China were incorrectly perceived as being directed against the United States. The importance of the Sino-Soviet rivalry in Angola prior to the American intervention is assessed by the British commentator Colin Legum:

> The collapse of the Portuguese dictatorship in April 1974 initiated a new phase in the Sino-Soviet struggle, with the Chinese initially making far the greater gains, particularly in Mozambique, and in consolidating their relations with Tanzania and Zambia. Given the strong Chinese position already established with two of Angola's liberation movements...[FNLA and UNITA] as well as with the Zaire government, the cards were heavily stacked in the Chinese favor at the end of 1974. In this context, and within what was already emerging as a much speeded-up timetable in southern Africa generally, the Soviets made their crucial decision in Angola in 1975....The key to these bold Soviet decisions lay above all in the Chinese factor. [66]

Besides misperceiving the catalytic effect Chinese support for the FNLA had on Soviet moves in Angola, the Secretary of State never fully understood why the Chinese withdrew in mid-1975. If China's withdrawal had been understood, it is unlikely that the United States would have intervened militarily. While China realized in mid-1975 that the FNLA army was a "paper tiger" and therefore made a hasty exit, Kissinger and others in the Administration were only too ready to pick up where the Chinese had left off, ignoring years of accumulated U.S. intelligence on the FNLA and their poor performance on the battlefield.

The failure to comprehend FNLA weaknesses apparently encouraged the erroneous belief early in 1975 that MPLA victories were attributable to Soviet assistance. Yet, as noted earlier, external assistance to the MPLA did not differ significantly from that to the FNLA through the first half of 1975. The MPLA's early victories can be explained in part by the qualitative difference between the two armies and by the fact that the FNLA chose to attack the MPLA on their own terrain, including within Luanda where the FNLA had practically no support. It was a serious mistake to credit Soviet assistance to the MPLA as the principal explanation for those early MPLA victories. It was an even greater mistake to characterize them publicly as victories for the Soviet Union and losses for the United States. This myopic perspective was the direct result of Kissinger's propensity, throughout the Angolan conflict, to view events through the optic of an inappropriate global framework.

The Administration compounded its error of inheriting what the Chinese considered to be a losing cause by justifying its continued escalation as a necessary demonstration to the Chinese that the U.S. still had the will and ability to resist the Soviet Union. President Ford, Henry Kissinger, George Bush (who succeeded Colby as Director of the CIA), and General Brown (Chairman of the Joint Chiefs of Staff) frequently expressed concern over the reaction of China and our western European allies if the U.S. "failed to demonstrate in Angola American will power to resist Soviet expansion."

What is still not clear is why the Administration ever accepted the interpretation that Angola represented a test of American strength and will power. Even if one were to begin with the premise (which I reject) that Angola was an example of Soviet aggression requiring a strong military response, why should it be assumed that the response was the responsibility of the United States? Moreover, if western allies assumed that an MPLA victory would greatly increase the Soviet Union's power in central and southern Africa and therefore pose a threat to the West, why did England and France look to the U.S., which has less at stake than they in the region and is much less vulnerable to any potential disruption of oil supplies transported around the Cape of Good Hope? It is interesting to note in light of the fears expressed about Chinese and western European impressions of American will power that in the Security Council vote of June 23, 1976, on the admission of Angola to the United Nations, England and France joined thirteen other nations in favoring admission, while China was not present. The U.S. was left to cast the sole veto.

The American veto of Angola's admission to the United Nations and refusal to recognize the Peoples Republic of Angola highlight another problem area in U.S. foreign policy, the implications of

which transcend U.S.-Angolan relations. There is no formula which
can be used with certainty to provide the optimal timing for establishing diplomatic relations with a country whose leaders or policies
are perceived as hostile to the United States. In general, the U.S.
attempts to maintain diplomatic relations with all countries without
regard to the character of their regimes. Notable exceptions include,
besides Angola, North Korea, Albania, the Peoples Republic of China,
Cuba, and Vietnam. The latter four countries have indicated that
they would welcome U.S. recognition but, for a variety of reasons,
the Administration does not believe that recognition is in the best
interests of the U.S.

Two imaginative arguments have been advanced recently which
advocate American recognition of China and Vietnam for reasons that
go well beyond the question of recognition itself. Tiziano Terzani,
correspondent for Der Spiegel and author of Giai Phong! The Fall and
Liberation of Saigon, avers that there is a power struggle within
Vietnam between the "gradualists" and those advocating a firm authoritarian political line ("Stalinist-Confucian"). He argues that the
"gradualists would be encouraged and strengthened if the Western
nations, and particularly the U.S., were to respond favorably to
Vietnamese offers of relations and its need for aid--while they will
become weaker if Vietnam remains isolated and thus dependent mainly
on the USSR." [67] In a similar vein Roger Brown, a senior analyst
in the CIA who presented his own (not official) views in an important
lead article in Foreign Policy, maintains that "U.S. moves to establish
full diplomatic relations with China would probably strengthen the
pragmatists' position and Peking's commitment to expanding ties with

non-Communist countries."[68]   Brown argues on the other hand,

> ...prolonged stagnation in Sino-Soviet relations could well
> contribute to undermining the political power of those
> individuals and groups within China which are favorably
> disposed toward Washington, and lead to an increase in the
> relative power of either pro-Soviet elements in the military,
> the radicals, or some coalition of both groups.[69]

Both analyses take into account the existence within the Vietnamese and Chinese regimes of competing groups representing alternative strategies for development and differing approaches to the
conduct of foreign affairs. One group--variously called "gradualists," "pragmatists," or "moderates"--favors economic and political
relations with the West and non-alignment in international affairs,
while the "radicals" or "leftists" advocate avoidance of economic
and political contacts with the West and prefer instead to establish
close ties with the Soviet Union. It would seem indisputable that
it is in the interest of the United States to do everything possible
to encourage the pragmatists in these and other countries. If the
establishment of diplomatic and economic relations will strengthen
their position internally, it should be done immediately.

A similar configuration of competition exists today in Angola.
The "moderates"--led by President Neto and Prime Minister Lopo de
Nascimento--favor the establishment of diplomatic and economic relations with all nations of the world who are prepared to respect
Angola's independence, the maintenance of a private economic sector,
cooperation among all classes, and the establishment of a truly
multiracial society in which advancement is based on merit, not
color. The "moderates" are being challenged   by a
more radical group of "leftists"--   led by two government

ministers, Nito Alves and David Aires Machado--who advocate the
immediate abolition of the private economic sector and the destruction
of the middle and upper classes, cessation of all contracts with multinationals such as Gulf Oil, a more exclusively pro-Soviet policy, the
removal of whites and mesticos and the rapid advancement of blacks
into positions of importance irrespective of merit. [70]

What is common to all these countries--China, Vietnam, and
Angola--is a desire for non-alignment on the part of "moderate"
factions within the ruling parties. What is important for U.S.
foreign policy is whether or not our government is capable of
establishing relations with these countries now, while those
advocating non-alignment are still in power.

The United States has made great strides in understanding
the Third World since the days of John Foster Dulles, who equated
non-alignment and socialism with enmity toward the United States.
However, we still have a long way to go. We apparently still do
not appreciate that Third World leaders, whom Americans may consider "radical" socialists or Marxists, believe that non-alignment
is the only way to guarantee their national independence and that
equitable economic cooperation with the West is not only possible
but desirable for the economic development of their countries.
It would be a tragic mistake for the United States to adopt a
posture which undermined their belief and which could force those
leaders to enter alliances, however reluctantly, in order to protect themselves from the U.S.

The history of Africa over the past decade and a half shows
that, with very few exceptions, the continent's 47 nations have

preferred non-alignment and some form of nominal socialism. "If there is one message African leaders want the United States Government to understand," Senator Clark astutely observes, "it is that they will not be pawns of either the Soviet Union or the United States. To regard them as such is wrong and can only lead to one mistake after another in our Africa policy."[71] There is no reason to suppose that the Neto faction of the MPLA will be any different; therefore the U.S. should cease reacting to them as an enemy and seek to normalize relations, based on mutual interests, immediately.

Henry Kissinger did not understand nor appreciate that prac- tically all African leaders are strongly committed to non-alignment and he therefore dismissed the advice of his Africa experts who urged him to support the OAU's unanimous opposition (in mid-1975) to all foreign intervention in Angola. The argument which Kiss- inger rejected was that if the U.S. were to stay out of Angola and keep its hands clean, African leaders would either prevent the Soviet Union from massively intervening unilaterally or deal them a diplomatic setback. Instead, he took the course of military intervention, which ended in an American setback which need never have occurred.

Fortunately the Secretary of State learned some important lessons from the Angolan debacle. His diplomatic efforts concern- ing southern Africa in the late summer and early fall of 1976 were premised squarely on the belief that if the U.S. did not choose sides in Rhodesia or Namibia, African leaders will ensure that no other superpower will unilaterally determine the outcome of these present struggles. This dramatic change was just in time for the

U.S. to contribute positively to solutions of southern Africa's complex problems. Hopefully, it came in time to avert another tragic imposition of superpower rivalries on African realities.

CHRONOLOGY OF MAJOR EVENTS MENTIONED IN TEXT

1969

21 January   Richard Nixon becomes the President of the United States.

April   The National Security Council Interdepartmental Group for Africa begins a major study of U.S. policy in southern Africa under the direction of Henry Kissinger.

1970

2 January   The National Security Council Study (NSSM 39) is presented to President Nixon. Kissinger recommends following an option which favors a relaxation in the political isolation and economic restrictions against the white-ruled states in southern Africa.

1973

4 December   An FNLA delegation, led by Holden Roberto, arrives in the People's Republic of China for an 18-day visit. China's embrace of Roberto is followed by the shipment of hundreds of tons of Chinese weapons to the FNLA in Zaire. Shortly after the Portuguese coup (25 April 1974) the first members of a 120-man military training mission (headed by a major general) arrive in Zaire to instruct FNLA troops.

Mid-December   Henry Kissinger visits Portugal to thank the Portuguese for use of the Azores base during the Yom Kippur war and promises the delivery of offensive weapons for use in Africa if the Portuguese Government will renew the Azores treaty with the U.S.

1974

February or March   The Soviet Union stops all military and financial aid to the MPLA.

March   Donald Easum replaces David Newsom as Assistant Secretary of State for African Affairs.

25 April   Caetano regime in Portugal is overthrown by Armed Forces Movement, which is dedicated to decolonization in Africa.

15 & 21 October   FNLA and MPLA sign cease-fire agreements with the Portuguese and begin to establish offices in Luanda. UNITA had signed the cease-fire on 17 June 1974.

<u>1974</u> continued

Oct. or November   The Soviet Union resumes aid to the MPLA.

2 & 19 November   Assistant Secretary of State for African Affairs Donald Easum, in
                      a speech in Dar es Salaam, urges the U.S. to work toward change in
                      southern Africa, rather than supporting the status quo. Two weeks
                      later he meets with the Transitional Government in Mozambique.

25 November   Secretary of State Henry Kissinger removes Donald Easum as Assis-
                      tant Secretary of State for African Affairs.

<u>1975</u>

8 January   Nathaniel Davis is nominated to be Assistant Secretary of State
                      for African Affairs.

15 January   Alvor Agreement is signed in Portugal by Portuguese Government,
                      MPLA, FNLA, and UNITA. It establishes mechanics for a transitional
                      government and sets date of independence for 11 November 1975.

Late January   40 Committee approves CIA request to channel $300,000 to FNLA.

31 January   Transitional Government (comprised of MPLA, FNLA, UNITA, and Por-
                      tuguese Government) is installed in Angola.

21 February   Organization of African Unity (OAU) unanimously condemns nomina-
                      tion of Nathaniel Davis as Assistant Secretary of State for Afri-
                      can Affairs.

21 February   Daniel Chipenda, leader of "Eastern Revolt" (dissident faction of
                      MPLA), integrates his approximately 3,000 troops with FNLA, placing
                      FNLA and MPLA on certain collision course.

11 March   General Spinola attempts abortive coup in Lisbon.

23 March   FNLA, supported by Zairien troops, captures Caxito (a town 35 miles
                      north of Luanda), killing and mutilating over 60 MPLA partisans.
                      Kissinger later describes this as first major clash in the war.
                      MPLA considers attack as beginning of war.

March/April   Substantial increase in Soviet aid to MPLA.

29 April   End of Vietnam war.

Early June   Defense Secretary James Schlesinger shows aerial photographs of
                      Soviet missile installations in Somalia and warns of danger of
                      Soviet expansion in Africa.

1975 continued

Early June	American intelligence learns that China is losing faith in FNLA.
Mid-June	President Mobutu sends U.S. Ambassador home from Zaire and threatens to sever relations with U.S.
16 June	African Subcommittee of Senate Foreign Relations Committee holds hearings on Angola.
June	40 Committee considers CIA request for massive increase in U.S. covert aid to Angola. Committee decides to postpone decision for a month and commissions State Department and National Security Council to study the issue.
June	Arrival of approximately 250 Cuban advisors in Angola.
June/July	State Department Bureaus of African Affairs, Policy Planning, and Intelligence and Research study and reject CIA proposal for major American military escalation. They recommend that U.S. employ diplomatic leverage instead.
June/July	National Security Council studies options for Angola and endorses a major increase in covert military aid to FNLA and UNITA, strongl rejecting diplomatic efforts until FNLA and UNITA ground forces can be built up.
12 July	Nathaniel Davis, testifying before Senate Foreign Relations Subcommittee on Africa, indicates that he has no knowledge that U.S. military equipment sent to Zaire is being passed on to FNLA.
17 July	40 Committee approves CIA request for major increase in U.S. cover aid to FNLA and UNITA of approximately $30 million.
Late July	Senator Clark receives CIA briefing on U.S. covert activities in Angola which he later claimed handcuffed him and actually became an impediment to effective congressional oversight of covert activities.
Late July	Nathaniel Davis asks Clark, during Senate hearing, not to press him on U.S. intervention in Angola because "we both know" about U.S. covert support.
Late July	Deputy Secretary of State Robert Ingersoll briefs Senate Foreign Relations Subcommittee on Africa and rejects Subcommittee's recommendation to pursue diplomatic course, rather than military course
August	Senator Clark travels to Angola where he meets with the leaders of MPLA, FNLA, and UNITA. He leaves even more convinced that U.S. should not intervene in the conflict.

1975 continued

9 August	First South African invasion of Angola. By end of August MPLA is convinced that this was precursor to a major South African invasion.
9 August	UNITA and FNLA withdraw from Luanda after weeks of attacks by MPLA.
Mid-August	Portugal assumes power in Angola in wake of collapse of Transitional Government.
Late August	Collapse of Gonçalves regime in Portugal. It had been generally supportive of MPLA, unlike its successor (the sixth provisional government).
31 August	Nathaniel Davis resigns as Assistant Secretary of State for African Affairs because of his strong opposition to U.S. policy of covert military intervention in Angola.
Late August- *Early September*	Major increase in arms for FNLA and UNITA, approved by 40 Committee on 17 July, begins to arrive in Angola.
25 September	Leslie Gelb, The New York Times reporter, publishes first major leak concerning CIA covert support of FNLA.
Early October	Approximately 700 Cuban military advisors arrive in Anogla, bringing total number of Cubans in Angola to approximately 1,000.
15 or 16 October	U.S. rejects Jonas Savimbi's (UNITA President) request for U.S. troops. Savimbi responds by telling his supporters that he has no other alternative than to ask South Africa for troops.
23 October	South African troops, some UNITA troops, the Chipenda faction of FNLA, and hundreds of mercenaries launch major attack in southern Angola. Within less than three weeks, attacking forces move 500 miles north, threatening the capital.
Late October	FNLA and 3,000 to 4,000 Zairien troops launch major attack in northern Angola, stopping only 12 miles from Luanda (at Quifangondo) days before independence.
Late October	Cuban military advisors are moved to front lines for the first time in an MPLA effort to stop the north-south pincer movement.
Late October	Ford Administration makes its first contacts with Soviet Union concerning Angola.
Early November	FNLA and Zaire move troops to Cabinda border. They finally attack the oil-rich enclave, with troops from FLEC, on 14 November.
5 November	First contingent of Cuban regular forces arrives in Angola.

1975 continued

5 November
: Acting Assistant Secretary of State for African Affairs Edward Mulcahy testifies during a House hearing that U.S. policy is against intervention in Angola. He refuses, however, to comment on whether or not the U.S. is, in fact, intervening.

6 November
: CIA Director William Colby and Undersecretary of State Joseph Sisco tell Senate Foreign Relations Committee the extent and rationale for U.S. intervention in Angola. Committee disagrees with military strategy of the Administration but little can be done to stop it.

7 November
: The New York Times leaks essence of Colby-Sisco testimony of previous day, which brings issue of U.S. intervention into public sphere and stimulates public and congressional debate.

8 November
: The Washington Post leaks other aspects of Colby-Sisco testimony, marking the beginning of a series of unprecedented media leaks on U.S. covert activities in Angola.

11 November
: Angolan Independence Day.

12 November
: Foreign diplomats in Luanda express fear that capital will be choked off by north-south pincer movement launched by South Africa, Zaire, FNLA, UNITA, and an assortment of mercenaries, including many former Portuguese commandos.

Mid-November
: Cuban Government begins to dispatch, in Fidel Castro's words, "the men and weapons necessary to win the struggle."

21 November
: Harris poll indicates that 72% of Americans feel the U.S. should avoid involvement in guerrilla wars when it appears that the U.S. is participating in another country's civil war.

23 November
: Reliable sources estimate the number of South African troops committed inside Angola to be between 4,000 and 6,000.

Early December
: Senator Clark, backed by most of the Senate Foreign Relations Committee, proposes amendment to Foreign Assistance Act to cut off all covert aid to Angola. Later President Ford vetoes the Act.

10 December
: First public acknowledgment by Henry Kissinger (during press conference) that the U.S. is involved in Angolan conflict.

12 December
: CIA Director William Colby testifies before House Select Committee on Intelligence that simplest answer to question of why China and U.S. support FNLA and UNITA is that "the Soviets are backing the MPLA."

1975 continued

19 December   By a vote of 54 to 22, Senate passes Tunney Amendment (to Defense
Appropriations bill) cutting off all covert aid to Angola.

23 December   Kissinger makes his first direct appeal for withdrawal of South
African troops from Angola. Many argue that this appeal comes too
late to be credible.

31 December   Number of Cuban troops in Angola estimated to be 7,000.

31 December   U.S. estimates total Soviet aid to MPLA to be $200 million.

1976

19 January   House Select Committee on Intelligence report is completed. It
indicates that CIA undervalued amount of U.S. covert aid and
quotes William Colby's testimony of 12 December 1975 on why U.S.
and China supported FNLA and UNITA.

27 January   House of Representatives votes 323 to 99 to join Senate in cutting
off American covert aid to Angola.

29 January   Henry Kissinger testifies before Senate Foreign Relations Committee.
He presents detailed analysis of events in Angola over past year.

Late January-
Early February   FNLA and UNITA are defeated militarily by MPLA and their Cuban
allies. Both FNLA and UNITA promise to return to guerrilla tac-
tics against the victors.

February   During Florida primary (where his major opponent is Ronald Reagan),
President Ford makes major issue of Cuban presence in Angola, a
theme he repeats throughout remaining primaries.

6 February   State Department rejects MPLA feeler to normalize relations (transmitted from Luanda by an aide to Senator John Tunney).

10 February   In an attempt to shift whatever "blame" there may be for a "loss"
in Angola away from his administration, President Ford accuses
Congress of lacking "guts" on Angola.

28 March   South Africa completes the withdrawal of its approximately 5,000
soldiers from Angola.

19 April   Fidel Castro, in a speech marking 15th anniversary of Bay of Pigs
invasion, answers Ford and Kissinger criticisms and asserts that
Cuba's decision to send troops to Angola was made by Cuba alone,
not the Soviet Union.

1976 continued

27 April   Secretary of State Henry Kissinger spells out his new African policy in Lusaka, Zambia. It includes a ten-point program in support of the goal of majority rule in Rhodesia and Namibia.

28 May   State Department adopts a harder line on Cuban presence in Angola by demanding a total withdrawal at the very time Cubans are preparing to initiate a gradual withdrawal.

23 June   U.S. vetoes Angola's application for membership in United Nations.

10 July   People's Republic of Angola executes four mercenaries, including an American, Daniel Gearhart. Both Ford and Kissinger announce that Gearhart's execution hurts any chance for an improvement in relations with Angola.

FOOTNOTES

1. Henry Kissinger, "Implications of Angola for U.S. Foreign Policy," in Department of State Bureau of Public Affairs, Office of Media Services, The Secretary of State, PR 40 (Washington, D.C.), 29 January 1976, p. 1.

2. Arthur Schlesinger, Jr., A Thousand Days, (New York: Fawcell Crest, 1965), p. 473.

   Another close Kennedy advisor and speech writer, Theodore Sorensen, noted the pressure which Portugal attempted to exert on the U.S. and Kennedy's reaction: "...the Portuguese tried every form of diplomatic blackmail to alter our position on Angola, using as a wedge our country's expiring lease on a key military base on the Azores Islands. The President finally felt that, if necessary, he was prepared to forgo the base entirely rather than permit Portugal to dictate his African policy." Kennedy, (New York: Bantam Books, 1965), p. 605, note 2.

3. See "CIA's Secret War in Angola," Intelligence Report, 1 (December 1975): 1.

4. While in the process of delivering the eighth of twenty B-26 bombers to Portugal, two alleged CIA agents were arrested in Miami by agents of the Treasury Department in September 1965. John Richard Hawke, an Englishman, stated during his trial for munitions smuggling in Federal Court at Buffalo, New York, "I flew B-26 bombers to Portugal for use in their African colonies, and the operation was arranged through the State Department and the CIA." Quoted in David Welsh, "Flyboys of the CIA," Ramparts, 5 (December 1966): 12.

5. NSSM 39 has been widely leaked and discussed in newspapers and schol journals. Some examples of extensive analyses of and quotes from the memorandum can be found in Edger Lockwood, "National Security Study Memorandum 39 and the Future of United States Policy toward Southern Africa," Issue, 4 (Fall 1974): 63-70; Tad Szulc, "Why Are We in Johannesburg," Esquire, 82 (October 1974): 48-66,91; and Bruce Oudes, "Southern African Policy Watershed," Africa Report, 19 (November-December 1974): 44-50. and Mohamed A. El-Khawas and Barry Cohen (eds.), The Kissinger Study of Southern Africa, (Westport: Lawrence Hill & Company, 1976)

6. Memorandum (attached to NSSM 39) from Henry A. Kissinger to Richard M. Nixon, "Subject: Policy Decisions on Southern Africa," 2 January 1970, Tab A.

There has been considerable controversy over the question of whether or not "option two" was ever "adopted" as policy. The State Department has staunchly denied that any of the six options was ever "adopted." In fact, Donald B. Easum, who served as Assistant Secretary of State for African Affairs throughout most of 1974, has explicitly stated that none of the six options "...was in fact adopted as such," although a "limited number of operational decisions" relating to the Portuguese territories were made. See Donald B. Easum, "U.S. Policy Toward South Africa," Issue, 5(Fall 1975): 71. More important than the question of option two actually being adopted is the fact that it does appear to have characterized U.S. Angolan policy between 1970 and 1974.

7. John A. Marcum, "Lessons of Angola," Foreign Affairs, 54(April 1976): 408.

8. During his brief visit to Lisbon, Kissinger referred to Portugal as a "good and reliable friend of the United States" and went on to predict that his visit would bring the two countries closer together. Kissinger told Foreign Minister Rui Patricio and other Portuguese officials that "On this trip through the Middle East, I was reminded of the fact that Portugal stood by its allies during the recent difficulties, and the United States is extremely grateful for that." The joint communiqué issued after Kissinger's visit reported that "there was a large area of agreement with respect to the problems of concern to the two countries." See Department of State Bulletin (Washington, D.C.), 14 January 1974, cited in Southern Africa, 7(March 1974): 18; and Noticias de Portugal, No. 1390 (22 December 1973): 2-3,7.

9. For Easum's remarks in Dar-es-Salaam and a report of his removal by Kissinger, see Bruce Oudes, "US Sacks its Africa Advisor," The Observer (London), 22 December 1974. For a comprehensive statement of Easum's views on southern Africa through early 1975, see Easum, pp. 66-72.

10. Naturally any brief composite of such a general subject as "perceptions in Washington" cannot do justice to all aspects or facets of opinion. This synthesis is derived from numerous personal interviews with officials in Washington involved with Angolan matters and a careful reading of all American press coverage. Also see Kenneth L. Adelman, "Report from Angola," Foreign Affairs, 53(April 1975): 558-574. This article was based largely on interviews he conducted with American officials in Angola and Zaire. (It is of interest to note that Adelman predicted that Savimbi and Roberto would almost certainly become the winners in Angola.) For a more comprehensive and objective analysis of the three nationalist parties throughout this period,

see John Marcum's presidential address to the African Studies
Association, "The Anguish of Angola: On Becoming Independent
in the Last Quarter of the Twentieth Century," Issue, 5(Winter
1975): 3-11, and his article in Foreign Affairs, loc. cit.
Further insights into the perceptions in Washington during this
period can be found in The New York Times, 24 November 1974 and
16 January 1975, and The Washington Post, 13 January 1975.

11. "Program assistance" is the term used when the CIA gives money
    to a party or organization to help it implement its program;
    this term is distinguished from "personal assistance" when money
    is given to an individual for information about the program and
    activities of a given party or organization. Thus, when the CIA
    switched from program assistance to the FNLA to personal assis-
    tance for Holden Roberto in 1970, it amounted to giving Roberto
    money for information about the activities of FNLA to defeat the
    Portuguese rather than money to actually help him carry out his
    program of ending the Portuguese colonization of Angola.

    The 40 Committee, a four-person subcommittee of the National
    Security Council, included at this time Henry Kissinger, William
    Colby, who was then Director of the CIA, General George S.
    Brown, Chairperson of the Joint Chiefs of Staff, and William
    Clement, Deputy Secretary of Defense.

12. Quoted in Roger Morris, "The Proxy War in Angola: Pathology of
    a Blunder," The New Republic, 31 January 1976, p. 21. This
    article, written by Kissinger's former African Affairs assis-
    tant in the National Security Council, is the most detailed
    account of the general climate and actual deliberations of the
    40 Committee's decision to intervene in Angola.

13. Quoted in Murrey Marder, "The Angolan Involvement," The Washing-
    ton Post, 6 January 1976.

14. Morris, p. 20.

15. Ibid., pp. 20-21.

16. There is no question that the aid was noticed by the Soviets.
    The American Consulate which had not been informed of the
    decision to covertly assist the FNLA, reported to Washington in
    early 1975 a noticeable increase in FNLA spending. They re-
    ported, for example, that the party purchased the leading news-
    paper (A Provincia de Angola) and a television station which
    prompted an inquiry to discover the source of the funds used
    to bankroll these purchases. The Consulate concluded (and re-
    ported back to the State Department) that the money must have
    been supplied by Portuguese coffee plantation owners in northern
    Angola!

17. One State Department source, intimately involved with Angolan matters, told me in early 1976 that "in retrospect it appears that the Soviet aid to the MPLA through April 1975 was merely an attempt to bring them up to parity--keep them in the game-- with the FNLA." Seymour M. Hersh, a journalist, has also suggested that Soviet aid to the MPLA in March/April was merely a response to the U.S. and Chinese aid to the FNLA. See "Early Angola Aid by U.S. Reported," The New York Times, 19 December 1975. Also see Morris and Marder for similar assertions.

18. Kissinger, 29 January 1976, p. 4.

19. Marcum, "The Lessons," p. 414.

20. The most severe early challenge to the MPLA in Luanda came from the breakaway faction of the party ("Eastern Revolt") headed by Daniel Chipenda, which had set up offices in the capital. Chipenda merged his faction with the FNLA in February (with Chipenda being named Secretary-General of the FNLA), a move which appeared to tip the military balance strongly in favor of the FNLA. In mid-February the MPLA began to close down Chipenda's offices, leading to many deaths in the ensuing clashes. Ultimately Chipenda and his forces were pushed out of the capital. See Fola Soremekun, "Angola: The Politics of Transition," a paper delivered to the UCLA International Conference on "Portuguese-Speaking Africa in Transition," 12 February 1976, pp. 26-27.

21. Ibid., pp. 26-30. In his 29 January testimony before the Senate Foreign Relations Committee, Kissinger stated: "On March 23 the first of repeated military clashes between the MPLA and FNLA occurred" (p. 4). Quite clearly there had been a number of "military clashes" before 23 March 1975 but the Secretary is correct to underscore the importance of this event because it did mark a significant escalation in the level of violence. The question--upon which hangs much of Kissinger's later rationale for U.S. intervention--is whether or not this act of "aggression" (by the FNLA) signaled the start of the civil war (as the MPLA maintains) or if this only occurred later in July when the MPLA's "aggression" drove the FNLA and UNITA out of Luanda. This dispute over "who started what and when" will undoubtedly continue for many years; however, what is less ambiguous is the impact this attack had on the MPLA and, most certainly, the Soviet Union. The atmosphere in Angola was highly charged at the time: General Spinola's abortive armed revolt in Lisbon on 11 March provoked, over the following weeks, unsuccessful right-wing attempts to overthrow the governments in both Mozambique and Guinea-Bissau. On 15 March the FNLA began a week-long celebration marking the anniversary of its formal launching of the Angolan nationalist war (15 March 1961), which included strong verbal attacks on the MPLA and which evoked

many uncomfortable memories of the carnage which had occurred in early 1961. The press coverage of the FNLA Caxito massacre is epitomized by the following description in the sober Financial Times (London), 29 March 1975:

> Eyewitness reports of the massacre by FNLA soldiers of civilians and others suggest beyond a reasonable doubt that what has occurred is a first terrifying attempt by FNLA to kill substantial numbers of MPLA soldiers and supporters and instill a climate of fear in the country such as it did in 1961 on the Zaire border.

The FNLA believed that it had to control Caxito in order to maintain a land link with its forces in Luanda.

22. "From March to July, fighting and Soviet arms shipments increased in tandem. Perhaps, as the Administration later asserted, the Soviet arms shipments were a major escalatory move. If so, they seemed at the time not an unreasonable response to Roberto's own escalation--and in any event were almost certainly encouraged by the continuing desire to head off the Chinese, a motive that never seems to have been taken into account in Washington." Marcum, "Lessons," p. 415.

23. Morris, pp. 21-22.

24. Ibid., p. 22. Schlesinger was eventually fired six months later but in June it was not clear which of the two antagonists in the Cabinet would prevail. Two examples of Schlesinger's views of the significance of Soviet moves in Angola can be found in: James R. Schlesinger, "The Continuing Challenge to America," The Reader's Digest, 108(April 1976):61-66; idem, "The Evolution of American Policy Towards the Soviet Union," International Security, 1(Summer 1976):3-14.

25. The most complete account of Nathaniel Davis's and the Africa Bureau's position against military escalation in Angola can be found in Seymour M. Hersh, "Angola-Aid Issue Opening Rifts in State Department," The New York Times, 14 December 1975. Also see note 29 below.

26. Ibid. For a comprehensive background on Nathaniel Davis's career, his position against U.S. escalation in Angola and Kissinger's rejection of his advice, see Roger Morris, "A Rare Resignation in Protest: Nat Davis and Angola," The Washington Monthly, 7(February 1976):22-32.

Morris uncovers some interesting perspectives on Kissinger and Davis with regard to Angola. Morris notes that while it is true that Davis objected to further escalation, some of his aides are quoted as believing he actually presented a very weak case: "there's no question that the arguments against it [military escalation] were weak." Morris also quotes some

sources who imply that Kissinger rejected Davis's opposition
to escalation on rather personal grounds. For example, Kissinger
is quoted as saying, "What does he know about Africa? . . . He's
only parroting the incompetents in the bureau." Moreover, one
witness even suggested that "Kissinger figured from the start
that Angola would be one Chile too many for Nat," assuming that
Davis had lost his nerve to judge the policy precisely because
of his experience in Chile (p. 30). Mr. Davis is currently the
U.S. Ambassador to Switzerland.

27. Notable and important exceptions include two of the three
    foreign service officers stationed at the American Consulate
    in Luanda in late 1974 and early 1975. While they reported to
    the State Department their views favoring U.S. intervention,
    they were unaware that any plans for intervention were under
    consideration at the time.

28. The June 16 testimony of the three academic witnesses (John
    Marcum, Douglas Wheeler, and Gerald J. Bender) appears in
    Committee on Foreign Relations, United States Senate, Subcommittee
    on African Affairs, U.S. Policy Toward Southern Africa, 94th
    Congress, first session (Washington, D.C.: U.S. Government
    Printing Office, 1976), pp. 69-119. Excerpts appear in Issue,
    5(Fall 1975): 16-23.

29. The exchange between Clark and Davis is recorded in U.S. Policy
    Toward Southern Africa, pp. 254-255.

30. In the House Select Committee on Intelligence report, footnote
    477 states:

    > Officials from the Department of State have told this
    > Committee that the majority of that task force [composed
    > of African experts within the Department of State, Defense
    > Department officials, CIA officials and others] recommended
    > diplomatic efforts to encourage a political settlement
    > rather than intervention. After they had prepared their
    > report for the Secretary of State containing this recommen-
    > dation, they were informed by National Security Council
    > aides that it was improper for them to make a recommenda-
    > tion on policy. Instead, they were instructed to simply
    > list diplomatic efforts as one option among many in their
    > final report. Thus, the African experts who made up the
    > task force were not allowed to place their recommendations
    > on paper to be reviewed by the Forty Committee.

    This quote is taken from the version of the report known as the
    "Pike Papers" which was leaked by former CBS newsman Daniel Schorr
    to The Village Voice, 21(20 February 1976): 40.

31. This passage relies upon a full account of the steps authorized
    by the 40 Committee in July by Seymour M. Hersh, "Early Angola
    Aid by U.S. Reported." See also Morris, "The Proxy War," p. 22,
    and Marder.

32. This quote can be found in the "Pike Papers," p. 37. The report indicates, for example, that .45 caliber automatic pistols were valued by the CIA at $5 each and .30 caliber semi-automatic carbines at $7.55. _Africa News_, normally reliable on southern Africa, reported that the actual value of U.S. aid to Angola may have totaled close to $100 million (6[26 January 1976]:5). A similar figure of $100 million was also reported in the _Los Angeles Times_, 21 December 1975.

33. Leslie H. Gelb, "U.S. Aides Tell of Covert European Help to Angolans," _New York Times_, 10 March 1976. The CIA estimate of Soviet assistance of $80 million as of October 1975 is reported in Marder. Marder also states that "French arms and money had come into the battle covertly with the French intelligence service, the SDECE, the counterpart of the CIA, cooperating with that agency and with Zaire President Mobutu to channel aid to Roberto's National Front. Belgian, British and West German aid [was also sent to the FNLA and UNITA]."

34. For a discussion of how the MPLA carried out this expansion, see René Pelissier, "Notes sur la deuxième guerre d'Angola," paper delivered at a conference on "The Crisis in Portugal," Toronto, Canada, 17 April 1976; and the excellent reporting by a number of journalists, especially David Ottaway of the Washington Post and Michael Kaufman of The New York Times. Also see Ernest Harsh and Tony Thomas, Angola: The Hidden History of Washington's War (New York: Pathfinder Press, 1976), pp. 61-108. This is an extremely detailed account of events in Angola and Washington (with a strong emphasis on 1975) from the perspective of the Socialist Workers Party.

    It should be noted that the MPLA did have a considerable advantage in arms over UNITA which, in part, accounted for MPLA's successful occupation of the major cities in southern Angola during the summer of 1975.

35. A detailed chronology of the South African invasion of Angola including dates, numbers of troops, descriptions of missions and breakdown of equipment, allegedly based on information from "highly placed officials within the U.S. Department of Defense who are opposed to U.S. policy in Angola," appears in the report by Sean Gervasi, "Continuing Escalation in the Angola Crisis," released 19 December 1975 by the American Committee on Africa.

36. The north-south attack against the MPLA near Luanda during the weeks before and after independence was widely reported in the American media. For specific reference to events described in the text see: Washington Post, 1 and 7 November 1975; Washington Star, 8 November 1975; New York Times, 9 November 1975; and Los Angeles Times, 13 November 1975. For a vivid account of conditions in Luanda during the ten months preceeding independence see Kevin Brown, "A New Angolan Society," The Nation (17 July 1976):42-46.

37. For a different periodization of Cuba's role in Angola, see
     Edward Gonzalez and David Ronfeldt, "Castro's Cuba: From
     Surrogate to Superclient," unpublished manuscript written in
     May 1976, pp. 16-33. Also see Edward Gonzalez, "Castro and
     Cuba's New Orthodoxy," Problems of Communism, 25(January-
     February 1976: 1-19. Both sources contain valuable analyses
     of the impact of Cuban domestic factors on the Angolan opera-
     tion. While I differ with Gonzalez and Ronfeldt on a variety
     of details, I am in complete agreement with their conclusion
     that "the actual policy behind Cuba's Angolan involvement
     appears to have been largely incremental and reactive" (p. 30).

38. For estimates of the timing and numbers of Cubans in Angola
     based on leaks from U.S. intelligence sources, see Newsweek,
     29 December 1975, p. 33, and The Washington Post, 18 February 1976.

39. Colin Legum dates the Russian and Cuban decisions to win in
     Angola much earlier than I do. He argues, for example:

          It is not yet possible to fix with certainty the exact
          date when Moscow first began to arrange with Fidel Castro
          to bring large numbers of Cubans. . . . By July, however,
          the Russians were almost certainly going for broke.
          By September, two months before the date set for inde-
          pendence on November 11, the Russian and Cuban military
          aid was of a size that promised military supremacy to the
          MPLA. The scale of the Soviet/Cuban intervention increased
          sharply in early October, three weeks before the South
          African forces entered Angola in any size. . . . The Russian
          and Cuban contention that their military intervention was
          the result of the South African invasion is clearly an
          ex post facto rationalization.

     "The Soviet Union, China and The West in Southern Africa,"
     Foreign Affairs, 54(July 1976): 750-751. Legum published
     similar views previously in an unsigned article "Angola:
     The International Dimension," in Africa Bureau Fact Sheet,
     No. 46 (March/April 1976).

40. In early May 1976 it was revealed in the South African Parlia-
     ment that Defense Minister Pieter Botha had boasted to an MP
     that South African troops could have easily gone to Luanda and
     were, in fact, poised to take the capital when they pulled
     back because "the United States had pleaded with South Africa
     not to send its forces to Luanda." Quoted in the Daily Telegraph
     (London), 7 May 1976. American officials later dismissed this
     story as "phony."

     One of the Americans serving in the Luanda Consulate reported
     to the State Department at the time that there was not the
     slightest chance the FNLA could capture and hold Luanda given
     the size of their forces and the impossibility of operating
     within the heartland of the MPLA's ethnic support. I have
     heard two reports from excellent sources, which I have been

unable to confirm, that the reason why South Africa did not
attempt to capture Luanda with the FNLA is that Jonas Savimbi
reached the same conclusion as the American official in the
Luanda Consulate and therefore urged his South African allies
not to attempt to capture Luanda.

41. Fidel Castro, "Angola African Girón," speech commemorating
    the 15th anniversary of the Cuban victory at Playa Girón
    (Bay of Pigs), Havana, 19 April 1976. The complete speech
    can be found in Gramma (Havana), 2 May 1976 (weekly review
    edition).

42. Kissinger, 29 January 1976, p. 4. The same perspective is
    apparent in his major policy statement on Angola delivered in
    San Francisco, 3 February 1976.

43. Ibid. Kissinger limited not only his analysis of outside inter-
    vention to the Cubans and Russians but his condemnations as
    well. In so doing, Kissinger signaled to the world that, until
    the final week of 1975, he viewed Cuban and Soviet intervention
    as "illegitimate" and threatening but not so the "continental"
    intervention of South Africa and Zaire. Through his selective
    criticism, Kissinger unwittingly tainted his Angolan policy with
    the scourge of South African racism. Despite his later calls
    for South African withdrawal, which appeared to be a half-
    hearted afterthought, and his adamant denials of any consulta-
    tion between the U.S. and South Africa over Angola, Kissinger
    was unable to convince the majority of African leaders or the
    U.S. Congress that American policies and goals were independent
    of South African actions in Angola. Moreover, President Ford,
    in his personal letters to African Heads of State on the eve of
    the OAU meeting in January, infuriated a number of African
    leaders (e.g., in Nigeria and Tanzania) by equating the "unin-
    vited" intervention of racist South Africa with the "invited"
    Cuban and Soviet assistance (which has been viewed generally
    by most Africans as legitimate help to the cause of African
    liberation). Thus, by appearing to have enlisted South African
    military intervention to resist "international communism," the
    U.S. communicated that it feared communism more than white racism
    in Africa. This alienated the majority of African leaders for
    whom the issue of white racism still remains paramount and
    tended to polarize African and world opinion along lines which
    generated little support for American objectives in Angola.

44. The quote from Kissinger's November 11th speech in Pittsburgh
    is cited in The Washington Star, 12 November 1975. For an in-
    cisive analysis of the importance of the support the MPLA re-
    ceived in the Luanda region, see John Marcum, The Angolan Revo-
    lution: The Anatomy of an Explosion (1950-1962), Vol. I, (Cam-
    bridge: The M.I.T. Press, 1969), pp. 13-48; and idem, "The
    Anguish of Angola," pp. 4-8.

45.   Castro, 19 April 1976.

46.   Newsweek, for example, noted that "most U.S. officials believe
      the Cubans are in Angola because the Soviets presented an IOU
      for the $5.4 billion in military and economic aid that Moscow
      has given them since 1960." (29 December 1975, p. 34.) Kis-
      singer flatly stated that Cuban troops would not have been in
      Angola without being "under Soviet advice." (Cited in the Los
      Angeles Times, 24 December 1975.) For an interesting discus-
      sion of the debate among U.S. government officials over the re-
      lationship between Cuba and the Soviet Union in Angola, see
      The Christian Science Monitor, 18 March 1976 and 7 April 1976.

47.   The Washington Post, 18 February 1976.

48.   The day before the Senate Foreign Relations Committee hearings
      on Angola (November 5), Edward Mulcahy, Acting Assistant Secre-
      tary of State for African Affairs, refused to admit U.S. inter-
      vention in Angola during a House hearing. When one Congressman
      asked if it were a proper summation of his position to say "it
      is our policy not to intervene but you have no comment on
      whether we are intervening," Mulcahy replied that this would be
      "substantially correct." Cited in The Washington Office on
      Africa, "Africa Action," newsletter, November 1975.

49.   The Secretary of State frequently stressed the large number of
      Congressmen who were briefed on American covert activities in
      Angola: "Altogether more than two dozen Senators, about 150
      Congressmen, and over 100 staff members of both Houses were in-
      formed." (29 January 1976, p. 7.) It should be noted, however,
      that most of those briefed had no, or only minor, reservations
      about the policy. Moreover, serious questions can be raised
      about the adequacy of the briefings. Senator Clark told me,
      for example, that he was not informed during his July briefing
      that the 40 Committee had decided on July 17th to support UNITA
      as well as the FNLA nor was he informed about the $300,000 given
      to the FNLA in early 1975.

      The quotes and information on Clark's experiences which appear
      in the next section of the text are drawn from: remarks he
      made during the various hearings he held as Chairman of the
      Senate Foreign Relations Committee's African Subcommittee (pub-
      lished in U.S. Policy Toward Southern Africa); observations he
      made at the Seven Springs Center's "Second Symposium on Southern
      Africa," Mount Kisco, New York, 8-10 May 1976 (see my report on
      the Symposium's proceedings, pp. 70-74); and personal conver-
      sations with the Senator. Most of the quotes in the text can
      be found in Dick Clark, "Frustration," The New York Times, 29
      January 1976.

50.   Leslie H. Gelb, "U.S. Aides Tell Senators of Arms Aid to Ango-
      lans," The New York Times, 7 November 1975; and Walter Pincus,
      "CIA Aid in Angola Defended," The Washington Post, 8 November
      1975. This was not Gelb's first revelation of CIA activities
      in Angola. Six weeks previously he had published some facts

about the CIA and Angola as part of a larger story on CIA aid
to Portugal (The New York Times, 25 September 1975). Gelb had
come across the Angolan information by accident and neither he
nor the general public seemed interested in pursuing the matter
before the Senate Foreign Relations Committee held its hearings.

51. The New York Times was unrivaled in terms of general coverage
    of the Angolan debate, providing most major leaks and offering
    numerous analyses of developments throughout the Angolan conflict.

52. Senator John Tunney articulated this viewpoint well when he said:

> I am not an isolationist. I, too, am deeply disturbed
> by the spectre of Soviet expansionism. But the course of
> American foreign policy must not be determined by blind
> reactive opposition to every movement from Moscow. We
> must not fall prey to the myopia which removes every civil
> war, every nationalist struggle from its own geopolitical
> and social context and places it instead in the realm of
> some grand Soviet strategem in a global superpower con-
> spiracy.

Senator John V. Tunney, "The Meaning of Detente," Speech at
American University, 5 February 1976.

Whatever the validity, Kissinger, Colby, and Sisco all stressed
early in the debate that the U.S. did not have important strategic or economic interests to pursue in Angola, but not all Administration spokesmen appeared to understand this point (e.g.,
Daniel Moynihan, U.N. Ambassador). For a discussion of American interests in Angola, see Gerald J. Bender, "Is U.S. Being
Drawn into Angolan Conflict?" Los Angeles Times, 23 November
1975.

53. The citation to the Lou Harris poll is found in Intelligence
    Report, p. 6.

54. When Zaire and South Africa sent military aid to UNITA in mid-
    September, both countries also had to send personnel to oper-
    ate the equipment. In fact, it was the poor quality of his
    army which prompted Savimbi one month later (October 15 or 16)
    to ask "an American friend" for U.S. troops to fight on his
    side. Savimbi met the "American friend" (whom he assumed to be
    from the CIA) at General Mobutu's palace in Kinshasa. When the
    "friend" turned down his request, Savimbi announced that he had
    no alternative but to seek further and more direct South Afri-
    can assistance. It is not clear whether or not he was encouraged
    in this direction by his "American friend." Most of this infor-
    mation was gathered by an aide to Senator Tunney, Bill Coughlin,
    who had extended conversations with Savimbi in Silva Porto and

Lobito, during the latter part of January 1976, and can be found in John Tunney, "Testimony Before African Subcommittee of Senate Foreign Relations Committee," 6 February 1976, pp. 1-4. Also see John Blair, "Unscrambling America's Role in the Angolan Fiasco," the _Times_ (London), 23 June 1976.

55. Tunney, "Testimony," p. 5

56. "Pike Papers," p. 40, note 481. Many Africa experts were incredulous and/or appalled to see so many Congressmen during the Angolan debate argue that there were "no differences" among the three competing factions. What the "experts" did not realize is that most of the Congressmen were merely repeating the assessment they had heard from the CIA. Moreover, many interpreted the open support of Gulf Oil for the MPLA as further proof that the MPLA was not significantly different or more threatening to the U.S. than its two rivals. By mid-1975 Gulf had concluded not only that the MPLA would win the war but also that it was the only party which could provide a stable government in Angola. Since Gulf accounted for most of the American investment in Angola, it made little sense to a number of Congressmen for the U.S. to spend tens of millions of dollars to opppose the party which was supported by Gulf Oil. As one conservative Senator who supported the Tunney Amendment remarked, "the MPLA can't be all that bad if Gulf is strongly backing them."

57. Henry Kissinger, speech in San Francisco, 3 February 1976, reprinted in the _Los Angeles Times_, 8 February 1976.

58. Quoted in Leslie H. Gelb, "The Boundaries of Détente Have Not Been Easy to Set," _The New York Times_, 14 December 1975.

59. For a full text of his speech in Lusaka on 27 April 1976, see Henry Kissinger, "Southern Africa and the United States: An Agenda for Cooperation," in Department of State, Bureau of Public Affairs, Office of Media Services, _The Secretary of State_, PR 205, (Washington, D.C.), 7 pp.

60. I would like to thank Mark Moran, an aide to Senator Tunney, who allowed me to see some of his notes on his discussions with Angolan leaders he met in Luanda in late January 1976. Moran considered President Agostinho Neto and Prime Minister Lopo de Nascimento to be within the moderate faction of the party--a view which has been repeated by most observers, including top Angola experts in the State Department. Moran noted while still in Angola, "My impression is that there are several positions in the MPLA and that the moderates are in a bit of a quandary over what they recognize as the need for eventual U.S. economic and financial assistance. They need a softening of Washington's position to legitimize their own standing in the

movement." Quoted in The New York Times, 26 January 1976.
Parts of Moran's notes were leaked in a column by Jack Anderson
and Les Whitten, "MPLA Seeking Talks with U.S." The Washington
Post, 17 February 1976.

Concerning past strains between Moscow and the MPLA, Colin Legum
observes:

> Moscow had a particularly troubled relationship with
> the Angolan leadership during the liberation struggle.
> Although they had consistently supported the Popular Move-
> ment for the Liberation of Angola (MPLA), they had never
> found it easy to get along with the rather secretive and
> prickly Agostinho Neto. For a time in 1973 they went so
> far as to support one of Neto's challengers, Daniel Chi-
> penda, and cut off all their aid to MPLA; but once it be-
> came clear that Chipenda could not win, Moscow switched
> its support back to Neto (p. 749).

61. The Director of the Washington Office on Africa, Ted Lockwood,
    noted that the Angolan Desk Officer in the State Department
    told him on 28 May 1976 that the U.S. was moving toward a harder
    line on Cubans in Angola. Cited in "Angolan News Summary," 25
    June 1976, p. 8.

    Ironically, just as the Cubans were preparing to begin their
    withdrawal from Angola, a number of reports appeared which sug-
    gested that the Cuban military and civilian personnel were a
    vital stabilizing influence in Angola. See The New York Times,
    16 May 1976; and the Los Angeles Times, 18 and 20 June 1976.

62. When Angola's membership to the United Nations first came up in
    May, 1976, Ambassador William Scranton recommended that the U.S.
    support the application in the Security Council while suggesting
    an abstention as a fallback position if Kissinger felt that it
    was too early to indicate such a positive act. The option of
    a veto was not even discussed as a possibility by Scranton.
    Nevertheless, the U.S. asked Angola to delay their request for
    membership in May and then proceeded to veto it when it was pro-
    posed in late June. [Anxious to avoid alienating African leaders
    during the sensitive Rhodesian negotiations, the Administration
    did not veto Angola's second application for U.N. membership in
    late November 1976.]
    posed in late June.

63. President Ford described the execution of the American mercen-
    ary Daniel Gearhart by the Angolan government as "unjustified
    and unwarranted," adding that it "will make even more difficult
    any steps toward the normalization of relations between Angola
    and the United States." Kissinger noted that the execution
    "hurt any chance of American aid to Angola or any other improve-
    ment in relations." (Both are quoted in the Los Angeles Times,
    11 July 1976.)

64. It is interesting to note that from his public pronouncements,
    it would appear that President Ford related to Angola almost

exclusively in terms of its impact on American domestic politics. Significantly, he never addressed the subject publicly
until the week of the Senate debate in mid-December, when it
was too late to affect Congressional and public opposition.
Following the passage of the Tunney Amendment, he said that if
the American people were "fully informed" about American objectives in Angola they would support the Administration. (Quoted
in The New York Times, 4 January 1976.) What he neglected to
point out here is that it was the Administration's policy to
try to prevent the American public and Congress from being
"fully informed."

Finally, during the primaries President Ford oversimplified and
distorted Angolan realities in order to present the Administration's Angolan policy in the most favorable light possible. He
argued, for example, that until Congress cut off funds "the
forces we were supporting were prevailing."

> But the minute the Congress said "no" and we couldn't
> provide our allies with what they needed, then the Soviet
> Union and Cuba won. It's just that simple. That is not
> the fault of the administration or the executive branch.
> The Congress just failed to stand up and do what they
> should have done. So there can't be any blame of the
> executive branch failing to challenge the Soviet Union.
> The Congress just bugged out. That is just what it
> amounted to.

Quoted in C. Robert Zelnick, "Who Lost Angola?" The Christian
Science Monitor, 8 March 1976.

65. The five failures, all elaborated in the text are: (1) his
recomendation of Option 2 in NSSM 39 to President Nixon in
January 1970; (2) his offer of offensive weapons to the
Portuguese for use in Africa in December 1973; (3) his approval
of the initial covert aid to the FNLA in January 1975; (4) his
approval of the major military escalation in aid to the FNLA and
UNITA in July 1975; and (5) his veto of Angola's application
for membership in the United Nations in June 1976.

It should be noted that the State Department made several
private attempts through Gulf Oil and Boeing Aircraft to
indicate that it desired an improvement in relations with
the Angolan Government. The State Department believed that
this was sufficient action to signal the moderates in the MPLA
that the U.S. supported them but it is unlikely that, given
the impossible conditions (e.g., removal of Cuban troops) the
U.S. set for an improvement in relations, any Angolans took
these representations seriously.

66. Legum, "The Soviet Union...," pp. 749-750. While Legum provides an extremely penetrating analysis of Sino-Soviet relations in Africa in general and in Angola through 1974, his assessment of Soviet motives and activities in Angola during 1975 closely parallels that of Henry Kissinger. In fact, he published a strong attack on American liberals in The New Republic at the end of the Angolan war accusing them of betraying liberal principles in Angola "...you liberals seem to be more concerned with limiting U.S. power in foreign affairs...rather than with putting forward constructive policies to meet foreign crises such as Angola." "Don't Write Off Angola Just Because Kissinger's Involved," reprinted in The Washington Star, 3 February 1976. Also see his unsigned article "Angola: The International Dimension," in Africa Bureau Fact Sheet, No. 46 (March/April 1976).

67. Tiziano Terzani, "Vietnam: The First Year," The New York Review of Books, 23(15 July 1976):9. The posture which Vietnam adopted at the August, 1976 meeting of non-aligned countries in Colombo, which The New York Times characterized as "refreshingly independent, moderately pro-American," sheds further light on "gradualists" in Vietnam. See the editorial in The New York Times, 4 September 1976, urging the U.S. Government not to veto Vietnam's admission to the U.N.

68. Roger Glenn Brown, "Chinese Politics and American Policy: A New Look at the Triangle," Foreign Policy, No. 23 (Summer 1976):20.

69. Ibid., p. 21.

70. For discussions of these two factions within the MPLA see: Kevin Brown, "A New Angolan Society," The Nation, 223 (17-24 July 1976):42-46; René Lefort, "En Angola, le M.P.L.A. affronte dans des conditions difficiles la tâche de 'reconstruction nationale,'" Le Monde (Paris), 12 March 1976; The Washington Post, 1 April 1976; The Economist (London), 31 July 1976; and Expresso (Lisbon), 29 May 1976, 30 July 1976, 27 August 1976.

[Editor's note: Alves and Machado provided part of the leadership for the abortive coup attempt against the Neto government in late May, 1977.]

71. Dick Clark, "U.S. Policy Toward Africa," Foreign Service Journal, (July 1976):9.

CHAPTER III

THE US, ZAIRE AND ANGOLA

BY Nzongola-Ntalaja

In its most vulgar usage, dependency theory restricts the role of Third World states in international relations to that of victims or instruments of the actions and interests of the major powers.* Aside from the theoretical difficulties arising from the concept of state implicit in such an interpretation, this view tends to convey the misleading impression that the leaders of these states are helpless cogs in the imperialist machine. Their ability to promote their own class interests, and to summon external backing for the same, is thereby neglected. Yet, the rivalry among the major powers, even within the western imperialist camp alone, and the heightened political awareness of the popular classes throughout the world allow Third World leaders greater room for manipulation and a greater political autonomy. In this contest, the imperialist states are just as vulnerable to the pressures exerted by their junior partners as they are capable of setting the limits beyond which these partners cannot modify the pattern of imperialist exploitation in their respective countries.

This essay attempts to show that Zaire's intervention in the Angolan civil war, far from being a simple execution of American directives by the government of President Mobutu Sese Seko, was primarily related to the latter's struggle for survival, a desire that coincided with the foreign policy objectives of the United States. This is to say that the Mobutu regime intervened in Angola to defend its own class interests as well as to

---

*The author would like to thank René Lemarchand, Kazu Wamba-dia-Wamba and Steve Weissman for their very helpful comments on an earlier version of this paper.

discharge its obligations as a junior partner of U.S. imperialism. Accordingly, the relatively autonomous manner in which the Zairian state has played this second role would seem to suggest that it is the mutually convenient relations developed since 1960 between Zaire and the United States, rather than a situation in which the first is the puppet of the second, that may offer a better explanation of their unity of action in Angola. Needless to say, this joint action, to which the racist state of South Africa was also associated, cannot be completely understood without reference to the higher stakes (strategic, economic, political) involved in central and southern Africa.

U.S. Neocolonialism in Africa

Whatever interest the United States might have in Angolan oil, coffee, diamonds and other natural resources, American intervention in Angola cannot be explained exclusively in terms of the actual economic interests of American corporations. Such an interpretation is inadequate at both the empirical and theoretical levels. Empirically, the American investment in Angola at the time of the civil war was not enormous. Only the Gulf Oil Corporation, the largest U.S. and foreign investor in Angola, had a lot at stake; it estimated its total investments to be around $209 million in 1972.[1] Theoretically, there is the danger of economism, of reducing every social phenomenon to a mere reflection of the economic, and every historical event to some economic causes.[2] This is not to deny the importance of economic factors in the Angolan conflict - for they are very significant - nor their determining influence within the capitalist system. It is only a warning against a narrow specific factor analysis of the complex nature of neocolonialism, defined here as the subordination, by all the means possible, of a politically independent country to the imperialist countries' overall aim of maintaining it within, and thereby preserving, the world captialist system.[3]

It is this primary goal that explains Dr. Henry Kissinger's rage when contemplating the Soviet Union's involvement in southern Africa, thousands of miles away from its borders, in an area where, according to the former American Secretary of State, the U.S.S.R. has no "traditional interests." Since the U.S.A. is equally thousands of miles away from Angola, the meaning of American intervention, and indeed, the cornerstone of U.S. foreign policy in the last thirty years, is that the United States considers it as its duty to maintain all the non-socialist countries within the world capitalist system. Consequently, if Western Europe becomes unable to retain its former colonial empire under neocolonial control, the United States should step

in to prevent "instability," "power vacuum," and "Communist subversion."
This is what led to American military interventions in Indochina, in the
Congo (Zaire), in the Dominican Republic, and more recently in Angola.

An adequate interpretation of American intervention in Angola becomes
possible, therefore, when viewed from this more general framework of neocolonialism. The interests to be protected are neither singly American nor
exclusively economic. They comprise all those interests necessary to the
preservation of the world captialist system. And these are economic, strategic, political and ideological. They include the interests of the international bourgeoisie as well as those of the state bourgeoisies of post-
colonial countries still subjected to imperialist exploitation.

The economic and strategic interests of the United States in central
and southern Africa reside in maintaining Western access to the strategic
resources of this minerally-rich area of the world, and in protecting the
economic health of Western Europe, which is greatly dependent on African
resources.[4] These interests constitute the rationale for the adoption of
the second option of the National Security Study Memorandum (NSSM) No. 39
of 1969, submitted to President Nixon by Kissinger on 2 January 1970. That
was the option calling for the strengthening of mutually beneficial ties
between the United States on the one hand, and Portugal, Rhodesia and South
Africa on the other. Reference is also made to the indispensability of
the strategic resources of these embargo-proof colonial settler states of
Rhodesia and South Africa in the December 1974 report of the Council on
International Economic Policy on "critical imported materials."

For U.S. policy-makers, the white settlers are clearly the best possible
allies, in a situation where no viable African "moderates" can be helped
to crush radical liberation movements. Not only would white settlers provide
easy access to mineral resources and a very cheap labor force to produce

them, the countries and strategic positions they occupy would also be
readily available for use in the event of an East-West war. Since 1909,
for example, Britain has tied its worries concerning the Suez Canal to the
need of maintaining a friendly government in South Africa, for purposes of
assuring a safe passage to British ships around the Cape of Good Hope. The
1967 Israeli-Arab war, which resulted in the closing of the canal, gave
proof of the correctness of the British viewpoint, and helped to intensify
Western fears of Soviet presence in the Indian Ocean.

Regardless of French displeasure with Dr. Kissinger's arrogance on the
question of Arab oil-fields much of capitalist Europe still recognizes
the United states as their major protector. This protection, as both John
Foster Dulles and Henry Kissinger has admitted, is not altruistic. Given
its enormous investments in Western Europe, the United States has a major
economic and strategic stake in those resources whose non-availability might
result in the "strangulation" of the highly industrial economies of Western
Europe.[5] American intervention in Angola, like its earlier intervention
in Zaire, was part of this general effort to maintain the availability of
some "essential" or strategic resources (e.g. oil, hydro-electric power,
diamonds, iron) to Western Europe and, in this particular case, to South
Africa.

If the economic and strategic interests are readily apparent, the
political and ideological aspects of neocolonialism are not always easy to
grasp. Nevertheless, the political and ideological instances are structu-
rally specific and autonomous vis-à-vis the economic and the strategic.
This is an important proposition, as it helps to explain imperialist aggression in areas where the economic stake may be negligible - e.g. American
intervention in Chad.[6]

In the political sphere, the United States prefers the orderly transfer of power from the colonialists to African "moderates" or those politicians whose class interests are not irreconcilable with imperialism. Having achieved their goal of Africanizing the state institutions from which they were for the most part excluded under colonialism, the petty bourgeois intellectuals who led the struggle for independence have betrayed their peoples' expectation that independence would bring about an amelioration in their material conditions of life.[7] Consequently, the principal contradiction in Africa today is that between the objective interests of the masses and those of the state bourgeoisie that exploits them economically in partnership with imperialism, and oppresses them politically, while at the same time attempting to legitimize its privileges by a skillful manipulation of traditional culture, values and ideologies.[8]

Whenever these ideological representations fail to diminish the bourgeoisie's isolation from the masses and thereby increasing the former's vulnerability to revolutionary struggle, the neocolonial state has recourse to greater repression and external protection. The weaker the regime, the deeper the external involvement, which may result in foreign military presence. However unpopular or discredited a regime may become, it remains politically useful to its external backers, as the legitimate popular struggle against it may be represented as a case of "Communist subversion." Moreover, the client rulers so protected may be counted upon to vote the American way at the United Nations, as members of Daniel P. Moynihan's club of the "free" and the "decent" in this barbarous world. Rewarding them for services rendered to the United States and the "Free World" becomes part of the "moral commitment" of the United States. Failure to defend them, according to this view, encourages the enemy to stir up trouble elsewhere, and may give the impression that the United States either cannot respect its

commitments or is no longer sufficiently strong to contain communism. Pushed
to its absurd limit, this is what may be termed the Mayaguez or Ford doctrine:
hitting the adversary so hard, no matter how small the latter is, to prove
that the United States has the ability and the will to protect the world
capitalist system.

In the ideological war between the capitalist and socialist camps, the
preservation of the anti-communist ideas once championed by the ideological
apparatuses of the colonial state is one of the major tasks that imperialism
has assigned to the neocolonial state. Thus, work among the "free" or
"Christian" trade unions, training programs in Israel (until 1973) and the
West for trade union leaders and journalists, and scholarships for university
students are part of the American and Western ideological stake in Africa.
Part of this ideological stake involves "the strangulation of the process
of knowledge itself," since the quest for knowledge implies a struggle
against the false ideas.[9] These are being pushed on the people under numerous forms of cultural revival and superstitions by politicans who, for
purposes of maintaining the stability of the established order, rely "on
circuses rather than on bread, on ideological claptrap rather than on
reason."[10] The Western powers are more than willing to help perpetuate
obscurantism in this fashion and to make ordinary people ignorant of the
realities of today's world. In a series of interviews by Barbara Walters
on NBC's Today Show in early May 1975, Kissinger stated that one of the
challenges facing the United States was the rapid growth and widespread
acceptance of Marxist ideas throughout the world, a development he thought
threatened the American way of life. To counteract such a cancerous growth,
one that might develop deep roots within the imperialist countries themselves and thus undermine the legitimacy of the system, you need to help
"moderate" leaders suppress the "extremists" and their Marxist ideas.

The United States and Zaire

How does Zaire fit in this grand scheme in general, and with respect to
the Angolan conflict in particular? To answer this question in a meaningful
way is to explain how the United States intervenes in African conflicts
alongside African partners whose interests are compatible with those of U.S.
imperialism.

It should be remembered, at the outset, that it was in Zaire, formerly
the Congo, where the United States first tested and perfected its neocolonialist strategy and tactics for Africa. Recounting how the United States began
its intervention there through the United Nations Congo Mission (ONUC)
in 1960, Seth Singleton writes that "Washington quite accruately perceived
that the United States' interests would best be served by a policy which
promoted African self-regulation of African conflicts, but only so long as
that self-regulation was clearly in the hands of African 'moderates'."[11]
This "African solution" option was a concrete application of the policy that
came to be known as the Guam or Nixon Doctrine. The Nixon Doctrine is a
strategy of indirect intervention, of using "moderates," non-American troops
and international organizations as means of maintaining a stable world situation favorable to American interests, without at the same time running the
risk of a costly direct intervention and that of a direct Soviet-American
confrontation. In Zaire, the United Nations provided the umbrella for the
American anti-communist or more precisely anti-Lumumbist policy.[12]

American intervention became more and more direct after the U.N. umbrella was removed in 1964. In the case of Angola, Zaire served as both the
precedent for, and the instrument of, indirect intervention.[13] An adequate
understanding of Zaire's role in Angola must, therefore, begin with the
lessons that Americans learned from their Zairian adventure, and the leadership group they helped to create and later used in the Angolan conflict.

In 1960, the major "moderate" elements in Zaire were, among others, Joseph Kasavubu, Joseph Ileo, Cyrille Adoula and Joseph Mobutu, all of whom were opposed to the more radical nationalism of Patrice Lumumba, Antoine Gizenga, Pierre Mulele and their followers. Since he was not thought to be a "moderate," Prime Minister Lumumba was not acceptable to the conservative Republican Administration in Washington. His removal from the political scene was actively sought by this Administration, which found support within the United Nations Secretariat. U.N. and U.S. officials in Kinshasa (then Leopoldville) acted to prevent reconciliation between Lumumba and Kasavubu and to nullify Colonel Mobutu's plan to "neutralize" both men, in favor of President Kasavubu.

Thus in keeping with the tactic of using African self-regulation through "moderates," the Kasavubu coup of 5 September 1969 against the Lumumba government was actually the work of American U.N. diplomat Andrew Cordier. Likewise, the Mobutu "neutralization" coup of 14 September 1960 had the enthusiastic backing of the U.S. Central Intelligence Agency (C.I.A.), the Belgian Security Policy and ONUC, with Moroccan General Kettani as the key man among those involved in its preparation and execution.

By January 1961, when the pro-Lumumba rival government headed by Gizenga in Kisangani (then Stanleyville) began expanding its control and authority in the eastern part of the Republic and thus encouraged Lumumba's followers all over the country, the American Embassy's displeasure over the course of events and rumors of a pro-Lumumba coup in Kinshasa resulted in Lumumba's transfer to Lubumbashi (then Elisabethville) on 17 January 1961.[15] He was murdered on the same day by the authorities of the secessionist state of Katanga, before the CIA-prepared cobra venom could reach him.

Just as they worked together to eliminate Lumumba, the Americans and their Zairian allies worked hard during the next seven months to bring about

his successor. U.S. officials have described the Lovanium University meeting
of the Parliament during which the choice of Adoula as Prime Minister was
approved as "really a U.S. operation but using outstanding U.N. personali-
ties."[16] According to Stephen Weissman, the American government "not only
supported Adoula; it was, in many different ways, part of his government."[17]
So when the U.N. umbrella that served to mask American intervention and tutelage was removed on 30 June 1964, the United States and Belgium had to step
in more forcefully to fill the "internal security gap" created by the departure of the U.N. force, in the midst of popular revolts for a "second independence" in Kwilu and in the east. To do this they decided to act through
the former secessionist Moise Tshombe, with the United States footing the
bill for his white mercenaries and the CIA's little air force, registered in
Liechtenstein as Western International Ground Maintenance Organization (WIGMO),
among other projects, while Belgium took it upon itself to help straighten
out Mobutu's army and the entire repressive apparatus of the state.

In spite of all this help, Tshombe failed to unite the moderate leadership and to end the political crisis. This failure once again demonstrated
the inability of the Zairian state bourgeoisie to govern the nation through
the internally divisive parliamentarian regime. It is at this juncture that
General Mobutu made his second dramatic appearance on the political scene,
this time to end instability and to give the bourgeoisie and organizational
unity that it had been unable to achieve on its own. The coup d' etat of
24 November 1965 allowed this class to meet its most serious threat to date,
namely, the organized struggle of peasants, workers and the lumpenproletariat
reflected in the "second independence" movement. This Ceasarist arbitration
clearly took the side of bourgeois interests, and resulted in the establishment of a Bonapartist regime.[18]

Within the framework of neocolonialism, this form of regime is primarily

geared to law and order functions, the depolitization of the masses and
capitalist development. Accordingly, the state bourgeoisie and multinational corporations were to become the major beneficiaries of this stabili-
zation process. U.S. investments in Zaire rose from less than $20 million
in 1960 to approximately $750 million in 1975.[19] As a junior partner in
this joint venture of economics exploitation, the Zairian bourgeoisie has a
stake in this enormous investment, as it allows this class to solidify its
hold over the state and maximizes the chances of its individual members to
enrich themselves. Its economic, political and ideological interests are
clearly compatible with those of U.S. imperialism.

This compatibility explains not only the existence of mutually convenient relations between the United States and Zaire, but also the willingness of the Zairian state to faithfully execute its role as the junior partner of imperialist exploitation vis-à-vis the inhabitants of its own
territory and vis-à-vis neighboring countries. There is an element of
reciprocity here, best exemplified by General Mobutu's ability to literally
compel the U.S. government to come to his rescue when, threatened by a severe
economic crisis in 1975, he was largely rewarded even after having accused
the CIA and the American ambassador as having plotted a coup against him with
a group of Zairian military officers.[20] Coming in the midst of revelations
concerning CIA doings around the world, Mobutu's action had the effect -
intended or not - of showing that his is not a puppet regime. And it is not.
Reciprocity and the interpenetration of interests are the keys that explain
the regime's pro-American actions.

Even before Angola, the pattern of Zairian foreign relations reflected
this basically pro-American bias, official declarations and dramatic actions
of a radical nature notwithstanding. Until November 1972, for example, the
People's Republic of China was continuously denounced as the greatest

perpetrator of subversion around the world. The Zairian government, accordingly, opposed China's admission to the United Nations. And yet, the surprise announcement of the establishment of diplomatic relations between the two countries in late 1972 - the year that Richard Nixon "normalized" American relations with China - was followed by two visits to the People's Republic by President Mobutu (January 1973 and December 1974) and by Chinese and North Korean economic and military assistance to Zaire.

Throughout 1973, the government of Zaire coupled its intensified drive for "authenticity" at home with an aggressively Third World stance on major international issues. Although never entirely consistent, as we shall see below, this radical stance was coherently stated in the now famous address by President Mobutu to the United Nations General Assembly on 4 October 1973. It was here the he reiterated Zaire's opposition to colonialism and racism, and publicly announced the breaking of diplomatic relations with Israel, two days before the October War. Israel's best friend in Africa became the first non-Arab chief of state to be invited as an observer to a summit meeting of the Arab League in December 1973 in Algiers, thus giving some substance to Mobutu's U.N. speech dictum that "between and friend and a brother, the choice is clear."

What, then, was Zaire's choice in the Arab-Israeli conflict? Only two years later, a government that had always stated its opposition to dialogue with the rulers of the colonial-settler states of southern Africa, and since 1973 denounced Zionism and the suppression of the national rights of the Palestinian people, was now opposing proposed moves to expel or suspend Israel and South Africa from the United Nations. Zaire began to openly defend the well-known American notion of "universality" with respect to U.N. membership, a concept, by the way, that American policy-makers ignored for two dozen years in their crusade against the People's Republic of China, and once more violated with regard to liberated Vietnam in 1975 and 1976.

On 20 September 1975, the then Zairian Foreign Affairs Commissioner, Mandungu Bula Nyati, stated in New York that his government opposed "any suspension or expulsion of any state from any international organization."[21] As for Israeli and South African intransigence with respect to their illegal occupation of Arab territories and Namibia, respectively, Commissioner Mandungu said that "it was preferable to put pressure on either Israel or South Africa inside the world organization than seek their expulsion."[22] Now this has always been the American position, particularly in relation to South Africa.

Coming at a time when the United States was crying against the alleged tyranny of the majority in the U.N. General Assembly, Mandungu's statement and Zaire's U.N. votes confirmed the then Secretary of State Henry Kissinger's confidence that he expected Zaire to defend American interests in international forums. With few exceptions, all the evidence tends to support this expectation.[23] Witness Zaire's basically neutral stand on the Vietnam war, and its strongly pro-American bias at the July 1973 summit of non-aligned countries in Algiers, and the 1975 Organization of African Unity (OAU) summit in Kampala. Zaire's role in facilitiating American intervention in Angola has to be understood within this general framework of the execution of its expected and freely accepted role as a defender of American interests, a role which is a function of the interpenetration of the interests of the Zairian state bourgeoisie with those of U.S. imperialism.

The Zaire/Angola Connection

What, then, were the specfiically Zairian interests in the Angolan conflict? As an underdeveloped capitalist-type of state, Zaire is in no position to exploit Angola economically. Much has been said of Mobutu's ambitions concerning oil-rich Cabinda. The question most people fail to raise is why is it that Zaire did very little to help liberate that territory until 1974, when the Front for the Liberation of Cabinda (FLEC) suddenly emerged from its obscurity to claim Zairian support. Even if Zaire had wanted to seize Cabinda in the manner that India took over Goa, the weakness of the Zairian army would have made it impossible to achieve this goal.[24] As the Popular Front for the Liberation of Angola (MPLA) had already establish- ed a strong revolutionary base inside Cabinda, the latter's annexation to Zaire could have come only as a result of a neocolonialist agreement on the Western Sahara model. It has been reported, but not fully substantiated, that former Portuguese President Antonio de Spinola and the National Front for the Liberation of Angola (FNLA) leader, Holden Roberto, were not unsympathetic to such an agreement.

But Zaire does have an important economic and strategic stake in Angola. It consists in maintaining access to the ports of Lobito in Angola and Matadi in Zaire. Of the four exit routes for Zairian copper exports, the Benguela Railway, from the southeastern frontier with Angola to Lobito on the Atlantic Ocean, is still the quickest and the best. It is much shorter than the Sakania-Beira line through Zambia, Zimbabwe and Mozambique, and does not involve the elaborate trans-shipments of the National Line which runs from Lumbumbashi to Matadi via Ilebo and Kinshasa, and of the Kigoma- Dar-es Salaam line. Its closure during the Angolan civil war resulted in costly delays of the copper exports of both Zaire and Zambia.

The port of Matadi and the 23-mile strip of land separating Angola from Cabinda constitute Zaire's only direct access to the Atlantic Ocean, through the Zaire/Congo River. An armed conflict between Zaire and Angola could effectively prevent any shipping in this area and thus cripple the export-oriented externally dependent Zairina economy. Just as in the case of the United States, the "access interest" takes precedence over any other economic interests.

However, the probability of an MPLA government deliberately denying Zaire access to the Atlantic has always been very low. If that indeed was the case in 1975, then Zaire's stake in Angola has to be more complex than just its economic and strategic interests. Without denying the importance of these interests, Jean Rymenam has suggested that since the time the MPLA launched its post-independence offensive, "it is the political future of the regime and of its chief that are at stake and, beyond Zaire, the balance of forces in Africa and in the world."[25] This refers to the specifically political and ideological aspects of Zairian intervention in Angola.

President Mobutu himself was reported to have confided that the way the Angolan conflict is resolved would determine his own political future. But he also had reason to believe that the United States would support him regardless of the outcome, because, as Rene Lefort suggests, "American presence in Zaire would depend on the survival of the Mobutu regime."[26]

Were Mobutu's fears justified? The question can meaningfully be approached from a short-run as well as a long-run perspective. In the short run, the Mobutu regime feared the possibility of a triumphant MPLA retaliating against Zairian aggression, either directly in the Matadi-Boma region, and thus denying Zaire access to the Ocean, or indirectly by supporting a move by the revengeful Katangese to march on Kinshasa for purpose of over-throwing Mobutu. The approximately 6,000 former Katanga gendarmes were brought out of their exile in Angola by their chief, Tshombe, to fight the Lumumbists and Mulelists in 1964, only to be forced to return there in 1966. This was the year that a mutiny within their ranks at Kisagnani resulted in a concerted effort to eliminate them physically. Their subsequent hostility to Mobutu is so great that they rejected the Zairian President's amnesty of 1975. Having worked as mercenaries for the Portuguese colonialists, they unhesitantly threw in their lot with the MPLA, fearing that a victory by the FNLA would mean total surrender to Mobutu.

Even before the Brazzaville Agreement of 28 February 1976 reached by Presidents Agostinho Neto of the People's Republic of Angola and Mobutu Sese Seko of Zaire, it was doubtful that the MPLA government would either attack Zaire or allow the Katangese to do so. Desirous of being recognized and accepted by all African states and fearful of any military adventure when their own hold on the new state was not yet secure, the Angolan authorities could not afford to take this option.

The same conclusion would seem to apply to the possibility of Luanda providing direct assistance to the Lumumbist Gizenga and the People's Revolutionary Party (PRP) led by Laurent Kabila. A remnant of the Simba or Eastern Rebellion of the "second independence" movement, the PRP's greatest feat to date has been the kidnapping of three American and one Dutch students in 1975 on the Tanzanian side of Lake Tanganyika. In spite of its harassment of Zairian troops in the Uvira area of Kivu Region, it did not seem to constitute a major threat to the regime.

As for Gizenga, he has never shown much ability in effective organization and leadership. His irresponsible statements of late January 1976 issued in the relative security of Geneva and Brussels to the effect that he was returning home to lead an armed struggle against Mobutu resulted in military repression in his home region of Bandundu, which borders on the north of Angola. Those Zairian troops defeated in Angola were reported to be taking vengeance against their own people in this area, accusing them of being MPLA sympathizers. Although Gizenga, the PRP, the Katangese and other opposition groupings are said to have formed an alliance in November 1975 for purposes of overthrowing the Mobutu regime, ideological and personality clashes between the various leaders prevented this loos alliance from meterializing into a viable resistance movement and from gaining active support from the People's Republic of Angola. The absence of these two crucial conditions provides a partial explanation for the failure of the premature Guevarist-type military action by the Katangese in March 1977.

If immediate economic, strategic and military threats seem to have been exaggerated, the major threat an Angola under MPLA rule presented to the Mobutu regime was a long-run political and ideological challenge. This consists above all in the consequences the MPLA victory may eventually have for the prestige and legitimacy of the Mobutu regime as well as for the strength of the repressive apparatus on which it relies. The defeat of Zairian troops by MPLA forces (and subsequently by General Nathanael Mbumba's "Katangese" army in March 1977) has thoroughly humiliated the Zairian armed forces. At the very least, it has contributed to the sharpening of class contradictions within the military organization, whose officers spent more time in pursuit of private wealth and luxury than in training their badly paid troops. Such contradictions cannot help but further reduce the fighting capability of the armed forces, while correspondingly baring their strictly repressive function.

Moreover, the establishment of a presumably Marxit regime in Luanda is likely to intensify the ideological debate in this part of Africa. Should the socialist experiment succeed in Angola, it would constitute a powerful demonstration effect for the Zairian people. Meanwhile, the apostal of authenticity cannot enjoy the thought of being surrounded on both the western and southern borders of Zaïre by advocates of scientific socialism, in theory hostile to the state capitalism option taken by his regime. The intermittent battle of the radio stations - la guerre des ondes, as it is known in French - between Kinshasa and Brazzaville, and one that Radio Luanda joined at the height of the civil war, does sometimes bring to the attention of ordinary people sensitive matters (such as foreign-owned properties) that Zairian

authorities would not wish to devulge to their citizens.[27] Newsworthy

items of this kind freely provided by a hostile neighbor may serve to under-

mine the legitimacy of the regime and/or that of its authorities.

Having invested so much in the effort to establish the FNLA as the dominant

nationalist group and help it to weaken, if not to eliminate, the MPLA,

Zaire stood to reap a moral defeat from the MPLA victory. For Zaire, this de-

feat is a deeply felt "loss" - for such is the notion in these political-ideo-

logical wars - inasmuch as the FNLA was more or less a Zairian political organi-

zation. As a perceptive political analyst has pointed out, the FNLA had

come "to incarnate Zairian expansionism toward Angola: the more progress the

MPLA made, the more the nationalist dimension of the FNLA diminished."[28] The

logical outcome of this substitution effect was direct Zairian military inter-

vention in Angola. The inability of the FNLA and its ally, the National Union

for the Total Independence of Angola (UNITA), to defeat the MPLA forced Zaire

and South Africa to send their regular troops. Without Zairian backing in

the first place, the FNLA could not have become an effective social force.[29]

No attempt is made here to deny the nationalist character of the FNLA.

This nationalism, however, has to be placed in its proper historical context.

Holden Roberto's movement originated in the reactionary nationalism of Kongo

royalists during their struggle to restore the old Kongo Kingdom or, failing

that, to be able to control its remnant in Angola. This nationalism was re-

actionary because the nation to be established has to be found in the precolonial

past. It was not the more universally accepted African new nation based on a

common specific history of colonial oppression and a common hope for the future.

These twentieth century royalists were first led by Miguel Nekaka, and later

by his son Manuel Barros Nekaka, who moved to Kinshasa in 1942.[30]

Manuel Nekaka was Holden Roberto's uncle and political tutor. The nephew

had been taken to Kinshasa at two years of age in 1925. It was here, in the
Belgian Congo, that he acquired his education, worked as a clerk in the
colonial apparatus and later became his uncle's top lieutenant in the separatist
movement for a free Kongo state, the Union of the Populations of Northern
Angola (UPNA), founded in 1957. A member of the évolué circles from which
the political ideas of Congolese independence emerged in the mid-1975's,
Roberto's political thinking was marked by the "reformist option" to which
nearly the entire Congolese petty bourgeoisie subscribed.

After George Houser of the American Committee on Africa in 1957, and
Kwane Nkrumah's All African People's Conference in 1958 convinced Roberto to
strip his movement of its "tribal anachronism," he was satisfied to change
its name from UPNA to UPA (Union of the Populations of Angola) but refused
all attemps to merge with the MPLA, which he labeled "Communist." With an
unshakeable faith in the ability of the United Nations and the United States
to compel Portugal into granting independence to Angola on the neocolonialist
model of mutually convenient relationships between the former colonialist
and the national petty bourgeoisie, Roberto saw no need of reconciling his
newly found reformist nationalism with the more revolutionary or people-oriented
nationalism of the MPLA.

Rejecting the MPLA, the UPA merged with another grouping of Angola émigrés,
the Zombo-based Angolan Democratic Party (PDA), to form the FNLA on 27 March
1962. From 5 April 1962 until 1971, the FNLA was to be known under its more
ambitious name of the Revolutionary Government of Angola in Exile (GRAE). In
spite of the FNLA/GRAE's recognition in 1963 as the only effective Angolan
liberation movement by the OAU, this attempt at monopolizing nationalist legitimacy was bound to fail, due to the superior organizational capabilities of the
MPLA. The FNLA finally acknowledged the MPLA's staying power by signing the
Kinshasa merger agreement of 14 December 1972 which, by the way, remained a

dead letter.[31] The non-observance of this Kinshasa accord, and of the Mombasa, Alvor and Nakuru accords which followed, demonstrates that national unity, like true independence, is not achieved through written agreements. The people of Angola were to define their true identity in their heroic struggle against foreign invaders: European, South African, and Zairian.

Conclusion

The political-ideological stake of the Mobutu regime in Angola, and by implication the maintenance of the bourgeoisie as a ruling class in Zaire, coincides with the overall neocolonial strategy of the United States in Africa. This, more than any other factor, explains why the Zairian state bourgeoisie intervened in Angola on the side of the American imperalists and the South African racists. The major aim of the intervention was to help defeat the MPLA and thereby insure the victory of the moderate FNLA-UNITA politicians. Since the FNLA leadership was on the whole composed of Angola-Zairians who tended to imitate the behavior of the Zairian state bourgeoisie, including the latter's thirst for private wealth, luxury and impeccable attire, there is no doubt that from the viewpoint of Mobutu's Zaire, they would have made better neighbors than the MPLA militants. The Zairians would prefer to see in Angola a political regime whose leadership not only shares a similar capitalist world view and common behavioral traits, but also which owes its survival as a viable organization to Zairian support. If the first of these two assets would have eliminated the danger of having a potentially hostile neighbor, the second could have served to enhance the prestige of the Mobutu regime by allowing it to claim credit for the liberation of Angola. Needless to say, all this would have strengthened the tendency to dissociate the national liberation struggle in southern Africa from the anti-imperialist struggle of the dominated classes in neocolonial countries. For the objective interests of the dominant classes of these countries, like those of U.S. imperialism, are in systematic conflict with revolutionary mobilization.

NOTES

1. Mohamed A. El-Khawas and Barry Cohen (eds.) The Kissinger Study of Southern Africa (Westport, Conn.: Lawrence Hill and Co., 1976), p. 50.

2. The notion of "economism" is used here, not in its Leninist conception of reformist trade union activities, but in its Marxist epistemological sense, as defined by Nicos Poulantzas in Political Power and Social Classes (London: NLB and Sheed and Ward, 1973), pp. 14, note 3, 38-39, and passim.

3. The major elements of this definition are borrowed from Stewart Smith, U.S. Neocolonialism in Africa (New York: International Publishers, 1974) pp. 37-43.

4. Sean Gervasi, "The Politics of Accelerated Economic Growth," in Leonard Thompson and Jeffrey Butler (eds.) Change in Contemporary South Africa (Berkeley: University of California Press, 1975), p. 353, estimates the value of the direct investments of the main western powers in southern Africa alone to have been around $15 billion in 1974. For a more detailed examination of the "access interest," especially as it relates to Zaire, see Stephen Weissman, American Foreign Policy in the Congo, 1960-1964 (Ithaca: Cornell University Press, 1974), pp. 28-31. See also G. Mennen Williams, "U.S. Objectives in the Congo, 1960-65," Africa Report, 10:8 (August 1965), 12-20, for a statement of what Weissman has termed the "sophisticated anti-communism" of the New Frontier liberals.

5. In a statement that anticipates Kissinger's well-publicized position concerning the significance of Middle East oil for U.S. foreign policy, former Secretary of State John Foster Dulles maintained that the United States had a stake in those resources "essential to the industrial life of Western Europe." The statement is quoted in Weissman, American Foreign Policy in the Congo, p. 30.

6. Although future uranium exploitation and the strategically located French military base at N'Djamena (then Fort Lamy) must be taken into account, they alone could not have justified the massive commitment of French troops to the defense of the Tombalbaye regime between 1968 and 1972.

7. I have already dealt at length with this contradiction in the perceptions of independence by the various social classes in Georges N. Nzongola, "The bourgeoisie and Revolution in the Congo," Journal of Modern African Studies, 8:4 (December 1970), 511-530.

8. For a stimulating discussion of this contradiction, see Jean-Pierre Oliver, "Afrique: Qui exploite qui?," Les Temps Modernes, 30:346 (May 1975), 1506-1551 and 30: 347 (June 1975), 1744-1775.

9. Personal communication from Wamba-dia-Wamba.

10. Paul A. Baran, The Political Economy of Growth (New York: Monthly Review Press, 1968), p. 254.

11. Seth Singleton, "Conflict Resolution in Africa: The Congo and the Rules of the Game," Pan-African Journal, 8:1 (Spring 1975), pp. 5-6.

12. Weissman, p. 60.

13. The word "instrument" should not convey the false impression that Zaire's actions were taken exclusively, or even primarily, for purposes of serving American interests. One example should suffice to elucidate the true relationship. The instrumental role of Israel in what has been termed the "third-country technique" in the transfer of South African goods to black African markets with a "Made in Israel" label did imply tangible benefits for the Zionist state, and did not imply any coercion from or subservience to, the apartheid state. This fact, long published only in the literature of progressive groups, was finally reported by Terence Smith in The New York Times of Sunday, 18 April 1976, p. 3. for a defense of the third-country technique as it relates to Israel, see Arnold Rivkin, Africa and the West (New York: Praeger, 1962), pp. 71-85.

14. Weissman, pp. 52-55 and 85-99.

15. Ibid, p. 110.

16. An unidentified U.S. Embassy official, quoted in Weissman, p. 147.

17. Weissman, p. 208.

18. For a more detailed analysis of these developments, and a definition of the concept of Caesarism, see Nzongola-Ntalaja, "Urban Administration in Zaire: A Study of Kananga, 1971-73," (Ph.D. dissertation, University of Wisconsin - Madison, 1975), pp. 18-44.

19. In a personal communication, Stephen Swissman writes that this "$750 million figure refers to investments, loans, and contracts. In 1974 the investment figure (alone) was put at about $200 million by the State Department."

20. The United States moved to grant economic assistance, and acted through international lending institutions to reschedule Zaire's debts. The editor of the "Week in Review" section of The New York Times of Sunday, 26 October 1975 found a perfect title for a Colin Legum article analyzing American policy: "U.S. TURNS CHEEK AND CHECKBOOK TO ZAIRE."

21. The New York Times, Sunday, 21 September 1975, p. 7.

22. Ibid. This is the Times' account of his statement, not a direct quotation.

23. The most notable exception was Mobutu's strong denunciation of the appointment of Nathaniel Davis as Assistant Secretary of State for African Affairs in January 1975. A worsening of Zaire-American relations following the expulsion mentioned above, of U.S. Ambassador Deane Hinton in June 1975 was averted, thanks in part to the skillful diplomacy of the former U.S. Ambassador to Zaire and former Under-Secretary of State Sheldon Vance, to the satisfaction of all parties concerned.

24. As Mahmoud Hussein points out in his analysis of the Nasserist regime, a bourgeois type army losis its fighting ability when the behavior of its officers is dominated by "capitalist self-interest, the pursuit of private profit, and a taste for luxury and personal prestige." Class Conflict in Egypt, 1945-1970 (New York: Monthly Review Press, 1973), p. 257, note 8.

25. Jean Rymenam, "Zaïre: Le pouvoir absolu d'un militaire d' occasion,"
    Le Monde Diplomatique, December 1975, p. 10.

26. René Lefort, "Angola: Les interventions étrangères menacent de faire
    déborder le conflit," Le Monde Diplomatique, December 1975, p. 6.

27. For example, when Brazzaville and European news media called attention
    to the ownership of several castles by General Mobutu in Europe, the
    Zairian propaganda machine made a considerable effort to convince the
    people that these castles were essential to our national security.
    How can one expect, they asked, the President of our great country to
    risk his life staying in hotels, when so many mentally unbalanced Euro-
    peans run around with guns?

28. Lefort, op. cit.

29. On Zairian efforts on behalf of the FNLA and against the MPLA, see Basil
    Davidson, In the Eye of the Storm (Garden City, N.Y.: Doubleday, 1972),
    pp. 208,221-222, 231-239 and passim.

30. The account of the FNLA history in this and subsequent paragraphs is based
    primarily on John Marcum, The Angolan Revolution, vol. 1 (Cambridge: M.I.T.
    Press, 1969), pp. 49-100.

31. The agreement provided for the establishment of a unified supreme council
    of the revolution having a dual executive with Roberto as the political
    leader and Neto as the military leader plus a unifed command of twelve
    members, equally divided between the FNLA and the MPLA. This unified
    front agreement was never implemented, as Zaire continued to deny the
    MPLA access to Zaire's long border with Angola.

CHAPTER IV

US POLICY TOWARDS RHODESIA

BY LARRY BOWMAN

Nowhere have American concerns about African issues come into sharper
focus than in Rhodesia. Here issues of racial discrimination, United Nations
sanctions, economic interest, the use of violence, and U.S.-Soviet rivalry
have been neatly joined in one complex political problem--the political
future of Rhodesia. The unilateral declaration of independence (UDI) by
white Rhodesians in 1965 made it impossible to ignore what was happening
there. Since that time Rhodesia has grown steadily as an issue of global
political importance and America has been unable to avoid being drawn
ever more tightly into the vortex of the Rhodesian crisis.

American policy over the past decade or so has taken several twists
and turns. Policy was often short-sighted and narrowly focused. Failure
was more frequently the rule than the exception. In 1974 American policy
in Southern Africa began unraveling and by the end of 1975 it was in a total
shambles. Efforts by former Secretary of State Henry Kissinger to reconstruct
U.S. policy began in 1976. But it will fall to the new Carter administration
to fundamentally face the consequences of past American policy failures in
Southern Africa and attempt a fresh start.

There has always been considerable difficulty, when addressing the
Rhodesian question, to adequately discern just what American interests are.
Trade ties are important to a few corporations but scarcely to the nation
as a whole. Our national security is not threatened by Rhodesian developments.
Our real interests in Rhodesia are more general and more subtle. As a

multi-racial nation ourselves, we do have some national interest in how
racial questions are handled elsewhere, and more explicitly, how our
policies affect such developments. More broadly we are a nation devoted
to the rule of law. The Rhodesian problem, in part, has been handled at
the United Nations and through legal mechanisms available there. We presumably have an interest in how these legal steps work out. And we certainly
have an interest in the broad shape of power and influence in the Southern
Africa region as a whole; Rhodesia is an important factor in this larger
picture.

Until recently these issues were ignored or only vaguely appreciated.
In an area perceived as non-vital to America, Rhodesian questions were
submerged beneath the claims of other actors and special interests. In
his valuable study of American policy toward Rhodesia, Anthony Lake pointed
out that

> The Rhodesian problem presents Americans with a
> series of conflicting choices: between immediate
> economic interests and the claims of international
> law; between American opposition to racial injustice
> abroad and the impulse to seek smooth relations with
> foreign powers-that-be, especially if they are "anti-
> Communist"' between calculations of short-term national
> interest and a longer view of what is good for us as
> well as for others.[1]

As Lake plainly indicates, America normally settles for the former of
his paired choices. Future options will be more complex, however, for in
the past year Rhodesia has moved from being a problem of only passing
American concern to one of considerable importance. Part of our story
will be about how this transition took place. It is not a particularly
edifying story for the obfuscations, compromises, and indifference of

years past are precisely the reasons why the problems are so intractable today.

The following discussion is set within the broader setting of general U.S. foreign policy concerns. How should we define our responsibilities in Rhodesia? On what basis can we intervene in Rhodesia and to what extent and at what cost? Can we really be effective in a region so removed from the U.S.? And what would being effective imply? These and other questions must be borne in mind as we endeavor to unravel the past shaping of American policy and attempt to discern our future lines of policy.

U. S. Policy Until 1974

With the advent of African nationalism, the U. S. generally adopted a position of support for African majority rule. This often meant little more than a verbal commitment to their cause. The colonial powers usually had American support to devolve power at their own speed and in any manner of their choosing. As far as Rhodesia was concerned, the U.S. was quite content to stay in the background and defer to the British. The fact that Rhodesia was proving to be a very difficult problem for Britian did not seem to evoke any unusual American concern.[2]

In 1965 the circumstances of Rhodesian politics were irrevocably altered by the declaration of independence by Prime Minister Ian D. Smith on November 11. In do doing Smith defied British colonial authority within Rhodesia and starkly claimed Rhodesian determination to remain a white-dominated state.

The U.S. orientation to Rhodesia after UDI was "to keep free of responsibility, to prejudice as little as possible conflicting U.S. sub-stantive stakes in the area, and to balance the opposing pressures of American advocates (within the government and outside it) who favored either more or less action against the Rhodesian regime by the United

States, the United Kingdom, and the United Nations." [3] This was a recipe for keeping in the background, doing as little as possible, and hoping for the best.

And so the government followed the British lead. Since the use of force to bring down Smith was ruled out from the beginning, the choices available centered on diplomacy and economic measures. The primary setting of U.S. policy toward Rhodesia after UDI was at the United Nations. Here we joined with Britain and most other nations of the world in implementing economic sanctions against the Smith regime. In our orientation to all this, however, we stayed safely behind Britain and helped them to forestall African attempts to push more vigorously against Rhodesia. We conveyed to Britain the message that they could not count on our help if they pushed South Africa on the Rhodesian issue and thereby jeopardized their own balance of payments position. [4] As America increasingly became absorbed with the Vietnam War, there was little high-level attention ever paid to the Rhodesian situation.

Economic sanctions against Rhodesia were initiated immediately after UDI. They were subsequently extended in 1966 and then made mandatory in May 1968. The U.S. government supported these measures. From 1965 to 1968 U.S. trade with Rhodesia dropped from about $33 million to less than $4 million; by 1970 it would fall under $1 million. There was some agitation from the right against U.S. support for sanctions and some liberal groups urged more aggressive policies toward Rhodesia, but neither side had much of an impact on policy-makers.

The fact that sanctions were not having the desired effect of inducing change in the Rhodesian government does not seem to have mattered much. With harsher measures ruled out, things just drifted. This suited the policy-makers of the time. The Rhodesian problem seemed to be contained--pressures to escalate the sanctions campaign to include Portugal and South Africa were given short shrift. No thought ever seemed to have been given to the possibility that by letting the Rhodesian problem fester, we would one day wind up with a far greater problem.

Despite the general indifference which the Johnson administration paid to Rhodesian matters, on balance it was a better and more fore-sighted policy than would be followed by its successor. Once they had taken office President Nixon and his national security advisor, Henry Kissinger, initiated a broad review of American policy toward Southern Africa. The upshot of all this was an explicit policy change that would have disastrous consequences for American policy in the region.

The origins, development, and implementation of National Security Study Memorandum 39 (NSSM-39) and its "Tar Baby" option 2 has been extensively analyzed elsewhere.[5] It became one of the foreign policy "leaks" of the Nixon years.[6] The heart of NSSM-39 lay in option 2 which would be adopted by the National Security Council at the end of 1969. The new Nixon/Kissinger policy orientation toward Southern Africa would emphasize "communication" with the white regimes.

Communication was a code word for strengthening U.S. ties with the white governments. South Africa and Portugal were more important here than Rhodesia, but Rhodesia rather got dragged along. Several assumptions underlay this tilt in policy. One was that the white governments were a permanent fixture in Southern Africa and they would not likely be threatened by the liberation movements. Another was that hostile actions against the white regimes would only be counterproductive. If you wanted to induce them to moderate their policies, you would be more effective if you had good relations with them. And it was further assumed that if change was to come in Southern Africa, it would most likely come by peaceful means

through the ongoing process of economic growth. Therefore economic ties
to the white governments should also be strengthened.[7]

Those who promoted and supported option 2 believed that a partial
relaxation of American pressure toward the white regimes would somehow
help promote peaceful change in Southern Africa. In reality, however,
American policies toward the white regimes had never been very threatening.
Our verbal commitments to majority rule were always juxtaposed with extensive economic ties with South Africa and, in the case of Portugal, military
ties through N.A.T.O. as well.

There were two main problems with option 2. One was that the
assumptions on which it was based were highly suspect. There was little
evidence to suggest that the white regimes were interested in changing
their racial policies. Economic growth had been taking place in the region
for decades without there being a moderating of discriminatory legislation
or practice. In discounting the liberation movements America was cutting
itself off from the real catalyst for change in the region. The other
problem with option 2 was that in moving closer to the white regimes,
we were seen to be indifferent to African protests about the nature of
these regimes and were risking the possibility that we might become further
tied to their defense.

Because of Rhodesia's unique status as a pariah state, it was somewhat
difficult for the U.S. to alter its policies in a direction favorable to
the Smith regime. Nevertheless, various initiatives were taken that were
readily interpreted by the Rhodesian government as a lessening of American
interest in bringing it to heel.

In 1969 Roger Morris of the National Security Council staff began
a series of meetings with Kenneth Towsey of the Rhodesian Information
Office in Washington.[8] This gave the Rhodesian government ongoing access

to Nixon/Kissinger thinking on Rhodesia. Coinciding with the foreign policy
review of 1969, there was a major struggle within the administration over
whether or not to close the American consulate in Salisbury. The consulate
was eventually closed in March 1970, but only after intense British
pressure; the British themselves had left nine months earlier after a
Rhodesian referendum declared itself in favor of becoming a republic.
This would be the only support that Rhodesia's Africans would get from
the Nixon administration, and its grudging attitude on even this matter
gave a cue about what was to follow.

On March 17, 1970--the same day the Salisbury consulate was closed--
the U.S. cast its first U.N. veto. It came on a resolution over Rhodesia.
At the U.N. African delegates had used the opportunity of the declaration
of a republic to renew their attack on the British government's failure
to reassert its authority in Rhodesia and crush the rebellion. The
African resolution condemned the British for their failure to use force,
extended sanctions to include South Africa and Portugal, made mandatory
the withdrawal of foreign consulates from Rhodesia, and called for a sever-
ance of communication and transportation ties with Rhodesia. Britain
joined America in vetoing this resolution and they would do so again in
1973 on another Rhodesian resolution.

But more important than either the consulate question
or the vetoes was the turn taken with respect to American adherence to
sanctions. There were numerous ways in which the sanctions program began
to falter during the Nixon/Kissinger years. In a complicated decision
taken in 1970, Union Carbide was allowed to import 150,000 tons of chromite
which it claimed it had paid for just days before sanctions embargoing
trade in Rhodesian minerals went into effect in 1966.[9] The amount involved was $2.5 million. A blind eye was turned to the activities of
the Rhodesian Information Office in Washington--even though it placed ads

in American journals urging business and trade ties with Rhodesia.[10]
From America, air travel, car rentals, and hotel accomodations could be
booked in Rhodesia. A more stringent concern for the success of sanctions
would have led to a far different U.S. attitude on these various questions.

The most damaging American action on Rhodesia, however, was the
1971 passage of the Byrd Amendment. The ostensible goal of the bill was
to protect the U.S. from becoming dependent on Soviet Union supplies for
specified strategic and critical materials. But the real purpose of the
bill was to open the way for U.S. imports of chrome from Rhodesia.

There were many explanations for why this bill was passed. But its
immediate and permanent effect (until it was repealed in the early days
of the new Carter administration) was to place the U.S. on record with
South Africa, and earlier Portugal, as the only states in the world openly
flouting U.N. mandatory sanctions against Rhodesia. As such it undercut
U.S. relations with African states, made hypocritical our statements
about supporting majority rule for Rhodesia, and unwidely undercut the
aspirations of those who would aspire to a working international rule
of law.

The passage of the Byrd Amendment was a tour de force of legislative
maneuvering, a tribute to the persistence of those within the U.S. who
supported Ian Smith, and a testimony to the enduring power of cold war
reasoning to sway congressmen. The debate about the bill touched all
manner of issues--chrome prices, the effect on U.S. jobs, national security,
the value of the U.N.--that served to obscure the reality that this was
about Rhodesia. The official administration stance on this bill was to oppose
it and keep America on record in support of U.N. sanctions. But in repeated
votes on the bill, both as it was initially being passed and then in
subsequent repeal efforts, the Nixon (and Ford) White House did nothing
to corner key congressional votes.[11]

The U. S. thus began violating sanctions as a matter of official policy. Trade, which had fallen to almost nothing, quickly resumed and went as high as $25 million per year. It undercut U. N. efforts to find a peaceful means to induce change in Rhodesia and gave heart to Rhodesian whites as they clung to power against the African majority. It was a real victory for the Smith regime and a blow to the African nationalists.

Anthony Lake has compiled a scorecard on the effects of the Byrd Amendment. He finds that it damaged both the American interest in international law and our diplomatic position at the U. N. and in Africa, it damaged the U. N., and it probably set back the chances for a peaceful settlement by encouraging the Smith regime.[12]

The Nixon/Kissinger policy from 1969-1974 was a lethargic policy in which white domination was accepted as a given, in which profits and short term interests were paramount, and in which independent assessment of the politics within Rhodesia and issues rising there were almost never considered. Rhodesia was a minor spot on a much larger map. There was no ongoing concern that Rhodesia itself might raise questions of lasting consequence to American policy makers. All of this indifference would soon change.

Kissinger Discovers Africa and Rhodesia, 1974-1976

The Portuguese coup in April 1974 marked the beginning of the end for NSSM-39, Option 2, and the whole structure of America's foreign policy in the region. The shambles of American foreign policy would not be fully apparent for another two years at the end of the Angolan debacle, but it had been long coming and was fully deserved. For while Johnson had been hiding behind Britain and hoping to avoid doing anything, and Nixon/ Kissinger had been doing something but with the wrong people, much else was changing throughout Southern Africa. These developments need to be briefly reviewed before turning to Kissinger's direct involvement with the

Rhodesian question.

Since the signing of the Lusaka Manifesto in 1969, the black African states had been committed to the liberation of their brothers in Southern Africa. With respect to Rhodesia the manifesto explicitly declared that "If the colonial power is unwilling or unable to effect such a transfer of power to the people, then the people themselves will have no alternative but to capture it as and when they can. And Africa has no alternative but to support them."[13]

For Rhodesia's Africans, there really had been little change in their position since 1965. Their leaders were in detention or in exile; the Smith regime remained firmly in power. But they had made their desires known in the most forceful way in 1972 when they rejected an agreement between Rhodesia's white government and Britain which would have granted Rhodesia independence under a minority regime.[14] There were two lessons drawn from this episode. One was that Britain was certainly not prepared to help the African peoples attain their freedom; and the second was that in their own strength there might be an alternate road to power. And that road was by the gun.

At the end of 1972 the Rhodesian nationalist movement ZANU (Zimbabwe African Nationalist Union) began opening up a front in the northeast of the country. This followed years of intermittent guerrilla activity that both ZANU and its main nationalist party rival ZAPU (Zimbabwe African Peoples Union) had engaged in since UDI. None of these earlier efforts had been sustained for any length of time.

The Portuguese coup in 1974, for which the liberation movements in Guinea-Bissau, Mozambique, and Angola could claim a large measure of credit, demonstrated the efficiency of armed struggle as a vehicle for African liberation. And it also changed all the political equations in Southern Africa. The tier of white dominated states that South Africa had seen as

its buffer zone began to fall away. The permanence of white domination--
the underlying assumption of the U.S.'s communication policy--had lasted
only four years. These two factors--the persistence and growth of armed
struggle within Rhodesia and the changed political realities of the region--
would soon lead toward new and markedly different policy attitudes about
Rhodesia.

In December 1974 it became known that Prime Minister John Vorster
of South Africa and President Kenneth Kaunda of Zambia were working together
to try to find a solution to the Rhodesian crisis. Despite longstanding
differences, they each had reasons for seeking a Rhodesian solution. With
Angola and Mozambique now soon to have African governments, South Africa's
foreign policy was changing. Now it emphasized building good relations
with moderate African countries and with major Western countries. It was
a policy of dialogue and detente and for it to have any chance at all of
success, it would require South African flexibility on the question of
white rule in Rhodesia and Namibia. For Zambia, its concerns were even
more pressing. The sanctions campaign against Rhodesia bore heavily on
Zambia; its border with Rhodesia was closed--its trade and transport ties
more costly and less efficient. Moreover, Zambia did not welcome becoming
a permanent basecamp for a long Rhodesian insurgency.[15]

The South Africa/Zambia initiative lasted all through 1975. South
Africa was able to get Ian Smith to release many of Rhodesia's important
nationalist leaders from detention. Zambia with the help of the leaders
of the other frontline states (President Julius Nyerere of Tanzania,
President Samora Machel of Mozambique, President Seretse Khama of Botswana--
President Agostinho Neto of Angola would later be added to the frontline
group) attempted to impose unity on Rhodesia's feuding nationalist factions.

The whole effort, however, soon stalled. The Africans remained split
into several factions despite a paper unity agreement. Smith and the

Rhodesian whites probably rightly saw that to participate in a constitutional conference could only mean their political suicide. Despite South
Africa's pressure on Smith and Zambia's crackdown on ZANU--who were urging
the continuation of the armed struggle rather than negotiations--no progress
was made. The fact of the matter was that local realities and mistrust
were sufficiently strong to overcome external pressures for a settlement.
Until it became clearer to Rhodesian whites on the one side and the Africans
on the other just how political change would affect them, they preferred
to stall and see what developed.[16]

Next came the Angolan crisis. Its main significance, from the standpoint of this discussion, is that it played out in full view of the nation
and the world the bankruptcy of American policy in Southern Africa.[17] The
victory of the MPLA in the Angolan civil war and the influence that victory
brought the Soviet Union and Cuba shook Washington enough to realize that
fundamental policy changes were needed. Africans in the region would have
to be considered and consulted in future planning. And the Cubans in
Angola, supplied with Soviet arms, certainly had the effect of drawing
the region to the attention of Secretary of State Kissinger.

The MPLA was installed in Luanda by early 1976; FRELIMO was in power
in Mozambique. The geopolitical situation was clear. Both of these
parties had come to power through armed struggle. Each was a radical
government closely aligned with the Eastern bloc who had supported their
struggle. If the same pattern was to play itself out in Rhodesia, there
would be a string of progressive governments encircling South Africa and
possibly even threatening the more pro-Western African regimes in the
region. It was to prevent this altogether likely scenario from developing
that Secretary Kissinger now turned his attention.

Two key developments marked Kissinger's Africa year--his last as

American Secretary of State. One was his important address in Lusaka
in April 1976 when he reversed the policy he had followed in Africa for the
preceding seven years. The second was his intense collaboration with
Prime Minister Vorster and the Presidents of the frontline states which
resulted, in September 1976, in an apparent breakthrough on the Rhodesian
constitutional issue. Though this effort appeared near collapse as
Kissinger left office in January 1977, his attention to Africa and especially
to Rhodesia marked a dramatic new stage in America's African policies.
And because of the new intensity of American involvement and the issues
that were growing within the continent, it seemed unlikely that the U. S.
could ever return to the indifference of previous years and decades.

In his African trip of April 1976 Kissinger stated "my journey is
intended. . .to usher in a new era of American policy." He categorically
stated American determination to support "self-determination, majority
rule, equal rights, and human dignity for all the peoples of southern
Africa--in the name of moral principle, international law, and world peace."
As far as Rhodesia was concerned, Kissinger explicitly supported proposals
made the previous month by James Callaghan, then Foreign Secretary of
Britain, which had called for independence under African majority rule.
This transition was to take place no later than two years following the
conclusion of negotiations between white and black Rhodesians.

In this Lusaka speech, Kissinger warned the white Rhodesians that they
could expect no assistance from America in their struggle against liberation
movements, and he said he would urge Congress to repeal the Byrd Amendment.
He offered economic assistance to Mozambique for the costs they would
have to bear for closing their border with Rhodesia in support of sanctions.
He reiterated the new American commitment to "bring about a rapid, just,
and African solution to the issue of Rhodesia." The only mention in his

long address that touched on the Angolan situation came when he stated that "Africans cannot want outsiders seeking to impose solutions or choosing among countries or movements. The United States for its part, does not seek any pro-American Africa bloc,. . .but neither should any other country pursue hegemonial aspirations or bloc politics. An attempt by one will inevitably be countered by the other."[18]

The main thrust of American policy throughout 1976 was to find a quick solution to the Rhodesian problem. As such it followed on, and complemented, the South African/Zambian initiatives of the preceding year. But the difficulties remained substantial and it always got back to the question: whose interests would be served by a quick solution?

As South Africa and America worked together during 1976 their goals were clear. They wanted to forestall a revolutionary victory by Zimbabwe liberation movements--either on their own or with external (possibly Cuban) assistance. At the same time an African majority rule government would be necessary if it was going to have any chance of gaining acceptance with Rhodesia's Africans or the frontline states. This in turn meant that Prime Minister Smith would have to go.

In September Kissinger brought his unique brand of shuttle diplomacy to Southern Africa. Working directly with Vorster, Nyerere, and Kaunda he attempted to develop a formula that would work. Finally in a head-to-head meeting with Smith in Pretoria on September 19, Kissinger and Vorster persuaded Smith to agree to a package deal which would lead the way to an African majority rule government within two years. The deal included a two tiered system of government during the transition stage in which both whites and Africans in Rhodesia would have a veto. The transition government would have the responsibility of drafting the independence constitution. And in a critical concession to Smith, Kissinger agreed that whites would control the ministries of defense and law enforcement during the transition stage.

When Smith announced on September 24 his acceptance of the principle
of majority rule within two years and outlined the package deal to which
he had agreed, it appeared for a moment that Kissinger had pulled off
an enormous diplomatic coup. A solution might now be in hand for the
eleven year-old Rhodesian rebellion. But it was not to be.

The African nationalists of Rhodesia quickly denounced the structure
of the transitional government as "legalizing the racist structure of
power." They categorically opposed any white domination of the ministries
of defense and law enforcement. And they feared that the power-sharing
formula in the transition government would give the whites too much influence
over the shaping of the new independence constitution.

It quickly became apparent that the frontline states had not been
fully consulted on the details of the package, and they backed up the
nationalists in their protests. The nationalists called for a "total
and immediate transfer of power." They feared that unless power was
firmly in African hands, Smith could always renege on his agreement. And,
moreover, they did not want to risk giving up the armed struggle for a
transition formula which was altogether unclear.

Both the accomplishment and the limitations of the Kissinger diplomacy
were there for all to see. With Vorster's obvious assistance, they had
convinced Smith that his position was untenable over the long haul. The
transition deal mentioned, plus financial guarantees for the white's land
and property, was the carrot offered. Smith accepted with considerable
reluctance, but he did accept.

But everything was not lined up. In a situation so fraught with hatred
and mistrust, things needed to be more fully agreed before they were
publicly displayed. And in fact the issues of power and control in an

independent Zimbabwe remained unresolved. The frontline states, let
alone the still feuding factions of Rhodesia's nationalists, had not
accepted the rules by which the transition would occur. Smith bought the
whole thing as a package deal; the frontline states and the nationalists
liked the idea of a two year transition, but they saw the rest of the
transition arrangements as but a basis for negotiation.

From October 1976 to January 1977, all of these conflicts were played
out to a deadlock at a conference in Geneva. Under the chairmanship of
the British government, four Rhodesian nationalists factions plus the
Smith government sought to find a way of implementing the Kissinger proposals.
The sense of urgency felt by the Americans and South Africans, or even the
sense of promise that one might justifiably have found in the overall deal
could not be transmitted to the Rhodesians.

For Smith's government it was an all or nothing deal; he would
negotiate nothing. For the Africans the situation was more complex.
Joshua Nkomo, leader of ZAPU, and Robert Mugabe, a former ZANU leader who
emerged as the primary political spokesman for the guerrilla forces, patched
together a tenuous alliance called the Patriotic Front. Also at the conference was Bishop Abel Muzorewa, leader of the African National Council
within Rhodesia. He had led the fight against the 1971-72 constitutional
proposals and had been an early favorite as a compromise leader of a united
nationalist movement. Rev. Ndabaningi Sithole, another ZANU leader and
a long-time foe of Nkomo, was also in attendance. For the African factions
the issue was: what political route is most likely to enhance my faction's
chances for winning ultimate control. Given this orientation of the nationalist factions, there was little chance for success.

In involving himself in the Rhodesia question, Kissinger was primarily
concerned with issues that really transcended Rhodesia. The growth of great

power rivalry in Southern Africa and the future political economy of
the region were clearly of far higher priority to him than any specific
settlement within Rhodesia. Yet to achieve his own goals, he was of
necessity forced to deal with local actors whose interests were far
different than his own. It was the impossibility of resolving their
endless differences that brought this Kissinger initiative to a grinding
halt.

Issues of power and privilege, of economic interest, and of ideology
are increasingly mixed into the Rhodesian cauldron. This involves not
only the various Rhodesian factions--white and black--but also external
actors like the frontline states, South Africa, and the growing international involvement of the U.S. and the Soviet Union. Interests are not
compatible and the chances of resolving them are slim. The Kissinger
style was not enough. Until rules can be devised that all will agree
to honor or until one faction or another can impose a solution on the
rest, the Rhodesian situation is going to continue to be difficult and
messy. This is as true for internal actors as for those outsiders who
are involved. It will be the responsibility of the new Carter administration
to try to find a way through the minefield that is Rhodesian politics at
the present time.

The Carter Administration and Rhodesia

All of the difficult questions that Henry Kissinger confronted, but
failed to resolve, were there as the new administration took power in
early 1977. The Geneva talks were stalemated and would soon collapse. The
Byrd Amendment remained in force and was a constant reminder to the world
of the ambiguities of U.S. policy toward Rhodesia. Relations with many
African countries were not good, and there was general skepticism about the
intensity with which the U.S. was willing to follow up the Kissinger in-

itiatives on Rhodesia. (The turning of the Geneva Conference over to Britain hinted at the limited extent to which the U.S. might be prepared to remain involved.) Finally there were the whole range of broader questions about Southern Africa—investment, access to raw materials, strategic matters, the role of violence in political change, the future of South Africa, Soviet penetration of the region, and the like—all of which in one way or another impinged on how the U.S. would view the narrower question of what policy to follow toward Rhodesia.

During its first months in office, the Carter administration has taken a number of steps—some direct and specific, others far more general and symbolic—that give us some idea about how it will persue Rhodesian matters. But there remain large unresolved questions—particularly as Rhodesian matters link to regional and indeed global concerns—on which there is still no clear direction.

In an action both symbolic and suggestive about America's future policy, Carter appointed Andrew Young as United Nations Ambassador.[19] Few other choices could have conveyed more stridently America's concern about racism to the world. In the past the U.N. Ambassador has stood outside the foreign policy process. But Young has been given cabinet rank. His close personal relationship with Carter makes it likely that he will be fully involved in policy making, especially with respect to Southern Africa.

A second step, symbolic in a way, but also having Southern African ramifications is the aggressive Carter administration position on human rights. In his Inaugural Address Carter stated "because we are free we can never be indifferent to the fate of freedom elsewhere."[20] And in his first major foreign policy address delivered, it should be noted, at the United Nations he declared, "The basic thrust of human affairs points toward a more universal demand for fundamental human rights. The United

States has a historical birthright to be associated with this process.
We in the United States accept this responsibility in the fullest and
most constructive sense."[21]

There seems little doubt now that Carter is prepared to make human
rights one of the major concerns of his administration.   Raising the
human rights issue so forcefully seems to be part of a basic Carter desire
to restore American confidence in our long held, but often ignored, ideals
of freedom. As such he taps a real current of American life. If human
rights remain on the Carter agenda, and it is hard so see how it can dis-
appear now that such fundamental questions have been raised, then the whites
of Southern Africa have a legitimate cause for concern.

A third step taken by the new administration has been to take a far
more activist focus than its predecessors in seeking to align the U.S. with
African states, to consult them about issues of mutual concern, and to generally upgrade Africa as an area of U.S. attention and interest. The first
major foreign tour taken by any top-ranking administration official was
Andrew Young's trip to Africa. Much of Young's trip was devoted to Southern
Africa matters, of which the Rhodesian question had the highest priority.

Young visited the frontline states of Tanzania and Zambia and had
extensive talks with both Julius Nyerere and Kenneth Kaunda. He also went
to Zaire and, perhaps most importantly, he visited Nigeria--the largest
of Africa's nations--which had curtly refused to receive Henry Kissinger.
At the end of extensive talks with Nigeria's leader, General Olusegun
Obasanjo, there was every indication of better relations between Washington
and Lagos.

This would tie in with the idea, articulated by Young, that a proper
U.S. role in the Southern Africa situation would be "to work with the
peoples of Africa and African nationalists in a supporting role."[22]

If indeed that is to be the U.S. orientation, then it is mandatory that
Nigeria and the frontline states (so crucial to Rhodesian developments)
be closely in touch with policy making circles in Washington.

So far Young seems to have done this. During the March 1977 Security
Council debate on South Africa, he was repeatedly in consultation with
African delegations. This effort to work together with African countries
stands in stark contrast with America's previously indifferent, if not
hostile, posture with respect to Third World countries. The Carter administration appears ready to use the U.N. as its base for asserting his
human rights stand and for working more closely with African nations.
If this remains the case then we can expect heightened pressure on all
Southern African questions for the U.N. has been a primary international
base of opposition to white rule in Southern Africa.[23]

A fourth step taken by the new administration was to actively work
for and achieve the repeal of the Byrd Amendment. This was accomplished
within two months of taking office. By repealing the Byrd Amendment the
American government brought itself into compliance with U.N. mandatory
sanctions and signaled to both whites and blacks in Rhodesia of our policy
shift. It could not be ignored in Salisbury that this was one of the first
foreign policy steps taken by the Carter administration. Although no one
expected this to bring Smith to his knees, it would deny the regime about
$25 million in export sales which now would have to be channeled more
circuitously and less profitably into world markets.

Finally the Carter administration quickly rejected the proposals
developed by Smith following the breakdown of the Geneva conference in
January 1977. Smith proposed to adhere to the September agreement with
Vorster and Kissinger and reach an "internal" settlement with "moderate"
Africans within Rhodesia. But he was deliberately vague on what he now

meant by African majority rule, and he specifically ruled out any dealing with the Patriotic Front who the Smith regime blamed for the failure of the Geneva conference. Since the Pretoria agreement is rejected by the frontline states and the Patriotic Front, the prospects for a settlement without their compliance are practically nil. Thus by taking a stand against an internal settlement, the administration was leaving the way open for continued talks with all Rhodesian factions and making clear to both the Rhodesian whites and the South Africans that no deal was possible if the frontline states and the Patriotic Front were not involved.

The steps taken so far by the new administration are direct, positive, and seem clearly to lead in one direction. But, what next? It is in shaping of actual policies that the administration will have to confront all the difficult, and so far unresolved, questions that arise in the context of our Rhodesian policy.

The first of these is the U.S. attitude toward the use of violence to achieve political change. The U.S. has always opposed violence in this region and the Carter administration is taking the same line. In his U.N. address Carter stated that "In Southern Africa we will work to help attain majority rule through peaceful means."[24] In a long, but often vague interview with _Africa_--Andrew Young called armed struggle "a no-win situation for all concerned" and not "a viable option".[25]

For many others, however, violence is not only a viable option, but the only one. The Patriotic Front is increasingly committed to the notion that only through armed struggle will Africans finally gain power in Rhodesia. The five frontline states, and the Liberation Committee of the Organization of African Unity, have now fully thrown their political backing behind the Patriotic Front, to the exclusion of Bishop Abel Muzorewa's African National Council which still seeks to find a negotiated road to African majority rule.

Our attitude toward violence puts us on the horns of a dilemma that
is not easy to resolve. Violence has worked elsewhere in Southern Africa,
not to mention many other places. If it is to be avoided in Rhodesia,
then sufficient pressures of other kinds must be amassed to engineer the
desired political transition. And, put quite bluntly, the U.S. and its
Western allies do not yet have a policy that as seriously, or with such
a sense of purpose and potential for success, comes to grip with this
question. As a consequences of our failures, others have taken up armed
struggle.

Our choices are really quite simple. We can stand aside and let the
armed struggle build against white Rhodesia. However long it takes, the
outcome is all but assured. A revolutionary army will one day march into
Salisbury with whom we will have few in any ties. Their allies will be
the socialist bloc and their African neighbors. Or we can evolve a plan,
presumably with the help of other interested parties, that guarantees the
ouster of Ian Smith and his Rhodesian Front government in Salisbury. Moreover, and this is critical, the plan must be seen by the liberation movements and the frontline states as one that can, and will, be accomplished
more speedily than victory through armed struggle.

This leads to a second dilemma that the Carter administration faces.
How big a role should America play? How much leverage do we have in this
situation? What are our responsibilities? There really are more questions
here than there are answers. It is sometimes articulated by American policy
makers that we should intervene in Rhodesia to prevent a race war. Leaving
aside the fact that the war has already begun, it is far from clear that
we have any national responsibility to stop it. The distinguished columist
David Broder has recently argued that the arguments now being made for
American action in Africa are precisely the arguments that led us into

Vietnam.[26]

America does have a certain power in the current situation in that
we are the one state that all factions in and around Rhodesia are willing
to deal with. This was most clearly evident at the time of the Kissinger
initiative. This may still be true though circumstances have already
changed. Perhaps there is the possibility of a much larger role for
America at a reconvened Geneva conference. But again, the time frame
is crucial--negotiations are only on if all key parties see it in their
interest to talk. Moreover, an expanded U.S. role runs counter to our
desire to have Britain, South Africa, and major African states take
the lead on Rhodesian matters.

The question of leverage in the current situation leads to the
third American dilemma. What is our policy toward South Africa going
to be?

We need South Africa's help to bring down Ian Smith. South Africa
alone has the power over Rhodesia to make Smith move. Kissinger and
Vorster were able to work closely together because both wanted to minimize
the level of violence in Rhodesia, prevent a successful insurgency, and
install a moderate African government. South Africa's inducement to work
with the U.S. on this rested with its larger desire to be close to the
West and be seen as a responsible international actor.

But the willingness of South Africa to join in this Rhodesian initiative may well have waned since the high point of September 1976. The
breakdown of the Geneva talks are seen by the South African government
as evidence of African untrustworthiness and Western weakness. The continued feuding between Rhodesian nationalist factions augments South African
fears that any agreement for a transfer of power in Rhodeisa will only lead
to a civil war, as in Angola. With the Patriotic Front increasingly trying

its fortunes to assistance from the Soviet Union, there is concern that
any transition will eventually lead to a radical African government in
Rhodesia.

Vorster would deal with Kissinger because of his prestige, his
vagueness about South Africa's future, and his apparent ability to
carry the frontline leaders with him. But the early Carter administration
comments about South Africa are far from encouraging to the authorities
in Pretoria. South Africa is as nervous about President Carter's human
rights campaign as are the Russians. If Vorster only sees himself as
the next target, his incentive to help the U.S. in Rhodesia may well
vanish. South Africa may well decide to take its chances on Smith, on
the internecine warfare among the Rhodesian nationalist groups, and on
toughing it out. Then what will the Carter administration do--back off
on Rhodesia or bite the bullet and reconjize that Rhodesia and South
Africa are part of the same problem?

It was this uncertainty that stalled Andrew Young's efforts at the
U.N. in March to get a Declaration of Principles on South Africa through
the Security Council. The declaration called on South Africa to abandon
apartheid, to grant independence to Namibia, and to stop supporting the
Smith regime. Young worked hard to gain African support, but when they
asked the appropriate and logical question, what will you do when South
Africa says no, he had no response. There was no American policy on the
issue of a mandatory arms embargo, on banning new investment, on review-
ing trade ties. Until these questions are answered in a way that seems
promising to Nigeria, to the frontline states, and to the liberation movements, the U.S. position with Africans is likely to remain tenuous.

America's fourth, and last, dilemma is in part related to the third.
Our uncertainty about South Africa is linked to the growing Soviet presence

in the region. In a little more than two years, the Soviet Union has become the dominant foreign power in Mozambique and, with Cuba, the dominant ally of Angola. It has increasingly close ties with SWAPO--the liberation movement fighting for Namibia, and with the Patriotic Front. Soviet President Nikolai Podgorny paid a notably successful trip to Tanzania, Zambia, and Mozambique in March 1977.

On the one hand America realizes that it is the persistence of white racism that heightens regional tensions and gives the Soviet Union the opportunity to advance its influence through its support of the liberation movements. But our historic trade, investment, and ideological ties with the white states makes it difficult to break with them.

The U.S. has suggested that it would like to strike a bargain with the Soviet Union to halt outside intervention in Africa. But intervention is not the key question to most Africans. Racism is. And as the Soviet Union and Cuba, and to a lesser degree China, concretely help Africans in their struggle against racism their influence naturally grows. Even so moderate and pro-Western an African leader as President Kaunda of Zambia now argues that the West supports "fascism and racism in Southern Africa."[27] Less than two years ago Kuanda was one of the main leaders opposing the Soviet and Cuban role in Angola. Now he welcomes Soviet assistance to the Patriotic Front so they can continue their struggle against white Rhodesia.

What lessons will the Carter administration draw from Soviet successes in Southern Africa? Will they adhere to past policies and traditional anti-Communist reflexes? Or will they realize that the present Soviet prestige derives from the fact that they alone at the present time are in alliance with the African people and offering them hope for a better future? The way to limit Soviet penetration in Southern Africa lies not in confrontation with the Soviet Union or in alliance with anti-Communist white states, but in support of African aspirations. Until we are ready to do that, the initiative for regional change will lie with Moscow and its allies, and to them will rightfully accrue the credit for any successes.

Each of these dilemmas pose hard questions and hard choices. It is perhaps not surprising that the Carter administration has paused a bit before jumping into the middle of all this. The stakes are high, the pressures are great, but American power is also limited. Until there is a decision within the administration about how much to play for and how much to risk in Southern Africa, prudence is perhaps warranted.

Yet none of the questions will go away. The most that will happen is that some options will be foreclosed. In Rhodesia it is simply a matter of what set of pressures will finally force Smith to give way. If America wants to be in on this, it will have to evolve clear policies on the four dilemmas raised.

The story of U.S. policy toward Rhodesia is not particularly flatter-ing. Our country is now paying a big price for years, if not decades, of neglect. Our historic values and ideals have for so long been tarnished and compromised in Southern Africa that it is not easy to recoup what has been lost.

It is the obligation of all Americans to try. Racial discrimination has corroded our own national life. We recognize from our own natioanl experience that to abandon the legalized structure of discrimination is but the first step taken in the much longer journey toward freedom and equality for all. But if the ideas we aspire to are to remain alive for us and have any transcendent meaning for the rest of the world, then we must be true to them elsewhere as well. Nowhere in the world are the issues of racism and inequality drawn as starkly as in Southern Africa. The success or failure of our Rhodesian policy will be easily measured by the degree to which our policies there are informed by the abiding strength of our own ideals.

FOOTNOTES

1. Anthony Lake, The "Tar Baby" Option: American Policy Toward
   Southern Rhodesia (New York, Columbia University Press, 1976),
   p. xii.

2. Larry W. Bowman, Politics in Rhodesia: White Power in an African
   State (Cambridge, Mass., Harvard University Press, 1973). All
   aspects of British relations with Rhodesia, from 1890-1972,
   are considered in my book.

3. Lake, p. 61. I have drawn regularly on this book for the first
   section of this paper.

4. Lake, p. 93.

5. Lake, pp. 123-157; Mohamed A. El-Khawas and Barry Cohen, eds., The
   Kissinger Study of Southern Africa (Westport, Ct., Lawrence
   Hill & Co., 1976); Edgar Lockwood, "National Security Study
   Memorandum 39 and the Future of United States Policy Toward
   Southern Africa", Issue 4, no. 3 (Fall 1974), pp. 63-72.

6. The first two articles were Ken Owen, The Star (Johannesburg),
   February 2, 1971 and Terence Smith, The New York Times, April
   2, 1972. Later Jack Anderson and Tad Szulc would provide
   further details.

7. I gave an early and skeptical appraisal of all of this in my "Southern
   Africa Policy for the Seventies," Issue 1, no. 1 (Fall 1971), pp.
   25-26.

8. Lake, p. 134 and passim.

9. Lake, pp. 148-157.

10. Lake, p. 190. The U.S. view was that general information dissemination,
    public relations activities or advertisements did not promote
    and were not calculated to promote business with Rhodesia.

11. Lake, pp. 198-285. This will tell you everything you ever want to
    know about the Byrd Amendment and more.

12. Lake, p. 264.

13. The Review (June 1969), The International Commission of Jurists,
    Geneva, p. 59.

14. Bowman, Politics in Rhodesia, pp. 122-129.

15. Larry W. Bowman, "Vorster and Kaunda--Strange American Bedfellows,"
    The Nation (April 12, 1975), pp. 426-429.

16. Larry W. Bowman, "Rhodesian Dentente," The Nation (January 10, 1976), pp. 9-12.

17. There is a fine article on U.S. policy in Angola. John Marcum, "Lessons of Angola," Foreign Affairs, 54, 3 (April 1976), 407-425.

18. All the quotes in the last two paragraphs are from Henry A. Kissinger, "Southern Africa and the United States: An Agenda for Cooperation," (April 27, 1976), (Washington, D.C., Dept. of State, Bureau of Public Affairs, 1976).

19. In addition to Anthony Lake, author of the previously mentioned book on American policy towards Rhodesia, was appointed director of the Dept. of State, Policy Planning Staff. From this position he could have substantial influence on policies toward Rhodesia.

20. International Herald Tribune (January 22-23, 1977).

21. New York Times (March 18, 1977).

22. International Herald Tribune (February 8, 1977).

23. Andrew Young also suggested that U.S. troops might be used as part of a U.N. peacekeeping force in Rhodesia. (Washington Post, March 8, 1977). It was quickly denied that this was actively being considered, but the incident does suggest the U.N. orientation on these matters.

24. New York Times (March 18, 1977).

25. Africa, no. 67 (March 1977), p. 16.

26. David Broder, "Intervention in Africa: Civilized Rational Way toward a New Vietnam," Washington Post (February 20, 1977).

27. Robin Wright, "Visit by Podgorny Indicates Major Zambian Policy Change," International Herald Tribune (March 28, 1977).

CHAPTER V

THE US AND SOUTH AFRICA: THE LIMITS OF "PEACEFUL CHANGE"

BY WINSTON NAGAN

Major changes are taking place in the political structure of Southern
Africa. The means by which change is brought about may have a major impact
on the future of race relations, not only in South Africa, but in the rest
of the world as well.

In response to the imminence of change in the white redoubt of Southern
Africa (Zimbabwe, Namibia and South Africa itself) American policy towards
South Africa is currently undergoing yet another "agonizing reappraisal".
The Carter Administration has apparently come to the position that human rights
and human dignity will have meaning in the context of South Africa only if it
endorses what has long been the cornerstone of black political demands inside
South Africa, that is full political participation by all South Africans.
Along with this commitment to the goal of full political participation there
has been an equally important commitment to the kinds of strategies of change
that might make these goals realizable. This involves a U.S. commitment to
the promotion of peaceful change in South Africa. As William Schaufele recently
put it, "unless the spiral of violence can be arrested and reversed, there will
be such a polarization of forces within South Africa that peaceful change will
become immeasurably more difficult than it is already".

Since the administration of John Kennedy, American foreign policy has,
at least verbally, opposed regimes in Southern Africa that are based on racial
and social injustice. It chose to endorse one or any combination of the following political principles:

(1) majority rule

(2) majority rule with institutional safeguards for minority rights

(3) full political participation (which may or may not envision one-
man, one-vote).

Although these principles appeared to have been rejected by the Nixon Administration, they have been reiterated in a way that suggests a fundamental change in American policy. Illustrative of this fundamental rethinking of the American stance in South Africa is the statement issued by Secretary Vance on July 1, 1977:

> We have expressed to the South African government our firm belief in the benefits of a progressive transformation of South African Society. This would mean an end to racial discrimination and the establishment of a new course toward full political participation by all South Africans.[1]

At the root of this policy lies the assumption that some form of change is inevitable in the internal South African political process, and furthermore that a meaningful transfer of power can be achieved in the context of existing political realities. Peaceful change, in short, is not only desirable but necessary.

Why does the U.S. consider peaceful change to be necessary in the context of South Africa? A skeptical view of this policy would maintain that strategies of peaceful change are bound to fail in the context of a political process (the apartheid process) which is committed to the optimal use of state violence to maintain the status quo. Hence, public posturing for peaceful change with respect to South Africa's internal political process may be seen to be a tacit underwriting of the apartheid regime, while our professed goals of freedom and equality maintain a veneer of moral righteousness. For example, how can one assume that blacks in South Africa will commit themselves to peaceful change when the Terrorism Act makes the advocacy of a social change an act of statuory terrorism, punishable by death?

Hence the skeptics may be inclined to see the American commitments to peaceful change as being primarily aimed at (1) preservation of the status quo, and (2) the prevention of revolution. The implication is that South Africa will remain in the orbit of special interest groups whose perception of world order is defined in either geoeconomic terms or bipolar, cold war terms.

A less cynical view would be to take professed American foreign policy

at its word. From this perspective the American commitment to human rights
must be assessed against the reality of slow and incremental change in the
direction of a human dignity postulate on the one hand, and the possibility
of traumatic revolutionary change with all of the potential for a racial holo-
caust. The tough policy decision then, involves an estimate that the cost of
human suffering in the long run is cheaper than the cost of traumatic violent
and social change not only for South Africa, but also for the larger world
community. This assumes that economic and strategic considerations, while important, can be sacrificed with ease when fundamental ideals relating to racial
justice and human rights imperatives are posed in sharp juxtaposition.

The Larger Goals of U.S. Foreign Policy.

Foreign policy is never neutral. Nor indeed is scholarship objectively
neutral. The most one can hope is for the scholar to clarify what is perceived
to be the most inclusive common interests envisioned in the formulation and
execution of foreign policy and to consider whether those objectives are compatible with one's own subjective vision of what is morally right. It is important that the scholar make the values to which he subscribes explicit, so
that his criticism of foreign policy is made with reference to clearly stated
assumptions.

It may be useful to see the principles and strategies of the Carter administration in Southern Africa against the broader framework of ideas that appear
to influence the U.S. world view. While concepts relating to strategic, economic,
and political interests are incorporated in the definition of national interest,
it is obvious that broader questions of political and social morality are often
seen to lend a more inclusive perspective to the more exclusivist focus on the
primacy of national interest.

The predominant world order model about foreign affairs since World War II
has been essentially a bipolar model. With the emergence of detente and the

concepts of mutual restraint among the super powers, there has emerged the
further recognition that the conditions of world power are becoming diffused
in "polycentric" fashion. These changing concepts are supported by such events
as the defeat of a superpower (the United States in Vietnam) in an essentially
colonial war, mischaracterized as a war against Soviet or Chinese imperialism;
the effective use by the third world countries of strategic raw materials to
secure political ends otherwise unobtainable (the Arab oil embargo). The
process of decolonization has also proceeded with dramatic haste impacting
upon the political profile of the metropolitan powers themselves (the change to
social democracy in Portugal); moreover, public opinion has been aroused by
the commitments to dictatorial regimes in the third world. Superpower mentors
have indeed become implicated in the atrocities and torture practices of third
world dictators (the Americans in Chile and Vietnam; the Russians in Uganda and
Ethiopia). These events have further rekindled the thought that U.S. foreign
policy ought to be more firmly and explicitly rooted in the moral foundations
of our political culture.

It is within the framework of perceived national interest and fundamental
political morality, on the one hand and a renewed debate within the U.S. about
future "world order models" on the other, that the Southern Africa problem
must be viewed. So far as one is able to discern, the search for new world order
models has centered upon the work of the Trilateral Commission, whose ostensible
goal is to "bring the best brains in the world to bear on the problems of the
future."[2] Professor Falk has determined that, when stripped of its verbal
felicity, the ideological outlook of the Trilateral Commission is essentially
that of the "cosmocorp" i.e., the multilateral corporation. And this involves,
in Falk's words,

"a geoeconomic search for a managerial formula that will keep (this)

concentration of wealth intact, given its non territorial character,
and in light of multiple challenges to it from Arab oil interests,
the Communist bloc, and various expressions of statism. In a sense,
the vistas of the Trilateral Commission can be understood as the
ideological perspective representing the transnational outlook of the
multinational corporation."[3]

The past record of the multinational corporate picture appears to vindicate the
view that it thrives on stability; that in a Third or Fourth world setting
there often appears to be a complicated interdependence, and sometimes inter-
stimulation between an extremely repressive and an exploitive state apparatus,
and the "well-being" of such a corporate contact.[4] Professor Falk and other
distinguished writers are highly skeptical that global solutions-e.g. to social
decay and poverty, to the extinction of widespread repression and torture
practices, to the ecological imperatives of preserving scarce global resources,
and to the promise of minimum conditions of world order (peace) - can be derived
from the managerial and technical finesse of an elite committed the global expansion of "cosmocorp" and the business or corporate values that sustain it.
It should not be forgotten that the President's national security advisor,
Zbigniew Brzezinski, is one of the intellectual architects of the Trilateral
Commission. And one of Mr. Brzezinski's patrons is Mr. David Rockefeller of
the Chase Manhatten Bank, a bank that has in the past had close connections
with South African corporate and governmental concerns.

The human rights emphasis of the Carter administration represents a key
point in the current effort to move foreign policy goals away from the excessive
preoccupation with national security issues. But the human rights focus has
special relevance to Southern Africa because of the massive and systematic
violation of such rights under the auspices of the South African State. This
issue presents an added sensitivity to U.S. policy makers because of its historic

relevance to American race relations, and to compound the complexities that underlie this whole question of human rights we have the apparent paradox of a white, southern Baptist president commanding the most solid ethnic constituency in the U.S., i.e. the constituency of black America. Black Americans have indeed extended their concern for civil rights within the U.S. to the larger world context and have been particularly articulate on racism in Southern Africa.

These then are some of the important elements that appear to influence the world view of President Carter and his foreign policy specialists. The picture that emerges in an untidy one, conditioned by the constraints of diverse domestic influences like the Trilateral Commission and a black America, unequivocally committed to racial justice at home and abroad. It is from this situational context that Mr. Carter has sought to give concrete leadership in the larger world arena. The key tension that confronts Carter's Southern Africa perspective is that policies designed to secure "World Peace through World Trade" (the objectives of Cosmocorp) may be in conflict with human rights priorities in Southern Africa. More specifically, the involvement of corporate America in the institutions of apartheid reflects the involvement of essentially global corporate interests in which Americans all too often predominate. American business may thus be perceived as being fully involved in the economy of apartheid and benefiting from it. To the extent that apartheid, as a system, is thought to represent an unvarnished and highly institutionalized deprivation of human rights, such corporate involvement constitutes a major challenge to either human rights values, or to geoeconomic values.

American Initiatives for the Promotion of Change in South Africa.

President Carter's policy with respect to peaceful change in South Africa was made explicit in the Vienna meeting with Mr. Vorster. The Vice-President, Mr. Walter Mondale, speaking for the President, stated that South Africa should

move toward "full participation" for all South Africans. The phrase was
clarified in a later press conference to include full franchise rights: one
man, one vote. The clarification was important. In the apartheid lexicon
"full participation" might be viewed as being not inconsistent with full participation in the black's own sphere of "separate" political and social development
under the apartheid scheme. The policy clarification made explicit that not
only does the U.S. consider that the apartheid policies ought to be halted, but
also that the institutions spawned by them be dismantled. The implications of
such a policy are that the United States entertains the expectation that South
Africa ought to move far and fast in the "other" political direction. It is
commonly forgotten that the apartheid system is not a static one; rather it is
a dynamic right-wing vision of desirable social and political relations based
on the politico-biological concept of race as understood in the white South
African lexicon. The system is designed for ever greater extensions of the rule
of white supremacy. And this is consolidated by a dynamic sensitivity to the
uses of sophisticated techniques of social control to ensure that goal for the
indefinite future.

From the perspective of the South African government, concepts such as
"petty apartheid"; "moving toward self-determination"; "full participation
in your own ethnic-group area"; "moving away from discrimination", are to be
seen as concepts designed to preserve the superstructure of apartheid; while
at the same time refining the system of controls so that its blatantly brutal
character is not so obvious to sympathetic public opinion in the West. By
preempting the very symbols of political rectitude that form an intrinsic
part of western political culture, the apartheid regime has aspired to project
the process of deprivation as fundamentally reasonable and compatible with
what is assumed to be a western standard of political morality. It is also a
propaganda tool to disarm opponents of apartheid who have in the past been so

successful in marshalling world opinion against the apartheid system. It
should be readily appreciated that the Mondale clarification represented
the sharpest rebuke to the so-called "Verligte" element in the broederbond
and the party, because it implied that full participation along apartheid
lines was incompatible with the American concept of what genuine democracy
means: one man, one vote. The further implication was that the apartheid
edifice was to be dismantled if the democratic aspirations of the blacks were
to be met. It should be noted that the most conservative black leaders have
taken the public position that "apartheid must go"; a position compatible
with the declared goals of American policy.

If there were any ambiguity in the American government's position on
South Africa, this was dispelled by Secretary of State Vance's recent speech
before the NAACP in St. Louis. There Vance called for "full political participation by all South Africans". He condemned the separate homelands policy,
reiterating that the U.S. would refuse to recognize the Transkei and Bophuta-
tswana.[5] As to the prospect of socialist intervention into the military balance
of power in Southern Africa, Vance said:

> I have heard some suggest that we must support the white
>
> governments of Southern Africa, come what may, since they
>
> are anti-communist. In fact the denial of racial justice
>
> in Southern Africa encourages the possibility of outside
>
> intervention.[6]

Persuasive and Coercive Strategies to Promote Peaceful Change in South Africa

According to administration officials, the Carter Administration is
strongly committed to racial justice in South Africa. To this end the Administration has put under review a number of measures to communicate in no uncertain
terms that the U.S. means to encourage South Africa to meaningfully change its
racial policies. These measures are designed to show that the U.S., in the

words of one official, is going to deliver some "stick instead of carrot" to white South Africa. The following measures are under active consideration: First, the withdrawal of U.S. military attaches from South Africa; second, the ending of exchanges of intelligence information; third, the reduction of Export-Import Bank guaranties for investments in South Africa; fourth, that the issuance of U.S. visas be issued on a basis of reciprocity; fifth, that corporations doing business inside South Africa improve their human relations profile; sixth, reevaluation of treaty commitments with respect to nuclear energy for peaceful purposes.

Essentially, the search has been for pressure points that may be applied with a kind of graduated intensity to either persuade or coerce the Vorster government to scrap the apartheid regime. Perhaps the most significant point scored by the Carter regime so far has been the formulation of a six-point code of conduct for American corporations doing business in South Africa. These six principles are as follows:

- Non-segration of the races in all eating, comfort and work facilities;
- Equal pay and fair employment practices for all employees;
- Equal pay for all employees doing equal and comparable work for the same period;
- Initiation of development training programmes that will prepare Blacks in substantial numbers for supervisory, administrative, clerical and technical jobs;
- Increasing the number of Blacks in management and supervisory positions; and;
- Improving the quality of employees' lives outside the work environment in such areas as housing, transport, schooling, recreation and health facilities.

The business code of conduct has, needless to say, been received with excessive hostility in South Africa. The Citizen for example, described the Carter

approach as mind boggling and "nutty" and suggested that America was being
hypocritical because of her "selective indignation".[7] The Afrikaans newspaper
Die Beeld opined that the code of conduct constituted "wisdom after the event".[8]
The editor suggested that Americans had in the past gleefully taken advantage
of black workers "shielding behind the government with excuses that it was preventing them from introducing greater equality in pay etc."[9]

The most recent pressure point to be used to promote "peaceful change"
inside South Africa is the "atoms for change"[10] concept. The essence of the
matter is this: President Carter has threatened to make the renegotiation of
South Africa's nuclear supply agreement dependent on the progress it makes in
its internal politics toward full participation. Again the reaction in the
opinion forming press of South Africa has been hostile and intransigent. Die
Burgher, for example, advised American policy makers that "compulsion" and
"ultimatums" would make white South Africans even more intransigent.[11]

American policy to promote peaceful change in South Africa has also to
be seen in the context of joint efforts (with the U.K. and other Western powers)
to effectuate a less violent transfer of power to majority rule in Zimbabwe
and Namibia.

These efforts involve securing South Africa's cooperation because of South
Africa's strategic and economic interests in these territories. The real problem
of this regional strategy is that it may crucially impact upon the substance of
policy with respect to South Africa. The U.S. is, of course, vigorously opposed
to change by armed struggle in Zimbabwe and Namibia. Indeed, the key focus of
policy as explained by Ambassador Young is that the U.S. "compete with those
people who advocate armed struggle".[12] In the light of prior policies of
other Administrations, a not implausible construction of this policy may, in
fact, place the U.S. in a completely adversary posture to all black aspirations
for majority rule which may include the most "reasonable" strategies of change

(and this may be seen in context to include the military instrument). Stated simply, the Administration's position is replete with tension and conflict. First, it advocates democratic rights for all Southern Africans; but it must at the same time cooperate with the chief offender (South Africa) to secure a hoped for peaceful shift to majority rule in Zimbabwe and Namibia. To secure a degree of cooperation, the U.S. will inevitably have to maintain a disjuncture between advocacy of human rights, condemnations of apartheid, and the application of concrete coercive strategies to stimulate change toward a democratic dispensation of political rights in South Africa. The Administration's condemnation of armed struggle is also made in the face of events that are themselves fact-creating ones. The armed struggle in Zimbabwe and Namibia is in an advanced stage; the blacks have not sought to monopolize the use of violence; state violence and terrorism are part of the scenario, too. Hence, the search for a peaceful transfer of power is actually taking place in a context in which the use of force is an intrinsic part of the scenario. To ask the blacks to renounce armed struggle as a mode of national liberation must appear hollow to black leaders when their continued subjugation is maintained by the full violence of the national security state apparatus. Moreover, one could hardly imagine South Africa or Smith's Rhodiesa being willing to negotiate at all about a power transfer, but for the actual and prospective armed capability that blacks are able to muster to secure their liberation by coercive or pursuasive means, or by a combination of the two.

These tensions are reflected in the manner in which American policy makers have equivocated as to matters of fundamental principle concerning Southern Africa. On the one hand, full political participation may or may not mean one man, one vote---and it may. On the other hand, when the state department acknowledges that we have strategic and economic interests in South Africa, and when these considerations are made the focus of attention, the official position becomes less than affirmative about black emancipation. For example, Philip

Habek told the Diggs House Africa Subcommittee that "the U.S. has no reason to

fear the necessary and inevitable achievement of racial equality and social

justice in Southern Africa," but cautioned that external pressures on white

South Africa would harden their already intransigent perspectives about change.

It should be noted that a recurrent theme of South African propaganda is that

outside pressures are making necessary political and social change harder to

realize! This raises difficult questions of principle for American foreign

policy. First, American foreign policy has always been a blend of self-interest

and morality; a coalescence of economic and strategic interest, buttressed by

a belief that the promotion of these ends is largely coterminous with human

rights and human dignity for all. Second, in the South African context this

connection may not be as manifestly sustainable. The interests of the Tri-

lateral Commission for world economic order may be thoroughly inconsistent with

the moral axioms of freedom that sustain American ideals.

The Official South African Response

The South African response has been mixed but predictable. R. F. Botha

took the view that one, man one vote meant in reality a commitment to black

majority rule; that such a commitment would involve white South Africa in

"negotiating our own destruction." Speaking to an American television audience

he described the call for one man, one vote the "height of immorality" and added:

"You want us to accept this new commitment---a commitment to suicide. Forget

it. No way. We shall not accept that; not now, not tomorrow, never, ever."[13]

Botha's reaction caused Hodding Carter of the State Department to issue a

clarification of Mondale's one man, one vote concept of full participation.

According to Carter the U.S. was not dogmatically insisting on a one man, one

vote formula; rather it wanted South Africa to move towards a "full democratic

society".[14]

Mr. Vorster reporting to the South African parliment on his talks with Mondale made it explicit that he would not take "orders from any other country" regarding the internal South African policy. He rejected categorically the idea that one man, one vote would be acceptable to white South Africa.[15]

More recently, Mr. Vorster launched a detailed and trenchant attack on American policy with respect to South Africa. Vorster accused the Carter Administration of promoting "chaos and anarchy" in Southern Africa.[16] Vorster described American initiatives as "strangulation with finesse." The speech signalled a shift from cooperation to defiance over South Africa's support for Rhodesia. What Mr. Vorster saw as perhaps more threatening was that in a recession---the worst South Africa has experienced in thirty years---the U.S. has encouraged curtailing trade credits for South Africa; there is little sign of a resurgence of private sector investment in South Africa, which might otherwise move South Africa out of the recession (soup kitchens have been established by philantropic groups in some black and coloured urban ghettos). Moreover, it is perhaps obvious to South Africa that Washington is discouraging banks from expanding their interests in South Africa. Even more threatening to the Vorster regime is the prospect that the arms embargo may widen and be made more effective by the purposeful use of American influence. Under non-crisis conditions these events would have enabled South Africa to simply ride out the storm. But today these measures assume a more ominous dimension for South Africa's rulers. Not the least of these dimensions is the fact that these trends and conditions reinforce resistance to white supremacy inside South Africa. According to Vorster,

> There is also evidence that certain people and organizations
> believe, and are encouraged to believe, that they are backing
> the same sources in bringing about radical change in South
> Africa by extra parliamentary means, and by exerting certain

pressures, even if such pressure leads to violence and disorder.[17]

The general thrust of these and other statements seems to concede that American policy (and the policies of other Western countries) and pressure from informal sources (lobbies, pressure groups in world politics) are serving the purpose of undermining "white rule" and indeed also encouraging civil disorders inside South Africa.[18]

How effective, in these circumstances, can the strategies designed to promote peaceful change in South Africa be? How realistic are they in the light of the trends and conditions affecting the disposition of power in Southern Africa? The rest of this paper seeks to synthesize the key factors operative in the domestic and transnational environment of South Africa, and to identify the key obstacles in the way of the progressive transformation of South African society in ways that are compatible with preferred human rights goals of American Foreign policy.

The Logic of Apartheid

The principal characteristics of race relations in South Africa encapsulate a social process of privilege for any person who according to the race classification system is deemed white, whether those whites, so classified, prefer it or not. The system is characterized by a social process of deprivations imposed on all non-whites; a system which, within limits, varies with intensity and frequency according to one's specific ethnic identification (Coloured, Indian, African, Honorary White) and the vagaries, through time, of cultural, class, personality and crisis. These deprivations visit non-white or Black South Africans whether they like it or not. The South African political process is a unique one in a great many respects. Foremost among these is the peculiarly sophisticated manner in which the juridical bureaucratic apparatus of state control has been converted into all encompassing instruments of coercion, thereby eroding the authority base of the state and at the same time extending its coercive-control potentials. The interaction between law, politics, and social control can only be adequately appreciated when it is realized that South Africa is not a conservative regime bent on maintaining the status quo. Rather, it is a radical regime of the right which has, since 1948, agressively sought to translate its vision of "proper" order; i.e., to translate it vision of "proper" social, political legal and racial relations, into the concrete facts of social life. To be sure, this radical vision has on occasion to be tempered by the reality of a hostile world; but temperence has in the past been modest and grudgingly conceded. There is far less reliance on "dialogue" than on "kragdadigheid," i.e. coercion.

To the extent that dialogue across racial lines exists inside South Africa, it is conditioned by the political culture of domination and subjugation that characterizes the apartheid regime in action. Such a structure is a massive barrier to direct communication between the white rulers and their black subjects. Peaceful change as presumably envisioned by the U.S. assumes the need for a dialogue among chief protagonists. However, the nature of the social process of apartheid assumes the irrelevance of transracial lines of communication to the process of social control. Indeed "dialogue" assumes, in some degree, a psychological identification of sorts between the parties. The prime ideological objective of the apartheid regime has been to destroy patterns of identification between groups, in which common loyalty symbols serve to identify common interests of the larger society.

Apartheid leaves no psychological room for the evolution of positive political sentiments between white and black because the common interests of all South Africans are inimical to the special interest Afrikaners have in the preservation and extention of their herrenvolk ideology. Hence the system feeds on isolation and domination; it precludes identification with an interlocutor.

From what I have said, it seems clear that the apartheid regime since 1948, has created a distinctive normative structure and has forced the social and political realities of South Africa into this normative mold. Some of these outcomes may or may not have been anticipated by the regime. These involve the polarization of the entire population along racial lines, and strict maintenance of such polarization by the rigor with which those who transgress apartheid norms are invariably punished. To summarize, the South African System precludes dialogue between the chief protagonists as a cultural-political objective; it excludes or severely restricts the advocacy of change by constitutional means; it punishes and tortures those who challenge these proscriptions. The result has been to create conditions for change by non-constitutional means. To talk about peaceful change or transition in such a setting is to ignore the psychological, social, and political facts that animate the essential substructure of apartheid. This is vividly illustrated by the insurrection that occurred in most of South Africa's urban ghettos, particularly in Soweto.

Soweto and the Student Insurrection.

The uniqueness of the revolt of the school children in South Africa's Black ghettos must be seen against a backdrop of two important socio-historical events. First, the political socialization of black students, especially those in high schools and their tradition of political organization. Second, the marginal sociological position of the urban black.

The emergence of student opposition to apartheid is a fact of which the nationalist government has always been keenly aware. Indeed, the creation of the Bantu education system and the separate universities bear testimony to this awareness. Direct action against students is embodied in the Fort Hare University record which has seen countless instances of expulsion, closure, police brutality, torture, and political trials from the late 1950's to the present.

By the early 1960's a number of black students groups were operating

in the universities and the schools. Student leaders like Thabo Mbeki and
others had recognized that the vast majority of black students were located
in the schools and not the universities; that organizing students in the schools
was a far more significant enterprise than organizing the relatively few who
were admitted into the university system. During the early 1960's, organizations like ASUSA--the African Students Union of South Africa; the PNSO--the
Progressive National Students Organization; SOYA--the Society of Young Africans;
ASA--the African Students Association, were all competing for the associational
and ideological loyalty of all non-white students in both the high schools and
the universities. It seems clear that these efforts established a strong
pattern of political socialization in the schools and probably laid the seeds
of black consciousness so vigorously asserted by the student leaders in SASO
and other groups in the early seventies. The technique of consciousness-rais-
ing to obvious political inequality by students to students from the university
level into the schools appears on the whole to have evaded or outwitted the
strict scrutiny of the Security Police, preoccupied as they were with bigger
issues.

Thus it is not at all surprising that non-while students in South Africa
appear to have established and maintained an unusually strong animosity and
skepticism for the status quo. But this does not altogether explain the scope
and intensity of the student revolt, or the necessity of crushing it by such
brutal means. Children occupy a unique role in urban ghetto life in South
Africa, their fundamental status is a contingent one; one dependent upon marginal parental privileges in the urban areas. Direct political action by
parents results not only in reprisals against the parent involved, but also
threatens the entire family's (often an extended family) capacity to survive,
given that under normal conditions the very presence of a black parent in an
urban context is a tenuous one because of statutes like Urban Areas Act and
other legislative enactments.

It is within the not-so-visible interstices of the ghetto social process, where the regulatory scheme has allowed a legal vacuum by default, that forms of political protest of an overt nature can evidently occur. Among these arenas in which the regulatory scheme is apparently ineffectual is the situational context of ghetto school children. Reprisals against individual students does not have the same sociological impact upon black survival that occurs when parents are the victims. It is within these structural gaps in the legal and political structures erected to render politically impotent the urban black, that the position of children appears to have become important. They have inherited an arena of political "movement" practically denied their parents; they have inherited a tradition of political socialization by a discrete student political tradition since, at least, the late 1950's; they appear to be exploiting this arena of movement to the hilt. They have shown a rare capacity to resist the institutions of white power in open defiance of a national security state.

It is difficult to know what the ultimate results of the Soweto events will protend. The following conclusions are tentatively advanced. First, the willingness of the government to use the philosophy of "kragdadigheid" to control the students resulted in an enormous loss of life. This may have great symbolic import for black expectations inside South Africa, about the nature and price of political freedom. The symbols of struggle may be felt with a greater immediacy and urgency because the persons killed were children--their children. It would seem that the necessity of struggle for political freedom may now be felt with a heightened collective intensity because the content of the childrens' demands was so thoroughly minimal, and modest, and because it provoked such an unreasoned and furious response. It is difficult to articulate the nature of collective emotions that have been stirred by the killing of the children. It is difficult to predict with precision the extent to which

these emotions may be converted into a new power predicate for black militants.
That they exist and are deeply felt is undisputed. The killing of and defiance
by children represented a new kind of political experience for both black and
white. The defiance crossed a threshold of fear; the slaughter had the para-
doxical effect of killing that "fear." It may be that the policy of kragdadigheid
as directed against the children of Soweto, Capetown, Port Elizabeth and other
centers of unrest has in effect forced black resistence to a situation in which
fear is no longer the pivotal controlling emotion in determining forms of
resistance. It may be that blacks are now past the "point of fear" and its
corollary, the "point of restraint." Are these concepts then obsolete in
South Africa's changing power-race relations? Soweto may well be the symbolic
harbinger of racial war. Eyewitnesses reporting on the mood among Soweto
students were struck by the fearlessness of the students; each killing seemed
to close out any avenue for turning back any kind of personal refuge in fear
and restraint: Kragdadigheid had killed off for urban black South Africa a
fundamental existential choice to be fearful and restrained. How far this
attitude has infused the adult black population of South Africa is difficult
to say, but the following hypothetical case may give readers of this paper
some situation sense of it. Assume that an iniquitous black tyrant had killed
600 white children: if the "white" west would be outraged; then consider the
black South African parents' response.

For those who still harbor thoughts that a racial war can be averted in
South Africa, the government's response must have been a frightening one. It
allowed a rent increase in Soweto during a period of unrest and economic
recession that is reportedly the worst South Africa has experienced since the
Great Depression. Moreover, the demand that blacks be given the right to own
real estate in Soweto (i.e., that some blacks be allowed to own their own homes)
was rejected, it should be noted, by a government that claimed before the world

that it would move away from discrimination; by a government whose propaganda now loudly proclaims the urgent necessity of cultivating a black middle class! It should also be parenthetically noted that one of the fundamental aims of Nationalist party policy since 1948 has been the progressive expropriation of the non-white middle classes and their extinction, a policy projection which did not entirely succeed only because it ran counter to the facts of economic life in post-war South Africa.

The Regional Context.

Prior to the extinction of the Portuguese presence in Southern Africa, all the countries under white rule maintained a cooperative regional system for their mutual security interests: the "white" cordon sanitaire. These security linkages between South Africa, Rhodesia, and the Portuguese empire were designed to establish and maintain the security of the white regimes against the threat of black revolution, which it was thought would be under-written by the communist powers. This arrangement implicated cold-war perspectives inasmuch as Portugal was a NATO member and was the recipient of NATO hardware and U.S. credits which served the function of freeing other resources for the fight against black liberation in the colonies.

The pattern of power relations changed fundamentally when the Portuguese withdrew from Angola and Mozambique leaving those states to their former adversaries, the black nationalists. These black states are socialist in outlook. They are experienced in the ways of armed struggle to achieve national liberation and are committed to the destruction of white supremacy in South Africa, Namibia and Zimbabwe. Moreover these states are geographically contiginous to the "shrunken" white redoubt, which means they pose a significant security threat to South Africa because of their potentials as sanctuaries from which freedom fighters might penetrate South African borders. The prospect that Angola and Mozambique are committed to full support of the national liberation movements

of the unliberated states is already a partial reality. The critical question
is, what is the nature of the South African response to these external threats?

Mozambique

The South African posture with respect to Mozambique has been cool and
correct. It has maintained much of the structure of economic relations that
obtained prior to the Portuguese coup. Mozambique workers still work in South
African mines and provide much needed foreign exchange to the Machel regime.
Yet Mozambique may one day be a staging post for the South African liberation
movement. The South African position here is clearly a flexible one. Mozambique
poses no immediate threat to the security of South Africa. Moreover, there is
a danger that if Machel feels directly threatened by South Africa, that this
might provide a convenient excuse for more affirmative and direct Soviet
involvment in securing the existence of the Machel regime. To do this effectively
may warrant even greater support for the South African liberation movement from
those quarters. The interim stratagem for handling Mozambique has been the policy
of flexible pragmatism. But the ability to be flexible may be preempted by
conditions over which South Africa's control is tangential at best.

Angola

The invasion of Angola by South African troops in the aftermath of
Portugal's cession of sovereignty to the Angolan liberation forces was both
a strategic and diplomatic blunder. The presence of South African troops
provided a prime excuse for Castro to extend Cuban and Soviet influence in
Angola. Militarily the South Africans were faced with seasoned Cuban troops
armed with sophisticated Soviet weapons and having the capability of using them
effectively. Faced with the prospect of being wiped out, white South Africa
soldiers were withdrawn in defeat from Angolan soil. That white soldiers were
infact defeated by "coloured" troops (Cuban or Angolan) is of high symbolic
import in a culture that has believed in the supremacy if not invincibility of

the herrenvolk. When the Neto regime consolidates its bases of power in Angola this country may be an important strategic archilles heel in the South African security system. Moreover, the presence of Cuban troops suggests that South Africa's capacity to retaliate against the Angolans will be a limited one.

Namabia

South Africa's apparent flexibility on the issue of independence for Namibia ought not to be misconstrued. The principal aim is for a kind of political independence that ensures military dependence on South Africa. It is not likely that South Africa will go further in fact as distinct from form than the constitutional dispensation envisioned in the Turnhalle proceedings.[19] Such a program will ensure that some "reliable" leaders may be called upon to protect Namibia's right to self-determination and independence from "communist" subversion. The critical function of such "puppet" leadership will be to legitimize the South African military presence in South West Africa. The role that South Africa thus envisions for Namibia is similar to that of the South African bantustans, i.e., a return to the 19th century concept of flexible suzerainty, under more fashionable labels. This will not be acceptable to SWAPO or the U.N., and a continuing armed struggle for national liberation will continue to be supported by most of the world community.

Zimbabwe

The policy of flexible pragmatism is basically aimed at maintaining a public posture of persuading Smith to transfer formal power to black leadership while encouraging Smith to cultivate a cadre of black leaders committed to moderate political goals, and who would be prepared to essentially remain within the South African security orbit. South Africa will not countenance a transfer of power to the Patriotic Front of Mugabe and Nkomo. Again the key factor in the Rhodesian context will be real power, rather than who "formally" heads the Rhodesian state in any kind of future settlement. It is probable that the key to success of moderate African leadership like Muzorewa or Sithole will be their ability to deliver goods and services and opportunities to the emergent black urban middle classes, and this in turn depends upon the stability with which such a regime could be maintained and its access to capital investment along the lines of the Kissinger proposal.

How long South Africa might be able to stall the African revolution in South Africa is hard to predict. The fact is that the guerillas of the Patriotic Front are growing stronger each month; the Socialistic regimes in Mozambique and Angola are consolidating themselves internally, and expect to play a role in the eventual liberation of South Africa. The greater infusion of sophisticated weapons from the Soviet bloc, and the infusion of Cuban troops into the Southern African sieve suggest that there are finite limits to South Africa's pragmatic flexibility in its regional diplomatic posture. Moreover, oil rich countries like Nigeria are prepared to devote more of their resources to the liberation struggle in the South.

The limits of pragmatic flexibility on regional issues should also be seen against the limits on growing inflexibility in internal South African issues. For the changes in the regional context have created relatively priviledged sanctuaries for black South Africans in South Africa. Moreover, this development will clearly strengthen the linkage between struggle for national liberation inside and outside South Africa.

The fundamental dilemma for American policy makers with respect to pragmatic felxibility is this. There is a tendency of U.S. policy makers to assume that such a posture may signal a desire to move toward a system of racial and social justice on the part of the South African government; that South African pragmatic flexibility means a change in principle and outlook with respect to the apartheid system. The reality of flexible pragmatism, however, has had as its principle goal the preservation of the apartheid status quo based on official state

violence. Given the right strategic circumstances, the South African authorities
will not hesitate to use their armed forces.

The current trends and conditions affecting the security regime of Southern
Africa suggest great instability, and portend major changes in the distribution
of power in that region in the immediate future. The major condition of change
has been the growth and emergence of powerful indigenous forces committed to
the extinction of white supremacy and the regime that sustains it. These forces
have historically cultivated inclusive symbols of black nationalism, and
national liberation. Working from these perspectives, they have cultivated
global support for the cause of self-determination and independence. They have
at the same time, managed to sustain a presence within the while redoubt and
have thereby laid an infrastructure of political loyalities unified by the
common symbols of national liberation and national oppression. It is essentially
the internal-external linkage pattern that suggests great vulnerability for the
white regimes maintaining minimum conditions of order in South Africa, Namibia,
Zimbabwe. Moreover, realities of power in South Africa cannot be divorced from
the radical shift in the regional balance of forces inaugurated by the demise
of Portuguese rule. Indeed a regional perspective is just as essential to an
understanding of the dynamics of change in South Africa as it is to an appreciation of the changing U.S. posture on the issue of apartheid. Ultimately, whether
or not American policy succeeds in setting a new course towards full political
participation of all South Africans will depend to a considerable extent on our
ability to respond constructively to political developments within and outside
South Africa.

A developmental construct setting out the most optimistic and pessimistic
predictions for the immediate future of South Africa are set out. This may
enable us to more realistically devise future strategies to approximate, what
according to our stated policies, may be the most optimistic outcome for South
Africa.

A Developmental Construct for the Future of South Africa

    (a) The most optimistic construct

There will be a gradual intensification of violence within South Africa, outbreaks of terrorism in the urban areas. Terrorism will be directed at creating a fear among whites that the government is incapable of securing their safety. Black support will be consolidated by a campaign directed at the security police informer network. Security police agents and torturers will become key targets for assassination squads. This will provoke a strong reaction from a coalition of forces within the white power structure. It will be seen that the white electorate is incapable of supporting any government which seeks to come to terms with the nationalist forces. A coalition of "ver-ligte" Afrikaners in combination with the active support of a business sector committed to a more liberal outlook will marshall the support of key elements in the army to suspend the constitution. With the army in control of the political process, these forces will inaugurate a national convention with the purpose of redesigning the constitutional structure of South Africa along the lines of a federal or confederal system. The objective of the convention as seen by its convenors will be firstly the gradual dismantling of the garrison security state constructed by the Nationalist regime; the introduction of a rule of law based on a rigid constitution embodying a Bill of Rights. Secondly, the convenors will seek the release of all political prisoners and the abolition of all torture practices. Thirdly, the convenors will envision an amnesty for all exiles and political parties in exile for full participation in the new national convention. The express aim of the convention will be to dismantle the apartheid regime and its superstructure of discriminatory laws and to develop a framework which accounts for past discrimination and which secures direct political participation for all races in the destiny of the country but which diffuses power so effectively that the dominance of one group by another will not be possible by constitutional means.

(b) The Pessimistic Developmental Construct.

As conditions of minimum order in Southern Africa continue to deteriorate, there will be a massive exodus of whites from South Africa whose perspectives are not as rigidly locked into concepts of white supremacy or Afrikaner nationalism. This will reduce the kinds of pressures on the Afrikaner elite for accommodation to black demands for meaningful change. With even less accountability to the white electorate, the Afrikaners will seek to maintain their power and authority by the increased use of force. This position will further harden as Western "friends" are perceived to be communistic fellow travellers in disguise; and as it becomes very apparent that South Africa has, within its grasp, a nuclear capability. The need to compromise on the question of black rights will herafter be seen to be irrelevant to the survival of the Afrikaner race. The Apartheid government will, in the meanwhile, do its utmost to shore up the Smith regime with stepped up support of arms and other strategic supplies. It will fight Smith's war by proxy, keeping the intensive fighting as far from the borders of South Africa as possible. It will also seek to cultivate client black leadership in Zimbabwe which along with Smith might pliantly request an even more direct South African military presence there. Vorster will then try to secure some sort of linkage between this leadership and the Savimbi's guerillas in Southern Angola. Cooperation with the effort of Western States to secure a peaceful withdrawal of South African control over Namibia will stall on the question of the withdrawal of South Africa's military presence. The expectations of violence inside South Africa will be greatly intensified as Zimbabwe falls under black rule. Front line states will now be flooded with refugees ready for training in the techniques of guerilla warfare and civilian insurrection. As these troops are infiltrated into South Africa in increasing numbers, leaders in quasi independent bantustans will either have to turn a blind eye to their territories being used as staging posts, or face reprisals from the guerillas. Their position will be highly tenuous, and it is hardly likely that, as the credibility of black military operations intensify, such leaders will commit themselves unequivocally to white supremacy. Inexorably, the key issues will more and more be resolved according to group and individual security. The need for complete geopysical separation of black and white will become critical as the expectations and actualities of violence intensify. Gradually the state will not be able to secure the safety of white populations and a trend toward geophysical security will be evidenced by shrinking white group areas.

As the state of racial violence intensifies, South Africa will threaten the use of nuclear weapons against front line states; it may threaten guerilla leaders by making certain black populations inside South Africa, hostage communities. As the authority of the state is gradually eroded and its reliance on force becomes almost total, the use of nuclear weapons ushers in a devastating destruction in some front line states and black areas in South Africa. The gradual withdrawal into a kind of "laager" of the bitter-end Afrikaners who have not deserted the volk is accomplished together with a systematic destruction of areas vacated. As the use of nuclear weapons clearly presents a threat to world peace the Major Powers, acting throught the security council will sanction U.N. intervention of a military nature. This construct does not predict whether in phoenix-like fashion, a new South Africa will emerge from the "ashes" of the old. Rather it focusses upon the price of change in terms of the net losses in human suffering.

If the optimistic construct is a realistic prognosis for the future of South Africa, that is in some measure compatible with President Carter's full participation/peaceful change formula, then collective economic coercion led by the U.S. together with other measurers short of the use of force, and directed against other pressure points in South Africa may be helpful in realizing this goal.

Moral and Ideological Jawboning

Andrew Young as Ambassador to the United Nations has and continues to be a vital asset of this administration in international affairs, particularly with respect to African policy. His key role so far has been to sensitize not only the U.S., but world public opinion on the issue of racism in international affairs. In discharging this function he has symbolized a fundamental connection between racial justice at home and abroad. If the optimistic construct is deemed a realizable goal for American policy-makers, clearly the vigorous articulation of the Young perspective is significant if leverage to use pressure points against South Africa is to be rung from the domestic constraints that limit the structure of political action in foreign affairs. What ought to be remembered is this. To black Africa, armed sturggle is one of the important though not exclusive instruments of change. Without access to this instrument there would be no hope of realizing the goals of African liberation, and the white regimes and pressure groups within them would see little need to consider seriously black political demands. Indeed, the peaceful change position that Young advocates--the so-called "Atlanta model"--is thought to be ludicrous by articulate white South African opinion.[20] The South African Broadcasting Corp. (the state-controlled radio) writes off the "Atlanta model" as nothing but the displacement of America's official guilt feelings on racial questions to South Africa.[21] The flaw in the Atlanta model lies in the assumption that political change and racial justice in South Africa can be achieved by constitutional means roughly anologous to the struggle in the United States. The facts of black South African history refute this. Constitutional struggle using the moral force of non-violence literally started in South Africa during the First World War under the leadership of Gandhi. That struggle

not only used the doctrine of non-violence and "love force" to change the
mindset of white supremacy, it also developed the struggle along many other
fronts including that of the trade union movement. The tradition of struggle
through passive resistance, the defiance of unjust laws and the anti-pass campaigns
have all accelerated the closure of licit avenues of political action. Civil
rights in the U.S.--a movement of recent vintage--occurred in a political
environment in which the national authority supported the civil rights leaders.
A liberal supreme court codified their demands as the law of the land and the
national guard enforced these initiatives. In South Africa the passive resisters
and those committed to its moral axioms--the political moderates--have been
unremittingly persecuted by the state. The moderates are in jail or under
banning orders, or in exile. Many have been tortured and abused by the police
and prison authorities. In short, Young himself violated provisions of the
South African Terrorism Act when he advocated social change along the lines
of the Atlanta model inside South Africa. Indeed, the point of the matter
is that the Atlanta model is insufficiently realistic to accomodate the real
trends and conditions that have politically, socially and psychologically
polarized black and white society. To some extent, Young conceeded as much
when he departed from the prepared text of his Maputo speech, and suggested
how far the U.S. had evolved away from the institutional patterns of racial
deprivation. Blacks will not realistically give up armed struggle as one of
the instruments of liberation, so long as white supremacy in South Africa
rests so unambigiously on the use of state violence to maintain itself. While
the Atlanta model is no panacea for change in South Africa, the overall framework does two important things. First, it provides some kind of reference
point for articulating the aggregate of black demands in South Africa in a
form that communicates to America. Second, political events are always un-
predictable. The Atlanta frame if viewed flexibly and in the context of other

initiatives aimed at the emergence of more accomodating voices among the
white South Africans may well be useful in realizing the optimistic construct
we have delineated. But this would be contingent upon the emergence of white
leadership outside the Afrikaner laager and with sufficient credibility and
power to be able to take the radical steps needed for real change in South
Africa.

International Pressure

For years the United Nations has sought to set in motion a program of
sanctions designed to coerce the South African authorities to move away from
apartheid. International law has moved in the direction of outlawing genocide,
racial discrimination and more recently formulating a convention declaring that
apartheid is a crime against humanity. The U.S., now in a minority position
in the General Assembly, has along with other Western powers sought to protect
South Africa from the full mandate of international law and morality. It seems
that the optimistic prognosis might only be realized if the program of international sanctions is fully implemented along the lines suggested by Colin
and Margaret Legum and further adumbrated by Professor Hunt Davis' paper in
this book. This requires a significant change in United States outlook. The
U.S. could do much to restore the U.N. role in South Africa by more affirmatively
endorsing the U.N. perspective rather than pursuing a bilateral or unilateral
modus operandi aimed at selective pressure points. Stripped of all details,
the collective interest in South Africa poses the sharpest questions about world
peace and global justice. South Africa presents a threat to world peace because
it provokes superpower confrontation. The South African situation brings to
mind the great questions of our time about optimal justice and human progress in
world affairs as well as the collective capacity of the world community to
respond decisively to this problem in ways that promote the common interest.
The United States could give commanding leadership in this enterprise.

Conclusion

The limits of peaceful change are apparent. The American position is by
nature inclined to work through established power structures in South Africa.
This means changing the ideological, Christian Nationalist perspectives of the
Broederbond--a secret society committed to racial polarization and white
supremacy. Morover, there is the strong belief that the Broederbond would
sooner secure the complete destruction of South Africa than share power in ways
campatible with optimal democratic ideals. The American posture takes insufficient
account of the psychological bases of white herrenvolkism in South Africa. The
position is even more unrealistic when it comes to black nationalism. The
Atlanta plan simply ignores traditional African political parties still recognized
as the legitimate heirs of the goals and aspirations of the African people: the
ANC, the PAC, the NEUM and a host of other organizations whose collective outlook incorporated the oldest black nationalist movement in Africa. As movements
operating covertly inside South Africa, and overtly abroad, many of these groups
are still the authentic though not necessarily exclusive voice of African liberation. Any political solution which seeks to exclude the principal organs
of national liberation in South Africa is, in light of these facts, an exercise
in futility. This is not to say that these movements speak exclusively for
the black majority. Rather, it is that these groups have maintained continuing
presence and legitimacy among black South Africans and have a deeply rooted
history of commitment to African liberation and democratic ideals. Moreover,
their leaders have and continue to exhibit the courage that is the price of such
struggle. They continue to be regarded as the authentic voices of the black
perspective. As Professor Carter has observed, it is hardly likely that any
solution can be found to South Africa's problem when men like Nelson Mandela
and others are in jail; when Robert Sobukwe is under permanent house arrest
and when men like Oliver Tambo and I.B. Tabata are still in exile. The

ideological block that encumbers U.S. policy makers is that in varying degrees
these groups are committed to political and social justice as well as economic
justice for all South Africans. Is such an aim really coterminous with that
of the cosmocorp? Can the ideology or world view of cosmocorp and the Trilateral
commission be reconciled with genuine human rights prescriptions in this context?
Ultimately human rights have a political, social and economic dimension. South
Africa poses all these facets as sharp as the razor's edge. And a human rights
policy that ignores this is not only a hollow one; it is supremely unrealistic.
If the United States is to lead the way toward human freedom in Southern Africa,
we must be willing to apply our own constitutional ideals to that situation,
and this means providing the fullest support for those groups---black and white---
who share our values.

FOOTNOTES

1. Reproduced in AF Press Clips, vol. xii, no. 28, July 12, 1977.

2. D. Rockefeller as quoted in Prospectus of the Trilateral Commission (1973). The commission is evidently composed of existing elite figures drained almost exclusively from the developed industrial world of North America, Western Europe and Japan. These influential "private" citizens have access to the highest policy-making arenas. See R. Falk, "A New Paradigm for International Studies" 84 Yale Law Journal (1975), passim.

3. Ibid., p. 961.

4. Ibid., p. 1005.

5. Ethel Payne, "Vance Speaks Out", Chicago Defender, July 9, 1977.

6. Payne, id.

7. The Citizen, March 3, 1977.

8. Die Beeld, March 2, 1977; South Africa Digest, March 11, 1977, p. 9.

9. Ibid.

10. The term is owed to the editorial writer of The Daily News, East London, South Africa, July 14, 1977.

11. Die Burgher, July 22, 1977, S.A. Digest, p. 22.

12. Washington Notes on Africa: The Carter Work on Southern Africa, The Washington Office on Africa, Spring, 1977, p. 1.

13. S. A. Digest, July 1, 1966, p. 1.

14. Ibid., p. 2.

15. S.A. Digest, June 3, 1977, p. 1-2. See John Bums, Carter Foreign Policies Assailed by Vorster As Payoff for Blacks.

16. New York Times, August 7, 1977, p. 1. col. 1 and p. 2, col. 1.

17. Burns, Ibid, New York Times, p. 2, col. 1, August 7, 1977.

18. Id. The reference was to Andrew Young's unofficial visit to Johannesburg, but it also refers to the more inclusive class foreign pressures that cannot be kept from the opinion leaders in black communities.

19. Recent reports indicate that South Africa scrapped the Turnhalle scheme. A Supreme Court justice has been appointed as Administrator General of the territory. One of his functions is to set up an election for a constituent assembly. Some movement has been made for the release of

19. (continued)
Namibian political prisoners and the United Nations will give added supervision to the proposed elections. However, South Africa does not plan to withdraw its troops so long as a threat to the security of Namibia exists. Clearly the existence of a socialist Angola constitutes such a threat in South African eyes. Hence it is unlikely that South Africa will withdraw its troops from Namibia by agreement.

20. See. J. Barrat, U.S. and South Africa Not Easily Compared, South Africa Digest, July 8, 1977, p. 18; Terreblanche, "Thats the Difference, Andy Young", S.A. Digest, June 3, 1977, p. 15.

21. See "The Guilt Factor in Washington", S.A. Digest, June 17, 1977, p. 15.

PART TWO:

THE INCIDENCE OF STRATEGIC AND CORPORATE INTERESTS

Editor's Note

American policy in Southern Africa has been singularly ineffective and wrongheaded on a number of issues, but the impression of ineptitude and moral indifference conveyed by the record is nowhere more painfully apparent than in the case of South Africa. To put it boldly, American policy has failed conspicuously to alter the South African position on apartheid and has consistently ignored the moral imperative of racial justice for Africans. If anything it has reinforced the conviction of the Pretoria authorities that its racial policies, and continued denial of the vote to 80 percent of the population, were not only viable but necessary. By the time the Carter administration came into office our South African policy had reached a total impasse.

No attempt at understanding the roots of our present dilemma can overlook the underlying motives that have shaped the American posture in South Africa. What, exactly, is the nature and significance of American interests in the region? Are American economic and strategic interests of such magnitude as to set fundamental limitations on our ability to initiate a more positive policy with regard to the race problem? How far can these interests be allowed to take precedence over the moral and political imperatives of American diplomacy in South Africa?

The conservative position on these issues has been articulated time and again by various spokesmen of American business interests. The least that can be said is that it leaves little doubt as to the desirability of maintaining the preeminence of our economic and strategic interests in the area, for these are inevitably seen as "vital" interests. According to Anthony Harrigan, executive vice-president of the United States Industrial Council,

South Africa is the mineral treasure house of the Continent. It is very much in the national interest of the United States

to maintain access to the gold, uranium, coal, chrome,
platinum and other strategic materials in the subcontinent.
Access will be denied if Marxist regimes extend their sway.
At the same time the United States has a special strategic
interest in the Cape of Good Hope. Despite the reopening
of the Suez Canal, the vast bulk of the tanker traffic will
continue to use the Cape route.

Among radicals this line of reasoning offers irrefutable proof of the subordin-

ation of American policy to the interests of American captialism: It is seen

as the basic rationale behind Option 2 of NSSM 39, in short as providing the

essential justification for American support of the racist regimes of Southern

Africa. What remains unclear, however, is the extent to which the conservative

claims rest on verifiable evidence, and by the same token, whether the criticisms

voiced on the left are really substantiated by the nature of the case.

This is the basic issue to which Professors Foltz and Davis address them-

selves in the chapters which follow. Rejecting the arguments invoked by radicals

and conservatives to either pillory or justify previous U.S. policies, Foltz

makes a strong case for the view that the economic and strategic interests at

stake do not in fact constitute insuperable constraints on US policies, and

therefore that a far greater flexibility and adaptability should guide American

strategies in the area. Hence, according to Foltz, there are no compelling

reasons for "not working with, rather than against, the indigenous African forces

of change". While fully endorsing this proposition, Professor Davis introduces

some major qualifiers to the argument. American diplomacy in South Africa does

face some major liabilities in its effort to shape the direction of change. For

a variety of reasons -- some having to do with African perceptions (or mispercep-

tions) of US intentions, others with the structure and scale of American invest-

ments in the area and their relationships with corporate interests outside the

United States, others concerning the legacy of suspicion inherited by the present

administration from our previous policies -- it will not be easy for the United

States to promote change in the direction of majority rule and racial justice.

Yet these are the only objectives that are really consonant with current historical trends, and indeed with our own political tradition and self-image. The questions raised in the following chapters lie at the heart of the dilemmas faced by the Carter administration in its effort to assist revolutionary change through peaceful means.

CHAPTER VI

US POLICY TOWARD SOUTHERN AFRICA:
ECONOMIC AND STRATEGIC CONSTRAINTS

BY WILLIAM FOLTZ

The Angolan civil war of 1975-1976 and the succeeding challenge to white rule in Rhodesia thrust southern Africa into American consciousness to a degree not matched since, perhaps, the Boer War. At the same time the contradictions and the general ineptitude of American foreign policy in southern Africa were revealed as never before. Only a small part of the ineptitude can be put down to "bad luck," an unfortunate guess as to Portugal's staying power in Africa. Rather, one must question why it is that American policy makers chose not only to believe that all the various forms of white rule in southern Africa would last, but to assume as well that American interests would best be served by helping them last. Such questions are not only of historical interest; even more urgently they must be asked about the assumptions on which American policy toward southern Africa continues to be based. Chief among these assumptions is that southern Africa is a part of the world in which the United States has definite "vital interests."

The purpose of this article is to disprove the claim that there are tight economic and strategic constraints on American policy toward southern Africa, especially the supposition that it is possible to identify economic and strategic interests that are clearly "vital" to the United States and to its policy makers. Such interests could be considered vital for two reasons: first, they may be of such real and compelling importance that no prudent policy maker could neglect to take them into account; second, they may be so important either to the elec- torate at large or to certain politically powerful individuals and institutions that, without them, the continuity of an administration or its ability to carry out a coherent foreign policy would be jeopardized. Either situation would naturally provide serious constraints on foreign policy toward a particular region of the world. The logical conclusion, then, is that those who make policy are to be faulted not for blindly responding to real economic and security constraints; but for failing to take advantage of the considerable latitude of policy innovation which in fact is available.

Both conservative and radical critics of United States policy toward southern Africa seem to agree that certain fundamental economic and strategic interests derived from the very nature of America's domestic and international situation must underlie this policy. They then disagree on everything else. On the economic side, conservatives lament the absence of "realistic" trade and investment policies, particularly toward Rhodesia and the Republic of South Africa, and decry the weakness of the "bleeding hearts" in the Department of State's African Bureau. Radical critics see the lobbyists of multinational corporations behind every policy change and with varying degrees of enthusiasm trace America's postwar economic preeminence to unsavory profits made from the sweat of oppressed black labor. On strategic questions, conservatives (not necessarily the same as those arguing the economic case) point to the growth of the Soviet fleet or even the building of the TanZam railway as a threat to American survival. While few of their radical opponents go so far as Admiral Gorshkov in seeing the Soviet fleet as a force for peace (most prefer not to see it at all), they agree that a "military-industrial complex" has gotten hold of American policy formulation and warped its African enterprises, so that the military protection of American capitalism overrides any concern with political or social issues. Both sides, finally, agree on the further assumption that these interests are part and parcel of America's own version of capitalism and democracy; they disagree only on whether or not that version should survive.

ECONOMIC FACTORS

The basic economic facts are relatively straightforward and have been ably discussed by others; a brief summary should suffice here.[1] In terms of overall American trade and investment, Africa as a whole continues to be the "least important continent," though some major changes may be taking place. The trade figures show the greatest recent movement: in 1972, Africa provided 2.87 percent of America's imports; in 1974, 6.55 percent. In 1972 Africa took 3.2 percent of American exports; in 1974 3.74 percent (arms exports not included). Of the $6.6 billion worth of African goods imported into the United States in 1974, about half came from one country, Nigeria. In third and fourth places respectively (behind Algeria), South Africa and Angola accounted for $600 million and $400 million. Southern Africa's total exports to the United States were, then, less than one-third of those coming from Nigeria alone, which ranked seventh in the world, between Mexico and Italy, as a supplier of the American market.

The American export side reveals a different profile. Of America's $3.6 billion exports to Africa, the Republic of South Africa bought about one-third ($1.15 billion), almost as much as the next four clients (Egypt, Algeria, Nigeria, and Morocco) combined. South Africa thus ranked eighteenth, between Israel and Switzerland, as a market for American goods.

The change in these figures over recent years may be as important for our purposes as the absolute position in the latest figures. Between 1969 and 1975 American trade with South Africa tripled to reach $2.16 billion; in the same period trade with the rest of Africa went up sevenfold to $11.6 billion. The turning point emerges as 1973, the year in which total American trade with Nigeria surpassed that with South Africa. The key, of course, is oil, with Nigeria now standing among the principal foreign suppliers of petroleum for the American market, a position which seems unlikely to be challenged in the foresee-

able future, and which presumably is of some relevance to American policies
toward Africa generally.

Even with Nigeria's decisive replacement of South Africa in American trade
relations, the argument can be made that South Africa still is essential as the
one major African country with which the United States enjoys a decidedly positive balance of payments. While not totally irrelevant, the argument must be
viewed with suspicion for two reasons. First, there is no rational economic
principle that says the United States should balance its payments with a particular continent, as opposed, say, to all countries whose names begin with
the letters A through F. Second, had the figures gone the other way, with the
United States depending on vital South African exports to fuel its industrial
machinery, while Nigeria bought our exports, the same economic determinists
would probably sieze on those facts to explain that we were in a dependent
relationship with Pretoria which thus called the tune in our foreign policies.

The following seems to be the only clear generalization one can make from
these gross statistics: to the degree that foreign policy is conditioned directly by the desire to maintain good relations with countries which are strong economic partners, South African needs and desires should have some influence over
United States policy, but that influence should have declined substantially during the 1970s by comparison with that of Nigeria. If this generalization holds,
then the degree of influence involved must be so slight as to escape all but the
most finely tuned analysis and to have only the most marginal influence on
policy making.[2] One must conclude that, from the perspective of overall American
economic involvements, the situation is politically permissive. That is to
say, within certain very wide limits, foreign policy toward southern Africa can
be made without fear of damaging vital American economic interests--unless perhaps both South Africa and Nigeria were to line up strongly on the same side
of a vital issue.

Of course one must look behind those aggregate figures to discern probable patterns of influence. Influence need not come directly from the host country; rather it can come indirectly through the American corporation involved or seeking involvement there. American corporate involvement in South Africa and its dependents is clearly of some economic significance, though rather more for South Africa than for the United States. The $1.24 billion of direct American private investment in South Africa in 1973 represented 1.12 percent of United States private investment overseas (yielding 1 percent of foreign earnings), but 17 percent of all foreign investment in South Africa. Some 340 South African firms were American owned, wholly or in significant part, and the American companies involved represented a cross section of the biggest of American big business. Out of the 10 largest American corporations, 9 were included, as were 136 of the Fortune top 500. Furthermore, although earnings have diminished somewhat in recent years, they still are noticeably higher than those in other parts of the world. In the manufacturing sector, which accounts for almost half of American investment, earnings in the 1960s averaged 20.2 percent, as opposed to 9.4 percent worldwide.[3]

The very size of the American corporations involved, which should augment their potential influence with the United States government, also means that the South African operations represent a fairly small portion of their total overseas investments and an even smaller part of their combined foreign and domestic operations. South Africa is important, but far from crucial, for these great corporations.[4] In the absence of competing interests and countervailing pressures such as those generated by investments in black African states like Nigeria and Zambia, Chrysler, Ford, Firestone, Cummins Engine, Standard Oil, and IBM, not to mention those who would like to imitate such giants, would certainly try to promote a rapprochement between American and South African interests. But the competing interests are actively or potentially there for all these corporations, and the countervailing pressures may be there, sooner or later, as well.[5]

Additionally, one must admit the hypothesis that highly particular interests may be effectively represented behind the scenes by a powerful or well-connected person or group. One man in particular, Charles Engelhard, whose name graces many of the gold ingots Americans are now able to buy directly, was often singled out. Engelhard was the last American member of the board of the Anglo-American Corporation and a liberal contributor to political campaigns according to the purest capitalist principles. He was in favor of the winner, whoever he might be. Engelhard was reportedly on good personal terms with Lyndon Johnson (whom he represented at Zambia's independence celebration) but had no difficulty in expressing equal admiration for Johnson's successor in the White House. For all the mystique surrounding Engelhard, however, there is little evidence that he had any major impact on United States policy in southern Africa, though it is quite likely that he did influence minor policy decisions to the advantage of his personal interests. Engelhard died in 1973, and no one has yet been able to step into his shoes.

Kenneth Rush, president of Union Carbine from 1966 to 1969, illustrates another pattern of business influence. He first spent a year in the largely honorific position as member of the Public Advisory Committee on U.S. Trade Policy for Lyndon Johnson; next, Richard Nixon made Rush in succession ambassador to Germany, deputy secretary of defense, deputy secretary of state, and counselor to the president for economic policy; and then Gerald Ford sent him to Paris as ambassador. In his Washington stints Rush was clearly in a position to have a say in American policy toward southern Africa, and doubtless had a particular interest in Rhodesia, from which his former company continued to export chrome to the United States under the so-called Byrd amendment allowing violation of sanctions for the importation of critical minerals. In confirmation testimony, however, Rush specifically denied "discussing, either formally or informally, the subject of chrome with anyone."[6] Although skeptics were not so sure, it would seem almost immaterial whether or not Rush was scrupulous about his conflict of interest. His position was well known, and indeed Nixon chose him because he was the sort of man who would enthusiastically carry out the kind of policy that the president himself favored.

Business has been good in South Africa and there continued to be opportunities for some to make it better, particularly if they can influence American policies. The Fluor Company of California has been actively lobbying, along with the South African government, for the reversal of a twelve-year-old policy denying Export-Import Bank loans to South Africa. On the outcome of their effort may depend a billion dollar contract for the construction of a coal gasification and petroleum production plant. So far the administration has stood firmly by its policy of denying such loans. One must ask why this should be an issue if business influence on American policy is all that weighty. Why has American business not been allowed to go in like their French counterparts, selling anything the South Africans are willing to buy with the explicit collusion of, among other groups, the Ministry of Defense? Surely it is not just the countervailing opposition of those who support the Washington Office on Africa, or of the World Council of Churches, or of the participants in university seminars on southern Africa. All such efforts can hardly be considered to have had a major effect on foreign policy.

Before abandoning economic explanations, we must look with some sophistication at the role of economic interests in setting the tone for the way in which leading Americans think about policy toward southern Africa. Bruce Russett and Elizabeth Hanson have recently completed a major empirical study of business and other elite attitudes toward a range of relevant foreign policy issues.[7] While their inquiry does not deal directly with southern African affairs, it does investigate the broader issues of the way these individuals see the world of

which such affairs are a part. The core of their research was a comparison of

a set of questionnaires administered to a variety of American elites, including

business executives, military officers, Republican and Democratic politicians,

labor leaders, civil servents, heads of voluntary organizations, and leaders

of the communications media. Their first positive finding, which had "moderate

support," contains few surprises:

> Businessmen will be more favorable than other elites toward United States
> government activities to protect American business interests abroad, and
> toward the promotion of governments in less developed countries that are
> well disposed to the activities of foreign investors and maintenance of
> the free enterprise system; similarly they will be more hostile toward
> socialist and communist governments in less developed countries.[8]

Two groups in the sample, however, went against the proposition; labor leaders

by and large shared business attitudes on these issues, and Republican party

officials were decidedly to the right of the businessmen. Something other than

economic motivation narrowly construed must be operating.

A second set of questions specifically separated out those executives whose

firms do substantial business in less developed countries and compared them with

domestically oriented business leaders. The former group, as might be expected,

were more favorable than their fellows "toward United States government activities

to protect American business interests abroad." Surprisingly, however, they

were not more favorable toward "the promotion of governments in less developed

countries than are well disposed to the activities of foreign investors and

maintenance of the free enterprise system." Neither were they "more hostile

toward socialist and communist governments in less developed countries than. . .

executives from other corporations." In short, with the exception of foreign

policy efforts to help the most narrow definition of their corporate goals,

the foreign-oriented business executives did not differ from their domestic-

oriented counterparts, nor were both groups substantially out of line with the

rest of elite opinion.[9]

A third part of the Russett-Hanson study sought to compare the degree of influence on business executives' foreign policy preferences produced by three factors: economic motiviations and interests, domestic political ideology, and strategic (military and anticommunist) motivations. Domestic ideology was clearly the most important factor, followed by strategic motivations. "In only a very few instances did economic interests and motivations account for even as much as 2 percent of the variance in foreign policy preference."[10] Strategic motivations, while often powerful, frequently produced contradictory policy preferences, as, for example, during both the Korean and Vietnamese wars when business executives, like others, were divided over whether "communism" had to be stopped then and there, or whether this was "the wrong war, in the wrong place, at the wrong time."

The most consistent finding of the Russett-Hanson study is that political ideology has the most powerful and independent effect of foreign policy preferences of all the variables tested. Specialists in conservative political ideology and practice, exemplified by professional Republican politicians, consistently take the most right-wing position on foreign policy questions of all elite groups. Conservative business leaders tend to agree with them, while more liberal or moderate executives tend to disagree with them irresptective of their corporate economic interests.

Let us be quite clear on what this means. It certainly does not mean that most business executives are either raving liberals nor in most of their affairs heedless of their economic interests. It does mean, however, that these economic interests are only very weakly translated into foreign policy preferences, and then through the more powerful intermediaries of political ideology and of geo-political strategic preferences, each of which has an independent force. And in this, they are not unlike other Americans. If we are to search for the impact of economic interests on American policy toward southern Africa, then, we

must expect to find its subordinated to, or at least heavily attenuated by,
more broadly held preferences derived from general political ideology and from
shared views of the relationship between such policies and the strategic interests of the United States via-a-vis Communist powers.

STRATEGIC FACTORS

One strategic concern takes a primarily economic form: the rare minerals
that the West buys, principally so far from South Africa, South West Africa, and
Rhodesia. In addition to gold and diamonds, these include chrome, ferrochrome,
nickel, berrylium, cobalt, and other "vitamin" minerals which go into making
high-performance alloys. The arguments over repeal of the Byrd amendment (allowing American corporations to violate sanction against Rhodesia by importing
metals and ores) have produced much conflicting testimony as to just which was
how vital for what and to whom.[11] Unfortunately, little of the argument focused
on the issue of long-term access to these resources, which presumably should
provide the principal serious constraints on the development of foreign policy.
Since the United States' strategic stockpiles of these minerals are ample, the
long term is indeed the major concern. In thinking about the long term, one
historic precedent is unambiguous: so far, at least, no regime anywhere in
Africa, of any ideological or dermatological pigmentation, has refused to sell
the United States any valuable mineral it produces when offered something like
the going international commodity price.

Past performance is, of course, an imperfect guide to the future, and policy
makers must think prudentially about keeping open the greatest number of possibilities for access in a troubled area. Should, nevertheless, one be forced
to choose sides, the hardheaded choice is not necessarily to cater to those who
at present control the most valuable resources; rather, it is to discriminate
against those who have the fewest alternative possibilities for disposing of
them elsewhere. Of course, the hardheaded businesslike attitude is not necessarily

the one that should prevail in this or other foreign policy decisions. But if one is to argue the hardheaded case with regard to access to strategic minerals, one must recognize that it works against automatic support for wobbly white minority regimes. Moderately prudent management of American foreign relations should make it possible to avoid such a clear choice as a desperate means to guarantee the right to purchase strategic minerals. If that is so, the evidence supports the proposition that foreign policy makers in fact have considerable latitude in designing southern African policy, if only they choose to take it.

The withdrawal of British military presence from east and south of Suez and the introduction of Cuban troops to Angola have increased the military component of strategic concerns in Washington as well as in Pretoria. The Republic of South Africa's government tirelessly expounds the argument that the defense of southern Africa and its attendant sea lanes is a crucial component of "the defense of Western civilization." Increasingly, South Africa seeks to bring its message to broad segments of American opinion. Thus, on February 9, 1976, as the outcome of the Angolan war became clear, a South African publicity front published a full-page advertisement in The New York Times and other leading newspapers. Under the heading "The Free World stands today in greater danger than at any time since the darkest days of World War II. . ." the advertisement extolled South Africa's fight against "Soviet colonisers" in Angola and recalled South Africa's heroic participation in the Korean war. Similarly, the South African Department of Information commissioned and in 1975 distributed widely in America a book entitled The Communist Strategy, with prose redolent of vintage J. Edgar Hoover. It was accompanied by a slightly more sophisticated volume, The Indian Ocean and the Treat to the West, edited by a British Conservative M.P., whose contents are predictable from the title.[12]

Such propaganda efforts are not particularly important by themselves. Their seeds will germinate only if they fall on fertile ground prepared by a propensity of the general population ot believe such arguments, and with specific groups having direct interests at stake. Within the general American population there exists indeed a diffuse propensity to see the Soviet Union, and to a lesser degree China, as expansionist threats, particularly in the Third World. Presidential candidates of both parties have sought to capitalize on popular concern that the Soviet Union is getting strategic advantage out of detente at the expense of the United States. When, early in January 1976, Americans and samples from twelve other nations were asked whether or not they expected the "power" of the United States, Russia and China to increase or decrease in 1976, Americans split 42 to 44 percent over whether or not their own nation's power would increase or decrease. They felt, however, that Soviet power would increase rather than decrease (63 to 18 percent) and that Chinese power would do the same (65 to 11 percent). Americans expressed these last two opinions more decisively than the citizens of the other twelve nations sampled.[13] It must be emphasized that these are vary diffuse attitudes, at many steps remove from any policy issues directly affecting southern Africa. Still, people do volunteer some connection. A 1973 study sponsored by the Overseas Development Council (ODC) asked a national sample the open-ended question of what Third World countries would do if American aid were suspended. Far and away the top negative answer (20 percent of all replies) was that they "would go communist."[14] From this scattered evidence one can conclude at least that there is some disposition to be concerned about strategic cold-war issues and to see them as relevant to areas like southern Africa. At the same time, there is clearly little disposition to go rushing in with American troops, or even with substantial military aid. This latter, however popular it may have been with some parts of Congress, is far and away the most unpopular form of aid among the American public (opposed flatly by 49 percent of the sample in the ODC study, a figure that would be no lower today).[15]

The principal elite interest group with a stake in accentuating the strategic component of American foreign policy is, of course, the military. Compared with business leaders or the population as a whole, military officers consistently favor higher defense spending and demonstrate willingness to use armed intervention as a policy instrument in peripheral areas of the world. Even with this group, however, there are important nuances. For example, in the Russett-Hanson study, military officers are far more inclined to see upheavals in the Third World as occasioned by nationalism than by communist penetration--and on this issue, at least, they adopt a more "liberal" position than politicians of either party or than business or labor leaders.[16] Furthermore, as students of the American military and of Washington bureaucratic politics remind us, the military is hardly a unified group. Getting the Air Force and the Navy to agree on any aspect of a strategic doctrine (except that ground forces should receive lowest priority) requires diplomatic skills and the exercise of raw power of a very high order. Still, while the services and other interest groups within the Department of Defense and some of the intelligence agencies may argue over the relative priorities of expenditures and of favorable arrangements with accommodating foreign governments, when pressed their arguments are likely to be less of the "either/or" variety than of the "both/and"; that is, they will, when pushed, reinforce one another in the hopes of picking up trade-off support for future higher-ranked priorities. Thus, if the Navy wants to get concerned about the safety of the Cape route, the Air Force may eventually be persuaded to go along with such an unpromising distraction in hopes of later Navy enthusiasm for high-performance bombers.

Southern Africa's noneconomic strategic interest for the United States should be considered under at least three quite distinct rubrics, each of which has potentially very different policy ramifications: (1) U.S.-USSR mutual nuclear deterrence; (2) protection of the shipping lanes; (3) competition for political and military influence in southern African countries.

Southern Africa enters the arcane calculus of the Soviet/American balance of terror principally through the possibility of stationing atomic missile-bearing submarines in the Indian Ocean. That body of water is blessed with a complicated bottom configuration which produces irregular currents and thermal layers capable of baffling listening devices; thus, the Indian Ocean is an attractive place to hide submarines. The escalation of Soviet surface movements along the eastern African littoral began in 1967, the same year in which the deployment of Poseidon submarines brought the central Soviet Union within the range of missiles launched from the Indian Ocean north of the equator. (Soviet ports visits have increased from one in 1966 to an average of forty-five in recent years.) Trident I missiles have a range of 4000 miles (putting Moscow in range of a submarine off Zanzibar) and the 1980s generation of Trident III missiles, with at 6000-mile range, would allow a submarine commander to devastate Petropavlovsk by pushing a button while cruising off Beira.[17]

The Soviet Navy is quite aware of such strategic calculus, and Admiral Gorshkov has doubtless used these points to argue for the establishment of the new Soviet surface (and presumably submarine) fleet in the Indian Ocean, with its principally defensive and antisubmarine warfare armament. (Whether or not this surface power actually would serve to catch any of the American submarines is another question.) Following suit, the American Navy, particularly the carrier Navy, has used the presence of the Soviet surface fleet to argue for the stationing of a nuclear carrier task force in the Indian Ocean and, of course, the construction of a major Indian Ocean base in the middle of the water at Diego Garcia.[18] Diego Garcia, as an uninhabited (or more precisely, recently depopulated) archipelago, offers the political attraction of no native population to cause diplomatic fusses. At the same time, it is unlikely to possess the extensive facilities

needed to service large numbers of ships in a major extended confrontation, so
the newly enlarged service yards at Simonstown on the Cape peninsula might yet
get the use the South Africans so ardently covet. Indeed, the presence of
Diego Garcia, rather than serving as a substitute for an African continent base,
might in time be used as an argument for a mainland backup facility.[19]

Many questions remain to be answered concerning the Indian Ocean's potential role in nuclear deterrence. For example, since the Indian Ocean lies
at a considerable distance from any American submarine base, a Polaris or Trident vessel must spend a substantial percentage of its cruising time just getting
to where it can be on station within range of a worthwhile target. At present
it seems likely that the United States views the Indian Ocean principally as
an open option to be used very occasionally, but with enough flexibility so that
the Soviets feel obliged to stretch their antisubmarine warfare resources to
patrol a large, distant, and frustrating body of water.[20] Given the financial
and political complications of such a strategy, except as a rationale for the
navies of both sides to increase their forces, its logic appears as shifting
as the Indian Ocean's currents.

The defense of the Cape route, once extolled as necessary for guarding
British control of India, has taken on renewed interest now that the Western
world has noticed how much it depends on oil. The Cape route is easily linked
in the public mind with the Indian Ocean, and the Indian Ocean with strategic
access to the oil-producing states of the Persian Gulf. These linkages must
be regarded with some skepticism. Diego Garcia is already 2000 miles away from
most of the oil-producing states, and any South African base is so far away
from that the only quick strike capability would have to come from a sea-launched
nuclear missile--not the best way of assuring a continued oil flow. Southern
African bases are simply irrelevant to the protection or intimidation of the
Gult states. The Cape shipping route is another matter, but again one must

look carefully at what the issues are. There are over 1000 miles of open water south of the Cape of Good Hope; while Antarctic gales increase the hazards of passage far off shore, hostile submarines would still have to be deployed in massive numbers in order to interdict passage of oil. Their activities could, of course, raise the cost of such shipment, particularly to Europe, but serious harassment would quickly be regarded as a casus belli by the afflicted nations, thereby transforming the conflict into one which would probably be fought elsewhere. If the Soviet Union were seriously going to interdict shipping from the Persian Gulf, it would do so at the Strait of Hormuz, reachable by airplanes based in the Soviet Union itself, or by ships operating some 6000 miles away from the Cape of Good Hope.

The final strategic concern that affects policy toward southern Africa is that involving the balance of influence between East and West in the southern African states themselves. This is primarily a political issue, but it has two separate military elements. The first of these, much heralded since the 1975 visit of the American congressmen to Somalia, is the threat that the Soviet Union will actually construct major military bases in the southern African area which would be used to augment Soviet strategic military power in opposition to that of the United States. The evidence seems very slight that the Soviets want such bases, even slighter than any countries in the area are prepared to give them such facilities, and slighter yet that such bases would serve any substantial military purpose, except possibly to increase the bureaucratic weight of the Navy within the Soviet military establishment. The existing Soviet military bases in Africa, in Conakry and Berbera are much further north where they bear some relation to European, Mediterranean, and Arabian sea interests, and in any case are smallscale service stations, in no way comparable to American bases like Rota, Subic Bay, or Yokosuka, or even potentially Diego Garcia.[21] One can hardly claim that the Conakry base has in any way interfered

with major American interests in Guinea, which have been confined to making
sure that Olin Mathiessen and Harvey Aluminum continue to enjoy profitable
access to Guinean bauxite. Given the games the two countries have been playing
in the Indian Ocean, it would seem that the best way of dissuading the Soviets
from wanting to establish any sort of military base in southern Africa is for
the United States to make it clear that it is not going to try to beat them to
the punch.

The second military aspect is, of course, the use of American military force,
through showing the flag and less subtle forms of gunboat diplomacy, to affect
the political course of the independent nations of southern Africa. The so-called
Nixon Doctrine of 1969 envisages the promotion of what it calls "orderly change"
through the combination of military support for "responsible" local powers, and
the coercive offshore influence of the U. S. Navy and the Marines. The political
background for this doctrine's application in southern Africa was laid in the
famous "option II" of the 1969 National Security Council study NSSM 39, which
advocated a "tilt" toward the white regimes.[22] The objections to the Nixon
Doctrine, particularly as it might be applied in southern Africa where the
definition of "responsible powers" is subject to varying interpretation, go beyond the subject of this article. Suffice it to say that simple political means
appear to be far and away more cost-effective than any major military presence in
the area, and that "disorderly" change in the area is likely to be of far greater concern to the Republic of South Africa than to the United States of America.

UNDERSTANDING THE POLITICAL DIMENTIONS

An influential study published in 1969 by the Council on Foreign Relations
began its discussion of American policy toward Africa thus: "Through most of
American history . . . Africa essentially did not exist as an independent concern
of foreign policy . . . Militarily, economically, and politically, Africa in
American governmental policy was only an adjunct to relationships with Europe."[23]

Despite sporadic flurries of interest during the Kennedy and Johnson years, one must conclude that this historic pattern has remained dominant, particularly in the political domain. American policy in southern Africa in particular has proceeded in the absence of any accepted political analysis of southern African issues on their own merits or as they directly relate to American political interests independent of its involvements with the rest of the world. When such analyses have been prepared, as by the Department of State's African Bureau and occasionally by the Central Intelligence Agency, they have been neglected by the secretary of state and the White House, and their future production has been discouraged. Congressional leaders concerned with Africa, such as Congressman Diggs and Senator Clark, have encouraged more independent analysis, but their public and intragovernmental impact has been largely confined to the already committed.

Without such a generally accepted political analysis, American leaders have reacted to southern African events in three different ways: by ideological projection, by denial of political reality, and by treating Africa as an adjunct of more pressing relationships. Consistent with the Russett-Hanson findings, they have reacted overwhelmingly by projecting their domestic political ideology onto Africa. A comparison of Senate voting on four southern African issues between 1971 and 1975 with an index of the conservatism of their overall voting records demonstrates this projection. Of the ninety-two senators for whom sufficient information could be obtained, sixty-one are given scores by the Americans for Constitutional Action (ACA) lying either between 0 and 20 (very liberal) or 80 and 100 (very conservative).[24] The scores are based on their 1974 votes on nineteen issues (none of them dealing with Africa) selected by the ACA as a test of true conservatism/liberalism. The direction of their voting on the southern African issues can be preducted accurately for all but two senators (both known mavericks) on the sole basis of degree of conservatism/

liberalism of their ideology as revealed in their votes. Nor is their degree
of conservatism merely a reflection of their states' corporate interests: if
one looks at the pairs of senators from those eight states in which the two
differ by more than 50 points on their ACA rating, the votes split in the predicted direction in fourteen of the sixteen cases. (Interestingly, the two
deviants were the more conservative senators from states containing corporations
with substantial investments in South Africa who nevertheless voted on the
liberal side of the southern African issues.) Recent presidents have tended
politically to treat Africa, if they treated it at all, as an area for vague
symbolization of an ideological or domestic policy position. Thus, John
Kennedy made his very first appointment that of the ebulliently liberal Soapy
Williams as assistant secretary of state for Africa. Lyndon Johnson halted
American naval visits to Simonstown after black sailors were denied permission
to go ashore, at the time when he was preoccupied with programs for racial
equality at home. And Richard Nixon's "southern strategy" could be beautifully
symbolized by his barely concealed support for the Byrd amendment and "tilt"
toward white rule displayed in option II of NSSM 39. Nor do the majority of
concerned constituents seem to behave much differently. The greatest volume
of congressional mail on a southern African issue has been generated by groups
opposing the repeal of the Byrd amendment. A very high percentage of these
letters also include paragraphs on other authentic conservative causes,
particularly the retention of the House Un-American Activities Committee and
rejection of domestic gun control legislation.[25]

In typical American fashion, this political ideological dimension is
scarcely articulated. Irrespective of ideology, American display a peculiar
tendency to play down long-range political and ideological issues and to prefer
to talk in economic and military terms, as if they were somehow more real,
hardheaded, and practical. In debates over the southern African policy this tendency

has often concealed America's own interests and covered up the premises on which much of its policy has been based. This was most startlingly apparent during the Nixon years when the State Department repeatedly articulated the formal fiction that African leaders' overwhelming interest in economic development relegated their concern with political issues like liberation of still-dependent territories and racial justice to peripheral status. In effect, this represented a wishful projection of official American thinking onto the African themselves. In November 1974 the then assistant secretary of state for African affairs, Donald Easum, publicly broke with this position by reporting after a southern African tour that "two major issues dominated the thoughts of my hosts. They concerned, first of all, human dignity and racial equality in southern African—and secondly, decolonization and national self-determination."[26] The speech was his swan song, as he was soon replaced in that post by the former ambassador to Chile, an appointment explained as part of Henry Kissinger's campaign to break up State Department area fiefs and to promote a more global political perspective within the department.

For Kissinger the global perspective has meant a subordination of African policy to considerations of America's more pressing relations with the Soviet Union and China, with the Western alliance, and with such priority concerns as the Middle East, Latin America, and residues of involvement in Asia. Ambassadors to Africa complain they they receive detailed instruction from Washington on what to say about the Panama Canal, Palestinian refugees, or democracy in South Korea, but very little about the issues that directly interest the governments to which they are accredited. The costs of such subordination of Africa's own concerns became abudnantly apparent in the Angolan war when the secretary of state refused to listen to his own African Bureau's recommendations and reacted entirely as if the issue were a U. S.-USSR confrontation.[27] Consistent with the Nixon doctrine, he backed South African intervention and thereby provided the ultimate justification in most African eyes for the introduction of Cuban troops. Nor did congressional opponents of Kissinger's Angolan policies come to grips with the African dimension of the war. The Congress earned itself Gerald Ford's description of "weak-kneed" not by challenging the political premises of policy, but by invoking symbols of congressional privilege, CIA dirty tricks, and American boys dying in Vietnam.

True to his supremely political nature, Kissinger developed his policy in disregard of the most prominent American economic interest in Angola, that of Gulf Oil. Here was a situation in which a major American multinational firm was pumping 144,000 barrels of oil a day from Cabinda and paying taxes and royalities to the government bank in Luanda. From all reports the relations between Gulf and the Soviet and Cuban-backed Movimento Popular de Liberacao (MPLA) were cordial, and Gulf's payments substantially exceeded the amount of money that the United States government was covertly funneling into the MPLA's opponents, the Frente Nacional de Liberação de Angola (FNLA) and the União para la Independência Total de Angola (UNITA). Through direct State Department pressure, Gulf was obliged to suspend operations and to pay its royalties and taxes into a special escrow account. These funds were eventually turned over to the Angolan government and operations resumed, at about one-third the previous level, only after the MPLA's victory was recognized by the world community. In the meantime Angola's MPLA leaders bitterly attacked the State Department as well as Gulf for acceding to the department's pressures, while praising the more cooperative attitudes of other multinational corporations.[28]

CONCLUSION

With no significant domestic constituency and little public concern or understanding, southern Africa is, in political terms, something of a "free-play area" for American political leaders. Most have reacted passively, as

we have seen, in terms of their domestic political ideology. The few who
have become more directly involved have in general received neither reprisals
nor rewards from their constituents. Kissinger eventually sought to capitalize
on this free-play characteristic by sharply reversing the "tilt" in his southern
African policy in his Lusaka speech of of April 27, 1976, and then following
up with his shuttle diplomacy on the Rhodesian issue. Characteristically,
Ronald Reagan's attempt in the 1976 primary elections to capitalize on Kissinger's
reversal evoked little voter interest in comparison to his jingoistic statements
on the Panama Canal, and neither Gerald Ford nor Jimmy Carter was able to turn
discussion of southern African policy to his advantage in their televised debate on foreign policy.

In light of the above, one may conclude that within very broad limits,
America's vital economic and strategic interest set few serious constraints on
the development of policy toward southern Africa. In the absence of such constraints and of general public awareness, overall policy is most likely to be
defined broadly (and somewhat irrelevantly) by the symbolic extension of domestic political ideology with the occasional interjection of considerations derived
from concerns with the international balance of power between the United States
and the Soviet Union. So long as no leader proposes anything approximating
direct American military involvement and massive foreign aid expenditures, public opinion is unlikely to react directly to a policy initiative one way or the
other. As with most international issues, southern Africa offers the ambitious
politician few rewards in the form of votes, and few deprivations either.[29]

Nevertheless, any American administration inclined to accept the view presented above that the most prudent and cost-effective policy to protect American
economic and strategic interests would be to work with, rather than against,
the indigenous African forces of change, should find such a policy politically
possible to implement. While it is beyond the scope of this article to lay out

the details, the following general principles ought to underly such a policy.

In the United States, any redirection of policy ought to be carried out with a minimum of fanfare. With little short-term political advantage to be gained, an administration should avoid the sort of rhetorical excess that invites opposition to mobilize on partisan or ideological lines. It is quite possible to carry out major policy initiatives without the drama of a secretary of state publicly flying between secret meetings and inviting reactions to his person and style, as much as to his policy.

In Africa, American policy should express a broad commitment to full political participation for all African populations, but beyond that eschew attempts to dictate specific outcomes. On the one hand this should permit the United States to avoid identification with any specific contending liberation group, as happened with such cost in Angola. Except at great expense, the United States has few direct means of control over outcomes where black groups oppose one another, and cannot hope to compete with the Soviet Union in terms of credit for past support. By a public and private willingness to cooperate with a variety of groups, the United States offers the eventual winner maximum opportunity to avoid dependence on Soviet support. As Kissinger came to appreciate, the "frontline presidents" (of Angola, Botswana, Mozambique, Tanzania, and Zambia) are the natural group through which to coordinate relations with liberation groups. On the other hand, this same broad commitment includes acceptance of the continued presence of white communities, particularly in South Africa.[30]

Those in Africa and in the United States who would support such a redirection of American policy over the long run might usefully concentrate their efforts on building a greater American understanding of African political issues in terms appropriate to the situation, so that public debate can be carried on in something other than cold-war rhetoric leavened with an occasional injunction

about the necessity of preventing a "racial bloodbath." It would also make
tactical sense to pay some attention to national elections. South Africa's
lobbyists have long understood that the best practical way to affect the overall "tilt" of American policy in southern Africa is to affect the balance in
the American government between conservative racists and liberal integration-
ists, irrespective of their interests in southern African questions per se.[31]
Their wisdom is borne out in the analysis of congressional voting presented
above. Finally, it is advisable, for practical as well as analytic purposes
to avoid blanket attacks on bogeymen like the "military-industrial complex."
However, soul-satisfying, such attacks not only miss the target, they miss
the opportunity to pick up tactically useful allies, including part of the
American business community as well as important segments of the military and
foreign policy bureaucracies. For once, progressive critics might find it
nice to have a Gulf Oil on their side.

FOOTNOTES

1. Trade figures given are from International Monetary Fund. Direction of Trade: Annual 1970-74 (Washington, D.C., 1975). A convenient summary is in Marches Tropicaux (November 21, 1975), 3363-3364. Useful discussions include Donald McHenry, United States Firms in South Africa (Bloomington, Ind., 1975) and Timothy H. Smith, The American Corporation in South Africa (New York, 1970).

2. One can also argue the converse: to the degree than American economic ties produce foreign policy compliance from America's partners, Nigeria should increasingly have aligned its foreign policies on those of the United States. One can, of course, construct much more complex variants of these propositions by introducing time-lag effects and policy-arena distinctions, but neither generalization looks like a promising statement about a major influence on anybody's foreign policy.

3. McHenry, United States Firms.

4. Both public and private statements by corporate officers tend to overstate the importance of southern African operations. Public statements usually proceed from an understandable premise of "don't yield an inch or they'll take a yard." Private statements usually are obtained from those corporate officers most directly involved in southern African operations. For those individuals' careers, maintaining the southern African connection may indeed be crucial. Members of large private bureaucracies are no less likely than their public counterparts to confuse the success of their own work group with that of the organization as a whole.

5. Several of the largest firms have interests in both Nigeria and South Africa, and others would clearly like to join the list. See Jean Herskovits, "An Overview of American and African Policies in Regard to Southern Africa," Issue: A Quarterly Journal of Africanist Opinion, 5, no. 3 (Fall, 1975), 58.

6. See the articles by Bruce J. Oudes, "Clark MacGregor's Vacation: 'Different' Might Be an Understatement," Africa Report, 18, no. 1 (January-February 1973) and "Nigeria, Humphrey, and the Chrome Caper," ibid., no. 2 (March-April 1973).

7. Bruce M. Russett and Elizabeth C. Hanson, Interest and Ideology: The Foreign Policy Beliefs of American Businessman (San Francisco, 1975). See also Raymond A. Bauer, Ithiel de Sola Pool, and Anthony Dexter, American Business and Public Policy (New York, 1963).

8. Russett and Hanson, Interest and Ideology, pp. 95-96.

9. Ibid., pp. 122-123.

10. Ibid., p. 249.

11. In addition to the extensive congressional testimony, see "Southern Rhodesia: The Question of Economic Sanctions," Current Foreign Policy,

Department of State Publication 8744, African Series 55 (December, 1973), and Edgar Lockwood, "An Inside Look at the Sanctions Campaign," Issue: A Quarterly Journal of Africanist Opinion, 4, no. 3 (Fall 1974) 73-75.

12. C. F. De Villiers, F. R. Metrowich, and J. A. Du Plessis, The Communist Strategy (Pretoria, South Africa, 1975). Patrick Wall (ed.), The Indian Ocean and the Threat to the West: Four Studies in Global Strategy (London, 1975).

13. The Gallup Opinion Index, no. 126 (January 1976) and Gallup Poll news release, January 18. 1976.

14. Paul A. Laudicina, World Poverty and Development: A Survey of American Opinion (Washington, D.C., 1973), p. 39.

15. Ibid., p. 42. For some roughly comparably 1975 attitudes toward United States military aid, see "U. S. Commitments Should REmain Unchanged in Post-Vietnam Era," The Gallup Opinion Index, no. 121 (July 1975), 14-29.

16. Russett and Hanson, Interest and Ideology, p. 71.

17. The writings on Indian Ocean strategic questions are voluminous. In addition to the indespensable hardware discussion in Jane's Weapon Systems in 1976 (London, 1976), a neophyte should see J. Bowyer Bell, "Strategic Implications of the Soviet Presence in Somalia," Orbis, 19 no. 2 (Summer 1975); A. J. Cottrell and R. M. Burrell, "The Soviet Navy and the Indian Ocean" Strategic Review, 2, no. 4 (Fall 1974); David Johnson, "Troubled Waters for the U. S. Navy," Africa Report, 20, no. 1 (January-February 1975); and Michael T. Klare, "Superpower Rivalry at Sea," Foreign Policy, 21 (Winter 1975-1976).

18. The U. S. Navy has paid much public attention to Admiral Gorshkov's ideas, including the translation, annotation, publication, and dissemination of a volume of his collected writings. Sergei G. Gorshkov, Red Star Rising at Sea (Annapolis, Md., 1974). One wonders if the Soviet Navy has been equally assiduous in spreading the thought of Admiral Zumwalt.

19. See U. S. House of Representatives, Hearings before the Sub-Committee on the Near East and South Asia of the Committee on Foreign Affairs, 83rd Congress, 2d sess., Proposed Expantion of U. S. Military Facilities in the Indian Ocean (Washington, D.C., 1974). The testimonies of Earl C. Ravenel, and Admirals Gene R. La Rocque and Elmo R. Zumwalt, Jr., are particularly relevant.

20. A concise discussion of such antisubmarine warfare considerations can be found in Geoffrey Kemp, Nuclear Forces for Medium Powers; Part II and III: Strategic Requirements and Options. Adelphi Papers, no. 107 (London, 1974), pp. 7-8.

21. Klare, "Superpower Rivalry at Sea."

22. The leaked text of NSSM 39 has been published as The Kissinger Study of Southern Africa, edited and introduced by Mohamed A. El-Khawas and

Barry Cohen, preface by Edgar Lockwood (Westport, Conn., 1976). The authenticity of the text is not seriously disputed.

23. Waldemar A. Nielsen, The Great Powers and Africa (New York, 1969), p. 245.

24. The African votes are reported by the Washington Office on Africa, "Congressional Voting Record on Southern African Issues," Washington, D.C., May 1976. A fifth vote, that on the Mansield resolution to prohibit the expansion of the Diego Garcia base, was not included as it seemed less clearly a southern African issue than the others. The ACA ratings are from Congressional Quarterly Weekly Report, 33 (February 22, 1975), 387-389. No votes in the ACA scale concern any African issue.

25. Personal communication, Albert Cover, University of Michigan.

26. Donald B. Easum, "Lusaka Manifesto Revisited," Patterson School of Diplomacy and International Commerce, University of Kentucky, November 26, 1974 (mimeo).

27. See, in particular, Kissinger's press conference remarks on Angola, December 23, 1975.

28. As Robert Keohane has pointed out in "Not 'Innocents Abroad': American Multinational Corporations and the United States Government." Comparative Politics, 8, no. 2 (January 1976), 307-320, political manipulation of American nultinational corporations, particularly the oil companies, by the U. S. government has been a recurrent feature of American policy in areas of the world where major political interests are deemed to be at stake. While in the long run the government may well find some way of sweetening Gulf's disappointment, we must not loose sight of the fact that the decision to halt production was imposed by State's Kissinger, not by the MPLA's Neto or Gulf's Dorsey.

29. David R. Mayhew, Congress the Electoral Connection (New Haven, Conn., 1974), especially the discussion of particularization of benefits and symbolization, pp. 122-138. Personal communication from some of those few politicians actively interested in African matters confirms the specific applicability of the generalization to Africa.

30. It should be noted that the 1969 Lusaka Manifesto on Southern Africa, in which thirteen chiefs of state of East and Central Africa laid out their rationale and strategy for ending white rule in southern Africa has publicly questioned the principle. Paragraph eight of the Manifesto begins: "Our stand towards Southern Africa thus involves a rejection of racialism, not a reversal of the existing racial domination. We believe that all the peoples who have made their homes in the countries of Southern Africa are Africans, regardless of the colour of their skins; and we would oppose a racialist majority government which adopted a philosophy of deliberate and permanent discrimination between its citizens on grounds of racial origin."
   The complete text of the manifesto may be found a Appendix Two in Kenneth Grundy, Confrontation and Accommodation in Southern Africa (Berkeley, Calif., 1973).

31. See, for example, "U.S. Democrats and R.S.A.," South Africa Foundation News, 2, no. 8 (August 1976).

CHAPTER VII

US POLICY TOWARD SOUTH AFRICA: A DISSENTING VIEW

BY HUNT DAVIS, JR.

This chapter is being written during the first anniversary week of the
Soweto insurrection. In Johannesburg three Africans have gunned down two
whites and seriously wounded a third; demonstrations in Soweto have led to
the death of one youth, eleven others being wounded by police gunfire; several
instances of sabotage of railway lines have occurred; police action in Uitenhage
has resulted in the death of seven Africans. This tragic procession of events
sheds a lurid light on the gravity of the situation existing in South Africa
today. As has been repeatedly emphasized, "Southern Africa is an area of
struggle and conflict"[1]; "the revolutionary situation in South Africa is
daily building toward a massive, country-wide crisis."[2] Because Soweto is
really a microcosm of the larger South African society, it provides a useful
reference point for an understanding of the building crisis in South Africa.
It also serves as a convenient starting point for a critical assessment of
the argument set forth by William Foltz in the previous chapter.

Soweto is a large sprawling urban African township on the outskirts of
Johannesburg with a population of more than a million people. Its very
existence says much about the African condition in South Africa and the future
that apartheid holds for blacks. Despite its size Soweto is not a city--in
fact, it came into being when the government forced Africans out of the city.
It lacks the structure and amenities of a city. It is one vast dormitory
designed to meet white urban and industrial needs. Soweto's inhabitants lack
any citizenship rights in the area they occupy, and even their right to reside

in the township is extremely tenuous. One gets to the heart of apartheid
in Soweto--the purpose of the black is to serve the white. Yet, Soweto in-
forms us about more than apartheid. Africans are a fully integrated although
heavily exploited part of the South African economy. While many will continue to live in the rural areas, even if the migrant labor system is dismantled,
the African future is primarily an urban one. Theirs is an industrial society.
The Vorster government seeks to obscure the increasingly urban and industrial
proletarian character of the African population through the fiction of separate
development and the bantustans, but those who count most in this matter, the
Africans, have seen through this fiction.

African rejection of separate development underlay last year's uprisings
that Soweto has come to symbolize. There has been a long history of African
resistance to white domination, so that the events of the last year came as
no surprise to those who have an understanding of the South African past.
Nor did the violence with which the South African government sought to suppress
the uprisings come as a surprise, for twentieth century South African history
is replete with examples of the use of overt force to keep the African populace
in line. Yet, there was also something new about the situation in 1976. For
one thing, Africans living in South Africa could point to the recent success
of the liberation movements on their borders to instill new vigor in their
struggle for their own liberation. Secondly, the list of African grievances
had grown too long for the government to crush the rebellion against its
authority in a single concerted effort as had been the case in 1960 with the
Sharpeville massacre and the declaration of a state of emergency.[3] Finally,
South Africa is no longer able to escape the world's attention as it was able
to do even as recently as 1960. The long years of the Africans' struggle for
their own liberation has forced the world community to make South Africa its

business. For the Africans, it has been "no easy walk to freedom,"[4] but
their insistence on setting out on that walk has brought them closer to
their objective. The situation that exists in South Africa today, symbolized
by Soweto, provides compelling reasons for the United States to take a
fresh start in its policy toward southern Africa.

Reduced to its simplest expression, the central argument which Foltz
develops is that U.S. policy makers are essentially free of serious economic
and strategic constraints when it comes to southern Africa. He views the
area as something of a "free-play area for American political leaders." If
so, according to Foltz, "the most prudent and cost-effective policy to protect
American economic and strategic interests would be to work with, rather than
against, the indigenous African forces of change."

While I find myself generally in agreement with this last proposition,
the premise from which it stems needs re-examination. For one thing, the
manner in which previous administrations have perceived our interests in
southern Africa suggests that they must have been substantially at variance
with the way in which Foltz assesses such interests. If for no other reason
our previous policies cannot be left out of the accounting. They have in fact
created a set of political constraints which, however unwarranted, continue
to cast serious discredit upon our image and generate suspicions about our
foreign policy objectives in the minds of African nationalists and other anti-
apartheid elements. Further, the question arises as to whether our economic
and strategic interests are really as marginal as Foltz would lead us to
believe. Here again the constraints on our policy-makers may not be as benign
as one might imagine. Presently, the United States stands accused of complicity in apartheid. The situation calls for the U.S., in its own best
interests as well as those of the people of South Africa, to abandon its

support of the <u>status quo</u> and to utilize whatever leverage it possesses
to help resolve the South African conflict in favor of the Africans.

These, at any rate, are the key arguments contained in this chapter.
A brief summary of previous U.S. policies will show the extent to which
official preceptions of our interests in South Africa have tended to disprove the view that the U.S. lacks definite vital interests in the area.
We shall then turn to a more detailed examination of the character and
significance of American economic and strategic interests in South Africa.
Finally we shall attempt to indicate in general terms what the implications
are from the standpoint of our future policies toward South Africa.

U.S. Southern African Policy in the 1960s and 1970s

The Nixon administration initiated a significant shift in U.S. foreign
policy toward South Africa--a backward shift. Outwardly, there appeared to
be a continuity with the policy of the Kennedy and Johnson administrations.
The U.S. continued to maintain a posture of public opposition to colonialism
and apartheid in southern Africa, and policy-makers generally adhered to the
familiar low-profile approach to African issues. However, the southern
Africa policy review initiated by National Security Study Memorandum 39 (NSSM
39) in 1969 ended in a decision to "relax political isolation and economic
restrictions on the white states" of southern Africa. The stated purpose for
this change was to increase communication with the white minority governments
in order to convince them ultimately to alter their internal policies toward
blacks. The underlying premise now appears to have been extremely myopic:

> The whites are here to stay and the only way that constructive change
> can come about is through them. There is no hope for the blacks to gain
> the political rights they seek through violence, which will only lead to

chaos and increased opportunities for the communists. We can, by selective relaxation of our stance toward the white regimes, encourage some modification of their current racial and colonial policies and through more substantial economic assistance to the black states (a total of about $5 million annually in technical assistance to the black states) help to draw the two groups together and exert some influence on both for peaceful change. Our tangible interests form a basis for our contacts in the region, and these can be maintained at and acceptable political cost.[5]

Clearly, then, the United States had tilted toward the white minority governments in a manner that meant an acceptance of and accomodation with the status quo in the region on the vague notion that peaceful change would take place as a result. As Sean Gervasi has noted, those who have advocated this theory of peaceful change (which in actuality amounts to only a set of slogans) "seem to be lost in a wilderness of confusion, vagueness, and wishful thinking." What lay behind the advocacy of peaceful change was a political campaign, in concert with other western powers, to shore up the white governments of southern Africa by convincing the world at large that evolutionary change was both possible and far preferable to the supposed chaos that would stem from success on the part of the liberation movements.[6] In short, the American government was seeking to undercut the liberation movements because it believed that American interests were best served by white minority rule in southern Africa.

Leading Department of State officials denied that any tilt had taken place in U.S. policy toward the white regimes of southern Africa, even after NSSM 39 had been made public.[7] Such disavowals, however, have a hollow ring, especially when contrasted with statements such as the one by Goler Butcher that the relevations of NSSM 39 "showed little that the watchers of U.S. policy were not aware of; namely, that since 1969, U.S. policy--whatever the verbal pronounce-ments on abhorrence of apartheid and support of majority rule may have been--U.S. policy has been supportive of the status quo."[8] The evidence supports the position of Butcher and other leading advocates of the anti-apartheid cause.

A few examples will suffice to illustrate this point.

One of the proposals of Option 2 (the option which was adopted) of the NSSM 39 -generated study was that the United States continue to enforce its arms embargo against South Africa. However, there should be a "liberal treatment of equipment which could serve either military or civilian purposes." Subsequently, in February 1970, the U.S. government authorized the sale of ten Lockheed "Hercules" C-130 transport aircraft to a South African charter air firm. Later Department of State reports showed that the firm had contracted out the planes to the South African military. The sale of Cessna and Piper light planes similarly helped South Africa to upgrade its military capabilities through the development of air commando units composed of volunteers who use their own planes.

Another "Option 2 suggestion" was that the U.S. expand Export-Import Bank facilities for South Africa, actively encourage exports to South Africa, and facilitate American investment in that country. In January 1972, the Bank guaranteed a ten-year loan to South Africa amounting to $48.6 million dollars for the purchase of diesel locomotives. This action constituted a reversal of a policy established in 1964 to limit Ex-Im Bank loans to South Africa to a maximum term of five years. There was also a recommendation in Option 2 that the U.S. conduct selected exchange programs with the South African military. The visit of South African Admiral Bierman to the United States in May 1974 to hold meetings with Joint Chiefs of Staff Chairman Admiral Thomas H. Moorer and other top military and civilian officials provided highly visible evidence that the administration was implementing yet another Option 2 recommendation. Concrete examples of a similar tilt toward the other white minority regimes of southern Africa are also available.[9] The conclusion that one reaches from an examination of NSSM 39 is that the United States was pursuing a policy, whatever

its public posture to the contrary, to use South Africa as its "proxy" in
southern and central Africa.

The Portuguese coup of April 25, 1974 reduced to nought the tenets which
had served as the basis for policy in southern Africa since 1969. It could no
longer be argued that the whites were in southern Africa to stay and that
Africans could not gain political rights through the liberation movements.
Yet, the United States was seemingly very slow to realize that the coup had
triggered a series of events which undercut its policy in southern Africa.
Indeed, the failure of Secretary of State Kissinger and other American policy-
makers to come seriously to grips with the reality of southern Africa--that
it is an area of struggle and conflict--helped lead the Ford administration
into its disastrous Angolan venture. Not until April 1976, did the United
States begin to "correct" its posture toward southern Africa. In Lusaka
(Zambia) Kissinger promised a vigorous American policy toward southern Africa
which would assist in bringing negotiated settlements to both the Rhodesian
and Namibian situations. There was a notable vagueness in the whole speech about
South Africa.[10] The reason for the vagueness soon became clear. Two months
later the Secretary of State was in West Germany to meet with Prime Minister
John Vorster for the purpose of enlisting his aid in working toward a "constructive settlement" in Rhodesia. In the words of the Secretary, "South
Africa must demonstrate its commitment to Africa by assisting a negotiated outcome."[11] Kissinger followed up his June meeting with Vorster with a trip to
South Africa in September.

Upon closer inspection, the new policy initiatives of 1976 appear to be
based on continued acceptance of the basic premises of Option 2. True, they
no longer applied to Angola and Mozambique, but policy toward Rhodesia, Namibia,
and South Africa seemed to accept the premises as still viable. What had

changed was the general posture. Take, for example, the assertion that
"the whites are here to stay and the only way that constructive change can
come about is through them." Secretary Kissinger's August 2, 1976 speech
to the National Urban League in Boston called on Rhodesian whites to recognize
the inevitable and to negotiate a settlement with Africans while there was
still time to protect their basic interests. Such a negotiated outcome would
avoid the chaos and foreign (i.e., communist) intervention that would supposed-
ly result from a Zimbabwe brought into being through a successful war of
liberation. South Africa was to assist in the process by putting pressure on
the Smith regime. The front-line African states were to do the same with the
African nationalist movements. There was also to be an internationally-financed
economic stabilazation fund that would be available to the Zimbabwe government,
if it came to power through negotiation. All of this was designed to bring
about a transition from a white-ruled Rhodesia to a Zimbabwe under a "moderate"
black government and with an economy that remained basically unaltered. In
the Secretary's own words, "What we seek is . . . negotiated settlement that
assures the rights of all Rhodesians, black and white; preserves the economic
strength of the country, and removes the opportunity for foreign intervention."
If all went well, Rhodesia would become another Kenya. When it came to South
Africa, there was even less of a departure from previous policy. An African
government for Zimbabwe and an independent Namibia were immediate goals of the
"new" U.S. southern African policy, but these very goals were designed to
strengthen the white position in South Africa. The policy he was molding also
did not challenge the right of whites to continue ruling South Africa for the
indefinite future, for it contained no demands for any concrete steps toward
majority rule. What was requested of South Africa was that it "recognize that
the wind of change is again blowing through Africa," that it end its increasing

isolation from the rest of the continent (here Kissinger sounded like an
advocate of South Africa's "outward policy"), and that it "demonstrate its
commitment to Africa by making a positive contribution to the humane evolution
of the continent."[12]

The Portuguese coup changed the conditions under which U.S. foreign policy
operated in southern Africa, but it did not produce much more than surface
changes in that policy. Even here, what changes eventually emerged came after
a two-year interval. What was principally new about American policy was that
the United States dropped its low-profile approach toward southern Africa as
its Secretary of State took his highly personal brand of shuttle diplomacy to
Africa. The level of international intervention in the affairs of the region
had finally forced the United States to intervene directly in a public manner
(as opposed to the sub rosa intervention implicit in NSSM 39). One way to
interpret the intervention and calls for international cooperation in the
Rhodesian and Namibian situations, however, is to see it as yet another way
to shield South Africa. To be sure, white South Africa was nudged a little
harder and a little more publicly in the direction of "peaceful change" than
before. The U.S. also refused to recognize the Transkei (thought it also
abstained on the U.N. General Assembly resolution on the Transkei, being the
only country to do so). Yet, the Vorster government could take comfort in
American policy. It remained predicated on the concept of constructive change,
which excluded the liberation movements and their backers in the international
community and which essentially left it up to South Africa's Nationalist regime to determine what constituted change and at what pace it should proceed.
South Africa indeed had a friend in Henry Kissinger.[13] This was the policy
which the Carter administration inherited in January, 1977. Has there been a
change in the five months since it has been in office?

President Carter and others in his administration have clearly set a
new tone for U.S. policy toward Africa, including the southern part of the
continent. Whereas in the Nixon-Ford years, the theory of peaceful change
seemed little more than an excuse for accomodation with the white minority
regimes, we see in the Carter policy "a new attitude, a sincere affirmation
of principles given lip service in the past."[14] Examples of this new attitude
abound. For instance, the present administration has jettisoned any notion of
a low-profile approach to South Africa and its neighbors in favor of making
Africa a highly visible area of American foreign policy. The emphasis on human
rights combined with the appointment of Andrew Young as Ambassador to the
United Nations assured that South Africa would be in the foreign policy spot-
light. The administration moved quickly and decisively to secure the repeal
of the Byrd Amendment and place the U.S. back in compliance with U.N. sanctions
on Rhodesia. Furthermore, the President has called for majority rule not only
in Rhodesia and Namibia but in South Africa as well. Vice-President Mondale
reiterated this message in his May meeting with Prime Minister Vorster. In
this sense, then, Carter has moved well beyond his two predecessors, who had
always stopped short of demanding majority rule in South Africa itself. One
can therefore conclude that there is a new direction in U.S. policy in terms
of placing real pressure on the white redoubts of southern Africa. In fact,
Vorster is already predicting a worsening of relations with the United States,
and within the U.S., individuals as diverse as Ronald Regan and Charles Percy
are beginning to rise to the defense of South Africa.[15]

The recent departures in American foreign policy constitute welcome news
for the anti-apartheid forces. But the question must be raised as to whether
the Carter policy pronouncements simply add up to a new tone, leaving intact
the substance of previous policy.[16] Option 2 of the NSSM 39 study has become

"inoperable", but a basic element of that policy--opposition to the liberation
movements and a search for moderate solutions in southern Africa--seems to in-
fuse the Carter policy. A case in point is a speech by Assistant Secretary
for African Affairs William E. Schaufele, Jr. before the American Academy of
Political and Social Science, April 16, 1977, in Philadelphia.[17] The central
theme of the speech was the necessity of peaceful transition to majority rule in
Rhodesia and Namibia on the assertions that both countries possessed viable
economic structures capable of sustained economic growth under independence
if they were not destroyed by prolonged strife; that the contending parties
were equal enough in strength that "untold human suffering and misery" would
result from a protracted armed struggle; that wars of liberation would lead to
intervention of non-African forces (i.e., communists); that peaceful solutions
in Namibia and Rhodesia would be conducive to orderly change in South Africa.
Peaceful change is even more vital for South Africa, "if only because the
alternative is so unacceptable." South Africa should solve its own problems,
and there have been encouraging signs that many whites have begun to rethink
the basic tenets of apartheid. Schaufele thus pinned his hopes for change on
pressures generated from within the white oligarchy. Intervention in South
Africa from the outside and internal pressure from African liberation forces
will only serve to drive whites into the laager and thus undercut the chances
for change in the foreseeable future.

A closer look at Schaufele's arguments shows that, as in the Kissinger
era, no fundamental change is envisioned in southern Africa, for such change
in effect would presuppose the acceptance of a radical redistribution of power
and wealth. By asserting that the transition to majority rule should take place
within the existing Namibian, Rhodesian, and South African economic structures,

Schaufele implicitly suggests that effective economic and political power should remain in the hands of the settler minority and their external economic allies. Under the Schaufele formula Africans in South Africa must be discouraged from seeking political liberation through their nationalist movements. Attempts at "internal solutions" in Rhodesia and Namibia are unacceptable to Schaufele, but they seem to represent the proper course for South Africa. To the extent that Africans are to have a voice, it is through leaders such as Gathsha Buthelezi. While not a stooge of the Vorster government, Buthelezi's position of leadership is clearly a direct result of Nationalist bantustan policy. Mostly, however, it is to be the whites who through a process of soul searching, reexamination, and so forth will bring about change. If this is to be the case, chances are that there will be only superficial changes. The South African situation is in "a condition of such structural rigidity that structural change appears to be impossible of internal generation."[18] Finally, there is the issue of violence. The assumption seems to be that violence has only been injected into the situation by the liberation forces and their allies. Otherwise, conditions would be peaceful. Such an assumption constitutes a very serious misreading of the nature of white supremacy in southern Africa.

As Secretary of State Vance's speech of July 1 to the National Association for the Advancement of Colored People once again demonstrated, the Carter administration clearly eschewes the endorsement of liberation movements committed to the principle of armed struggle. Yet, it publicly proclaims its commitment to change in southern Africa.[19] If it is to avoid the gap between rhetoric and reality that characterized the Kennedy administration's southern African policy, then it will have to back up its words with concrete actions designed to promote significant change in southern Africa. Furthermore, it must do so in the recognition that a revolutionary situation exists in the southern part of the continent. As Colin and Margaret Legum pointed out it will not be possible for the West to prevent intervention by outside forces into the affairs of southern Africa. The choice confronting the United States and other western powers is either to insure that external intervention takes place in an orderly manner or to face a chaotic situation which will ultimately force the West to intervene directly.[20] The former pattern offers the best possibility for peaceful change and will, in fact, allow the opportunity for South Africans to solve their own problems; the latter pattern is sure to bring violence. Either way, however, it will be the liberation forces, as the voice of the African people, who will determine South Africa's future. Before discussing the specifics of a future course for U.S. policy, let us consider American corporate and strategic interests in South Africa.

U. S. Corporate and Strategic Interests in South Africa

During the years that U.S. foreign policy was "tilting" toward South Africa, there was also a tremendous increase in American investments in that country and elsewhere in the region. In addition, there was a growing emphasis on the strategic value of the area to the United States. For example, in 1974 a study on U.S. mineral dependence carried out on Presidential orders pointed out that South Africa was both a major and a dependable supplier of strategic materials. About the same time, Secretary Kissinger began to seek out support within the American financial community to provide the type of financial capital that would help insure moderate rather than radical changes in the region.[21] Yet, as William Foltz points out, the United States has neither vital economic nor vital strategic interests in southern Africa. Indeed, the NSSM 39 study contains the same conclusion. Not that American interests in South Africa are unimportant, but rather, Foltz argues, they place no significant restraints on

on American foreign policy makers. He thus comes to his conclusion that
southern Africa represents "something of a 'free-play area' for American
political leaders." Certainly, he is correct to assume that a direct American
private investment which represents slightly over one percent of all such
overseas investment does not constitute a vital interest, though he did overlook indirect investment which now totals more than direct investment. He
also quite clearly demonstrates the weakness of arguments that place heavy
emphasis on the strategic importance of the region to the United States. But,
Foltz is too quick to conclude that the lack of such vital interests makes
southern Africa an area generally free of serious foreign policy constraints.
When viewed from the perspective of South Africa, American corporate and
strategic interests along with those of the other western powers are very
substantial. It is precisely this western investment in apartheid that places
serious constraints on American policy.

Direct American private investment has grown at a steady pace since World
War II, with the most dramatic growth taking place during the early 1970s. In
1943, the American stake in South Africa was small, amounting to $50.7 million.
From this base, the book value of direct dollar investment (the actual value
was much higher) began to expand: $140 million in 1950, which more than doubled
by 1957; $353 million in 1961; $601 million in 1966; $750 million in 1970;
$1.24 billion in 1973; approximately $1.6 billion in 1976, though there are
indications that corporate investment leveled out in 1976 and may even have
declined. Significant additional sums have been invested elsewhere in southern
Africa. In recent years, the American share was slightly under one-fifth of the
total direct foreign investment in South Africa. For example, in 1972 U.S.
investment constituted 17 percent of the total of $6.828 billion invested in
the Republic of South Africa. About half of this amount came from Great Britian,

representing nearly 13 percent of the total British foreign investment (only

Australia was a larger recipient of British capital). Moreover, American

concern about Britain's economic health places another set of constraints on

our South African policy because of the potential ramifications for Great

Britain. Contributing to the American investment in South Africa are approxi-

mately 350 corporations, including nine of the ten largest corporations on the

Fortune 500 list (only tenth-ranked Western Electric was absent). The number

350 is somewhat misleading, however, for twelve corporation probably supply

70 percent of all American capital invested in South Africa, and probably no

more than 30 corporations are significant in terms of total capital invested.

The leading investor is America's largest corporation--General Motors--which

has South African assets that would place it in 11th place among the leading

100 companies, domestic and foreign, with holdings in South Africa. About 50

percent of the American corporate investment is in manufacturing, 20 percent

in petroleum, 10 percent in mining and smelting, and 20 percent in other areas.

This investment has been extremely profitable, especially in the area of mining

and smelting were the rate of return (earnings as a percentage of book value)

from 1961-1971 averaged 41.2 percent. While it was less for the principal area

of American investment, manufacturing, the rate of return still averaged 20.2

percent for the same period. In 1970, the rate of return in manufacturing was

16 percent for South Africa, compared to earnings of 9.4 percent worldwide for

American manufacturing firms.

Until recently, the principle form of American corporate involvement in

South Africa was through direct investment in the private sector. During 1976,

however, there was a quiet but dramatic shift in the nature of American economic

involvement in South Africa. The South African economic slump of 1976, growing

pressures for increasing black pay, and the political uncertainties stemming

from the urban and student revolt have combined to produce a leveling off
of corporate investment. Chrysler Corporation has negotiated the sale of
the greater share of its estimated $35 million in assets to the Anglo-American
Corporation, and General Motors, with $125 million in South African assets,
has announced that it will undertake no new expansion. American banks, however, led by Citibank, Chase Manhatten, Manufacturers Hanover Trust, and
Morgan Guaranty, have taken an opposite tack. In 1976 alone, American indirect
investment in the form of bank loans amounted to $800 million dollars. This
raised the total lending of American banks and their overseas subsidiaries to
South Africa over the $2 billion mark. For the first time, American _indirect_
investment surpassed American direct investment in South Africa. Furthermore,
most of these loans have gone to the government and to state-owned enterprises,
making 1976 the first year that the private sector in South Africa accounted
for less capital inflow than the public sector. South Africa has not been
able to get all of the credit facilities it wants (e.g., the Export-Import
Bank turned down its request for a 15-year, $375 million loan guarantee to
help finance a coal gasification project which the Fluor Corporation is helping build), but American financial institutions are heavily involved in helping the Vorster government solve its pressing economic problems.

Apologists for American investment in apartheid argue that the western
economic presence there assists in the development of a complex industrial
society which in turn will undermine apartheid because the two are incompatible.
Thus, western investment is an agent of peaceful change. Furthermore, they
aver, Africans have benefitted directly. Imperial Chemical Industries chairman
Sir Rowland Wright recently phrased the matter in a manner which would have
the agreement of most American businessmen involved with South Africa: "I am
convinced that Black workers have benefited by our presence. We provide about
15,000 jobs there, of which 9,000 are held by Blacks, and we have been instru-

mental in substantially improving their pay, housing and other benefits."

Yet decades of industrial growth have been accompanied not by a weakening but

by a strengthening of apartheid. The lion's share of economic benefits have

gone to the shareholders of the firms doing the investing and to white South

Africans who control the domestic economy. Control of a sophisticated though

dependent economy has greatly strengthened the white minority position in

South Africa. Not only have whites been able to enjoy a steadily increasing

standard of living, perhaps the highest in the world, but the steady transfer

of technological skills has increased white power in absolute terms. Thanks

to the investment of American oil firms (notably Mobil and Caltex), South

Africa has major refineries and storage capacities that would help it withstand

an oil boycott much better than it could in 1973. Indirect investment is

even more closely tailored to South African political and economic needs than

direct investment, since it is the government that is borrowing most of the

money and thus determining how it is to be spent. South Africa has been borrow-

ing heavily to finance strategic development projects such as the $2 billion

SASOL II coal gasification project and the $690 million nuclear generating plant

project for the Electricity Supply Commission. Foreign loans have also helped

South Africa to increase its defense spending by 21.3 percent to $1.8 billion

for 1977-78 (18 percent of the total budget) and to increase the African educa-

tion outlay by 52 percent to $134 million in an effort to defuse further student

unrest. Unable to generate sufficient financing from internal sources to meet

strategic needs, "it is", according to Reed Kramer, "hard to imagine where it

(South Africa) would be right now without borrowed funds." In short, American

investment is helping perpetuate apartheid in South Africa. The existence of

such support places serious constraints on U.S. foreign policy toward South

Africa.[22]

South Africa and its friends in the western world seek to strengthen the

the expanding economic links with the United States and other western countries by stressing the strategic importance of South Africa to the West. One of their strongest arguments is the existence of vast mineral resources in South Africa, including 70 percent of the noncommunist world's gold, half of its platinum, one-third of its diamonds, and important amounts of chrome, uranium, manganese, and other minerals. These mineral resources form a trump card that South Africa is playing for all that it is worth. For example, every recent issue of the South African Digest carries items that convey the following message: "The West's strategic and economic position would suffer immeasurable damage if South Africa's gold and other mineral resources fell into the hands of the communist bloc [which is what will happen if the whites lose control]" (April 8, 1977). Access to South Africa's mineral resources is obviously important, but nonetheless, as studies have shown, the loss of these supplies would not seriously harm the American economy. Secondly, South Africa needs the revenue from the sale of its mineral resources, and the present regime is hardly in a position to find customers other than its current ones. Finally, a black government would also need markets for its mineral production. But, if as Foltz states, long-range access to South Africa's minerals is dependent upon who the U.S. supports in the struggle for control of the area, then the wisest course would seem to be support of the liberation movements. If anything, the strategic mineral resource argument should lead the West to distance itself from the Vorster government rather than drawing closer to it.

The other principal argument concerning the strategic importance of South Africa to the United States is the military one. "South Africa is extremely important on a regional scale and is becoming increasingly vital on a global scale."[23] This statement fairly accurately sums up the approach of those who argue that South Africa is vital to American defense. There are several major components to their argument: the Cape sea route is vital to western energy needs, since most of Europe's oil comes by sea via the Cape; South Africa offers major naval facilities for the protection of American interests in the Indian Ocean; South Africa is a dependable ally in the struggle against communism, both on a world-wide basis and on the African continent. The Angolan-based invasion of Zaire as part of a supposed Soviet attempt to establish a communist belt across central Africa has tended in some circles to strengthen calls for incorporating South Africa as an ally in efforts to contain communism. Close scrutiny of the position taken by proponents of the strategic necessities of the South African case demonstrates that it is extremely short-range in its outlook and constructed on a number of fallacious assumptions. Foltz, for example, notes the almost mythical nature of the arguments about defending the Cape route. Or, as Leonard Thompson has phrased it, "One has had very emotional, far-reaching assertions by senior officers, especially naval officers, but with great respect, having been a junior officer in the British Navy, my respect for the judgement of senior naval officers has not always been justified by the facts."[24] Furthermore, the invocation of communist threats as a brush with which to tar African nationalism has been a consistent tactic of pro-colonial elements for the last three decades. South Africa and its supporters have used this technique in a particularly heavy-handed manner. To the extent, however, that the United States is concerned with the issue of communist penetration of the southern African region, the surest way to see such penetration stepped up is to strengthen defense ties with the current South African regime. Intervention even more fully on the side of the white minority will force African nationalists to secure countervailing support for which the Soviet Union and China are obvious sources. To take the steps proposed by South Africa and its friends in the West would lead to a new set of constraints on U.S. foreign policy that do not presently exist.

Toward a New South Africa Policy

As the foregoing makes clear, Foltz's conclusion about American policy makers being essentially free of serious economic and strategic constraints when it comes to southern Africa is not entirely convincing. American economic involvement in South Africa and the deviousness of the Kissinger era have left the Carter administration a legacy of American complicity in apartheid which imposes serious limitations on U.S. policy. Another equally important limiting factor has to do with the very nature of the turmoil that presently engulfs southern Africa. Even if the United States had been in earnest about its disapproval of apartheid during the Nixon-Ford years, it would still find itself faced with a situation where a policy advocating peaceful change in an atmosphere free of outside intervention would be insufficient. The Carter administration has placed a new face on America's South African policy, but the substance remains much the same. Efforts to persuade white South Africans by force of logic to initiate fundamental change are bound to produce minimal results. What the Legums noted in 1964, namely that "the power structure inside the Republic rules out any hope of inter-racial agreement without intervention,"[25] is even more true today. Even though the inhibitions on American policy toward South Africa may not be tied exclusively to economic and strategic considerations of the sort which Foltz describes, they are none the less real.

Soweto might be regarded by some as an inconsequential episode in the larger struggle unfolding south of the Zambezi; but it is hardly inconsequential for the people of Soweto, least of all for those who mourn their dead and live in fear of further repression. Soweto epitomizes, in dramatic fashion, the race/economic problem of South Africa. Its moral and political implications far outweigh whatever material and strategic interests the U.S. may have in

South Africa. Yet, the United States has long avoided coming to grips with
the reality of the South African situation. Hence, American policy has had
little relevance to the dynamics of events in the region. If the Carter administration is to establish a policy which meets American aspirations and needs,
it first must develop a realistic view of the revolutionary conditions now
existing in South Africa and the neighboring countries. It also should realize
that the settler regimes are dependent for their very survival on the United
States and other western countries. Any western dependence of southern African
mineral resources or on trade and investment in the region pales by comparison.
Such an understanding should provide a clear perception of the serious results
that will stem from a failure to initiate a genuinely new policy. The United
States and its allies are already deeply implicated in southern Africa through
existing links and established policy. It is therefore incumbent upon them to
take positive steps to institute racial and social justice, or they will find
the region's burgeoning racial conflagration engulfing them as well.[26]

A new policy must necessarily repudiate the basic premise of NSSM 39, that
of relying on the white regime as a vehicle for the type of change which would
promote western interests. Nor can policy-makers hope that the growing economic
complexity of the South African economy will somehow promote a liberalization
of the country's racial policies. Disengagement seems an attractive option
to some, but the United States cannot absolve itself so readily from its
responsibilities in southern Africa. As George Shephard has pointed out,
"some variation on the liberation-through-sanctions policy . . . appears to offer
the best alternatives."[27] There are those who accept the need for some form
of American sanctions on South Africa but who think in terms of a gradualist
approach: complete opposition to any acceptance or endorsement of the bantustan
style fragmentation of South Africa; discouragement of new investments coupled
with pressure on firms with existing operations to improve conditions for the

black employees, especially through the promotion of trade unions; expand
communication with South Africans to include increased contacts with black
organizations both within and outside the country.[28] Such an approach offers
too little and is too late. It might have been adequate a decade ago, but
today the best it could do would be to lower suspicions of American connivance
with apartheid. This would represent an improvement, but it would not address
the basic issues.

The United States must, in its own self-interest as well as in the interest
of the peoples of southern Africa, develop a policy directed toward achieving
fundamental change in South Africa. The policy should also be one that provides
all the peoples of South Africa with the opportunity to determine their own
future in an atmosphere as free from violence as conditions realistically warrant. In short, the United States must accept the legitimacy of African
nationalism. Sooner or later the force of events will compel the U.S. to support African liberation. Delay in doing so will only serve to promote the
intervention of non-African parties and to escalate existing patterns of violence,
developments which American policy makers all along have stated they wish to
avoid. What pattern, then, should American intervention take? Thirteen years
ago, Colin and Margaret Legum put forward a solution that strikes us as the
most pertinent for the U.S. to adopt. It is one that would generally have the
support of the anti-apartheid forces.[29]

In brief, the Legums called for a program of collective sanctions against
South Africa mounted through the United Nations. The ultimate objective would
be "to produce a situation inside South Africa which will facilitate the
transfer of power to a representative form of government under conditions which
will ensure a minimum of disruption and provide optimum opportunities for
inter-racial cooperation." The means to acheiving this end would be a National
Convention of the type proposed by the African National Congress. It would

consist of representatives of all groups within South Africa for the purpose
of drafting a new democratic constitution.[30] The role of United Nations would
be to serve as a catalyst to get all of the parties together for purposes of
negotiation and to assure that the basic conditions necessary to satisfy the
legitimate interest of all South Africans would be met: each community to be
totally free to determine the composition of its representatives; any agreement
reached should be submitted to a referendum; the constitution should establish
a representative and democratic government; the constitution should contain en-
forceable safeguards of minority rights. To compel the South African government
to accede to demands for a National Convention (and just not one of the phony
Turnhalle variety), which at present is unacceptable to the Vorster regime,
will require "a sanctions programme capable of inflicting real economic damage."
Half-measures of the sort applied to Rhodesia would undermine the whole effort.
The United Nations, then, should resort to economic warfare against South Africa
and avoid the use of military force. It should, however, have a peace-keeping
force in reserve in case civil disorders in South Africa should reach a point
where the parties were amenable to having the United Nations move in to keep
the peace.[31]

Imposing sanctions will not be an easy task, for South Africa is in a
much better position to withstand them than it was in 1964. For one thing,
it has expanded the offensive military capability of its air force and navy
with modern fighter bombers, submarines, and torpedo boats so that it could,
if it chose, attack ships participating in a naval blockade. South Africa
can also meet almost all of its light armament needs through its own manufacturing processes. Nor is it as vulnerable to an oil embargo as it was a few
years ago. Furthermore, the multi-national corporations have the resources
and the ability to frustrate economic sanctions for some time, as many of
them would undoubtedly choose to do. Also, France and/or Great Britain might

well veto in the Security Council any sanctions effort, at least initially.[32] Thus, the almost immediate capitulation which the Legums envisaged would likely instead turn out to be a much longer term program. Yet, delay will make the inevitable task of dealing forcefully with the South African issue even more difficult. Should South Africa develop a nuclear capacity as it is now seeking to do, should it complete the SASOL II coal gasification project, should it build up still further its military strength, then intervention shall become even more costly and the risks of a racial conflagration even greater.

Aside from the challenge posed to continued white domination by the black population, South Africa's greatest weaknesses are its dependence on western capital and external sources of energy. A sanctions program should therefore seek to curtail both direct and indirect investment in South Africa and to bring a halt to all form of assistance to South Africa in developing its energy resources, especially nuclear energy. Once such a sanctions program is in operation, it should be made clear to South Africa that the next step, if necessary, will be an oil embargo enforced by a naval blockade. The United Nations should also institute a mandatory arms embargo that extends to non-military items such as cargo planes, light aircraft and helicopters, heavy trucks, and sophisticated communications and computer equipment that have clear utility for military purposes. Support for the process of further isolating South Africa from the world community such as the recent decision by the Commonwealth to ban sports events with South Africa should also be stepped up. During the whole sanctions process, it should repeatedly be made clear that the target is not the white population but rather white domination. As the Lusaka Manifesto and other important African nationalist pronouncements have stated, there is no quarrel with a continued white presence in South Africa as long as it is not at the expense of the rights of the majority.

The United States can embark upon a number of specific steps to ensure the success of a sanctions program. In the diplomatic field it can take the lead by cooperating with those countries which presently favor sanctions by developing a workable program and then attempting to persuade its allies to commit themselves to the program. Full support should also be given to a U.N. occupation of Namibia should South Africa persist in refusal to allow its peoples freely to determine their future. Needless to say, the U.S. should be firmly opposed to the bantustans. It can also take direct steps to change current U.S. policy. Economic measures would include: abandonment of the current stance of neither encouraging nor discouraging investment and adopting a policy of actively discouraging new investments; withdrawal of economic/commercial officers attached to the U.S. consulates in South Africa; ending Export-Import Bank guarantees; revocation of the South African sugar quota; passage of legislation which would enforce minimum standards for U.S. firms operating overseas that would cover working conditions and human rights. Feasible steps in the area of energy could include the following: ending all assistance to South African efforts to develop a nuclear capacity (this has obvious military implications as well); ending any exchange of technical information by government agencies and federally-supported institutions in the area of energy development; putting pressure on American oil firms to stop further expansion of their South African facilities and to withdraw from oil exploration ventures, following the precedent set by State Department pressures on the Gulf Oil Corporation during the Angolan crisis. In the area of military/strategic matters, the United States should expand its current voluntary arms embargo to include all equipment that can be used for military as well as civilian purposes; end all exchanges of military and intelligence information; close down Air Force and NASA tracking stations; stop all official contacts between American and South African military personnel. Other assorted measures could include: prohibiting the South African Department of Information from further distribution of its propaganda in the United States; denying visas to South African government officials and civil servants; dissuading Americans, particularly those with technological skills, from working in South Africa; according quasi-official status to the ANC, the PAC, and other African nationalist movements. The United States should not embark upon such a sanctions program in a piecemeal fashion. Rather, it should plan the program carefully and be prepared to provide whatever assistance possible to minimise the human suffering and economic disruption which will inevitably result from its application. This country should also make clear that the foe is apartheid and not the people of South Africa, and that we stand ready to offer assistance in helping South Africans solve their problems once white domination has been abandoned.

Adoption of a new South African policy based on a commitment to fundamental change and incorporating a sanctions program in conjunction with the United Nations has major advantages for the United States. There will be vehement opposition to such a policy from several quarters in the United States and elsewhere in the western world, to say nothing of South Africa. But the merits of a policy along these lines commend it as the most viable option open to the United States. In the first place, it has the best chances of achieving two frequently stated objectives of this country's policy toward South Africa, namely the fostering of peaceful change and allowing South Africans to determine their own future. Secondly, it is a policy that is in keeping with the American commitment to human rights and to the principles embodied in the Constitution and the Declaration of Independence. Third, it offers a long-range policy that is in keeping with the realities of the southern African situation and is therefore in the best self-interests of the United States. Specifically, it will ensure continued access to the mineral resources of the southern part of the continent, if such access ever has really been in

question; it will enhance America's standing among the former colonial
peoples, a grouping that has a growing say in world affairs; it offers the
best means of coping with an increasingly threatening crisis which will have
serious repurcussions for the United States, both domestically and externally.
Finally, the South African situation offers an opportunity for strengthening
the United Nations' role in world affairs through a cooperative effort centered on an issue about which most of that organization's members are potentially
in fundamental agreement. Vice President Mondale conveyed two veiled warnings
to Prime Minister Vorster at their May meeting. The first was that South
Africa should be under no illusion that the United States will ultimately
intervene on behalf of apartheid. The second was that "our paths will diverge
and our policies come into conflict" if South Africa persists in its current
policies.[33] It is time to cease making veiled warnings and to embark boldly
upon a policy that deals with South Africa in terms of its true identity--
that of a predominantly African nation fully determined to liberate itself
from the exploitation and oppression of a white settler minority.

NOTES

1.   Testimony of George Houser in U.S. Congress, Senate, Committee on
     Foreign Relations, U.S. Policy Toward Southern Africa, Hearings, before
     the Subcommittee on African Affairs, Senate, 94th Cong., 1st Sess.,
     1975, p. 494.

2.   George W. Shepherd, Jr., "The Struggle for a New Southern Africa Policy:
     The Carter Task," Journal of Southern African Affairs. Vol. II, No. 1,

3.   Ibid.

4.   The phrase is Nelson Mandela's, from the title of his book, No Easy Walk
     to Freedom (London: Heinemann Educational Books, 1965).

5.   The Kissinger Study on Southern Africa, intro. by Barry Cohen and Mohamed
     A. El-Khawas (Nottingham: Spokesman Books, 1975), pp. 66-67. This book
     contains a complete and unabridged text of the study by the National
     Security Council Interdepartmental Group for Africa that resulted from
     NSSM 39.

6.   Sean Gervasi, "The Politics of 'Accelerated Economic Growth,'" in Change
     in Contemporary South Africa, ed. by Leonard Thompson and Jeffrey Butler
     (Berkeley and Los Angeles: University of California Press, 1975), pp. 366-
     67. Elsewhere in the article (pp. 356-59), Gervasi argues that about 1970
     the western powers began a deliberate process of intervention in southern
     Africa in order to prevent the collapse of the white minority regimes.
     This intervention, exemplified by NSSM 30, was occurring concurrently with
     a public posture of non-intervention.

7.   See for instance the testimony of Nathaniel Davis, Assistant Secretary
     of State for African Affairs, U.S. Policy Toward Southern Africa, Hearings,
     p. 347.

8.   Testimony of Goler Teal Butcher in ibid., p. 265.

9.   Kissinger Study, pp. 13-33, 67-68; Jennifer Davis, testimony, U.S. Policy
     Toward Southern Africa, Hearings, pp. 372-74; Bruce Oudes, "Southern Africa
     Policy Watershed," Africa Report (Nov.-Dec., 1974), pp. 47-48; Anthony
     Lake, The "Tar Baby" Option (New York: Columbia University Press, 1976),
     pp. 123-57.

10. For details on the Lusaka speech, see Africa Report (May-June, 1976),pp.
     21-23; Southern Africa (June-July, 1976), pp. 35-37.

11. Henry A. Kissinger, "South Africa" An American Perspective," Africa
     Report (Sept.-Oct., 1976), p. 18.

12. Ibid., pp. 18-20.

13. Southern Africa (Nov., 1976), pp. 12-14.

14. Charles Mohr, "U.S. Policy in Africa is Broadly Advanced," New York Times, May 29, 1977.

15. Baltimore Sun, May 22, 1977; CBS Evening News, June 8, 1977.

16. Southern Africa (May, 1977), pp. 12-14, and "Washington Notes on Africa" (Spring, 1977) address this question.

17. U.S., Department of State, "U.S. Relations in Southern Africa," Bureau of Public Affairs, Office of Media Services. Schaufele is to be appointed Ambassador to Greece upon confirmation of Richard M. Moose as Assistant Secretary of State for African Affairs.

18. David Welsh, "The Politics of White Supremacy," in Change in Contemporary South Africa, pp. 75-76.

19. New York Times, July 2, 1977.

20. Colin and Margaret Legum, South Africa: Crisis for the West (London: Pall Mall Press, 1964), pp. 1-5, 258-60.

21. Reed Kramer, "In Hock to the U.S. Banks," The Nation, Dec. 11, 1976.

22. The information on investment in the foregoing paragraphs comes from the following sources: Ian Mackler, Pattern for Profit in South Africa (New York: Atheneum, 1975); Ruth First, Jonathan Steele, and Christabel Gurney, The South African Connection (New York: Barnes & Noble, 1973); Donald McHenry, United States Firms in South Africa (Bloomington: Indiana University African Studies Program on behalf of the Africa Publications Trust, 1975); Kramer, "In Hock to the U.S. Banks"; Africa Report (Nov.-Dec., 1976), p. 29, (Jan.-Feb., 1977), p. 25, (May-June, 1977), pp. 27-35; Business Week, Feb. 14, 1977; Manchester Guardian Weekly, April 24, 1977.

23. Jacques A. Rondeau, "Apartheid: Shadow over South Africa," United States Naval Institute Proceedings (Sept., 1976), p. 19. Rondeau, a captain in the U.S. Air Force, has served in the U.S. Defense Attaché Office, Pretoria.

24. Testimony, U.S. Policy Toward Southern Africa, Hearings, p. 303. Africa Report (Jan.-Feb., 1975), contains a series of articles on the issue of the strategic value of the Indian Ocean.

25. Legum, South Africa, p. 5.

26. Testimony of Houser, in U.S. Policy Toward Southern Africa, Hearings, pp. 496-97; Shepherd, "New Southern Africa Policy," p. 109.

27. Shepherd, "New Southern Africa Policy," p. 109.

28. Gwendolen M. Carter, American Policy and the Search for Justice and Reconciliation in South Africa (Racine, Wisconsin: The Johnson Foundation, 1975), pp. 29-48, offers an example of such an approach. For an elaboration of her arguments, see her "South Africa: Battleground of Rival Nationalisms," in Southern Africa in Crisis, edited by Gwendolen M. Carter and Patrick O'Meara (Bloomington: Indiana University Press, 1977), pp. 89-135.

306

29. Shepherd, "New Southern Africa Policy," p. 112.

30. Mandela, No Easy Walk to Freedom, p. 91.

31. Legum, South Africa, pp. 283-85, Carter, "South Africa,"p. 135, also urges that the U.S. take the lead in calling for a national convention. She sees a long-term process.

32. Jim Hoagland, reporting on the Mondale-Vorster meeting in the Washington Post, May 31, 1977, saw this as a definite reaction of France and Britain should sanctions be attempted.

33. Mohr, New York Times, May 29, 1977.

PART THREE

THE POTENTIAL SIGNIFICANCE OF U.S. BLACK CONSTITUENCIES

Editor's Note

In recent time public attention has been repeatedly drawn to the parallel between the race problem in South Africa and the civil rights movement in the American South. Much of the credit for this goes to Ambassador Andrew Young: No one has been more instrumental in giving official approval to the view that the strategies pursued by supporters of the civil rights movement offer the best hope for racial harmony in South Africa. The analogy, however, has failed to elicit anything approaching consensual agreement here and abroad. While some readily point to the very different ratio of whites to blacks in the US as compared with South Africa -- where the blacks are five times as numerous as the whites -- and then underscore the radically different character of the South African political environment as yet another factor militating against the successful use of civil rights tactics in South Africa, others would maintain that the sheer inability of the civil rights movement to move beyond its initial gains is enough to explain the general impotence of US policy on Southern Africa. According to this view a fundamental alteration in the racist character of American society is an absolute precondition for the initiation of a meaningful change in US policy.

Whatever merits can be attributed to these contrasting positions, the role of US black constituencies in shaping US policy in Southern Africa deserves serious examination. The appointment of Andrew Young to the post of US Ambassador to the UN is clearly indicative of the growing significance of the black vote in US domestic politics and of the potential leverage thereby made available to American blacks in the elaboration of our Africa policy. What remains to be specified is the extent to which, collectively, American blacks can bring their influence to bear on the direction of US policies. Or, as Martin Weil would put it, "Can the Blacks do for Africa what the Jews did for Israel?"

Taking as his frame of reference the strategies pursued by Jewish and
Polish minorities in their efforts to influence US policies, Weil sees American
blacks as being on the whole "quiescent and ineffective". The reason for this,
we are told, lies in (1) the failure of American blacks to pose a credible
electoral threat to aspiring politicans, thus depriving themselves of the leverage they might otherwise gain through their votes; (2) the absence of an effective black lobbying apparatus; and (3) the unwillingness or inability of most
American blacks to adjust their foreign policy objectives to the symbolic framework of American nationhood. But one is impelled to wonder whether these conditions can be met within the present context of American race relations. Per-
suasive as the argument may seem on the surface, for many American blacks, including Professor Tilden LeMelle, it is fundamentally question-begging. As LeMelle
points out, "Can American blacks, a subordinate racial group, influence the
foreign policy of the US, a white dominant and racially stratified society, in
the interest of black Africans when such interests are in conflict with those
of whites in Africa?" Which brings us back to the classic argument advanced
by the more radical critics of the civil rights movement: No meaningful change
in US policy towards Africa can be anticipated as long as American society
remains predominently racist in its ethos.

It is only fair to note that the debate introduced in the following pages
took place before the Carter administration came to power--that is before
Andrew Young had a chance to make his voice heard (more stridently than any
American Jew or Pole of comparable rank in any previous administration on issues
concerning Israel or Poland), and before Professor LeMelle's brother was given
the opportunity to serve as American Ambassador to Kenya (his involuntary subservience to a white dominant and racially stratified society notwithstanding).
As these and other developments tend to suggest, American blacks can no longer
be dismissed as "quiescent and ineffective" in the sense in which Professor

Weil used these terms. Yet the question of how much influence American blacks can bring to bear on our Africa policy, through what means, and for what ends, remains highly controversial and emotionally-laden. Not the least of the merits of the contributions that follow is to bring the issue to a more dispassionate level of discourse, and to focus attention on the increasingly significant role which American blacks are being called upon to play in the articulation and overall direction of American policy in Southern Africa.

CHAPTER VIII

CAN THE BLACKS DO FOR AFRICA WHAT THE JEWS DID FOR ISRAEL?

BY MARTIN WEIL

...American blacks have had no visible impact on American policy toward Africa. The Poles and Jews have been active and successful; the blacks, quiescent and in-effective . The reasons for this disparity and the likelihood of change are the subject of this article. This is not a fanciful exercise. Sooner or later, the United States will have to confront the emergence of powerful poticical pressure hostile to American policy in Africa. Whether the response is evenhanded or antagonistic (it is unlikely to be sympathetic) will depend greatly on whether or not an effective black lobby for Africa exists.

Ethnic influence over American foreign policy requires (1) an electoral threat, (2) a lobbying apparatus, and (3) a successful appeal to the symbols of American nationhood. An examination of the sources of Polish Catholic and Jewish leverage over postwar American foreign policy will describe the conditions necessary for a comparable African lobby...

...The skill of the Poles and the Jews in exploiting the American system of open politics guaranteed that they would get the maximum mileage out of the votes they represented. But more fundamentally, their success in attributable to an ideological harmony with the American psyche, an intense Americanism that attracted supporters from a broad spectrum of the electorate...

...The Poles and the Zionists were both celebrators of the American way. They sought a revivified homeland as a refuge for those of their ethnic kin who had not been so fortunate as to enjoy the blessings of life in the United States. Jews did not struggle for Israel out of a desire to leave the United States; nor did Rozmarek wish a restored Poland so that Chicago Polonia might emigrate. Jews and Poles alike loved America and praised the blessings it had provided to those fortunate enough to make their way to the New World. The new Poland and the Zionist homeland were envisioned as an extension of America, not a repudiation of it. In a real sense these ethnic leaders were American nationalists with an area specialization, exporters of the American tradition to a familiar overseas market. And from this derived their powerful appeal to a proud and morally supercilious citizenry glorying in the magnificence of the American way of life after a global military triumph. The Jews and the Poles channeled this chauvinistic enthusiasm into their own causes. Anti-Communism (aimed at Russia) and anti-imperialism (aimed at Britain) were two variants of the traditional American missionary zeal to transform the world in its own image. The Poles and the Jews were wise enough to flow with the current of American nationalism, not against it...

...Looming on the horizon, perhaps still a generation away, is a black lobby for Africa. What is required for the blacks to emulate the Poles's and the Jews's success?

First of all, the electoral threat must be made credible to politicians. This requires a sufficient level of concern with African affairs among black leadership groups, to convince politicians that a substantial number of blacks might vote according to their Afro-American loyalties on election day. The feeling of kinship with overseas forebears is undoubtedly less strong in the black community than it was in the Polish and Jewish communities. Polish-Americans were one generation removed from Poland as were American Jews from their European breathern. Black Americans are centuries removed from their African ancestors, across a cultural and historical divide that dampens the sense of sharing a common heritage. But the romantic attachment to Africa among ethnically proud young blacks may overcome this distance. Black organizations visibly dedicated to African liberation, speaking and fund-raising tours by African leaders to ghetto communities, and a lobbying arm in Washington linked to local politicans can bolster the image of an "African vote." Earlier politicians had no hard evidence that the Polish or Jewish voter actually performed as a foreign policy issue machine at the polls. They simply ran scared before a well-organized leadership. Blacks can accomplish the same.

Most effective of all would be the election of a black politician to statewide office who had chastised his unsuccessful opponent for insufficient dedication to

African problems. Joseph McCarthy's 1950 "defeat" of Millard Tydings in Maryland
and Richard Nixon's victory over Helen Gahangan Douglas did much to convince
politicians---correctly or not---that anti-Communism was decisive at the polls.
A contest of this sort would rivet the attention of politicians with black
constituencies on the power of the "African vote." An African side trip could
become a required adjunct to the traditional "three-I's" junket---Israel, Italy,
and Ireland.

Since the black community is more solidly Democratic today than the Jewish
community, little electoral leverage can be exerted on the Republican party. But
within the Democratic party much may be gained by a concerted campaign to dramatize
black concern for Africa. White Democrats, accustomed to dealing with brokers
for the black vote, will be especially susceptible to a carefully orchestrated effort
The opportunity exists for a respected black community leader to make a career for
himself in the Rozmarek tradition by organizing an ongoing Afro-American Congress
based on black fraternal and religious organizations.

Equally important is an African interest in cultivating the American black
community. The timidity of African diplomats in approaching black leaders contrasts
sharply with the intimate ties between American Jews and Israeli representatives in
the United States, and the former connections between American Polonia and the Polish
exiles. Embassies from other parts of the world readily grant requests from their
ethnic constituents to use embassy facilities for a benefit, noted one restive
Ghanian diplomat, but certain African ambassadors "think" that they should either
clear such requests with the State Department or reject them outright. Some even
refuse to take groups of blacks on a tour of their embassies. This, they fear,
would mean "involvement in American politics!" This fear is not wholly misplaced.
African diplomats shrink from providing excuses for a renewal of the racial incidents
that have plagued them since the opening of the first embassies in Washington in the
1950's. In the years ahead, as black advances in American life parallel the growth

of political and economic strength in black Africa, these inhibitions will decline.
The bonds between black Africa and black America will tighten. When the African
nations decide to make a serious issue of American commitments to white minority
regimes, an Afro-American apparatus may be at hand to reinforce their efforts.
King Faisal is teaching a lesson to African nationalists which may hasten that day.

Currently, the black lobbying apparatus is minimal. Nowhere does it combine
electoral threats with skillful organization. Representative Charles Diggs (D.-
Michigan), chairman of the House Foreign Affairs Subcommittee on Africa, has the
potential of becoming a shadow Assistant Secretary of State for African Affairs if
he develops the ability to play the legislative game with the same skill as some of
his more experienced colleagues. Indeed, the Afrophile African Bureau of the State
Department would welcome a more effective African lobby among black Americans. An
astute black lobby would force greater attention to African affairs, a situation
greatly desired by State's own Africanists, and provide them with a political
counterweight to the skillful lobbying of military and industrial interests working
through powerful southern congressmen. (The racially stratified American military
establishment would look on racial upheaval in white-ruled Africa with no less
distaste than the southern establishment. On the other hand, blacks account for
18.6 percent of enlisted men, and a third of new recruits.)

Diggs' effort so far have been isolated and largely rhetorical. His current
bill which, in effect, cuts off all government contracts to firms which conduct
operations in South Africa, is utterly fanciful. It may win the acclaim of exile
groups and black militants, but it is a far cry from the political finesse of the
southerners as demonstrated by the 1971 passage of the Byrd Amendment, permitting
American import of Rhodesian chrome in violation of U.N. sanctions. Spurred on by
the Rhodesian Information Office and two American firms with Rhodesian subsidiaries
--Union Carbide and Foote Mineral--Byrd introduced a bill prohibiting the United
States government from barring the import of any strategic material from a free

world country as long as the same item was being imported from a Communist country. Since much high-grade chromium comes from the Soviet Union, the intent was clear. By this wily stratagem, Byrd converted the issue from support of racism to opposition to Communism. After the bill failed in the liberal Senate Foreign Relations Committee, John Stennis of Mississippi attached it to the Military Procurement Bill in the more conservative Armed Forces Committee. A last-minute bit of parliamentary legerdmain garnered the few votes needed to back a striking motion and the amendment passed. The parliamentary skill of the southerners contrasted sharply with the absence of any comparable tactics by the black caucus. Once again ethnic politics triumphed, but this time it was the sympathy of American white supremacists for their African counterparts.

Keeping the Faith

In the area of symbolic politics, black efforts are, if anything, counterproductive. The supporters of white minority rule have attached their cause to the symbols of American nationhood. Rhodesia's Unilateral Declaration of Independence in 1965 has been protrayed as a parallel to the Declaration of Independence (Elizabeth II being the latterday George III, and Ian Smith being the Rhodesian George Washington). By contrast, arguments for African nationalism have come most vocally from black radicals bent on world revolution. These media wizards have no enduring roots in the black community and judge even black-ruled regimes by ideological dogmas that alienate many African officials. Furthermore, the black African exiles headquartered in London and New York practice the same apocalyptic politics. Some are in the pay of the Soviet Union; most espouse Communist doctrines that guarantee them impotence in the American Political arena. Marxist rhetoric, however titillating to the media and hothouse student audiences, is totally counterproductive and ultimately futile in creating public support for African nationalism. To be successful, a black movement for reform of American policy toward Africa must be perceived as a vehicle for exporting American ideals. It must be an

affirmation of black faith in the United States and a demonstration of black
ability to manipulate the fine structure of American politics with the astuteness
and finesse of previous practitioners. Blacks as blacks may identify with Africa,
but it is only as Americans that they can change United States policy in Africa.
If Afro-Americans ever gain leverage in foreign policy, it will be those black
politicians who are most successful within the system who will do so--those who
can command the respect of their black constituents and reassure white America
at the same time. To aid the revolution abroad, blacks must first join the
establishment at home.

Until the Africanists learn to play the legislative and publicity games as
well as their enemies, they will suffer an unnecessary handicap in moving American
policy toward a more liberal position. To some, liberalism may seem a pitifully
inadequate answer to the situation in Africa, but it is all that the American
political system will allow, and it is certainly an improvement over abandoning
the field to racists. More important, a progressive American policy will prepare
the public for a passive role should a race war erupt on the African continent.
So far the situation has received little attention. The Nigerian civil war and
fratricidal tribal bloodbaths in Rwanda and Burundi scarcely created a ripple in
American politics. As long as blacks slaughter blacks, the American public yawns.
But if blacks start killing whites, attention will pick up. When whites were
threatened in the Congo, Lyndon Johnson had the air transports flying within hours
and the story was front-page news. The domestic reverberations in the United
States of a war aimed at overthrowing the ruling white minorities in Rhodesia and
South Africa could have terrifying consequences.

The presence of a respected cadre of black political leaders to guide American
opinion in such a crisis and calm the more hysterical elements would have important
consequences. If black leaders had not become accepted participants in the executive
as well as the legislative politics of African policy, one could expect a less

measured response. Unlike the Israeli case, American blacks cannot seek actively
to aid revolutionary movements in Africa. The ideology of these movements will
be alien to most Americans and the prospect of a black underground shipping arms
to Africa will hardly meet with the friendly indifference that shielded Jewish
efforts to supply the Haganah. The best that can be hoped for is the gradual
withdrawal of American military and business interests from white Africa in the
years ahead, and a scrupulous neutrality if war does break out. Such a policy is
inadequate to some liberationists, but it is the only one that ultimately can
help them. The active sympathy of white America for the plight of black Africa
can only be won by a nonintimidating strategy. White America will judge Africa
by the American representatives who speak for her. As in other areas of American
life, blacks must be twice as careful to achieve half as much.

And this is particularly true of the most liberal of American minorities--
the Jews. Militant American blacks and some African leaders, espousing the cause
of Arab nationalism and black liberation in Africa, see the Jews as the oppressors
in the Middle East and in American cities. The Israelis may come to see themselves
as a besieged white community on the rim of Africa facing a new threat of extermi-
nation based on color rather than religion. They may have very mixed feelings
about the outcome of a war in South Africa or even in the Portuguese colonies.
And their brethren in the United States could scarcely feel differently. Liberal
Jews--the traditional political allies of ghetto-bound blacks--would quickly
unite with other whites in fear of the black community. The liberal buffer between
black resentment and white racism would dissolve, exposing the raw edges of race
conflict. The first fights that erupted in Harlem during Mussolini's invasion of
Ethiopia in 1935 would be but a faint foretaste of domestic tension that might
attend a bloody race war in Africa. Black indulgence of anti-Jewish feeling would
only harden American opinion against African liberation.

Since the Jews and the blacks are both in the Democratic party, it will be in the interest of blacks running for office above the local level to reconcile this conflict. State Senator Mervin Dymally of Los Angeles is a harbinger of this theory. He needs the support of both Beverly Hills and Watts in his bid to win the Democratic nomination for Lieutenant Governor in 1974. He is carefully straddling the issue, planning the ritual trip to Israel but also promising to report on Israel treatment of Arab refugees. On the one hand, he argues to blacks that they should actively back Israel. "The Jewish people were very active in many of our causes, like civil rights, labor, and the farmworkers' cause, and it will be a great mistake to allow Israel to have their independence jeopardized." On the other hand, he acknowledges: "I would like to see better communication between Jews and blacks. The Arab-Israeli situation has definite domestic. implications directly related to my constituents." As other black politicians seek state office, similar efforts at reconciliation are liable to occur. And this can only help reassure white America that a black revolution in Africa need not threaten riots in American cities nor support an assault on the state of Israel.

A successful black lobby for Africa must maintain a certain distance from the African liberation movements in order to maintain its own credibility with the American public, demonstrating by its own actions the hands-off posture that is the most forward policy America can support. Certainly, there is vast room for progress when the United States joins Greece, Portugal, South Africa, and Spain on the negative end of an 88 to 7 General Assembly vote on recognition of the black-control Republic of Guinea Bissau in Portuguese Guinea. A quarter century after the smaller Jewish community enjoyed instantaneous recognition of Israel, the black community has not even made an issue of Guinea Bissau, let alone mustered public support for defiance of Portuguese colonialism. The British were not so fortunate, nor was the Russian-sponsored government in Warsaw.

CHAPTER IX

AMERICAN BLACK CONSTITUENCIES AND AFRICA: A REJOINDER

BY TILDEN LEMELLE

The popular wisdom of much of U. S. social science analysis of the political behavior of Black Americans has been to compare them with white ethnic groups. So much so that the Black American is now being viewed as the "new immigrant" in the U. S. The ethnic group most frequently chosen for comparative purposes is the American Jew. The normative axiom derived from this choice of reference group is that Black Americans must emulate the European immigrants, particularly the Jews, in order to change their subordinate status in U. S. society. At other times it is expressed in the form of the question raised by Martin Weil: Can the Blacks do for Africa what the Jews did for Israel?

While the ethnic politics framework and the new immigrant concept are merely tools of analysis and should not be viewed as reality itself, they do tend to remove the analyst far from the reality of the Black American experience. Central to analyzing and understanding Black political behavior are certain simple givens: In the U.S. Black Americans are not just another ethnic group, they are a separate racial sub-group. Black Americans are not new immigrants, they are descendants of ancestors whose presence and parti- cipation in what is now the U.S. are traceable to the inception of European colonial rule in North America some 400 years ago. The choice of the ethnic and new immigrant concepts is itself a reflection of the inability and/or unwillingness of many social scientists to come to grips with the fundamental considerations of race and racial discrimination that must be made in any study of Black American participation in U.S. political processes.

In addition to the conceptual irrelevancy of Weil's attempt to compare Black American political behavior with that of American Jews, Weil's over

all analysis disregards two important historical realities about Black Americans
and U.S. African policy:

1. Until very recently the Afro-American, individually or as a group,
has played little or no direct role in the formation and/or implementation
of U.S. public policy, be it domestic or international, or be that policy
concerned or not with Africa.

2. Until the climaxing of the African independence movements in the
two decades following World War II, the United States had no active African
Foreign Policy. For all intents and purposes Africa was treated as a
subordinate subsystem, subject to the vagaries of U.S. relations with the
European colonial powers. In fact, it was not until July 10, 1958, that a
congressional bill was finally adopted establishing in the State Department
a separate Bureau of African Affairs with its own assistant secretary.

Any discussion of the part played by Afro-Americans in shaping U.S.
policy toward Africa must therefore focus on their very indirect role and
limit itself, of necessity, to the relatively short period of time during
which Black Americans have become citizens of the U.S. and African people
citizens of their respective states, a process still awaiting completion in
much of Southern Africa.

Before going any further, however, we should look a bit more closely at
those two realities because they have implications not only for an understanding
of the role Afro Americans might have played in the past but, more importantly,
for what that role may become in the near future.

That Afro Americans were unable to influence U.S. policies toward Africa
otherwise than in the most marginal fashion is not too surprising. The U.S.

has been from its birth, 200 years ago, to the present day a white dominant, racially stratified polity. Which is to say that there has existed, and still exists, a dominant/subordinate relationship between white and non white (Black) which affects not only attitudes but power and mobility relationships between them. It means that values and interests perceived or characterized as Black have been relegated to a subordinate status. It means that access to and use of the levers of political and economic power to maximize one's individual and/or group values and interests have been primarily a function of racial membership. In terms of white and Afro American power relationships, that means a dominant/subordinate relationship. The dominant/subordinate nature of the attitudinal and power relationships between whites and Blacks in the U.S. has always meant for Blacks a limited and controlled mobility which for all practical purposes has excluded Blacks from those positions in the public and private sectors from which effective influence could be brought to bear upon public policy, domestic and/or international. In short, the white dominant, racially stratified nature of the U.S. has meant with rare and questionable exceptions, the practical exclusion of Black Americans individually or as a group from direct participation in the making and implementing of U.S. foreign policy in Africa or anywhere else. This is where the position of Black Americans differs fundamentally from that of other ethnic minorities.

A close scrutiny of the argument advanced by Weil reveals more concretely the vacuity of the ethnic analysis as applied to American Blacks. He argues that "ethnic influence over American foreign policy requires (1) an electoral threat, (2) a lobbying apparatus, and (3) a successful appeal to the symbols of American nationhood."

First of all, there is nothing uniquely ethnic about the three requirements for success enumerated by Weil. Any group, ethnic or otherwise, that
can effectively b ing the three stated requirements to converge on the foreign
policy process can expect some measure of success. The ethnic variable
manifests itself primarily in an ethnic group's ability to identify a transnational ethnic interest in the external relations of the U.S. In that regard,
there has always been an African-American identification and involvement with
Africa. The nature of that identification and involvement has changed with
the changing fortunes of American Blacks just as their concern with U.S.
involvement in Africa has increased in proportion to that involvement. The
impact of the American Black's concern about U.S. involvement in Africa,
however, has been negligible if not non-existent. In addition, that concern
has not always been in the best interest of Africa or of the United States.

The salient question to be posed by anyone studying or concerned with the
American Black's impact on U.S. foreign policy is: Can a subordinate racial
group in a racially stratified system maximize its transnational racial interests
within the established or acceptable framework with a view to influencing
foreign policy? More specifically, can American Blacks, a subordinate racial
group, influence the foreign policy of the U.S., a white dominant and racially
stratified society, in the interests of Black Africans when such interests
are in conflict with those of whites in Africa? In the light of these questions,
the relevance of Weil's criteria becomes increasingly dubious.

As Weil rightly points out the credibility of an electoral threat by Blacks
would be dependent on the link between a well organized pro-African Black
leadership and a Black American African vote. But that's like saying: "to

be successful one must succeed!" No argument! The fundamental problem is
that Black Americans are ethnically American though racially Black. American
Blacks are culturally (ethnically) American and only American. Even the
ethnically dominant Anglo-Saxon American has his ethnic ties to some part of
what the anthropologist identifies as "African survivalisms", is probably
the only American who is wholly American. Even where an African connection
does exist, it is recognized only by a handful of Blacks who have studied
African culture and/or visited the continent. The inability of the vast
majority of American Blacks to develop an informed ethnic identification with
Africa is not just a matter of time or of the Americanization process. It is
a matter of an inability to identify with a whole continent (larger that
Europe and the U.S. combined) of ethnic groups. By contrast, the Pole identifies with Poland, not Europe; the Jew identifies with Israel, not the Middle
East. Africa is not a nation-state, but a continent. Thus to speak of the
"Afro-American loyalties" of ethnically proud young Blacks who have a romantic
tie to Africa, is to suggest an inherent contradiction. The "ethnic" ties of
the American Black is to America, not to Africa or any part of Africa. The
romantic ties of Africa are racial and can only be racial. Accordingly, any
link between a Black leadership group and an American Black "African vote"
in the interest of Africa must of necessity be based on a racial appeal
however that may be couched. Such an appeal to Black American unity in
support of a Black African interest would spell doom for any Black lobbying
effort. In a racially stratified white dominant society, a pro-Black stance
automatically is perceived to be anti-white since pro-white is the only
legitimate racial point of reference in such a society.

Weil suggests that the Black political leaders like Congressman
Charles Diggs might learn from the likes of Harry Byrd who couched their
white supremacist interests in the guise of anti-communism in passing
legislation supportive of the interests of white supremacist domination
in southern Africa. The obvious problem with that suggestion is that the
Byrd Amendment succeeded in the Senate in spite of the fact that it was
clearly anti-Black in its intent and effect. No one in the Senate or
White House was unaware of the racist thrust of the amendment. Yet it
succeeded. On the other hand, the choice and the attempt of Congressman
Diggs and other Blacks in Congress have been to equate white minority
domination in southern Africa with the racial totalitarianism and facism
that it is. Presumably those "isms" are just as counter to the American
ideal as is communism. The fact is, however, that a policy of accomodation
with totalitarian and fascist states is not nearly as repugnant to
decision-makers in Congress and in the White House as some might think.
Witness the U. S. support for dictatorships such as existed in Portugal,
Spain and South Vietnam and as exists in Chile, South Korea, etc. In
addition, Africans and their supporters in the U. S. have not only always
presented the African case as neither communist nor fascist but they have
in fact rejected both in favor of Africanism. Africanism, however, has
been seen as largely irrelevant by U. S. policy makers the latter
insisting that U. S. on foreign policy should "tile" in support of continuing
white supremacy in southern Africa. On that score the wording of NSSM
39 leaves very little room to the imagination.

The success of the white supremacist and the failure of the pro-
African forces in the elaboration of U. S. policy in Africa are not a
function of parliamentary skills or the lack thereof. Both sides have

used the same tactics. The appeal of those who have succeeded has
been to the reality of the continuing support for white domination over
Blacks in the name of anti-communism. The appeal of those who have
failed has been to the U. S. ideals of majority rule and racial pluralism
in the name of African self-determination. It proved more important and
more beneficial to be anti-communist in Washington than to uphold U. S.
ideals.

By neglecting this cardinal fact Weil is led to misjudge the significance of "keeping the faith" through symbolic manipulation. Keeping
the faith in anti-communism is far more decisive than keeping the faith
in American symbols. Thus the tribute paid by Weil to Ian Smith's
manipulative skills in drawing a parallel between the Rhodesian minority's
UDI (Unilateral Declaration of Independence) and the American Revolution
is misplaced if not irrelevant. Is it not equally in line with the American
tradition for the spokesmen of the African masses of Zimbabwe to seek to
achieve self-determination? UDI was aimed at establishing white minority
rule to the exclusion of the Black majority; the Zimbabwe liberation effort
has been aimed at establishing Black majority rule while protecting white
minority rights. To label support for African nationalism as the radical
vocalizing of dogmatic idealogues bent on world revolution seems like a
travesty, of African political realities; in fact it could easily be seen
as an insult by the many black and black/white individuals and organizations
that have worked for African interests long before and since UDI. The Pan
African Movement under the leadership of internationally famous scholars
like W. E. B. Dubois, the N.A.A.C.P. under James W. Johnson, the Council
on African Affairs under Paul Robeson and Max Yergan (who later joined
the Board of the South African Foundation), the Adlai Stevenson inspired

American Negro Leadership Conference, The African Heritage Studies Association of Black Academicians, The American Committee on Africa, and the
Washington Office on Africa, the National Council of Churches and the
denominational units like the Episcopal and the United Church of Christ
--to name a few - have been the most active and most vocal in support of
African nationalism and African liberation. Needless to say, on matters
pertaining to the liberation of Africa from European domination, all of
these groups are indeed "radical" since to support African aspiration for
self-determination is by definition radical in a white dominant society
such as the U.S. It is only natural that Weil should label them as
"radical". Ideological demogagues they are not. They have worked for
African interests openly and legally and have always eschewed the illegal
and clandestine activities that Weil points out were employed by U. S.
Zionists to bribe and corrupt U. S. Pentagon and intelligence officials.
Weil too easily confuses corruption of the system with working within the
system even though he acknowledges that American Blacks could not get away
with the same activities as the Zionists did.

Despite the irrelevancy of the comparative ethnic analysis and the
omissions and contradictions it engenders, Weil is quite perceptive on
two counts: White America would respond if white interests in Africa are
credibly threatened and the Israeli would seek closer ties with S. A. if
racial war were escalated in Africa. Both observations have become reality.
In both instances race has been the salient factor and not ethnicity. The
independence of Guinea Bisau, Mozambique and Angola was achieved in the
name of Black majority rule. The struggle for independence in Zimbabwe
(Rhodesia) and Namibia (Southwest Africa) has been conducted in the name

of Black majority rule as opposed to minority white rule. And the showdown
is soon to come in South Africa itself on the same issue. All along, Israel
and South Africa have publicly strengthened ties that have existed for a long
time though not so publicly. At the same time, American Blacks and American
Jews have grown farther apart with American Jews being petitioners and/or
amicus curiae in the legal fight against Affirmative Action programs for
Blacks. That the same opposition has not been brought against women or other
groups identified by the HEW Affirmative Action Guidelines is not all that
coincidental.

To suggest finally, as Weil does, that in addition to working "within"
the system American Blacks should nurture alliances with American Jews, "the
most liberal of American minorities," is less than political naivete. The
history of domestic Black politics clearly reveals that when any issue is to
its lowest common denominator--black vs. white interest--the white "liberal"
including American Jews and their organization have quickly disengaged themselves from support for American Black interests. Many, indeed, have joined
the anti-Black forces. It is highly questionable whether the "liberal buffer
between Black resentment and white racism" has ever been more than a benign
racism that quickly becomes blatant when Blacks begin to define for themselves
a uniquely pro-Black interest.

The fundamental problem facing the development of a Black American constituency for Africa is the problem of race. In Africa, the fundamental issue
since the imposition of European domination has been the restoration of Black
majority control over the destinies of Black people. That could only be
achieved by the elimination of white minority rule. For the African, the
issue has never been communism vs. capitalism or the U. S. vs. the U.S.S.R.

or China. Simply Black African rule vs. white European rule. Because the
U. S. itself has been and is a white dominant and racially stratified
system in terms of race, American Blacks who have sought to aid African
liberation and independence have had to do so outside of the established
processes for making and implementing U. S. foreign policy. Though not
stated explicitly until NSSM 39, U.S. foreign policy toward Africa has
always been based on the premise that "the whites are here to stay and the
only way constructive change can come about is through them." Invariably,
then, and with rare exceptions, American Blacks who have attempted to work
"within" the system have found that their efforts resulted in maintaining
continued white domination in Africa. Because American Blacks are ethnically
American and only a few have an informed racial identification with Africa,
many who have attempted to work "within" the system wittingly or unwittingly
have worked against African interests. AMSAC, the American Negro Leadership
Conference, the more recent pro-South Africa posturing by publicly prominent
American Blacks like Andrew Hatcher, Kenneth Clark and others are but a few
manifestations of the anti-Black rationale consequent to the Americanization
(ethnicity) of the Black man in the U.S.

The outlook for a broad American Black constituency for African interest
is not very hopeful for the near future. It probably will take another generation for the establishment of the kinds of transnational racial ties that are
a pre-condition for the emergence of such a constituency in the U. S. Anti-
Black racism is a profitable business (psychologically and economically) at
home and abroad. The U. S. will not really stop supporting white racism in
Africa (or at home) until that support becomes less profitable than opposition
to it. As in the past, it is the Africans themselves with the support in the

U. S. of a small but committed number of Blacks and non-Blacks of different ethnic origins who will have to pose a credible threat to the profitability of white racism. The ethnic comparison with the American Jew's support for Israel is meaningless and misleading. The question for the analyst of American Blacks and Africa vis a vis U. S. foreign policy is race and its psychological and power implications for political behavior.

PART FOUR

THE USE AND MISUSE OF SECRECY

Editor's Note

"America has perenially engaged in a search of its conscience", wrote
Secretary Kissinger in 1976. Although one may legitimately wonder whether
such noble preoccupations have had any perceptible impact on the policies pursued by Kissinger during the Angolan crisis, the question of how best to reconcile
our foreign policies with moral ends is too important to be left to policy-makers,
particularly when they cast themselves in the role of moralists.

In Southern Africa the issue is inextricably bound up with, though evidently
not limited to, the role of the CIA. Although the evidence is still too sketchy
to permit anything like a final assessment of the significance of the CIA in
the whole of Southern Africa, what we know of the Agency's activities in Angola
and Zaire is enough to disabuse ourselves of the notion that our policies have
always served ethical principles of the highest order. Seen from another
perspective, the intrusion of clandestine activities into the African Continent
raises strong doubts about the extent to which the short-run goals of the
CIA can be reconciled with the long-term objectives that are generally sub-
sumed under the rubric of political and economic development. Again, such
covert activities as have occurred in Angola and Zaire under the cloak of the
Agency inevitably call into question the scientific and ethical concerns of
social scientists. The point here is not simply that social scientists have
often failed to recognize the CIA for what it is, i.e. a key element in the
political equation of African states, but that in specific instances, this very
neglect may conceivably be intended to conceal their direct or indirect association with some of the more objectionable activities conducted under the auspices
of the Agency.

To ignore altogether the part played by the Agency in shaping the course
of events in states like Zaire and Angola would be just as naive and unwarranted
as to read into its more widely publicized activities irrefutable evidence of
a ubiquitous and all-powerful CIA presence throughout the African Continent.
As Professor Weissman's discussion suggests, Zaire and Angola were the principal
spheres of CIA involvement from 1960 to 1975.

For those of us who once tried to comprehend the byzantine complexities of
post-independence Zairian politics through the conventional tools of political
science analysis, Weissmann's chilling account will no doubt provide considerable food for thought. Even more importantly, however, his analysis lays bare
some of the major contradictions involved in the efforts of American policy-
makers as they seek to normalize our relationships with Angola while at the
same time living up to the expectations of our Zairian client. For if the
CIA intervention in Angola may well be regarded as the price exacted by
Mobutu to lend credibility to our Zairian commitment, the costs of the operation
far outweigh the short-term benefits derived from this last-minute effort to
turn the tide of Angolan nationalism. Not only has US policy in Angola suffered
irreparable discredit, but in the meantime, as Weissmann demonstrates, much of
the anti-Mobutu sentiment currently building up in Zaire takes on a decidedly
anti-American coloration, with the CIA seen as the major villain.

Much as we would like to evacuate all traces of clandestine activities from
the sphere of political analysis, whether for reasons of convenience or of
conscience, there is no gainsaying the continuing significance of such activities
in the realm of international politics. Just how far they have contaminated our
African policies and mortgaged our relationships with specific African states
is what the following chapters attempt to evaluate.

CHAPTER X

THE CIA IN AFRICA: HOW CENTRAL? HOW INTELLIGENT?

BY RENÉ LEMARCHAND

In an African continent understandably sensitive on the
issue of sovereignty, we Americans have had a special myth to
overcome: the myth of manipulation. I hope that this is dead.
I hope that we have been able to convince the African governments that we are not involved in any way in seeking to determine how they are governed and by whom"

Thus spoke former Assistant Secretary of State for African Affairs,

David Newsom, on March 14, 1973.[1] In the context of the post-Watergate

era -- when Americans are reminded almost day after day of the massive

and direct involvement of the CIA in the Angolan civil war, when they are

told of the assassination plans of the same agency against the late Patrice

Lumumba, and even get word of less publicized instances of clandestine

activities in Gabon and Madagascar -- the least that one can say of such

a statement is that it strains credulity. The virtuousness of the inten-

tions conveyed by Newsom's homily is indeed difficult to reconcile with

the staggering evidence to the contrary recently disclosed through senator-

ial investigations, press reports and various other sources.[2]

The crux of the problem, from the standpoint of the social science

community, is no longer whether or not we can dispel the "myth of manipula-

tion" from popular perceptions of US foreign policy, but whether, in the

light of recent disclosures, the extent of US manipulations abroad and its

effect on the domestic politics of Third World countries lend themselves

to an objective assessment.

For those of us accustomed to engage in more conventional modes of

social science investigation, prying into the murky underworld of CIA

activities raises obvious difficulties. Aside from the limitations inherent
in the very nature of the subject under consideration, not the least of
these difficulties stems from the emotional tone of the debate surrounding
CIA activities at home and abroad. Popular reactions to the evidence disclosed by the Church Committee mirror varying shades of indignation, cynicism and embarassment, all of which tend to reflect a generalized sense of
uneasiness about the credibility of the moral image we seek to project.
Yet there is clearly more at issue here than just a distortion of our
national self-image. If the ethical, normative and scientific concerns
of social scientists are recognized as part of the public controversy, as
I believe they should, a level of discourse must be established that
transcends invective and moral recrimination. In short, if social scientists are to exercize effectively the kind of independent critical function
which is normally expected of them, a note of dispassionate inquisitiveness
needs to be injected into the debate.

The initiation of a constructive dialogue about the effect of CIA
activities on US foreign policy is too important to be left to CIA officials,
or former officials, however repentant they may be. The significance of
such a dialogue, from the standpoint of the political science community, is
three-fold: to the extent that the retrieval and processing of political
information can be regarded as part of the routine intelligence gathering
activities of the CIA, and because some of us have been directly approached
and sollicited by CIA agents to provide them with such information, the
question arises as to whether political scientists have not contributed,
witttingly or unwittingly, directly or indirectly, to shape the posture
of the agency, as well as some of its more sordid policies, in specific
arenas of CIA involvement. [3]

The latest disclosures coming out of Washington also provide significant lessons about the relevance of the conventional models, methods and
approaches used by political scientists in their attempt to explain, or
explain away, the political realities of the Third World. To put the matter
more concretely, one is impelled to wonder whether, in particular instances,
CIA funds, shellfish toxin and cobra venom, falsified information and
"private" airlines, are not the really critical components of the stock
of resources at the disposal of Third World political actors, and whether
terms like "legitimacy", "authority", "charisma" and the like are not to be
treated as mere euphemisms for a far more sinister and effective type of
political resource. All this is not meant as an attempt to rehabilitate
conspiracy theories, only to suggest that, insofar as the existence of
such conspiracies can be established, they should not be left out of the
"accounting". As we now realize, "creating political order" [4] in Africa
and elsewhere is a process in which clandestine political and paramilitary activities have often played a determining role.

What remains highly debatable is whether the fostering of political
order through such means is at all compatible with political development.
How can one reconcile the involvement of the CIA in the internal politics
of African states with the development strategies pursued by AID agencies?
To what extent does it violate the assumptions held by AID officials about
how best to promote economic and political development? Is the CIA a
"rogue elephant" roaming over the African landscape, making a shambles of
the most carefully planned development strategies -- or is it, in the words
of one commentator, "an agency rich in intellectual talent... drawn deeply
into economic analysis and estimation" which, though admittedly guilty of
"misdemeanors or something worse", [5] has nonetheless contributed significantly

to the realization of specific developmental objectives?

This paper focusses primarily on the last two sets of issues. The aim, in brief, is to assess the scope and centrality of CIA covert activities in the internal politics of independent African states, and, where the evidence affords sufficient grounds for such an evaluation, to examine the bearing of such activities on development strategies in their broadest sense.

Before going any further a few caveats need to be entered. Despite all the sensationalism attending the disclosures of the Church Committee the truth of the matter is that our knowledge of CIA activities in Africa is still very limited, both in terms of areal coverage and of the circumstancial evidence thus far produced for public consumption. Although I have tried to supplement the facts that are now part of the public record with what little information I was able to collect in the course of my occasional (but deliberately distant) contacts with CIA officials in Africa and the US, what follows is obviously a very speculative discussion. Furthermore, by virtue of my own geographical area of specialization, and because it happens to include two of the states about which evidence of CIA involvement is most readily accessible, my analysis draws heavily from Angola, Zaire, Rwanda and Burundi. Finally, the reader should bear in mind that much of what I have to say about the effect of CIA activities might conceivably apply to its Soviet, British, Belgian and French counterparts. Indeed, judging from the extensive and apparently reliable evidence recently disclosed by Patrice Chairoff, [6] there seems to be some striking parallels between the style and methods of the CIA in Africa and those of its Franch equivalent, the Service de Documentation Exterieure et de Contre-Espionage (SDECE). Although their significance in the internal politics of

African states cannot be denied (nor proven), the covert activities of the SDECE and other foreign intelligence agencies only have a tangential bearing on the scope of this discussion; their main relevance lies in the manner in which US officials have perceived the role of these agencies in specific settings at particular times, and the impact this has had on the scope and character of CIA activities.

The Scope and Centrality of CIA Operations

Insofar as most African states share the characteristics of developing polities they rank relatively high on the list of polities most vulnerable to CIA penetration. What makes them ideal targets for covert operations is their inherent fragility. The point has been articulated by the former chief of the agency's Clandestine Services, Richard Bissell, as follows: [7]

> The underdeveloped world presents greater opportunities for covert intelligence collection simply because governments are much less highly oriented; there is less security consciousness; and there is apt to be more actual or potential diffusion of power among parties, localities, organizations and individuals outside the central governments.

Bissel's characterization is an apt summary of the state of affairs prevailing in the Congo (now Zaire) from 1960 to 1965, in Madagascar in early 1975, in Angola in 1975-76: it seems hardly a matter of coincidence that all three countries experienced a relatively high level of CIA involvement precisely when their political systems were least stable. The absence of supplementary evidence is of course no reason to assume that such involvement did not occur elsewhere in Africa; what does need to be emphasized is that political fragmentation, latent or actual instability, and a low degree of legitimacy are sufficient but by no means necessary conditions for the CIA to engage in subversion. Or else one would have to assume an

equally high incidence of covert operations in states like Chad, Dahomey,
Upper Volta or the Central African Republic. Few knowledgeable observers
would entertain such an assumption.

Any attempt to delimit the scope of CIA cover activities in Africa
is clearly a matter of conjecture, but what further complicates this task
is that it involves not only conjectural but conjunctural elements. Whether
or not covert operations are launched in a foreign state depends on the
choices made by Washington in response to particular crisis situations or
combinations of events. Spheres of CIA involvement thus tend to contract
and expand, in an accordian-like fashion, depending on a variety of factors,
including the saliency of perceived threats to US interests. In their quest
for quantifiable evidence some commentators have drawn attention to personnel
figures and budgetary appropriations as possible indices of the agency's
involvement; yet, both sets of figures being extremely flexible, one wonders
what profit, if any, can be drawn from reliance on this kind of data. What,
for example, is one to make of Bruce Oudes' contention that "the CIA African
budget is in the vicinity of $25 to 20 million a year", and that "no more
that a handful, if that, of CIA stations in Africa could have a budget running
$1 million or more",[8] when we learn that $25 million in arms were shipped by
the CIA to the pro-Western factions in Angola during the last three months of
1975? Similarly, to argue that "the CIA's African division consists of only
300 of the 4,500 employees of the CIA's clandestine services operations, making it the smallest of the CIA's geographic regions in terms of personnel,"[9]
tells us very little about the actual distribution of CIA personnel in the
field, their specific assignments, resources, and activities.

A more fruitful way of approaching the question is to focus on the
following combination of situational variables: (1) the extent to which
the field of intelligence operations has been effectively pre-empted by the
agencies of the former colonial power, and the degree of cooperation that
US policy-makers can expect of such agencies in matters involving East-West
rivalries; (2) the saliency of cold war issues (or issues that are defined
in these terms by US policy makers) discernible in the political conjuncture
of any given African state; (3) the magnitude of US economic and strategic
interests at stake in specific areas. All three factors, as we shall see,
are intimately connected.

The first of these variables takes on special significance in the
former French territories, particularly where French economic, strategic
or cultural interests are being pursued most vigorously and systematically
(e.g. the Ivory Coast, Gabon, Senegal and, until recently, Chad). The
nearly ubiquitous presence in these states of SDECE   and SAC
(Service d'Action Civique) "men" -- both forming in effect the armature
of the Foccard "machine" in Africa [10] --, together with the intricate network
of informal cooperative relationships that have developed over the years
between French intelligence agents, technical assistants, embassy officials
and businessmen, has had a strong inhibiting effect on the propensity of
the CIA to manipulate African actors. The situation is evidently more
complex in those territories where the French presence is no longer much in
evidence (Guinea, Congo), and this is equally true, mutatis mutandis, of
states like Uganda, Tanzania or Zanzibar, where British interests have been
drastically reduced if not eliminated. Inasmuch as the residual involvement
of Western interests in these states has implied corresponding limitations
on the presence of US corporate interests the result has been to seriously

narrow the range of opportunities for CIA intervention.

How far "pre-emption" by European intelligence networks has in fact operated to limit the spread of CIA covert activities in Africa can best be understood in the light of the impact of cold war issues on the attitude of European and American policy-makers, and of the resulting patterns of relationships that have developed between their respective intelligence communities.

The intrusion of cold war rivalries in Africa has given rise to two very different types of relationships between the CIA and Western intelligence agencies. The first may be referred to as the "Gehlen syndrome": just as after World War II the head of the Nazi intelligence apparatus, Richard Gehlen, delivered his organization "virtually intact into American hands" [11], and then went on to cooperate actively with the US intelligence community, in some instances Western intelligence agencies seem to have established much the same kind of cooperative relationships with CIA officials. I refer specifically to the situation that developed in Rwanda from 1962 to 1965. During these years the Rwanda elites were almost entirely dependent on Belgian security officials for information concerning the guerrilla activities mounted by "pro-Chinese" Tutsi exiles from Zaire, Uganda, Tanzania and Burundi. The head of the Rwanda Sureté was a Belgian national, a former Force Publique Major, who had   close relationships with CIA operatives in Rwanda, Burundi and Zaire. He stayed on the job until 1968. Until then it was the Belgian-manned Sureté which in fact constituted the eyes and ears of the CIA in Rwanda. The "Gehlen formula" was clearly an ideal one from the standpoint of US interests: not only were Belgian intelligence agents appropriately aware of the danger of Communist penetration by "proxy", but also remarkably adept at the art of collecting information, recruiting informants, penetrating _inyenzi_ [12] networks in exile, and occasionally indulging in the same kind of lethal gamesmanship that has come to characterize some of the CIA operations elsewhere in Africa.

A similar type of cooperative relationships appears to have developed between CIA and Belgian intelligence agents in Burundi from 1962 to 1964. By 1964, however, the rebellion in eastern Zaire had reached alarming proportions, and the emergence of a "pro-Chinese" faction in Burundi made it imperative for the US to take the initiative in the conduct of covert operations in Burundi and Zaire. Cuban pilots were hired by the CIA to fly bombing missions against rebel positions along the Fizi-Baraka axis; the agency set up its own "private" airline, the so-called Western International Ground Maintenance Operations (WIGMO), which served as a convenient cover for a variety of CIA-related activities, including the training of mercenaries near Albertville; [13] CIA operatives were hastily dispatched to Bukavu, Goma, Bujumbura and Kigali (in a re-enactment of the measures taken after the advent of Lumumba to power, in the summer of 1960); and ultimate responsibility for the coordination of these and other activities was vested in the hands of the CIA "boss" in Zaire, Mr. Lawrence Devlin. Throughout the duration of the rebellion very cozy relations existed between CIA officials and their Belgian counterparts; a particularly friendly rapport was established with the former head of the Belgian Sureté in Zaire, Colonel Vandewalle, who later assumed the dubious distinction of leading the Fifth Mechanised Brigade of mercenaries into Stanleyville in November 1964. [14]

In sharp contrast with the "Gehlen syndrome", in which one of the partners freely puts himself in the service of the other, a highly competitive if not openly antagonistic relationship emerged between Portuguese and US intelligence officials during the brief term of office of Rosa Coutinho as

Governor of Angola in 1974. That Coutinho used his authority to facilitate the entry into Angola of substantial though unknown quantities of Soviet military hardware for the MPLA is a well established fact. The nexus of interests between Coutinho and Neto, backed by strong ideological affinities, was seen by Kissinger as thoroughly incompatible with the spirit of detente, ultimately resulting in what one observer described as "one of the largest covert operations undertaken by the US outside Indo-China". [15] Whether there is any truth to the intriguing thesis (advanced in private by a foreign diplomat) that Kissinger's move in Angola was really intended to placate the Chinese Communists, so as to allay the latter's suspicion that the US was too accomodating towards the Soviets, is difficult to say. What is beyond dispute is that the initial involvement of the CIA in Angola stemmed from the radically divergent appraisals made by US and Portuguese officials of the cold-war implications of the struggle between pro-Soviet and pro-Western (and pro-Chinese) factions.

Somewhere between these extreme forms of cooperation and competition lies a more ambiguous spectrum of relationships, perhaps best illustrated by the kind of arms-length rapport established between the French and American intelligence communities during the Gaullist era. It is as yet impossible to get a full picture of the many ups and downs that have accompanied their dealings with each other, and their respective "deals" with African politicians. Yet there can be no gainsaying the sense of mutual hostility that marked their relationships in Gabon in 1964 and in Madagascar in 1971. In each case the activities of the CIA were seen by French intelligence operatives as posing a direct threat to their protégés, to Leon Mba in Gabon, and to Tsiranana in Madagascar, and hence as an indirect threat to themselves. Commenting on this state of affairs, one observer remarked that "it frequently seemed during the 1960's that CIA operatives in Africa spent more time countering alleged French espionage activities directed against the US than they were studying the Soviets and Chinese". [16] By contrast, the involvement of French "barbouzes" in the internal politics of Zaire in 1963-64 was viewed as little more than a mild irritant by Washington, as a fumbling attempt on the part of the Foccard networks to steal the thunder of the CIA in an area where the latter had already acquired a far stronger position than the French could possible hope to gain for themselves, no matter how hard they tried. [17] The outcome of these maneuverings in any event, was precisely the opposite of what had happened in Gabon and Madagascar a few years earlier. In both states French efforts to denounce the existence of alleged CIA "tricks" resulted in a drastic curtailing of the agency's activities; in Zaire, on the other hand, the CIA station emerged as all-powerful, with little effort on its part to add to the discredit which SDECE and SAC agents had already cast upon themselves through their own ineptitude.

On the whole, the scope and intensity of CIA involvement in Africa seem partly determined by the perceived threats to US interests posed by African actors -- who, rightly or wrongly, are identified as "enemies" -- and partly by the extent of cooperation that can be expected of European intelligence agencies in coping with such threats. But this leaves open the question of what causes Washington to perceive specific African actors as "enemies" and their policies as sufficiently "threatening" to warrant the conduct of covert operations against them. The mere identification of African actors as "Marxist", "Communist", "pro-Soviet" or "pro-Chinese" is clearly not sufficient as a criterion for judgement and evaluation. As the repurcussions of the US enterprise in Angola demonstrate, even where there

is substantial agreement about the ideological sympathies of African leaders,
fundamental disagreements may occur at the highest level as to the advisi-
bility of CIA operations .   The circumstances that led to the resignation of Assistant Secretary of State for African Affairs, Nathaniel Davis,
in 1975, give us a hint of the significance of such disagreements, irrespective of the motives which, in this case, prompted Davis to hand in his resignation -- e.g. his very low estimate of the chances of success of a CIA
operation in Angola, the damaging effect that such failure would have on
the political image of Mobutu of Zaire and Kaunda of Zambia, and the very
negative implications of a policy that would inevitably cast the US in the
role of an ally of South Africa. [18]

Decisive as such considerations may be in shaping particular US responses,
whether African actors are seen as "friends" or "enemies" also depends on
the relative compatibility of their policies with the magnitude of US
economic and strategic interests at stake in specific areas.   Thus Zaire,
Nigeria and Ethiopia are generally seen as areas where a basic reorientation
of economic and diplomatic choices by African actors would meet strong resistance from US policy makers, and possibly lead to countermoves by the CIA.
This is particularly true of Zaire, strategically located in the heart of
the continent, and where American investments are substantial. Not unnatur-
ally, a very cozy relationship has developed over the years between Mobutu
and his CIA patrons: aside from the fact that Zaire "is presumed to be a
symbolic battleground between East and West, where the success or failure
of one's clients would have repercussions throughout Africa",[19] the important
fact is that the CIA did play a determining role in "winning the battle",
largely because in picking Mobutu as its ally it also "came up with the
right man at the right place". [20] Mobutu owes a very large personal and

political debt to his CIA mentors, and whatever efforts and resources were "spent" on Mobutu turned out to be a highly productive investment from the standpoint of US corporate interests. While the CIA continues to play a critically important role in making Zaire "safe for US capitalism", the very magnitude of US corporate interests in Zaire constitutes an additional motive -- as well as an excellent "cover" -- for the maintenance of an extensive CIA network on the scene. If the case of Zaire is any index, the relationship between CIA activities and US corporate interests is a circular one: while CIA operations may play a decisive part in preparing the ground for the intrusion of US corporate interests, these in turn provide further justification for CIA involvement -- as well as the alibis and technological facilities deemed necessary for the conduct of intelligence operations.

The use of business corporations as an intelligence cover is a standard CIA practice: if we are to believe a recent New York Times article, about 200 CIA agents abroad make use of such a cover. As further evidence of this symbiotic relationship one only needs to look at the organizational structure of the agency and its avenues of recruitment. According to Barnet and Muller, "the CIA has a special office that does nothing but maintain contact with corporations overseas; this office is responsible for the placing of agents on corporation payrolls, frequently without the knowledge of top management." [21] Equally instructive is the number of top-ranking CIA officials recruited from the private corporate sector. As shown by Gabriel Kolko's examination of recruitment patterns from 1944 to 1960, out of a combined total of 13 top CIA officials, five were recruited from key law firms, one from a banking and investment firm, one from an industrial corporation, and seven from "miscellaneous business and commercial corporations". [22] The most notorious illustration of how

this sort of corporate linkage is liable to affect US policy abroad is
the Chilean destabilization plan concocted by John McCone, former Head
of the CIA and Director of ITT in 1970: McCone reportedly offered the
CIA a $1 million contribution to help finance a major convert operation
against the late Allende. Typical, also, is the case of Kermitt Roosevelt,
grandson of Teddy Roosevelt, Grotonian and recently Vice-President of Gulf
Oil: It was Kermitt Roosevelt who, in his capacity as Head of the Near
East section of the clandestine branch of the CIA, engineered the "destabilization" of Mossadegh in Iran in 1953, and who, after joining Northrop as
a business consultant in 1965, played a decisive role in persuading King
Faisal of Saudi Arabia to purchase the Northrop Freedom Fighter instead
of the Lockheed F-104 Starfighter. In return Northrop paid $400,000.00 in
consulting fees to Kermitt Roosevelt, who reportedly assured his benefactor:
"my friends in the CIA are also keeping an eye on things".[23] Admittedly,
Chile is not Zaire, nor is the Middle East indentifiable with Africa. But
what the Chilean case suggests, and what recent disclosures about the
ramification of US corporate involvement in the Middle East tend to
confirm, is the existence of significant linkages between the CIA and
US business interests. Just how significant these linkages are in specific
African settings, and how competitive they may be with foreign coporate-
intelligence networks, is what remains to be established.

To delimit the scope of CIA involvement is one thing; to assess its
impact on the course of events in any given state is a very different
matter. What are sufficient grounds to demonstrate that involvement did
occur may be totally inadequate to evaluate the resulting consequences.
In some instances one might even argue that there exist an inverse relationship between the amount of information available and the significance
of its bearing on the internal politics of African states. The quality of

the evidence poses yet another problem. It is not because the evidence happens to be plausible that it is necessarily conclusive. At times the element of fraud is easy to detect (as when the assassination of Prime Minister Pierre Ngendadumwe in Burundi in 1965 was blamed on the CIA by his political opponents); sometimes, however, the sorce from which the evidence is drawn gives us no hint of whether it is accurate or not -- only an impression of plausibility. Thus the information leaked to the French press in 1971 that the US Ambassador to Madagascar, Anthony Marshall might have acted hand in had with the CIA station chief in Tanarive, John F. "Jack" Hasey, to plot Tsiranana's rival, the Vice-President Andre Resampa",[24] but it is equally reasonable to assume that the evidence was fabricated by French intelligence operatives.

Again, the evidence may be "revelant" but incomplete. It may leave out some critically important qualifiers, along with the suplementary information that one would need to make sense of what is being revealed. One is left with bits and pieces of information that are hardly sufficient to get "the Full picture". Consider, for example, the statement made by Sidney Gottlieb in his testimony before the Senate Intelligence Committee in October 1975: Gottlieb, who in 1961 happened to be the head of the CIA's Chemical Division, said that "the agency prepared and sent to Zaire a dose of lethal poison intended for use in an assassination attempt against former premier Patrice Lumumba in 1961".[25] This extraordinary disclosure certainly tells us a great deal about Washington's attitude towards Lumumba, and about what might have been the role of the CIA had not Lumumba been done away with through other means. But this may only be the tip of the iceberg. Gottlieb's testimony tells us nothing of the alternate plans which might have been developed by the CIA, of the part which CIA agents might have played in those or other "contingency plans", of the relationships existing at the time between US and Belgian intelligence networks, of what part, if any, the CIA played in operating the transfer of Lumumba to the Katanga, of the allegation I heard in Kinshasa in 1960 that the CIA provided Mobutu with the money he needed to pay his troops in exchange for shipping Lumumba to his executioners. Nor indeed does Gottlieb's testimony give us as much as a hint of the sub-rosa activities he was conducting in Bukavu in late August 1960. [26] In brief, the mere fact that the CIA did contemplate to get rid of Lumumba through a dose of lethal poison still leaves open the question of the role actually played by the agency at this critical juncture of Zaire's political life.

In spite of these reservations the evidence is not always so fragmentary or unreliable as to preclude a rough reconstruction of sequences of events in which the role of the CIA appears to have been central, or at least signifi-cant from the standpoint of the internal politics of African states. For example: (1) the CIA played a direct role in influencing Kasavubu's decision to depose Lumumba on September 5, 1960, and in ushering in Mobutu as the "impartial arbiter" of the conflict between the President and Prime Minister; (2) CIA operations -- ranging from the hiring and training of mercenaries to the procurement and maintenance of Skyraider bomber fighters and B-26s -- were certainly instrumental in defeating Soumialot's Popular Liberation Army during the 1964 Zairian rebellion; (3) CIA agents, mostly operating from Rwanda, not only kept in close touch with opposition leaders in Burundi during the "pro-Chinese" interlude of 1964-65 but provided them with "technical advice" and probably financial support in an attempt to turn back the tide; (4) CIA agents were largely responsible for planning Moise Tshombe's hi-jacking in June 1967, and therefore indirectly responsible for the abortive anti-Mobutu mercenary-led coup that followed Tshombe's surrender to the Algerian authorities; (5) CIA agents played a significant role in manipulating the outcome of the 1967 elections in Somalia: the rise to power of Prime Minister Muhammed Egal was said to have been "facilitated" by "thousands of dollars in covert support to Egal and other pro-Western elements in the ruling Somali Youth League party prior to the 1967 presidential elections"; [27] (6) similarly, the CIA was directly involved in "facilitating" the rise to power of Col. Richard Ratsimandrava, in Madagascar, in February 1975 -- shortly before members of the Mobile Police Group killed him and replaced him with Didier Ratsiraka; [28] (7) to this must be added the well publicized and wide-ranging activities of the agency in Angola: the shipment of massive quantities of arms and ammunition through Zaire, cash payments to Holden Roberto and Jonas Savimbi, the hiring of mercenaries in Europe and the US, and the supervision of logistical operations on the ground both in Zaire and Angola.

Much of the evidence for these other examples of CIA involvement in the internal affairs of African states is part of the public record. So far, however, surprisingly little has been said of what it all means from the standpoint of political development: Must the CIA be viewed as yet another obstructive element in the list of "obstacles to development" discussed by some political scientists? Or could it conceivably be seen as an instrument of nation-building, as was privately suggested by a senior Foreign Service Officer? [29]

Implications for Development

It will be useful, for purposes of analysis, to look at these questions first from the vantage point of US AID development doctrines and then from the perspective of the academic literature on political development.

The problems involved in meshing US intelligence and developmental goals intrude themselves at different levels and in different forms; further compounding this difficulty is the extreme vagueness of US policy formulations on development: what, exactly, is meant by "political development" cannot be easily detected from statements like "our new aid policy aims at strengthening the political and economic independence of developing nations", or to the effect that foreign aid seeks to "create a peaceful world community of free and independent states, free to choose their own future and their own system so long as it does not threaten the freedom of others". [30] A more candid assessment emerges from Robert Packenham's interview with an AID office director: "We're somewhat schizophrenic here. We want governments that are free and independent, but also non-Communists, preferably a democratic one". [31] Summing up the level at which AID officials tend to conceptualize political development, Packenham notes that it usually means "short-term political or economic development: nearly all AID officials see the uses of aid primarily in terms of this dichotomy. As a result few officials even conceive of a third alternative, namely political development". [32]

It is easy to see in these conditions how intelligence activities might fit into the context of US aid policies (assuming that slogans can be elevated to the level of policies): their primary purpose is to make sure that Third World governments will not succumb to Communist subversion, a goal

which apparently can best be achieved through another kind of subversion.
Although the logic of this proposition is of course highly questionable,
it also raises the question of whether preventing Third World governments
from "going Communist" automatically carries with it the promise of
"freedom and independence". My own experience of the climate of freedom
prevailing in specific African states generally identified as allies of the
West prompts me to entertain rather strong reservations on this matter. A
more realistic appraisal of what development currently means in the official
thinking of US policy makers must take into account the growing irrelevance
of "freedom and democracy" as goals for developing polities, and the
corresponding emphasis placed on order and stability. Especially in point
here is Donal Cruise O'Brien's contention that a fundamental shift has
taken place over the last decade in the scale of priorities of US policy
makers, with the notion of "institutional order" taking precedence over
"democracy". [33] It is at this level that one can best grasp the nature of
the contribution made by intelligence activities to the developmental
goals of US policies in Africa: If development requires organizational
strength, covert manipulation is presumably one of the ways in which the
latter can be attained.

Another point concerns the economic side of the developmental equation.
Leaving aside for the time being the covert activities of the agency, and
focussing instead on its policy prescriptions, it may be worth our while to
consider the implications of the 1974 CIA study on the strategic aspects of
food resources. In the terms of the report, these resources "could give the
US a measure of power it never had before, possibly an economic and political
dominance greater than that of the immediate post-World War II period". [34]
That food has indeed become one "of the principal negotiating tools in our

kit", as Secretary of Agriculture Earl Butz put it in 1974, is by now common knowledge, and the implications of this policy are by no means confined to the African continent. What is significant is that the CIA should engage in this kind of general policy recommendations instead of confining its role to intelligence analysis; equally noteworthy are the repercussions which the implementation of such a policy might have on those African states that are most cruelly affected by resource scarcities. I am unable to say whether the 1974 CIA study had had any negative effect on the volume of agricultural surpluses shipped to Africa under Public Law 480; and even if it did not I am not trying to suggest that the kind of foreign assistance identified with PL 480 is the best or only road to economic development. The only point I wish to emphasize is that the maintenance of "institutional order" through covert manipulation abroad would seem to tie in logically with the sort of leverage accruing from the use of food as a strategic weapon, the former acting as the stick and the latter as the carrot.

Although covert intervention is perfectly consonant with the official tendency noted earlier to conceptualize development in terms of short-run political benefits, and with the primacy accorded to institutional order, this policy is obviously very difficult to reconcile with the requirements of long-run political and economic development. The dilemma is perhaps best expressed in Richard Bissell's own words: [35]

> Covert intervention is usually designed to operate on the internal power balance, often with fairly short-term objectives in view. An effort to build the economy of an underdeveloped country must be subtle, long continued, probably quite costly and must openly enlist the cooperation of major groups within the country... It is not surprising that the practitioners within the US government of these two types of intervention differ temperamentally and in their preferences for friends, methods and ideologies.

The dilemma cannot be resolved by an act of faith -- by a sense of
confidence in the long-term benefits of a transplanted form of democracy
-- or by an act of contrition -- by the recognition that since the "dirty
tricks" of the CIA are incompatible with our value system they ought to
be corrected and sanctioned. The setting up of guidelines and procedures
to control CIA activities abroad is no substitute for the elaboration of a
meaningful set of long-term developmental policies. In much of Africa CIA
activities occurred by default as much as by design.

The vacuousness of US development doctrines is all the more surprising
when one considers the sheer volume of US academic writings on political
development. Yet there is in a sense a close intellectual affinity between
them, suggesting that the wisdom emanating from the groves of academe might
have obviated the need for further elaboration at the official level. Basically, this element of affinity lies in the emphasis placed on institutional
stability as a precondition to development. One is reminded once again of
Donal Cruise O'Brien arresting thesis that "the emergence of political
order as an ideal in the literature on underdevelopment may be related not
only to new perspectives on American interests in dealing with the new states...
but also to changes within the US over the past decade (1960-1970)".[36]

As a means of countering institutional instability the CIA has seldom
if ever been taken into account by American political scientists (even
though some were probably aware of its actual or potential influence in
specific settings). This omission, however, does not detract from the per-
suasiveness of their argument about the need to create strong and effective
political institutions before one can entertain any hope about political
development.[37] Though some might object on moral grounds to the means employed

by the CIA in specific situations, quite a few would probably take the position that, in spite of such objections, CIA activities have often proved eminently functional in terms of creating short-term institutional stability. Judicious allocations of CIA resources to African politicians may thus be viewed as an important stabilizing influence where fragmentation and chaos threaten to tear apart the political system.

The problem with this line of reasoning is not simply that it provides social scientists and policy-makers with a convenient justification for supporting the most ruthlessly authoritarian regimes; it also tends to prejudge a number of issues that have a very direct and obvious bearing on political development.

This is not the place to engage in a critique of various development theories, except to note the critical significance of legitimacy as a precondition to, or expression of development. Legitimacy, in brief, is what allows political actors to enhance their capacity to fulfill certain developmental goals; although this may sound like a truism, what is perhaps less obvious is that the most likely candidates to claim the mantle of legitimacy in Africa are seldom those that are considered the "safest" from the standpoint of CIA standards. It is, after all, in the logic of a natio-nalist movement that its degree of popular legitimacy will tend to increase in proportion to its anti-imperialist, and by implication anti-Western, orien-tation -- at least in the early stages. When power is deflected from its original source of authority its quotient of coercion increases; or else the distributive output of the political system must somehow compensate for its loss of legitimacy. It is quite true, of course, that the coercive and distributive capacities of African actors have at times increased spectacularly as a result of their clientelistic ties with the CIA. Yet to the extent that this relationship becomes public knowledge, the legitimacy of the political system is inevitably called into question. Bribery and repression become routinized, and political actors tend to look upon their CIA connections as the best guarantees of their own political survival. A vicious circle develops in which every effort made by African clients to restore the credibility of their public image leads them to rely more and more heavily on their CIA patron.

Although the case of Zaire is sometimes cited by US officials as a prime example of successful covert intervention, it also shows just how counterproductive CIA connections may be in terms of legitimacy. Consider, for example, the sequence of events that took place in 1967: in an effort to allay suspicions that he was overwhelmingly dependent on the CIA (a fact that had become patently clear during the 1964 rebellion if not earlier) Mobutu decided in 1967 to assume a more radical stance, and in order to give a substance of "authenticity" to this new look, plans were made to bring Tshombe back from Spain and then stage a public execution of the "neo-imperialist" stooge. For this primary reliance was placed on the CIA. The operation proved eminently successful, at least in its initial stage: On June 30, Tshombe's plane was hi-jacked over the Mediterannean and after a forced landing in Algier the leader of the Katanga secession was surrendered to the Algerian government. At this point, however, it became apparent that Boumedienne was unwilling to deliver Tshombe unconditionally to Mobutu, a fact which the CIA had failed to anticipate. Nor did the CIA forsee that, as a consequence of the hi-jacking, an attempt would be made a few weeks later by mercenary forces to bring off a coup against the Kinshasa regime, and which in effect made Mobutu all the more dependent on his CIA patrons. Mobutu's determined efforts to prove that he is not a stooge of the CIA is also the most

plausible explanation for his allegation, in 1975, that a plot had been
hatched within the Forces Armees Zairoises involving the hand of the CIA.
Not only did this patently fabulous claim enable him to publicly dissociate
himself from the CIA at a time when congressional hearings threatened to
bring into the open his occult relationship with the agency, but it also
gave him a convenient pretext to get rid of a number of high-ranking officers
within the army who, for a variety of reasons, had to be eliminated. What
remains unclear is the extent to which Mobutu's latest ploy is liable to
backfire, and whether the expiatory victims chosen by Mobutu will not find
supporters within and outside the army to seek some sort of revenge, possibly
in the form of an army coup. Extolling the virtues of authenticite is barely
enough to conceal the fragility of Mobutu's rule.

In addition to the threats which the CIA poses to the legitimacy of its
African clients, the question arises as to what impact CIA connections may
have on processes of national integration. On the surface the evidence appears
anything but conclusive. At no time, to my knowledge did the CIA try to encourage the Katanga secession; indeed the support which the agency gave to
Mobutu was entirely consistent with Washington's policy of restoring and
maintaining the territorial integrity of the Zairian state. The Angola situation, on the other hand, offers a classic example of the divisive effect of
covert activities on the process of national unification. As I have argued
elsewhere,[38]

> the effect of our policies in Angola has been to render the task
> of national reconciliation an impossible one. By giving massive
> unilateral support to the FNLA-UNITA faction -- through CIA chan-
> nels and thus even before the Soviet-MPLA military connection was
> firmly established -- American policy makers (in effect Kissinger)
> have fordeited whatever opportunities existed at the time of pro-
> moting a rapprochement. Once we made it clear to Holden Roberto

and Jonas Savimbi that the US government would support them to
the hilt, financially and militarily, their expectations of
success were raised to the point where any concession to their
rival appeared unnecessary if not downright counterproductive.

But if this situation could not have arisen without the assistance of the

CIA, it could just as well be described as a consequence of Kissinger's own

policy decisions. And if so the blame lies perhaps more with Kissinger than

with the CIA men in charge of executing his policies. Furthermore, except

for Angola where contacts with Holden Roberto were established by the CIA

long before independence, I know of no example of a deliberate and systematic

effort on the part of the CIA to create or exploit ethnic or political divi-

sions within a nationalist movement prior to independence. The same cannot

be said of the PIDE or SDECE.[39] Where the divisive implications of CIA activi-

ties emerge in their most sinister light is at the level of elite interactions

in the period immediately following independence.

In a number of instances the contacts established by African leaders with

CIA operatives enabled them to raise their stock of resources as well as their

expectations to the point where they felt sufficiently confident to create new

parties, concoct plots and coups, or simply refuse to agree to a compromise

which under different circumstances would seem the most rational option avail-

able. This, at least, is what my reading of CIA involvement in states like

Zaire, Burundi, Angola, and Madagascar tends to suggest.

The "divide ut impera" facet of CIA involvement must be analysed not only

in terms of the political exchange relationships worked out with political op-

ponents or factions within any given state, but also, and perhaps more impor-

tantly, at the level of the attitudes that are fostered by the CIA among its

indigenous clients. What is involved here, in essence, is nothing less than

an attempt to hamper the growth of individual loyalties to the newly emergent state. The following statement by Bissell is again instructive in this respect:[40]

> The US should make increasing use of non-nationals, who, with effort
> at indoctrination and training, should be encouraged to develop a
> second loyalty... Such career agents should be encouraged... with a
> prospect of long-term employment to develop a second loyalty... The
> central task is that of identifying potential indigenous allies --
> both individuals and organizations -- making contact with them, and
> establishing the fact of a community of interests.

What this statement reveals is a conscious and deliberate attempt on the part

of the CIA bureaucracy to manipulate the attitudes of "potential indigenous

allies" in ways that are profoundly detrimental to the growth of national

loyalties. It brings to light the importance of "indoctrination and training"

in operating appropriate shifts of loyalty, and shows how prospects of "long-

term employment" may be used by CIA officials to nurture a proper cast of

mind among their potential allies. The implication is that only throuth con-

tinuous and intimate contacts with non-nationals can "career agents" be recrui-

ted into the agency and transformed into "loyal" auxiliaries in their home

states. One is impelled to wonder whether such practices do not constitute one

of the most serious disabilities faced by Third World governments in their

attempt to achieve a minimum level of national integration. If there is any

truth to the notion that "acute ambiguities in the normative and value systems

(of African countries)... have a profoundly negative effect on both the inte-

grative and performance capacities of these countries",[41] Bissel's exhortations

lay bare at least one major element in the background of such ambiguities.

Finally something must be said of the institutional constraints imposed

upon African client governments as a result of their CIA connections. I refer

specifically to the manner in which CIA covert activities are liable to affect

the process of institutionalization, that is the "process by which organizations

and procedures acquire value and stability".[42] If we accept the argument, set

forth by Samuel Huntington, that the existence of adaptable, complex, autonomous and coherent organizations and procedures is an essential prerequisite
of development, the question immediately arises as to whether an environment
permeated by CIA agents is in any way congenial to the growth of strong and
stable institutions.

There is no way one can assess the exact relationship between CIA networks and specific African institutions; nor is there any way of determining
what type of covert activity was operative in any particular context at a
particular time. Until that kind of evidence becomes available any attempt
to generalize about the relationship between CIA intervention and political
institutionalization is bound to involve a large element of speculation. In
particular the effect of indigenous factors (such as ethnicity, factionalism
or corruption) cannot be clearly segregated from exogenous (i.e. CIA) influences. Nonetheless, given the range of activities included under the rubric of
"covert action" -- namely, (1) political advice and counsel; (2) subsidies to
an individual; (3) financial support and technical assistance; (4) support of
private organizations, including labor unions, business firms, cooperatives,
etc. (5) covert propaganda; (6) private training of individuals and exchange
of persons; (7) economic operations; and (8) paramilitary or political action
designed to overthrow or to support a regime[43] -- it is easy to see how such
activities, whether individually or cumulatively, might positively hamper the
adaptability, autonomy and coherence of African institutions. Unless one takes
the view that penetration of an institution by the CIA is itself proof of its
adaptability, it seems fairly evident that the kind of "goal replacement" which
is brought about through CIA infiltration is bound to have a very negative effect
on the capacity of institutions to adapt themselves to sociopolitical change.

Trade union, student associations, church organizations may become so heavily dependent on CIA subsidies and advice as to lose all responsiveness to their respective constituencies. Their organizational goals may become almost exclusively geared towards the collection of secret information, espionage, propaganda, and so forth, to the detriment of their normal brokerage functions. Coordinated responses to environmental challenges become virtually impossible in these circumstances, if only because of the very nature of the reward system which operates to substitute external goals for internal ones, and individual gratifications for collective ones.

Not only the adaptability but the autonomy of political institutions is likely to be endangered by the spread of covert operations. The point here is not merely that the autonomy of an institution diminishes in proportion to its degree of dependence on an external agency; even more pertinent is the extent to which CIA activities operate to strengthen the dependence of political institutions on particularlistic groups and interests -- ethnic, regional, family or clan interests. Quite obviously, the saliency of particularistic interests is not solely attributable to CIA involvement; institutions can lose their autonomy for a variety of other reasons. Yet in a number of cases the net result of CIA involvement in the internal politics of African states has been to greatly accentuate the dependence of their institutions on ethnic and regional particularisms, and sometimes on a very special category of occupational groups -- i.e. mercenaries. The case of Zaire from 1964 to 1967, and Angola in 1975-76, are obvious examples. The intrusion of mercenary forces into the political process of these states has yet to be fully elucidated;[44] that it has had a profoundly detrimental influence on the stability of their political and military institutions is nonetheless undeniable.

The vulnerability of African institutions to CIA penetration threatens their cohesiveness for much the same reason that it lessens their autonomy. Sub-rosa maneuverings, personal animosities and conspiratorial attitudes are expected patterns of behavior among individuals engaged in covert activities. The injection of valued resources (usually in the form of cash) into the domestic environment of African states introduces a new structure of opportunities for opportunists at the same time that it sets the stage for underhand maneuverings and mutual suspicions among them. The competitive impulses unleashed through various forms of covert "assistance" or "advice" carry profoundly disruptive implications; further adding to the fragility of political institutions is the sense of cynicism and self-centeredness which inevitably accompanies involvement in covert operations. Maintaining a proper esprit de corps and solidarity in these circumstances is an impossible task. What happens to the cohesiveness of political institutions in an environment saturated by CIA influences is perhaps best illustrated by the so-called "Binza Group" in Zaire -- a loose assemblage of politicians whose only bond of solidarity stemmed from their various connections with CIA agents, and whose brief life-span in the early sixties testifies to its utter lack of cohesion, discipline and efficiency. [45] The "Binza Group" is indeed a prime example of institutional anemia.

What is sometimes referred to in the literature on development as the "crisis of penetration" -- meaning in its broadest sense the geographical extension of state structures along with the sociopsychological disposition to conform with public policies [46] -- is clearly in need of reformulation. Some of the most serious crises faced by African states are indeed crises of penetration. But the question that needs to be faced is whether the penetration of African institutions by foreign intelligence agencies does not represent a major element in the so-called "crisis of penetration" in the sense we just indicated. The time has come to recognize the CIA for what it is -- not just a "spook factory" but an institution which in varying degrees and through different instrumentalities has had and continues to have a largely negative effect on the process of development of Third World countries. And the same, of course, applies to its foreign counterparts, most notably its French counterpart. If so, it is no longer possible to accept at face value the disputable claim made by some analysts, either explicitly or implicitly, that the main impediments to Third World development are essentially internal. At a time when the economist P.T. Bauer, in what can only be described as a blatant case of special pleading, seeks to exculpate the West of its sense of guilt with regard to "Third World poverty", [47] it is appropriate to remind ourselves of the wide range of clandestine political, financial and paramilitary activities for which the West bears direct responsibility, and whose comulative impact appears to have been highly detrimental from the standpoint of economic and political development.

Conclusion

Among the several issues raised in this discussion, one of the most critical concerns the relationship of the social scientist with the realities of power. I am reminded in this connection of the argument set forth by the late Peter Nettl in his essay on "Power and the Intellectuals": [48]

> The major disability from which intellectuals suffer in modern society is their awkward and incongruous relationship with problems of modern power; intellectuals and power are incompatible. Since one is more sharply sensitive to what is intolerable than what is natural or congenial, it is perhaps natural that intellectuals should wince and cry at power, while social scientists should attempt to bury it among the antiquities.

This "incongruous relationship" is nowhere more evident than when the exercise of power involves stealth, coercion and "dirty tricks". These, after all, are categories which seldom enter into the conceptual arsenal of model builders and devotees of structural functionalism. While social scientists are everywhere drawn into an ever closer relationship with governmental agencies, and are becoming every day more aware of the seamier side of governmental and corporate power, they tend on the whole to display a remarkable degree of intellectual indifference to those very forms of power which violate their models as well as their ethical sensitivities.

The highly elusive, contingent character of the phenomena we just discussed is certainly a major element in the background of this paradoxecal situation. The problem of evidence, as noted earlier, is obviously a very real one. Yet few political scientists with experience on the ground, whether in Washington or in the Third World, can honestly claim to be unaware of the existence of covert activities, or incapable of intelligent speculation about their overall effect in specific situational contexts. That many such activities are by their very nature beyond the pale of scientific research does not make them less significant; nor can one invoke their "illegitimate" or "deviant" character as a pretext for leaving them out of the accounting.

If the incidence of covert activities on the political process of Third World countries is almost never mentioned in American political science writings, this is in part because of the highly sensitive nature of the evidence pertaining to these activities, and the prevalent assumption held by scholars that serious professional liabilities might result from the disclosure of such evidence. Another and perhaps even more significant reason is that this type of evidence detracts from the general assumptions underlying the various theories, scenarios and models that form the stock in trade of respectable political scientists. "Philosophical contemplation",

said Hegel, "has no other intention than to eliminate the accidental".
The same might be said of most theoretical formulations in the social
sciences. These formulations are seldom receptive to the accidental, and
when accidents take the form of "dirty tricks" the need to eliminate them
becomes all the more imperative. This is why the impression of theoretical
elegance conveyed by some of the theories offered by social scientists is
at times so difficult to reconcile with the contingent and disorderly nature
of political realities. The point has been made by the late Hannah Arendt
with characteristic forcefulness: "What these problem-solvers have in common
with down-to-earth liars is the attempt to get rid of facts, and the confidence that this should be possible because of the inherent contingency of
those facts". [49] Attempts at generalization are bound to involve some
degree of selectiveness in the choice of empirical data; this does not make
them synonymous with intellectual deception. The crux of the problem lies
in the manner in which selectivity is employed. It is one thing to discuss
problems of development from the standpoint of ethnicity and regionalism;
it is quite another to "explain" the Angolan civil war solely in terms of
ethnic and personality differences, or for that matter the failure of the
1964-65 rebellion in Zaire solely by reference to internal variables. The
latter type of explanation brings selectivity very close to the level of
intellectual deception. The point, in short, is that in a number of instances
our attempt to fit political realities into our theories results in a highly
distorted view of what constitutes power. However disconcerting or unpalat-
able, contingencies of the kind we discussed in this paper cannot be
eliminated from the ethical and intellectual concerns of political scientists;
or else their relationship with the realities of power are bound to involve
a good deal of intellectual sterility and moral cynicism.

Which brings us to another dimension of the paradox noted earlier,
i.e. the inability or unwillingness of American social scientists to
recognize and come to grips with what Martin Kilson calls "the hypocrisy
of power in American society". [50] Referring to the status of Afro-Americans
in the wider political system of the United States, Kilson notes that the
Afro-American subsystem constitutes "a veritable laboratory in which to
deepen our understanding of the hypocrisy of power -- normlessness and the
failure of political morality -- in a major modern political culture". [51]
How to deal with this "pervasive deviation by political actors from the
reputed norms of the political system", [52] is also the major problem confronting social scientists in the face of the intensifying debate over the
propriety of covert activities at home and abroad. Although the analysis
of forms of behavior that somehow diverge from established constitutional
or ethical standards has long been recognized as a legitimate concern of
social scientists, in this case the "norm gap" is so wide as to inspire in
most of us a degree of distaste and abhorrence which operates to inhibit
rational discourse. Critical analysis gives way to moral indignation or
silent consternation. Yet to divide humanity into the pure and the corrupt,
a la Robespierre, is scarcely appropriate to bridge the gap between "dirty
tricks" and accepted norms of political morality, least of all when the former
become a standard practice. Nor is the mere recognition of "the hypocricy
of power" sufficient to salve our conscience. There remains the more arduous
task of rescuing from our political system the sense of decency, and of
ultimate purpose that is supposed to govern our relationships with ourselves
and with others: if this discussion has in any way contributed to the
realization of this task, one of its main purposes has been achieved.

FOOTNOTES

1. Quoted in Current Foreign Policy (Department of State: Office of Media Services) Publication 8701, May 1973, p. 4.

2. See in particular, Victor Marchetti and John Marks, The CIA and the Cult of Intelligence (New York, 1974), and Robert L. Borosage and John Marks eds., The CIA File (New York, 1976). Other works of interest on the CIA, but of a lesser caliber, include Patrick McGarvey CIA: The Myth and the Madness (Baltimore 1972), Andrew Tully, CIA: The Inside Story (New York, 1962), and David Wise and Thomas Ross, The Espionage Establishment (New York, 1967).

3. For further thoughts on this matter, see the mock issue of Africa Report produced by the Harvard-based Africa Research Group, Africa Retort: A Tribal Analysis of US Africanists (n.d.); though highly polemical, much of the information conveyed in this publication needs to be taken seriously, at least seriously enough to promote debate and discussion among Africanists.

4. The phrase is borrowed from the much quoted work by Professor A. Zolberg, Creating Political Order (New York, 1965).

5. Charles J.V. Murphy, "Unlocking the CIA", Fortune, June 1975, p. 88, 91.

6. Patrice Chairoff, B... Comme Barbouzes (Paris, 1976), esp. pp. 69-91; see also, "Les pions de la France a Cabinda", Le Nouvel Observateur, January 20, 1976, p. 27.

7. See Appendix 1, in Marchetti and Marks, op. cit., p. 362.

8. Bruce Oudes, "The CIA in Africa", Africa Report, July-August 1974, p. 49.

9. Ibid.

10. The origins of the Service d'Action Civique and its relationship to the SDECE are vividly described in Chairoff, op. cit., p. 11 ff.; the determining role played by Jacques Foccart in the implantation of French intelligence networks throughout French West and Equatorial Africa -- partly through fake corporations, partly through personal connections, and partly through the infiltration of development agencies such as the Bureau pour le Développement de la Production Agricole (BDPA) -- emerges with special clarity from Chairoff's narrative, pp. 83-94.

11. See Heinz Hohne and Hermann Zolling, The General was a Spy (New York, 1972); the quote is from Tully's preface to the American edition, p. 2.

12. Inyenzi, meaning "cockroach" in Kinyarwanda, was the term commonly used in Rwanda to refer to the armed raids mounted by Tutsi refugees in exile against the government of Gregoire Kayibanda. For further information on the etymology of the term, see F. Rodegem, "Sens et role des noms propres en Histoire du Burundi", Etudes d'Histoire Africaine, VII (1975), pp. 79. For a discussion of the historical background to the Rwanda revolution, see my Rwanda and Burundi (London and New York, 1970).

13. See the comments by Ted B. Braden, himself hired in Brussels through CIA agents to serve in Zaire in the mid-sixties, in Ramparts, Octover 1967; further references to WIGMO are found in Congo 1967 (Bruxelles, 1968), p. 341, 350, 356, 362, 510.

14. Vandewalle's role during the rebellion is made abundantly clear by his candid and highly instructive account of mercenary activities, L'Ommegang: Odyssee et Reconquete de Stanleyville, 1964 (Bruxelles, n.d.).

15. Gerald Bender, "Angola: A New Quagmire for US?", Los Angeles Times, December 21, 1975.

16. Bruce Oudes, "The CIA in Africa", op. cit., p. 51.

17. A specific example of the activities conducted in Zaire by French intelligence operative, is the abortive plot reportedly carried out against Mobutu by a former OAS (Organization de l'Armée Secrete) Delta commando (known under the nickname of "Petite Soupe"); for further details, see Chairoff, op. cit., p. 78-79.

18. See New York Times.

19. Roger Morris and Richard Mauzy, "Following the Scenario: Reflections on Five Case Histories in the Mode and Aftermath of CIA Intervention", in Borosage and Marks, The CIA File, op. cit., p. 35.

20. Tully, CIA: The Inside Story, op. cit.

21. Richard Barnet and Ronald Muller, Global Reach (New York, 1974), p. 102.

22. Gabriel Kolko, The Roots of American Foreign Policy (Boston, 1959), p. 20.

23. See Joseph P. Albright "How to get a new plane (and its maker) off the Ground", The New York Times Magazine, Feb. 8, 1976. Also, Ann Crittenden, "Closing in on Corporate Payoffs Overseas", The New York Times, Feb. 15, 1976 (Section 3).

24. Bruce Oudes, "The CIA in Africa", op. cit.

25. Quoted in Saint Petersburg Times, Oct. 12, 1975.

26. I met Mr. Gottlieb in Bukavu in August 1960: he introduced himself as a Canadian businessman, who knew Lumumba, and eager to displace Belgian interests in the Kivu. He later on surfaced in the headlines as head of the Chemical Division of the CIA...

27. Morris and Mauzy, "Following the Scenario...", op. cit., p. 38.

28. See Tad Szulc, "Kissinger's Secret Empire", Penthouse, June 1975, p. 50.

29. Referring to the role of the CIA in Zaire, an unidentified Foreign Service Officer reportedly admitted to Morris and Mauzy, "It's been a good exercize in nation-building". Morris and Mauzy, "Following the Scenario...", op. cit., p. 36.

30. The first quote is from Dennedy's 1962 Foreign Aid Message to Congress; the second is from second State of the Union address. Both are quoted in Robert Packenham, "Political Development Doctrines in the American Foreign Aid Program," World Politics, XVIII, 2(January 1966), p. 211.

31. Ibid., p. 212.

32. Ibid., p. 214.

33. Donal Cruise O'Brien, "Modernization, Order and the Erosion of a Democratic Ideal", Journal of Development Studies, VIII, 4 (July 1972), pp. 352-378.

34. See The Manchester Guardian, January 4, 1976 (weekly edition).

35. Marchetti and Marks, The CIA and the Cult of Intelligence, op. cit., p. 365.

36. Donal Cruise O'Brien, "Modernization, Order and the Erosion of a Democratic Ideal", op. cit., p. 370.

37. This idea is articulated with special forcefulness and cogency in Huntington, Political Order in Changing Societies (New Haven, 1968), pp. 1-24.

38. In a letter to the Editor of the Gainesville Sun, December 28, 1975.

39. See for example the extraordinary account of the so-called "Operacao Safira" mounted by the Portuguese secret service (PIDE) against the PAIGC in Guinea Bissau in 1973, in _Expresso_ (Lisbon), January 24, 1976. Organized by Barbieri Cardoso, Deputy Director of the PIDE, (who apparently derived part of his inspiration from Edward Luttwak's _Coup d'Etat_, a kind of do-it-yourself instruction manual published in 1968), the aim of the operation was to take advantage of the tensions allegedly existing between Cape Verdian and Guinean elements so as to encourage the capture of the party leadership by pro-Portuguese Guinean elements. The April 1974 coup in Portugal was apparently the decisive factor preventing the operation from being carried out. Interestingly, SDECE was tangentially involved in the operation. See also the account of the so-called "Operacao Mar Verde" directed against Sekou Toure's regime in 1970, with the active cooperation of the PIDE and General Spinola, in _Expresso_, January 3, 1976.

40. Marchetti and Marks, _The CIA and the Cult of Intelligence,_ op. cit., p. 367-8.

41. James S. Coleman, "The Development Syndrome: Differentiation, Equality, Capacity", in Leonard Binder et al. eds, _Crises and Sequences in Political Development_ (Princeton, 1971), p. 99.

42. Huntington, _Political Order in Changing Societies, op. cit._, p. 12.

43. Marchetti and Marks, _The CIA and the Cult of Intelligence_, op. cit., p. 364.

44. See, however, the instructive discussion by J. Gerard-Libois and B. Verhaegen, "La Revolte des Mercenaires" in _Congo 1967_, op. cit., and Vandewalle, _L'Ommegang_, op. cit.

45. For a more detailed discussion, see M. Crawford Young "Political Systems Development" in John N. Paden & Edward W. Soja eds., _The African Experience_, Vol. I (Evanston 1970) pp. 467-8.

46. See Joseph LaPalombara, "Penetration: A Crisis of Governmental Capacity", in _Crises and Sequences of Development_, op. cit., pp. 205-232.

47. P.T. Bauer, "Western Guilt and Third World Poverty", _Commentary_, 61 (January 1976), pp. 31-8.

48. In Conor Cruise O'Brien and William Dean Vanech, _Power and Consciousness_ (London and New York, 1969), p. 16.

49. Hannah Arendt, "Lying in Politics", _The New York Review of Books,_ Nov. 18, 1971, p. 32.

50. Martin Kilson, "Political Science and Afro-American Studies", a paper presented at the University of Iowa Conference on "Political Science: The Teacher and the Polity", Oct. 17-19, 1974, p. 9.

51. Ibid.

52. Ibid.

CHAPTER XI

THE CIA AND US POLICY IN ZAIRE AND ANGOLA

BY STEPHEN WEISSMAN

Introduction

"Covert action" as practiced by the United States Central Intelligence
Agency has been defined as "clandestine activity designed to influence foreign
governments, events, organizations or persons in support of U.S. foreign policy
conducted in such a way that the involvement of the U.S. Government is not apparent."[1]
The CIA has pursued its most substantial African covert actions in Zaire (the
former Belgian Congo) and Angola. As the recent paramilitary, political and propaganda operation unfolded in Angola, both U.S. policymakers and distressed African
observers were struck by its connection to earlier American intervention in Zaire.
Secretary of State Henry Kissinger suggested that Angolan independence was fraught
with the same dangers for U.S. security as Zairian independence in 1960: "We
cannot ignore, for example, the substantial Soviet build-up of weapons in Angola,
which has introduced great power rivalry into Africa for the first time in 15 years."[2]
Assistant Secretary of State for African Affairs William Schaufele, Jr., discerned
"obvious parallels between Soviet efforts to move in on the Congo after independence
in 1960 and Moscow's behavior in Angola today."[3] From another perspective, an
editorial in a Government-owned newspaper in "pro-Western" Ghana complained, "The
U.S. is now fighting tooth and nail to prevent the Popular Movement for the
Liberation of Angola from taking the reins of government just as it used Tshombe
to destroy Patrice Lumumba in order to prevent his socialist-oriented party from taking
power at independence in the Congo."[4]

This essay compares covert action policies in Zaire and Angola in contexts of
overt U.S. and Western support, Soviet and other Communist power competition, and
indigenous political and economic forces.   The fundamental and long range
implications of intervention for U.S. diplomatic interests are also examined. An

opportunity for greater breadth of generalization is provided through reference
to other well-documented cases of covert action in the Third World.

In the previous chapter, Lemarchand described the problems posed to social
science research by the "murky underworld" of clandestine struggle. My own
presentation of specific covert exploits in Zaire and Angola is based on public
documents, including recently declassified papers from the Eisenhower, Kennedy
and Johnson Administrations, and confidential personal interviews with policymakers
and other informed individuals. When referring to interviews I always indicate
the general nature of the source. I make no reference to covert action without
either documentary proof or the testimony of at least two informed diplomatic or
other U.S. Government officials.

The evidence is inadequate for in-depth analysis of two important issues:
Executive and Congressional review and control of the CIA, and the rationale for
choosing covert rather than overt means. In general, the available documentary
and interview evidence suggests that with two possible exceptions[5] the major
Zairian and Angolan covert actions were known to top Executive officials. But
there is little information about the process of review, command and control in the
supervisory 40 Committee of the National Security Council and its predecessors.
As for the choice of covert technology, it is reasonable to infer that several
considerations were influential, depending upon the type of covert action and its
environment: effectiveness of proceeding secretly, avoidance of diplomatic problems
and an open confrontation with the Soviet Union, and evasion of domestic political
accountability.[6]

Covert Action in Context

Zaire

On June 30, 1960 the Belgian Congo received its Independence under a democratic
coalition Government headed by the militant nationalist, Patrice Lumumba.

"Shortly thereafter", Lawrence Devlin arrived in Leopoldville to assume his duties as Chief of the CIA Station in the American Embassy.[7] Within a few weeks he was deeply involved in an effort to overthrow the Government and assassinate some of its top officials, the first of a series of covert action and related "intelligence" programs that would continue into the 1970s.

Soon after independence the Congolese army mutinied; Belgian troops reoccupied the country, organizing the secession of the Katanga province; and Prime Minister Lumumba and Chief of State Joseph Kasavubu called in United Nations forces to help reorganize the army and remove the Belgians. The U.N., however, delayed in replacing the Belgian troops and refused to move against the Belgian-led Katanga secession. This policy received crucial backing from the Republican Eisenhower Administration which shared Belgium's vision of conservative order and was disposed to follow NATO leads in black Africa. As Belgian-organized secessionist and political pressures mounted against his Government, Lumumba threatened to dispense with the U.N. Force except for sympathetic African left-nationalist contingents and to invade Katanga with Afro-Asian and Soviet military assistance.

In the view of U.S. policymakers, Lumumba's persistent, emotional, and shifting pleas for outside help against Belgium revealed his "personal instability" which the Soviet Union came to exploit through "leftist", "anti-white", "Communist" and "Pro-Communist" advisers in the Prime Minister's entourage.[8] Referring to incidents in which elements of the Congolese army arrested Belgian and U.N. personnel, Ambassador Clare Timberlake warned,

> ...If the U.N. does not immediately act to take the army out of Government control...most of the handful of Europeans still in Leopoldville will leave and the remainder would be some foreign embassy personnel, Communist agents and carpetbaggers. We are convinced that the foregoing is the Communist plan. Lumumba (Minister of Information)Kashamura, Ghanaian Ambassador Djin and (Chief of Protocol)Madame Blouin are all anti-white and the latter is a Communist. So are their Guinean advisers. Our latest arrival (French press secretary) Serge Michel of the (Algerian National Liberation Front) is even more in the Commie camp and

anti-Western. They seem to have no trouble urging Lumumba
further down roads which his own instincts direct him at least
part of the way.[9]

The State Department noted that Lumumba "was receiving advice and encouragement

not only from Guinean and other African leftists but also from European Communists

and of course from the Soviet and other Communist representatives in Leopoldiville."[10]

On August 18th, Devlin cabled CIA headquarters,

Embassy and Station believe Congo experiencing classic Communist
takeover Government...Whether or not Lumumba actually Commie
or just playing Commie game to assist his solidifying power,
anti-west forces rapidly increasing power Congo and there may be
little time left in which take action to avoid another Cuba.[11]

At a National Security Council meeting the same day, Undersecretary of State

Douglas Dillon remarked, "If the U.N. were forced out, we might be faced with a

situation where the Soviets intervened by invitation of the Congo", and further

observed that Lumumba "was working to serve the purposes of the Soviets".

President Eisenhower exhibited acute concern that "one man supported by the Soviets"

could threaten the UN operation, and one top aide in attendance remembered the

President seeming to issue an assassination order. In any event, other forms

of covert action were apparently approved since CIA headquarters on the following

day authorized the Station "to proceed with operation (to replace Lumumba "with

pro-Western group") and the resulting activities were discussed August 25th at a

meeting of the NSC Special Group which oversees CIA covert actions.[12]

The CIA Station quickly undertook "covert operations through certain labor

groups" and "the planned attempt to arrange a vote of no confidence in Lumumba"

in the Congolese Senate. After August 25th when the Special Group agreed at

Eisenhower's behest that "planning for the Congo would not necessarily rule out

consideration of any particular kind of activity which might contribute to

getting rid of Lumuba", a series of assassination plots were encouraged, developed

and put into effect.[13] If any additional impetus were necessary, news arrived on

August 26th that an estimated 100 Soviet Bloc technicians in the Congo would soon be joined by 10 IL-18 Soviet transport planes to be used in a planned Central

Government invasion of Katanga.[14]

Unfortunately, the Senate Select Committee on Intelligence Report on

Alleged Assassinations Plots ignores, save for a few unanalyzed suggestions, CIA

political action programs against Lumumba and his followers in the fall and winter

of 1960 and the role of U.S.-financed leaders with respect to assassination.

As I have shown elsewhere, there is strong circumstantial evidence of a U.S. role

in the Kasavubu coup of September 5th against Lumumba; and there is the direct

testimony of a U.S. diplomat on the scene as well as two former U.S. officials that

the CIA was involved in the decisive Mobutu coup of September 14th.[15] A

recently declassified State Department Chronology of the Congo crisis seems generally

confirmatory:

> Planning, of an operational nature, dealt with covert activities
> to bring about the overthrow of Lumumba and install a pro-Western
> Government...(Operations under this plan were gradually put into
> effect by CIA).

Two reliable U.S. diplomatic sources have now confirmed that the Special Group

authorized payment to Kasavubu shortly before his coup. This certainly casts

light upon the Assassinations Report's observation that, on the day following

Kasavubu's initiative, two CIA officers approached "a high level Congolese

politician to warn him of the Lumumba danger", offer assistance "in preparation

new government program" and provide assurances that the U.S. "would supply

technicians" [17]

Several American and foreign diplomats agree that Colonel Joseph Mobutu and

his "Binza Group" of political allies (including Foreign Minister Bomboko,

Finance Commissioner Ndele, and Security chiefs Nendaka and Kandolo) constituted

a compact and frequently cooperative vehicle of CIA funds and counsel.[18] As

the State Department Chronology relates,

> The UAR and Ghana were not the only ones to pump money (in
> their case to the Lumumbists) into the political picture. By
> mid-November, U.S. activities on the political scene in Leopoldville

were of sizeable proportions and may have been fairly conspicuous...

> Ambassador Timberlake and the representatives of another Agency
> (Authors note: clearly the CIA) had intensive discussions with
> Kasavubu, Mobutu, Ileo, Bomboko, Adoula, Bolikango and others...
> (Timberlake cabled) I hope the Department is not assuming from
> a few modest successes that the Embassy has Kasavubu, Mobutu,
> or any other Congolese "in the pocket". While we have con-
> sistently endeavored through counsel and advice to guide moderate
> elements along a reasonable path, they rarely consult us voluntarily
> regarding their prospective moves...

> (U.N. Representative Rajeshar Dayal) in an interview with the
> New York Times correspondent (not printed) broadly implied that
> he knew the U.S. was financing Mobutu...

> (U.N. Secretary-General Dag Hammarskjold) told the American
> Ambassador to the U.N. it would be most helpful particularly
> if we could put some "fire" into Kasavubu (to help in forming
> a new Government acceptable to parliament) so long as we could
> do it "delicately" and not "visibly" and so long as we "put
> nothing in his pocket"---an apparent reference to U.S. "covert"
> activities in Leopoldville....[19]

Among the "modest successes" of the Americans were the frustration of African

and Congolese efforts to reconcile Kasavubu and Lumumba, and efforts by Congolese

"moderates" to expand the base of Mobutu's regime.[20]

CIA financed and counseled leaders also seem to have gone along with more force-

ful entreaties although their role has been obscured by the Assassinations Report.

The latter notes that Devlin "warned a key Congolese leader" about coup plotting

by Lumumba and two of his supporters, and "urged arrest or other more permanent

disposal of Lumumba, Gizenga and Mulele"[21]---a good example of the linkage between

CIA "intelligence" and "covert action" programs. But it fails to mention that

Deputy Prime Minister Gizenga was in fact arrested by Mobutu and a decision was

made to transfer him to his bitter enemies in Katanga. At the last minute he was

released by sympathetic U.N. troops from Ghana.[22] Similarly, Devlin is portrayed

as an "adviser" to a Congolese effort to "eliminate" Lumumba on the day after

Mobutu's coup. But there is no indication in the Report that Lumumba was arrested

on the following day, but managed to escape his captors.[23]

In late November Lumumba left U.N. protective custody to try and return to his political base at Stanleyville. The CIA Station worked with the Mobutu Government to get roads blocked and troops alerted to possible escape routes. After Lumumba's capture it appeared that the troops guarding him would mutiny and return him to power, so he was transferred to Katanga where he was murdered probably on the evening on January 17-18th.[24]

The authors of the Assassinations Report failed to consider this powerful context of CIA political action and influence in reaching their conclusion that,

> Despite the fact that (Devlin) knew of a (Government) plan to deliver Lumumba into the hands of his enemies at a time when the CIA was convinced that "drastic steps" were necessary to prevent Lumumba's retrun to power, there is no evidence of CIA involvement in this plan or in bringing about the death of Lumumba in Katanga.[25]

The CIA was subsidizing and advising (with "modest" success) the top Congolese leadership which decided to transfer Lumumba. It was a "Congolese Government leader'' who voluntarily informed Devlin of the plan. The CIA had been working with some of its political protégés---as well as other Congolese and a European--from August through November in efforts to assassinate or abduct Lumumba.[26] Its recommendation for "permanent disposal" of Lumumba's deputy had been followed by his arrest and a Government decision to deliver him to his "bitterest enemies" in Katanga. Given this background of covert political influence including specific assassination plots, the CIA's failure to question its clients' plan to dispose of Lumumba must have appeared as an expression of tacit consent. In any case it is hard to avoid the judgment that it represented a definite complicity in murder.

Overt diplomacy made an essential contribution to the success of covert operations in this period. The U.N. controlled potentially decisive military and financial resources in Leopoldiville. But its dependence upon American economic, political, logistical and administrative support ensured these trumps would be used either directly in behalf of American objectives or indirectly in the manner of benign neutrality. Thus U.N. Representative Andrew Cordier did not discourage

Kasavubu from his CIA-supported coup and gave it a probably decisive boost by closing the airports and radio station, preventing Lumumba from mobilizing his supporters. Having invoked the shibboleth of "law and order" this time, the U.N. fell silent and remained impassive when its military protege, Mobutu, pulled off another CIA coup several days later. Although certain political and administrative changes enabled the U.N. to assume a more even-handed stance in the following weeks (e.g. it offered protective custody to Lumumba before his escape and capture), it nevertheless gave considerable de facto support to the U.S.-sponsored Mobutu regime.[27]

The advent of the Democratic Kennedy Administration did not bring any lessening of concern about Soviet exploitation of the Lumumbist movement. After all Gizenga had set up a regime in Stanleyville which received financial and political support from the Soviet Union and United Arab Republic. But the Kennedy Administration had more confidence than its predecessor in the perseverance of civilian moderates and it possessed a new sensitivity to African relations. It decided to bring about a legal parliamentary regime under Cyrille Adoula that would absorb Gizenga and his allies, and to gradually move the U.N. and reluctant NATO allies to deal with Katangan secession. Covert CIA and U.N. bribery of parliamentarians at the meeting which selected Adoula has been confirmed by a member of the American Embassy and several unofficial sources, and received the following tribute in a CIA Memorandum in President Kennedy's files: "The U.N. and the United States, in closely coordinated activities, played essential roles in this significant success over Gizenga". This document also revealed the CIA program for Adoula as of November 1961:

> The (State) Department, in conjunction with other branches of
> the Government (Author's Note: clearly the CIA) is endeavoring
> to help Adoula improve his political base of support and enhance
> his domestic power and stature. This activity is in the areas
> of political organization with connected trade union and youth
> groups, public relations and security apparatus.[28]

The propaganda component would appear to have sufaced in mid-1964 when the Angolan leader Jonas Savimbi, then resident in Leopoldiville, revealed the presence of an American public relations adviser named Muller in Adoula's office.[29] The Prime Minister's key political supporters, the Binza Group, continued to receive CIA subsides according to several diplomatic sources. In addition, political action funds were used to keep parliament in line and to launch RADECO, a pro-Adoula political party. Another example of uses of "intelligence" for "covert action" was provided by the CIA's discovery of a plot to assassinate Mobutu. The information was passed on to Mobutu whose gratitude was said to make him more receptive to CIA suggestions.[30]

Again conventional diplomacy was a crucial backdrop for covert action to stabilize a pro-Western regime. American support enabled the U.N. Force to subdue Katanga secession, bringing new financial means and nationalist prestige to Adoula's Government. U.S. economic aid, at first through voluntary contributions to the U.N., then bilaterally, greatly increased the Government's resources. A military assistance program of equipment and training started in 1963, in conjuction with Belgium and Italy. The American Ambassador and U.N. Representative took the lead in urging Adoula to purge Gizenga from his cabinet and remove him from the political scene. The U.N. would collaborate in his arrest.[31]

After the subjugation of Katanga, Afro-Asian support for a U.N. military presence in the Congo flagged and the Operation was phased out by mid-1964. Lumumbist rebels, encouraged by Soviet and Chinese diplomats in neighboring countries, quickly spread across half the country and threatened the capital.

Under President Johnson, the CIA conducted a major paramilitary campaign against the Kwilu and Eastern rebellions for nearly four years. Covert action and planning focused mainly on direct combat operations, and were coordinated with overt U.S. and Belgian military assistance in the areas of equipment and support functions. Thus in early 1964 a CIA front organization in Miami furnished Cuban exile pilots to the Congo Government to fly armed Italian T-6 training planes

against "Mulelist" insurgents in the western Kwilu Province. (The Government had

no pilots of its own). In the Spring, rebel advances in the East led to the

dispatch of U.S. Department of Defense T-28 fighter planes armed with rockets

and machine guns, (6), C-47 military transport planes (10), H-21 heavy duty

helicopters (6), vehicle spare parts, 100 "military technicians" to show the

Congolese how to operate and maintain their new equipment, and "several"

counterinsurgency advisers for Congolese commanders. While Belgium sent

pilots and maintenance personnel for the non-combat aircraft, the CIA obtained

additional Cubans to fly the T-28 fighters under Station supervision.[32]

Following the fall of Stanleyville to the rebels in August, Secretary of State

Dean Rusk approved an "immediate effort... to concert with (the) Belgians to

help Tshombe (who had just replaced Adoula as Prime Minister with the backing of

Kasavubu and the Binza Group) raise gendarme-mercenary force along with bolstering

whatever force there is to hold present strong points and to start rebel roll back".[33]

Again the interdependent overt-covert pattern of support appeared. Four American

C-130 military transports with full crews and parachutist "guard" arrived in

Leopoldville, along with 4-5 B-26 bombers, ground vehicles, arms and ammunition.

The Belgians also supplied equipment as well as 300-400 officers who assumed

background roles of command and logistical support. Nearly all this overt assis-

tance was in behalf of a 700 man force of South African, Rhodesian and European

mercenaries which did much of the fighting as "spearheads" of selected Government

troops. CIA Station Chief Benjamin Hilton Cushing told the Belgian Commander that

he was prepared to subsidize Tshombe's entire mercenary recruitment if hard

currency were lacking (it wasn't). The Agency did supply more Cuban pilots for the

B-26s which joined the rest of the CIA Air Force in support of the mercenary

advance.[34] (By January 1965, two additional T-28s were operating in the Congo

as were 3-4 more B-26s apparently provided by Intermountain Aviation, a CIA (proprietary).[35]

As certain African countries began to ship arms to the rebels across Lake Tanganyika with apparent promises of Soviet replacement, the CIA engaged pilots and crews, reportedly South African, for patrol boat operations. A CIA front organization, Western International Ground Maintenance Organization(WIGMO) chartered in Lichtenstein, handled maintenance for the boats as well as the fighter planes with a staff of 50-100 Europeans.[36] The WIGMO mechanics and maintenance personnel enabled U.S. and Belgian military personnel to escape direct association with air and sea combat operations; they also represented an attempt by the CIA to get away from its increasingly visible Cuban connections.[37] Yet the CIA also formed a force of 17-18 Cubans for a possible operation to rescue U.S. diplomatic hostages, including CIA personnel, in Stanleyville. This objective was achieved on November 24, 1964 when U.S. C-130s dropped Belgian paratroops on the city. At that moment, the Cubans were accompanying a mercenary force just hours away, and prepared to act if the airdrop was canceled.[38]

By mid-1966 there were said to be a dozen Cuban aviators and 100 other WIGMO personnel in the Congo,[39] but the paramilitary campaign ended, according to Special Group Member Cyrus Vance, around mid-1967.[40] However in July 1967 a mutiny of white mercenaries against the Government raised a new threat of dismemberment and dangerous instability. Three C-130s with "supporting personnel" were rushed in to fly armored cars and troops to battle. But senior Congressmen fearing a new Vietnam forced President Johnson to withdraw two of the planes in August and the third in December.[41] Johnson also issued an order that the U.S. "would not again get so involved in Africa except out of the most overwhelming necessity".[42] Still, according to a high State Department official and another diplomatic source, the temptations of covert action were strong enough to sanction a return of several Cuban combat pilots to the Congo in late 1967.

On the political action side, say reliable diplomatic sources, the CIA continued to assist the Binza Group during the Tshombe era (1964-65). In view of a Constitution which vested great power in the President's Office, there was increasing competition between Prime Minister Tshombe and President Kasavubu, both of whom looked forward to a future Presidency. The Americans were "concerned" when Kasavubu sought "an opening to the left" by dismissing Tshombe and appointing a Government ready to consider the dismissal of mercenaries, recognition of Communist China, and improved relations with left-nationalist African states.[43] According to three informed individuals-- a U.S. official then in Washington, a Western diplomatic Congo specialist, and an American businessman who talked with the returned CIA man Devlin-- the CIA was involved in the second Mobutu coup of November 25, 1965.

As the CIA-assisted repression succeeded, Mobutu began to consolidate his political and financial hold. Trained Congolese pilots started returning from European military schools. There seemed to be a decreasing need for covert action. A U.S. diplomat whose information has always proved reliable states that CIA political action payments to Mobutu ceased "at the end of the 1960s." Still, according to a State Department official and a foreign diplomat in Zaire, the Agency was in charge of training Mobutu's personal bodyguard "during the 1970s". The aforementioned diplomat personally observed that the CIA Station Chief James Kim continued to furnish Mobutu with "intelligence" regarding both African and internal political developments, and "tried to influence him" partly through such contacts as Dr. William Close, an American citizen who was Mobutu's long-time personal physician and political counselor. A 1967 White House memorandum referred to Close's letter to President Johnson "commending" him on his decision to send C-130s to the Congo that summer. It noted that Close "exercises considerable influence on President Mobutu, has been used by him as an emissary on many occasions, and has always been helpful and cooperative with our Embassy at Kinshasa."[44]

By 1975 when the political crisis in neighboring Angola exploded, the

rationale for American support of Mobutu was no longer confined to the dangers of
Soviet subversion in Zaire and its consequences for other African countries. As
the Deputy Assistant Secretary of State for African Affairs explained at a Senate
hearing,

> Despite temporary aberrations (Zaire) has been a good friend to
> the United States...We do have...a warm spot in our hearts for
> President Mobutu. At a time when our aid and advice were critical
> to the development of Zaire, he was good enough--- and I might
> say wise enough--- to accept our suggestions and our counsel to
> the great profit of the state...(There is) a basic commonality
> of attitudes and policies in foreign affairs (between our two
> countries)..45

Given such outstanding reliability Secretary of State Kissinger was reportedly
"banking" on Mobutu "to oppose Moscow's interests" in Africa generally and "to
further Washington's interests in various international forums"---particularly
those where the U.S. was being assailed by Third World forces.46 Since Zaire
was to bear much of the burden of anti-Communism in Africa and moderation in the
Third World, a high State Department official noted " a thrust " in Washington
to bolster the country "in the hope that it could extend its hegemony throughout
the continent."47 In the same vein, CIA Director William Colby designated Zaire
"a future regional big power".48 The Republican Administration was also sensitive
to growing U.S. economic interests in Zaire including over $200 million in direct
private investment with more planned, and a deepening involvement on the part of
private and public creditors. Of concern to the U.S., remarked the Deputy
Assistant Secretary, "are not only Zaire's stability and development but also the
security of three-quarters of a billion dollars in U.S. investments, loans and
contracts and our access on favorable terms to Zaire's mineral resources."49
For all these reasons the U.S. rushed to Mobutu's aid in 1975 when copper prices
and Government revenues fell, debt repayment problems with U.S. and foreign
creditors arose, popular discontent became increasingly overt, and Mobutu worried
about the presence and example of a post-colonial leftist regime in neighboring
Angola. Abondoning its "low profile" in Africa, the Administration provided more

than $100 million in overt aid (nearly $30 million in military sales credits and $21.5 million in security supporting assistance for FY 1976 and the Transitional Quarter, about $29 million in Food for Peace and Commodity Credit Corporation loans for FY 1976, and a $20 million Export-Import Bank loan in process), and played an active role in the rescheduling of Zaire's foreign debt.[50] Covertly, one reason for the surprising CIA operation in Angola was to psychologically boost the Zairian regime, as we shall see below. It remained to be seen whether in light of Mobutu's continuing precariousness the Carter Administration would expand CIA programs in behalf of either Mobutu or a replacement team. Ironically, Lawrence Devlin was now back on the scene as the American Representative of U.S. business man Maurice Templesman--a major supporter and beneficiary of Mobutu's regime. Devlin has risen to the top of the CIA's clandestine Africa Division before finding his upward mobility in the Agency stalled. According to diplomatic sources, Mobutu relies upon him to make contacts with U.S. officials at moments of "misunderstanding" or strain between the two countries, and considers him a "second CIA" to keep an eye on the first one in the event of changing U.S. policies.

As we have seen, CIA covert operations and inter-related overt diplomacy played essential roles in the triumph of American-approved leadership. After 1967 they continued to sustain the Zairian Government. Even though their immediate impact was probably not decisive, their retrospective and potential influence were undoubtedly intimidating. By 1975 Mobutu's external fears (and hegemonial ambitions)[51] and his internal difficulties had provoked an escalation of U.S. support which again threatened to become the arbiter of Zaire's political destiny.

Yet even this heavy external involvement might not have been sufficient had the Lumumbist opposition been more effective and its external supporters more vigorous. Lumumbism in its various guises was the most popular political force in Zaire during the early 1960s. While it has not been possible to take a public opinion poll in recent years a serious potential for left-nationalist politics

remains in the form of a continuing rebel stronghold in the eastern Fizi-Baraka

region (Popular Revolutionary Party), exile activism on the part of Gizenga, the

ex-Kantanga soldiers in Angola reportedly radicalized by the MPLA (which recruited

them when Zairian troops intervened in the Angola civil war) and linked to the

eastern rebels, certain military officers with "progressive" views and, above all,

the increasingly overt expression of popular discontent. But the Lumumbists had

difficulty in creating a reasonably unified political movement. While fomenting

rebellion during the 1960s they were unable to overcome political, ethnic and social

divisions to forge a strong, modern organization for revolutionary warfare,

although the Kwilu Mulelists, Popular Revolutionary Party, and/perhaps the ex-Katanga
later

soldiers in Angola progressed further along these lines.[52] Also, considering the

scale of U.S., U.N. and Belgian involvment only the Soviet Union among the pro-

Lumumbist powers had the capacity to bring to bear an effective external counter-

weight. But the Soviets assigned Africa a low strategic priority and until

June 1964 African support of the United Nations Operation presented serious political

and logistical obstacles to a unilateral Soviet role. Furthermore, the Soviets

were skeptical about the trustworthiness and political effectiveness of some of

their new-found Zairian friends. For example, in October 1961 the American Embassy

reported to Washington: "There is evidence some disillusionment among Communist

bloc and neutralists with Gizenga's force and effectiveness." It also communicated

this piece of relevant evidence:

> Canadian (Consul General) Gauvin whom we have found to be
> accurate well-informed colleague showed Embassy officer today
> telegram reporting ninety minute conversation with Canadian
> Charge Rahman who has represented Soviet interests Congo since
> expulsion Soviet diplomats. Rahman indicated Communists have
> given up Gizenga as third rate theorist.[53]

In 1965, even Che Guevara and his band of more than 100 Cubans in the Eastern Congo

were said to be disillusioned with the rebel forces.[54]

Angola

Until 1975 Portugal refused to follow in the path of peaceful European

decolonization of black Africa. Portuguese President Salazar told the American

Ambassador in 1961 that the "only nationalism" in Angola and Mozamibque "was

Portuguese, deriving from centuries of close association with Portugal."[55]

This dogma was enforced by the suppression of any political activity that seemed

to have a modern, African nationalist, tone.

Influenced in part by the achievement of Independence in the neighboring ex-

Belgian Congo, various clandestine Angolan movements participated in the violent

revolts of February and March 1961 in Luanda, the capital, and the northern section

of the country. The Portuguese responded to these poorly prepared uprisings with a

veritable bloodbath. However, as we have seen, the liberal Kennedy Administration

had decided to fight the Cold War with a new emphasis upon Afro-Asian sentiment.

So the U.S. voted for the March 1961 U.N. resolution calling for self-determination

in Portuguese Africa. In July Assistant Secretary of State for African Affairs

G. Mennen Williams exhorted his colleagues,

> Angola has become for much of the world, as Berlin is for Europe,
> the center of the great battle between freedom and oppression...
> Angola in the eyes of much of the world is the test case of America's
> committment to freedom...The unacceptable alternative is to temporize
> and see Soviet Communism come on the scene as the spurious and
> cynical champion of "freedom" for Portuguese Africa.[56]

With National Security Action Memorandum No. 60 of July 14, 1961, the U.S.

launched a quiet diplomatic campaign, including promises of economic aid, to

persuade Portugal to institute reforms leading "eventually to self-determination".[57]

Military assistance and sales to Portugal were restricted to materials filling

"actual needs of Portuguese NATO forces remaining in Europe", and commercial arms

export licenses were screened for items "not clearly for NATO needs". Overt support

for the Angolans themselves included an emergency food and humanitarian assistance

program for the estimated 125,000 Angolan refugees in Zaire and a pre-university

training program for Portuguese Africans at Lincoln University in Pennsylvania.[58]
By May 1963, the latter had provided scholarships to 24 students, 9 of whom were
Angolan.[59] Finally, as Secretary Kissinger acknowledged, the U.S. soon began to
supply covert "financial, non-military aid" through the CIA to Holden Roberto,
the leader of an Angolan political movement based in Zaire[60]. As early as April
1961 the American Embassy in Leopoldville was in close contact with Roberto. When
the Portuguese Foreign Minister privately accused "U.S. services" of being
involved with "Portugal's enemies", the State Department ordered the Embassy "to
initiate no further contacts with Roberto unless otherwise instructed" although
he still could be seen at his own request.[61] For Secretary of State Rusk, Roberto
came to represent the "moderate" alternative to the opposing "de Andrade extremist
group tied to Moscow".[62]

In contrast with Zaire, overt support for America's favorites was limited
by the persistence of colonialism and the military importance of a Portuguese air
base to the United States. The diplomatic effort rapidly ebbed, leaving covert action
an isolated and ineffective strand of U.S. policy. Already in December 1961
Assistant Secretary Williams was complaining that "the importance to the United
States position of the Azores Air Base" had resulted in "too great constraints"
against "a full and open statement of our arms policy towards Portugal", and
protesting "our inability to hold a 'press backgrounder' on Angola" and "(the)
witholding (of) public mention of our Lincoln University training program...".[63]
By mid-1963 Williams observed that, "Responding to Portuguese sensitivities...we
have softened our approach during the past year."[64] This was evident in the failure
to maintain a consistent anti-colonial position at the U.N., to "expand modestly"
on "the very limited contacts we have with Portuguese Africans", and to "give
assistance to Portuguese African refugees and students."[65] Roberto himself
wrote President Kennedy in December 1962 complaining about these developments.[66]

With Portugal steadfast and the U.S. faint-hearted, Roberto depended
increasingly upon the hospitality and assistance of the Zairian Government. Of

course top Zairian leaders were on the CIA payroll and their relationship with
Roberto could only be enhanced by the sense of a common benefactor. But the
Zairians also had independent interests of their own. For instance, Prime
Minister Adoula was a close friend of Roberto and worried that the Angolan would
be "pushed aside by less moderate (forces)" and Adoula would "find himself with (a)
Communist-oriented government in exile" in Zaire.[67] Apparently acting on its own
initiative, Zaire permitted Roberto's GRAE to send men and material over the
Angolan border and established a training base at Kinkuzu where Algerian-trained
Angolans instructed the GRAE army, which was supplied with Algerian, Tunisian and
Moroccan weaponry.[68] According to Professor John Marcum, Adoula even financed
Roberto out of his own funds when necessary.[69] Zaire's 1963 decision to recognize
the GRAE as the sole legitimate Angolan nationalist movement seems to have been
taken against the advice of Assistant Secretary Williams and the American Embassy.
At this moment the State Department was encouraged by the efforts of the Soviet-
assisted MPLA "extremists" to diversify their international backing:

> U.S. has been under impression GRAE and Roberto represented
> a pro-Western stand in resistance movement...MPLA has received
> Communist support and has some Communist sympathizers in it.
> However in the last ten months some extreme leftists have been
> removed. Recent expulsion da Cruz and Migueis and Neto visit U.S.
> and Western Europe last year indicate MPLA seeking contacts
> with West. U.S. policy is rpt (sic) not to discourage MPLA
> (Neto-Andrade faction) move toward West and not to choose between
> these movements. Difficult to assess degree of support each
> group has in Angola... (and) how flexible groups would be in
> dealing with Portuguese.[70]

The Department was also concerned that Zairian recognition would lead to a diplomatic
break between Zaire and Portugal and prevent "meaningful talks" between the Portuguese
and their nationalist opponents.[71]

The inadequacy of a largely covert, financial and non-military, U.S. role
was underlined at the end of the year when Roberto appeared to the American
Embassy in Leopoldville to be "considering basic reorientation Angolan nationalist
policy in favor closer cooperation with Communist bloc.".[72] Roberto's labor

adviser, Carlos Kassel, approached Embassy officers with the information that,

> Since Roberto's recent return from New York he had found him
> changed man...completely disillusioned with western, and
> specifically U.S. policy on Angola. He was convinced that the
> U.S. would never jeopardize its military ties with Portugal and
> that, in last analysis, it was U.S. military aid to Portuguese
> that enabled them to hold Angola.[73]

At Kenya Independence ceremonies in Nairobi, Chinese Foreign Minister Chen Yi

was supposed to have offered Roberto "large scale military aid", and a visit to

Peking by a GRAE delegation was envisioned. Kassel himself was instructed to

"establish contact" with the Communist-controlled World Federation of Trade

Unions.[74] At this point, the Zairian authorities themselves came under attack by

Chinese-encouraged rebels, and "indicated their concern re Chicom involvement

with Angolan nationalists, and stated that Chicom technicians would not be welcome

in (Zaire)"[75]. Yet the U.S. and Zaire remained concerned that Roberto "might

soon be ousted by extremists...mortgaging their future to the Communists,"

and ultimately reaching "a stage where they will no longer be disposed to negotiate

a moderate and evolutionary settlement when Portugal finally comes around to offering

one."[76]

Given the constraints on overt diplomacy and the liberals' preference for

non-violent nationalism, Williams could only suggest, in May 1964, that a new

and expanded covert political action programs be launched in Angola and Mozambique.

The Assistant Secretary's proposal seems, in retrospect, to have been rooted in

some wishful thinking which failed to take account of the difference between

Portuguese and other European colonialisms in Africa:

> We believe that the nationalists should alter their present
> (violent) tactics and concentrate their energies, with our
> clandestine assistance, in setting up an extensive political
> organization within and outside the territories. This organi-
> zation should be based on non-racial principles...Inside the
> territories (it should conduct) political campaigns designed to
> bring about a political consciousness and manifestations of
> public support for self-determination.
>
> The difficulties involved inside the territories are not under-
> estimated: how to reorient the whole strategy and tactics of an

> organization which until now has been patterned on the Algerian
> rebellion and has concentrated on violence; how to overcome
> the insistence of extremist and pro-Communist elements to step
> up terrorism; how to organize an effective, resourceful,
> secret and extensive underground network; how to undertake
> strikes and other public demonstrations in the face of the ubiquitous
> and ruthless Portuguese secret police; how to obtain wide-
> spread public support in the face of fear of retaliation
> against the civilian population, etc.

> Nevertheless, violence has paid off. Moreover... by and large
> the newly emerging nationalism, particularly in Africa, have
> won their independence through broadly based political and non-
> violence movements that won indigenous and then worldwide backing.[77]

The fate of Williams' proposal is not known.

Later on in the Johnson Administration, even covert assistance took on an air of ambivalence. CIA funds continued to flow to Roberto: according to a former official of the State Department's African Bureau, doubts about Roberto's "leadership quality" were not sufficient to jeopardize "our historic relationship". On the other hand, Marchetti and Marks state--- and two former officials confirm--- that the U.S. decided to sell Portugal 20 B-26 bombers for use in her African territories. CIA employees delivered 7 planes to Portugal before they were arrested by U.S. Customs personnel in a bureaucratic snafu.[78] This break with the last vestige of overt pressure on Portugal--- the arms embargo--- was protested in vain by Williams.[79] While the specific motivation for this sale is not known, there is some evidence that it _might_ have had to do with the provision of certain facilities for Polaris submarine forces by Portugal.[80]

In spite of having gained recognition from the Organization of African Unity (OAU) in 1964, the GRAE remained largely dependent upon one African country, Zaire. The Mobutu regime provided limited funds and weapons. More important, it arrested Roberto's internal opposition which was imprisoned at the Kinkuzu base, and it continued an earlier policy of denying the MPLA access to the Zaire-Angola border, the most suitable frontier for guerilla operations.[81] Nevertheless, the Soviet-assisted MPLA was finally able to mount revolutionary warfare from bases in Congo-Brazzaville and, most significant, Zambia. By 1969 the latter operations were "rated by the Portuguese as the most effective guerilla force they face",[82] and Roberto was increasingly accused of lassitude and _embourgeoisement_.[83] In 1971. the OAU withdrew recognition for his movement.

Both overtly and covertly, U.S. policy in Southern Africa moved even further away from African nationalism during the Nixon and early Ford Administrations. Conservative Republican policymakers found it covenient to accept such assumptions as: "The whites are here to stay and the only way that constructive change can come about is through them", and "Violence in the area will not increase greatly because the blacks recognize the military superiority of the whites, and will not risk their security in confrontation".[84] From these they drew the policy implication that the U.S. could adopt "a general posture of partial relaxation (of restrictions on dealing with the white regimes)...balancing our relations in the area by compensating for---rather than abandoning--- our tangible interests in the white states." In the case of Angola, this meant "avoiding pressures on the Portuguese" particularly "as the Azores negotiations come forward."[85] Hence the Republican Administrations eased the arms embargo on Portugal by exempting non-lethal equipment which had dual civilian and military uses such as Boeing 707 transport planes.[86] And, according to intelligence sources, CIA covert action subsides for Roberto were scaled down to "minimal" payments of about $10,000 per year for "intelligence collection."

With the diminution of American support, Roberto's movement came even more under the influence of Mobutu whose dependence on the U.S. in the early 1970s was merely ultimate. Zaire took the initiative in training and supplying Roberto's forces, and putting down a mutiny of 1,000 GRAE troops in 1972.[87] Zaire's importance rose further in 1974 when a revolutionary military Government in Portugal commenced decolonization and Roberto's historic opportunity seemed to have arrived. Mobutu had followed Nixon to China in 1973 and, in turn, prepared the way for a subsequent visit by Roberto. Between May 1974 and October 1975 the Chinese, previously unsuccessful in exploiting divisions within MPLA and GRAE, provided approximately

120 military instructors for Roberto's forces---now called FNLA--- in Zaire. They also trained an estimated 5,000 FNLA troops and equipped them with small arms (AK-47 rifles, machine guns, rocket-propelled grenades and light mortars). Mobutu intervened with President Spinola in a vain effort to procure Portuguese recognition for MPLA dissident Chipenda who would later join the FNLA.[88]

By January 1975, when the Portuguese set up a transitional tripartite coalition government in Angola, the Chinese and Zairian-assisted FNLA had a large edge over the Soviet-aided MPLA in troops trained or in training, amount and quality of military equipment, and the number of nearby foreign advisers. The third major group, Jonas Savimbi's UNITA, had a very small and poorly armed force.[89] According to American diplomats in Luanda, the MPLA did not achieve parity in military resources until late Spring. Nevertheless a CIA proposal to bolster Roberto with $3000,000 in political action funds was approved by the 40 Committee and President Ford in late January. (The CIA's request for a $100,000 subsidy to Savimbi was rejected). An official of the 40 Committee recalls that the "basic concern" in this decision was not to respond to the Soviet-assisted MPLA but rather to "bolster psychologically our immediate ally", Zaire. Thus U.S. covert and overt "successes" in Zaire were now leading toward further intervention in Angola.

Elsewhere in this volume, Gerald Bender shows that after a couple of rounds of Soviet-Cuban and U.S.-Zairian-South African escalation, the MPLA did not have a significant advantage in military supplies and training, but its political and organizational superiority helped it drive the opposition from Luanda, Cabinda, and key Southern ports and district capitals. As Bender also indicates, the 40 Committee approved a $14 million two stage program of arms and other aid to Roberto and Savimbi on July 17th, and President Ford signed off on July 27th. An additional $10.7 million was approved in early September.[90] Secretary Kissinger's public statements and interviews with two members of the 40 Committee suggested a three-fold objective of covert action: to avoid a precedent of Soviet expansion

that could lead to pressures--- and accomodationist tendencies --- elsewhere
in the world; to work with the "moderate" anti-Communist leaders of Zaire and
Zambia who feared the consequences of a Soviet-assisted MPLA victory on their own
political positions; and to prevent Soviet and MPLA-assisted black extremists from
making gains in Namibia, Rhodesia and the rest of Southern Africa.[91] The second
concern, for Zaire and Zambia, was highlighted in Administration briefings to
Congressional committees at the end of July. Considering the relative depth of
past U.S. committment to Zaire, and published remarks by Kissinger aides, it is
reasonable to suppose that Zambia was of secondary importance.[92]

Unlike the Zaire operations of 1964-67 U.S. military aid was _entirely_ covert
in nature although CIA Director Colby warned that the chances for exposure were
"considerable".[93] Kissinger justified the attempt at total secrecy by referring to
legal obstacles to military assistance to insurgents, especially through neighboring
states, and by contending that overt aid could have led to an "unmanageable" and
"open" confrontation with the Soviet Union.[94] Still, legal barriers might have
been surmounted and the risks of disproportionate Soviet reaction to some overt aid
lessened if Congress and the public had been as Supportive as in the days of the
Zaire Rebellions. Indeed the Secretary himself pointed out that Soviet and Cuban
intervention was "an attempt to take advantage of our continuing domestic division
and self-torment".[95]

Various American diplomatic sources provided the following breakdown and
description of covert action expenditures by the middle of the fall:

$5.80 million	-	political action support
.50 "	-	other propaganda
.90 "	-	travel, miscellaneous
10.00 "	-	arms and equipment
.35 "	-	communications gear
5.40 "	-	shipping of arms and equipment

$22.95 million

Arms were provided to FNLA and UNITA both directly and through replacement of arms supplied by Zaire and Zambia. The latter course had the virtue of speed and, by providing much non-American equipment, helped submerge the U.S. role. The first direct U.S. arms shipments went in C-130s to the go-between countries, Zaire and Zambia. It was thought that Mobutu would "know we were serious" when he saw the large planes. A propaganda compaign to expose Soviet arming of MPLA and embarass the conduit countries was launched. Savimbi and Roberto received regular monthly political action payments for internal propaganda, organizational sustenance etc. These subsidies were also used to hire white mercenary "military technicians"--- former Portuguese sergeants, Brazilians and others. Although paid with CIA money, the mercenaries were not hired or directed by CIA personnel. The U.S. was covertly financing 3rd country nationals as it had in Zaire, but this time the CIA did not take on a direct supervisory role a la WIGMO. Instead the pattern was one which had been foreshadowed by the CIA's 1964 offer to subsidize Tshombe's own recruitment of white mercenaries. As in Zaire, American CIA personnel were forbidden to give in-country military advice or training to their clients. According to American diplomats, U.S. CIA personnel did help assure the delivery of airlifted equipment from Zaire to their proteges in Angola. Finally, although the CIA ran its Angolan operation out of its Kinshasa station, there was also a CIA station in Luanda which "did intelligence collection feeding into FNLA and UNITA". Again "intelligence" was deeply entwined with covert action.

By mid-November the 40 Committee and the President had authorized a final dose of $7 million, making a total of $32 million for covert action in Angola during 1975.[96] However the arrival of South African combat troops to bolster the increasingly desperate FNLA-UNITA coalition, had already begun to undermine both African and domestic tolerance for U.S. policy. The Soviets and Cubans were further encouraged by the relatively impressive performance of the MPLA, a group they had known and aided for more than a decade though not always without reservation. In these circumstances, so different from those which had obtained in Zaire, the two Communist powers provided massive military assistance in the form of arms and troops. In late January, a Congressional coalition of liberals and conservatives succeeded in stopping the covert action program. Shortly the South Africans, anxious to resurrect their policy of detente with moderate black Africa, also withdrew. The MPLA was victorious.

Patterns

The rationale, mechanisms and short-term local results of covert action in Zaire and Angola bear comparison with similar U.S. efforts in other parts of the Third World. As in Vietnam, Laos, Chile, Cuba etc., a prime motive of covert intervention was fear of external Communist subversion and its international implications. Each Administration sought to deal with this fear in conformity with its own political ideology. Beyond this negative sort of preoccupation, the Mobutu regime was increasingly counted on to oppose Moscow's interests and advance Washington's in continental and Third World arenas. Zaire's position as a regional strong point for American policy--- in many ways reminiscent of the Chilean "showcase" in Latin America---helped stimulate the abortive CIA paramilitary operation in Angola.

Together Zaire and Angola have constituted the terrain for a particularly wide variety of covert action techniques employed by the CIA in the Third World. These included: propaganda, manipulation of labor unions and student associations, subsidization of political leaders and parties, military and internal security functionaries, and coup- makers, political assassination plots, technical assistance for a Presidential bodyguard and security apparatus, provision of 3rd country foreign military combat and combat-support personnel, arms and related equipment. In addition, CIA "intelligence" activities were often difficult to distinguish from covert action since the political and military information gathered might be consumed by the CIA's local allies as well as U.S. analysts. And in a period of diminished covert action, "intelligence" support could help sustain a favorable disposition on the part of a Mobutu or a Roberto pending future occassions for clandestine struggle. Similarly the CIA "intelligence" program for the Chilean military during the leftist Allende Government included the passing of anti-Government information to a Chilean officer, and was partly designed "to put the U.S. Government in a position to take future advantage of either a political or military solution depending on developments within the country and the latter's impact on the military themselves."[97] Just as covert action support of Mobutu and Roberto escalated in the period of Angolan decolonization, so too did covert assistance to the Chilean military in the aftermath of the 1973 coup against Allende.

Covert action provided the most direct and aggressive U.S. assistance to political leaders in Zaire and Angola. But realization of its proximate objectives also depended upon:

- the degree of significant, often closely coordinated, overt
  support from the U.S. and other pro-Western countries
- the relative effectiveness of local political groups
- the scale of Soviet and other foreign Communist intervention

In Zaire, conventional U.S. economic and military aid, at first in cooperation with the U.N. and then with Belgium, created a powerful context for CIA manipulations. Although the regime foundered more than once, the more popular Lumumbists were unable to mount a well-organized challenge or to provoke a foreign Communist involvement commensurate with international aid to the "pro-Western moderates". The Soviets in particular were constrained by African resistance to intervention outside the U.N. and doubts about the political capacity of certain Lumumbist leaders. But in Angola things were different. There was a dearth of U.S. and other overt support for the FNLA against their colonial overlords, and even CIA assistance dropped off at the end of the 1960s. A burst of Chinese and CIA aid for FNLA-UNITA in 1974-75 produced a competitive Soviet effort in behalf of MPLA, whose political and military superiority was increasingly evident. This fact, and the ramifications fo South African intervention, laid the African and U.S. domestic bases for a low risk, decisive military thrust by the Soviet Union and Cuba.

Elsewhere in the Third World the CIA's immediate achievements have been influenced by a similar set of factors. For example, in Chile covert and overt assistance to the centrist Frei Government could not overcome the growing internal crisis that assured the election of leftist President Allende. Subsequently, internal polarization exacerbated by diplomatic and CIA tactics, and the Soviets' unwillingness to provide massive financial aid, helped pave the way for a right-wing military coup. On the other hand, the Communist-led Vietnamese, backed by current and potential Soviet and Chinese aid, were able to stand off massive CIA and other intervention until the latter's domestic support eroded.

Covert Action and the Long Run

So far, covert action has been evaluated in terms of its contribution to such proximate goals of U.S. policy as: overthrowing a government, building up its replacement, and strengthening a friendly group in its drive for political power. But these CIA operations must also be judged in light of more fundamental and long-term consequences for American interests.

For instance, in opposing the Lumumbists and the MPLA has the U.S. really prevented or delayed "Soviet takeovers" in Central Africa as the principal rationale for intervention suggests? Or has it simply frustrated strong nationalistic forces which would have pursued independent foreign policies?

Political viability, "development", and African acceptance have been instrumental goals of U.S. anti-Communism in Zaire and Angola, and with increasing consciousness of America's economic, political and military interdependence with the Third World, they are also becoming terminal objectives.* But have U.S.-backed

---

*As C. Fred Bergsten has observed, it is the growing cooperation of the Less Developed Countries in producer cartels, the U.S., and other world forums on hunger, exports, commodity prices, international monetary and environmental problems -- and their increasing military volatility -- which require significant adjustments by the somewhat weakened and divided induatrial states.

leaders significantly contributed to the political stability of their respective states? Have they really made any progress in the direction of an efficient and humane political economy? Or have their actions led to an increasingly successful opposition which is by force of circumstance, anti-American as well as to severe economic mismanagement, and embarrasing violations of human rights? Has U.S. involvement with its Zairian and Angolan friends generally improved American relations with Africa, or has it tended to complicate them?

The International Communist Threat

In both Zaire and Angola, American intervention stemmed from the conviction that foreign Communists, (especially the Soviets) were willing and able to exert massive, long-term influence over politically strong African left-nationalists, effectively blocking good relations with the U.S. and ultimately jeopardizing the world political balance. Yet Lumumba was neither a Communist nor the leader of a political organization which would yield readily to foreign control. The vision which Lumumba and his successors had of their country was conditioned by their strong belief that equality and dignity could never be achieved within a framework of foreign domination. Their political ideology was a militant, populist nationalism, and their preference for "positive neutralism" and non-alignment was therefore an integral part of their whole approach to politics. If they had a preferred external identification it was with other African leaders. Beyond their political creed, the Lumumbists' political talents and relative popular success implied that they would not have to depend on external support as much as other politicians.

Lumumba's appeal for Soviet military aid to counter a much larger Western intervention in Katanga may have been unrealistic given the U.S.'s violent reaction; but it was not the result of Soviet-exploited "personal instability" since it arose from his group's basic political formula of militant nationalism. Nor were his actions guided by "pro-Soviet" advisers as the Americans charged. For example, two of the most distrusted counselors, Press Secretary Michel and Ghanaian Ambassador Djin, opposed Lumumba's decision to accept Soviet aid. The Prime Minister's most influential colleagues were other Zairian nationalists. Even after the arrival of Soviet military equipment and technicians Lumumba manifested his independence by inviting Western technical assistance, recalling Belgian judges and teachers, and meeting with African diplomats who hoped to achieve a compromise between the impatient Prime Minister and the cautious U.N. Secretariat.

In succeeding years Lumumba's heirs, now in opposition, received limited Soviet, Chinese and Cuban diplomatic and material aid. But they generally adhered to the Lumumbist platform of 1960. In 1961-63 they associated themselves with the Nehru-Nasser brand of neutralism and appealed to President Kennedy for support. In the 1964-67 rebellions they sought Belgian backing and established their closest relations with 10 African states. Even those few Lumumbists who came to profess some form of African Marxism, such as Mulele's Kwilu group and the eastern Popular Revolutionary Party, were forced by circumstances to create national adaptations of Marxist doctrine and vowed to remain independent of the Soviets and Chinese.[98]

Born out of discussions between African nationalists and Portuguese Communists and leftists, compelled to organize guerilla warfare against Portuguese colonialism, the MPLA also developed its own brand of African Marxism --- and a stronger politico-military organization than the Lumubists ever had. Spurned too by the U.S. and the West in their long war against colonialism, the MPLA turned to the Soviet Union and Cuba for arms and advisers. But they also received significant arms supplies from anti-Soviet Yugoslavia as well as bases, sanctuary and other aid from African states (Guinea, Tanzania, Zambia, Congo-Brazzaville) and liberation movements (Mozambique's FRELIMO, Guinea-Bissau's PAIGC). As we have seen, Cuban troops appeared in large numbers only as the South Africans began to assist MPLA's opponents.

In 1963 the State Department had noted a degree of flexibility in MPLA that seemed to belie U.S. identification with the "anti-Communist" FNLA. Later these MPLA veterans of a long political and military battle against foreign domination continued to declare both publicly and in their internal documents that they were not communist puppets and would pursue an independent foreign policy open to good relations with the West. The leading scholarly observers of the movement, John Marcum and Basil Davidson, were in agreement on this point and they were joined, reports Bender, by some of the African experts in the American Government.[99]

Skeptics may wonder whether these elements of ideology and internally-rooted strength are sufficient to forestall a determined Soviet or Cuban advance. However on the Soviet side there is a lack of evidence of any major effort to achieve a degree of satellization in Central and Southern Africa. In Zaire, the late CIA Director Allen Dulles, publicly admitted, that "we overrated the danger" and while "it looked as though they were going to make a serious attempt at takeover in the Belgian Congo, well it did not work out that way at all".[100] Richard Loewenthal concluded that Soviet and Chinese objectives in the early 1960s "were mainly propagandistic".[101] Although decisive Soviet and Cuban military aid was provided to the MPLA in 1975, Administration briefings to Congress did not mention any drive for strategic military bases or other long term interests compatible with a major effort at satellization.[102] Indeed, in the likely event that Soviet objectives continue to be propagandistic--designed to weaken Western influence and curry favor with the perceived "wave of the future" in Southern Africa --any effort to establish significant control would be counterproductive. As it was, the new Angolan Government conferred "special stature" on its external backers but also tried to build bridges to U.S. private and public aid, pledging not to allow foreign bases on its territory.[103] Finally, it is important to remember that it was U.S. and Western hostility to the left-nationalists in Zaire and Angola which opened the doors to even limited Soviet and Cuban gains.

Political Capacity and Political Economy of U.S.-Supported Leadership

Against the popular but "pro-Communist" Lumumbist nationalists, the U.S. sponsored alternative "moderate" leadership, hoping it would be politically effective and broadly disposed to such objectives as orderly economic growth, social advancement, and some kind of representative government. But the principal figures, the Binza Group and its associates, had either failed the test of mass politics (Adoula, Bomboko) or had their power base in the army and security apparatus (Mobutu, Nendaka, Kandolo). They installed an increasingly narrow ethno-political regime and were consequently led to govern without parliament and normal political life. The remaining opposition was imprisoned or threatened with imprisonment. Without an organized mass political and counterweight, the army, politicians and higher civil servants absorbed a greater proportion of the budget even as receipts declined due to the continuing political and economic crisis. The resulting inflation and devaluation were paid for by the average person while the elite's income was adapted to the price increases. The denouement was the Lumumbist-led Rebellions of 1964.[104] There is little doubt that the rebels would have been victorious if the U.S.-Belgian-white mercenary operation had not taken place. Although Lumumbism was becoming more anti-American, it was only at the "moment when Belgo-American military assistance broke the power of the Eastern popular army" that "the Americans became the prime adversaries."[105] According to Professor Benoit Verhaegen, the leading expert on the Rebellions, the CIA's aggressive role contributed greatly to anti-American reactions. After the intervention of the Cuban exile-piloted T-28s, "attacks upon foreigners became more precise and more virulent and the rebels began to use the foreign population as hostages against further bombardments."[106]

In the last decade, political power has been centralized under the Presidential dictatorship of Mobutu. According to development economist J. Peemans, writing in African Affairs (April 1975), there has been an accompanying reinforcement of

economic power and concentration of income in favor of a limited class of people
who belong to the privileged circles of power. This elite, from the President on
down, drains the rest of the country and forestalls balanced economic development
through high salaries, corruption ("It has been estimated that an equivalent of 60
per cent of ordinary state revenues were lost in 1971 or at least diverted to other
programs than the official ones"), tranfers of money abroad and spending on luxury
consumption goods ("which together represent 50 per cent of the gross annual formation of capital"), and investment in trading activities which are highly profitable because the government holds down prices to agricultural producers.
While the regime lavishly spends mineral revenues on foreign prestige goods like
jumbo jets and Ali-Foreman heavyweight fight, agricultural investment represents
less than a third of the budget proportion it did in 1958, private wage employment
has declined from 11 to 8 per cent of the active population since 1959, real wages
are a third lower than in 1965, and peasant producers, with very low incomes of
$2-6 per month, have reduced agricultural output by 10% since 1969.[107] The
economic situation deteriorated further in the last two years due to falling copper
prices (the regime has maintained Zaire's dependence on revenues from one mineral),
rising oil costs, and a bungled attempt to take over foreign commercial and
agricultural enterprises.[108]

Again, economic policy has had a political counterpart. Repressive measures
have included: "almost a return to 'compulsory crops' system which existed
during the colonial period and which was so detested by the peasants",[109] controls
on the movement of desperate rural folk to the cities,[110] the abolition of all
significant political and non-political organizations save for the single party
which lacks a representative function,[111] the shooting and conscription of student
protesters,[112] and the "reportedly common practice", according to the recent State
Department "Human Rights" profile of Zaire, of using "force and threat of force in
the interrogation of suspected criminals" as well as alleged brutal treatment of

political prisoners, extended incarceration without trial, and "death of prisoners under interrogation.". Zairians, this official report suggests, dare not criticize President Mobutu or his Government.[113] Within the top political stratum a climate of paranoia and generalized insecurity has resulted in such dramas as the 1966 "Hanging of Pentecost" in which a former Prime Minister and others were publicly executed for a doubtful conspiracy,[114] and the alleged coup plot of 1975 in which 7 top officials of the army and security apparatus were condemned and 27 others were imprisoned.[115]

Despite large-scale U.S. aid beginning in 1975, the Zairian regime was considered "less stable" by State Department officers in 1977 than at anytime in the last 10 years. On March 9th a leading authority on Zairian politics wrote me, "The economic and social situation continues to deteriorate but the political regime miraculously survives--- till when?" A long-time diplomatic friend of Mobutu's recently told me that Mobutu "is doomed". The threat comes mainly from the discontented populace which is now openly critical of Mobutu,[116] the potentiality of the Popular Revolutionary Party rebels in the East, and the critical, even progressive views of a group of educated top military men. As Ntalaja Nzongola has pointed out, these forces may draw encouragement from the Angolan example, and even some marginal aid.

For reasons of circumstance rather than doctrine much of the anti-Mobutu sentiment is also anti-American, with the CIA a major villain. Thus the literature of the Eastern rebels lambastes "Belgo-American Imperialism" and "the government of the man of the CIA".[117] The university students I met in Zaire during 1969-71 were aware, and generally critical, of CIA and U.S. policies. Mobutu himself may have been worried about this aspect of his reputation when, in the wake of increasing American revelations of his past, he implausibly accused the CIA of fomenting a plot against him and expelled the American Ambassador. A month later he would be the principal authorized intermediary for the CIA's paramilitary operation in Angola! If the U.S. preserves its close association with the regime,

its eventual successor is likely to have, or take account of, anti-American
feeling.

Marcum has aptly described Holden Roberto's FNLA as "an extension or branch of
Zairian politics". Originally inspired by Frantz Fanon and associated with Lumumba,
Roberto subsequently became identified with the powers that be in Zaire. Unfortunately
their elitist political model excluded some basic elements of successful anti-
colonial guerilla warfare in Africa: multiethnic organization, modern political
education rooted in concrete problems, and reliance on the armed masses. Roberto
behaved in the manner of an established Zairian politician, surrounding himself
with his loyal ethnic brothers (just 11% of the Angolan population), giving "only
minimal attention" to political education,[118] succumbing to the lure of individual
enrichment by investing funds in several apartment houses in the Zairian capital[119]
--- which apparently detracted from his committment to collective armed struggle
against Portugal[120]--and ruthlessly repressing his internal and external opponents.[121]

After breaking with Roberto, in 1964, Savimbi formed UNITA whose leadership
came from the biggest ethnic group in Angola, a third of the population. But
UNITA too was unable to get away from its ethnic isolation, and its guerilla
activities were less organized and extensive than even the sparadic outbursts of
FNLA. Nor was political education Savimbi's strong point as he opportunistically
shifted from Maoism to black power to recruitment of white settler support, to
ethnic manipulation to an appeal for inclusion in an MPLA regime.[122]

Without idealizing the MPLA, it was by comparison less ethnic, more political
and more aggressive militarily than the other movements. It attracted not only a
large ethnic base (nearly a quarter of the population) which was strategically
located in and around the capital, but also numerous mulattoes, urban dewellers,
educated bureaucrats, and reportedly more than its share of black Portuguese Army
veterans.[123] Although there was an ethnic and mulatto concentration in the top
leadership, MPLA was the only movement to conduct extensive guerilla warfare in areas

outside its own ethnic redoubt. Its Eastern Operations, prepared by a long

period of political education, were considered the most effective in the entire

anti-colonial struggle.[124] Even though it traversed a serious internal crisis

during 1974, the MPLA would again show its political-military superiority over

its rivals in the fractious Spring and Summer of 1975.

U.S., including CIA, support of Roberto and his Zairian sponsors, and

tolerance of Portugal, made a bad impression on the MPLA. Marcum writes that

President Neto "considered himself and his movement to be the victims of 'American

imperialism' acting through the intermediary of a Congolese Government that had

given the [FNLA] a military base, exclusive access to the Angolan border, __

jure recognition and energetic support within the OAU".[125] Actually it was Savimbi,

breaking with Roberto in 1964, who not only echoed these sentiments but also provided

the names of Roberto's (and in one case Adoula's) alleged CIA advisers.[126] In the

post-war Angolan Government, the important but not yet predominant Alves faction

appeared to reject the possibility of good relations with the Americans. By with-

holding diplomatic recognition of MPLA's victory, the U.S. obtusele strengthened/case.[127] their

A final caveat: The self-defeating policies of CIA and U.S. supported

leaders were usually not the results of specific American direction. Rather they

tended to reflect the political inclinations and circumstances of the "moderates"

themselves. Thus while the U.S. had, as we have seen, some policy influence

with its inexperienced Zairian allies in the early 1960, its advice was often

rejected, as in Adoula's imprisonment of labor leaders and refusal to let an

American oil company build a refinery in 1963, and the Binza Group's selection of

Tshombe as Prime Minister in 1964.[128] As the Zairians consolidated their hold,

and relied less immediately on CIA and U.S. aid, they often seemed to think that

the Americans depended on them more than they on the Americans. For example,

as early as October 1961 Foreign Minister and Binza Group leader Bomboko, who

had countersigned Kasavubu's dismissal of Lumumba, warned his American patrons,

...If the (government of Zaire) were to fall (due to U.S.
temporization on Katanga) he personally would never again accept
the help of Americans who might then wish to restore moderates
to power. Now is the time to help. Bomboko said he did not
want to go through a 1960 again. Why do Americans sell out
Africa for the interests of a few people in Europe? Bomboko
said that he fought subversion once, and, if he spoke frankly,
it was not an effort at blackmail but to explain that if the
moderates failed now the U.S. can never again count on their
assistance.[128]

In 1966 Mobutu obtained the recall of Ambassador Godley who was said to be too

forward in his political recommendations. In 1975 he criticized the appointment of

former Ambassador to Chile Nathaniel Davis as Assistant Secretary of State for

African Affairs, and expelled Ambassador Hinton. (According to two diplomatic

accounts, Hinton was perhaps "too forward" in his efforts to obtain Mobutu's

cooperation in arranging the release of American students held by PRP rebels).

When the Arab oil boycott and price rise seemed to promise a new source of external

assistance, Mobutu broke off relations with pro-American Israel. As for Roberto,

he received CIA money for his Portuguese military advisers but he failed to heed

their recommendations in his ill-fated attack on Luanda's water supply in November

1975.[129]

African Relations

The initial impact of the Congo crisis was to "reveal and intensify" divisions

between the new African states.[130] The U.S. was presumably able to strengthen its

relations with "moderate" governments while sacrificing ties with "radical" ones.

If it were necessary to fight the Cold War in/Africa this was worthwhile because
                                          Central

one needed allies. If, as I have argued, Cold War diplomacy was a mistake and the

U.S. has an "interdependence" interest in the Third World, then relations with the

"radicals" need not and should not have been strained. A similar case can be made

regarding Angola policy.

It is also true that the most aggressive forms of American intervention,

particularly covert action, antagonized even the "moderates". The overthrow and

murder of Lumumba--- and suspicions of U.S. complicity--- helped move the "moderate" states closer to the "radicals' " position. During the Rebellions, the white

mercenaries (offered money by the CIA) and Cuban exile pilots (paid by the CIA and

acting in support of the mercenary force) helped estrange such friends as Kenyatta's

Kenya from American policy. The Stanleyville rescue, synchronized with a mercenary

assault, was almost universally condemned in Africa.[131] Tainted by de facto

cooperation with South Africa, the CIA paramilitary operation in Angola was

rejected by most African Governments including such traditional "moderates" as

Nigeria and Ghana. "Shut Up, President Ford " exclaimed the headline in a Government-

owned newspaper in Nigeria, which contributed $20 million to the MPLA.[132]

American policymakers hoped that negative reactions to U.S. and CIA intervention

would not be cumulative. And often the storm did seem to pass. But there is

increasing evidence that it had only subsided, and would break out with new fervor

as conditions warranted. The CIA intervention in Angola and official revelations

of past misdeeds in Zaire were sufficient for "moderate" Ghana to draw the critical

parallel between U.S. opposition to Lumumba and the MPLA quoted at the beginning of

this essay. In politically ambiguous Ethiopia and Uganda, the credibility of

official accusations of CIA plotting could only be furthered by past behavior in

Zaire and Angola---the major African theaters for covert action.[133] Two more or

less "radical" leaders who receive some American aid also illustrate the cumulative

effects of intervention. President Machel of Mozambique has noted the impact of

Zairian events on his own political thinking:

> We bagan to discover the capacity of Africans, through the radio
> and the press. This capacity, to organize, to direct the destiny
> of a nation, we felt close at hand with the independence of the
> Congo. And what horrified us most of all was the imperialist
> intervention in the Congo which liquidated its eminent leader.[134]

President Nyerere of Tanzania gave aid to the U.S.-opposed Zairian rebels of

1964, but eventually came to terms, publicly, with this relatively powerful

Zairian neighbor. Yet according to American diplomats in Tanzania, he is privately

contemptuous of the Mobutu regime. When he discovered, in the early 1970s, that

an extradited PRP rebel was thrown out of a plane by Mobutu's army, he terminated
the policy of extradition. After Angola and recent aid to Mobutu, the continuing
American-support for a repressive government must be clearer than ever to him.

Patterns

In numerous other Third World countries, CIA and overt diplomacy have also
proceeded on the assumption that politically strong left-nationalism will be more
or less subverted by external Communist supporters. There is good reason to
question this premise even outside of Zaire and Angola. For instance, the Senate
Select Intelligence Committee Staff Report on Covert Action in Chile revealed
CIA and State Department intelligence memoranda challenging policy-maker's
expectations of a Soviet-Cuban takeover of Allende's Government. These appreciations
portray Allende as a strong nationalist and the Soviets as unwilling to overcommit
themselves in behalf of a new, financially draining, nationalistic Marxism.[135]

Actually the most conspicuous Soviet "successes" in the Third World have
been the products of extremely unusual circumstances: Soviet wartime occupation
of North Korea and the combination of a strong indigenous Communist party used
to following Soviet leads and continuing Western economic and military intervention in behalf of a discredited status quo in Vietnam and Cuba. These conditions
exist in no African countries and few other places. And under contemporary
circumstances of nuclear stalemate, quasi-detente, and polycentrise, even the
special cases do not exclude good relations with the U.S.

Of course there have been areas of reputed "Soviet influence" in the Third
World like Nasser's Egypt, Barre's Somalia, Nkrumak's Ghana, and Toure's Guinea.
Yet in each case, the Soviet advance has been prepared by U.S. and Western
hostility to certain nationalist objectives. Typically, the Soviets manage to make
modest gains but do not come near to controlling the Government. Soon the political
leaders realize that the Soviets have not been able to get them the goods, or the
presence of Soviet advisers begins to ruffle nationalist nerves. The stage is set

for new initiatives and an attempted oscillation toward the West.

Many other U.S. and CIA interventions in the Third World have foundered on client incapacity, inefficiency and inhumanity and subsequently reaped a whirlwind of anti-Americanism. The familiar case is Vietnam. In Chile, the U.S.-supported Frei Government was unable to implement promised economic and social reforms, underwent internal strain, and plummeted in popularity. The CIA had spent approximately $6 million in its behalf for 8 years,[136] was visibly implicated in its failure, and may even have contributed to its demise:

> In a country where nationalism, "economic independence" and anti-imperialism" claimed almost universal support, the persistent allegations that the Christian Democrats and other parties of the center and right were linked to the CIA may have played a part in undercutting popular support for them.[137]

Covert subsidies were provided to the pro-Western Egal group in Somalia. But its political success was short-lived and the long-run reaction proved unfavorable to the Americans.[138] On the other hand there are some CIA-U.S.-aided regimes which have managed to endure despite stern political repression and mixed economic performances, e.g. Iran. Somewhere in between one finds Governments which are currently pro-Western but have from time to time undergone leftist political change, e.g. Peru and Bolivia.[139]

Regarding the overall diplomatic consequences of covert action, the Senate Select Intelligence Committee reached conclusions similar to those of the specific analysis of Zaire and Angola:

> ...Certain covert operations have been incompatible with American principles and ideology and, when exposed, have resulted in damaging this nation's ability to exercise moral and ethical leadership throughout the world. The U.S. involvement in assassination plots against foreign leaders and the attempt to foment a military coup in Chile in 1970 against a democratically elected government were two examples of such failures in purposes and ideals. Further because of widespread exposure of covert operations and suspicion that others are taking place, the CIA is blamed for virtually every foreign internal crisis.[140]

Concluding Note

In March 1977, an estimated 800-1500 armed, leftish Katangan exiles returned to their home province from neighboring Angola and nearly toppled the Mobutu Government. As the poorly paid and politically demoralized 60,000 man Zairian army proved to be ineffective, the regime was forced to call upon 1200 Moroccan troops, 80 French military advisers, about 50 Egyptian pilots and mechanics, French transport planes, and Belgian and Chinese arms. Although the new U.S. Administration was reluctant to lead the counterrevolution (no arms or advisers were dispatched), it did provide tangible aid: $15 million of combat support equipment including a G-130 plane to fly troops and arms into battle, spare parts for previously delivered C-130s, airplane fuel, parachutes for paratroops, rations and clothing for soldiers, communications gear etc. And President Carter's request for $32.5 million in military aid for Zaire in Fiscal Year 1978 -- half the total for Africa -- indicated a continuing commitment to the Mobutu regime. Furthermore, there is some evidence of CIA covert action planning in the days before Mobutu was able to clinch his French and Moroccan personnel support. In an open letter of resignation to the CIA Director, covert operator and CIA Angola Task Force Chief John Stockwell charged,

> Yes, I know you are attempting to generate token support
> to help Zaire meet its crisis -- that you are seeking out
> the same French mercenaries the CIA sent into Angola in
> early 1976. These are the men who took the CIA money but
> fled the first time they encountered heavy shelling.[141]

By June, Mobutu's foreign supporters had managed to contain the immediate threat as the exiles retreated rather than waste their forces in conventional warfare. Old problems of political fragmentation also prevented the Kantangana from gaining the active support of similarly disposed forces in other areas of the country such as the PRP in the East. Still the regime's military humiliation and demonstrated political weakness suggested that its days were numbered.

Most of the relevant academic experts and many diplomats expected a military
or military-civilian _coup_ in the near future, or even a complete collapse of
order in the penurious urban centers leading to a new Government. If the U.S.
persevered in its close association with the regime, its eventual successor
was likely to have, or take account of, anti-U.S. and anti-CIA sentiment.

Western and U.S. intervention in behalf of Mobutu intensified political
cleavages in Africa, fueled the suspicions of several leading states about
Western objectives, and appeared to complicate the task of accomodation
and avoidance of great power proxy way in Southern Africa. While a number of
small, conservative, French-speaking African governments encouraged the Western
intervention, it was criticized by spokesmen for several leading countries,
not all of them "leftist". For example, the official newspaper of "moderate"
Zambia stated:

> The almost obscene haste with which the west has rushed to pour
> arms into Zaire reinforces the argument of many Africans that be-
> hind every attempted or successful coup on this continent is the
> hand of a foreign power. . . Although Cyrus Vance and others have
> not come out and said so bluntly, there is little doubt that they
> are hoping for a full-scale confrontation between Zaire and Angola.
> It gives them an opportunity to make amends for alleged betrayal
> of the anti-MPLA forces during the civil war. It is to be hoped
> that President Carter puts a halt to this political adverturism
> before is is saddled with his own Vietnam. If he and his adminis-
> tration hope to come out of such a confrontation with their image
> in Africa unscathed, they need to do some rethinking. [142]

Significant reservations were also expressed by Nigeria, Tanzania and
Algeria. Soviet statements, as well as past actions in Angola, raised the
possibility of a future counteraction in such favorable settings as Rhodesia,
Southwest Africa, and Angola-Zaire.

The preponderant rationale for U.S. aid to Mobutu was anti-Communism. It
was clear that behind such official slogans as "friendship", "historic ties"
and "territorial integrity", lurked the fear of a "pro-Soviet" regeme in the
geographic center of Africa. Yet there was no evidence that the anti-Mobutu
Katangans were Soviet-influenced. Indeed the populist flavor of their propa-

ganda was more reminiscent of Lumumbism than of even Angolan Marxism. Ironically,
U.S. support of "anti-Communist" Zaire probably contributed to the Katangan
invasion itself. According to an informed American official, the U.S. did not
examine very closely Angolan charges that Mobutu was permitting exile attacks
on Northern Angola. Mobutu's assurances that he had "cut back" support of the
Angolan exiles were simply accepted. However the sequence of events suggests
that Angola allowed the Katangans to return to Zaire in response to these
incursions.

The latest Zaire crisis has dramatized the long term risks for U.S.
interests of two decades of U.S.-CIA intervention in Zaire and Angola. By
sticking to a well worn path of overt intervention in the area (with only
modest refinements) and apparently continuing to contemplate covert action,
the U.S. is in danger of re-enacting the Ethiopian syndrome: Continuing
American identification with a Government that is increasingly perceived by
its people as oppressive, revolutionary change, and the emergence of a successor
regime which is deeply suspicious of U.S. diplomacy. By contributing to inter-
African polarization and Cold War tension, the U.S. was increasing the chances
for a great power proxy war in Central and Southern Africa and diverting its
attention from the new, multilateral issues of Third World interdependence
that were becoming more and more urgent. By basing its African policy on an
obsolete anti-Communism, it ignored abundant evidence that the Soviet Union
has been unable to acquire even one satellite on the continent, let alone a
constant friend.

FOOTNOTES

1. U.S. Congress, Senate, Select Committee to Study Governmental
    Operations with Respect to Intelligence Activities, Final Report:
    Foreign and Military Intelligence, Book I, 94th Congress, 2nd
    Session, April 26, 1976, p. 131.

2. New York Times, November 25, 1975, p. 1.

3. U.S. Congress, Senate, Subcommittee on African Affairs of the
    Foreign Relations Committee, Angola, 94th Congress, 1st Session,
    January 29, February 3,4,6, 1976, p. 174.

4. New York Times, January 4, 1976, p. 17.

5. These are: The CIA assassination plot against Lumumba (see below,
    n. 13) and the temporary use of American CIA personnel as pilots
    in the Congo civil war of 1964 (see Stephen R. Weissman, American
    Foreign Policy in the Congo 1960-64 (Ithaca, N.Y.: Cornell University
    Press, 1974, pp. 229-230.

6. Senate Select Intelligence Committee, op.cit., pp. 50, 156-57;
    see also below, n. 94.

7. U.S. Congress, Senate, Select Committee to Study Governmental
    Operations with Respect to Intelligence Activities, Interim
    Report: Alleged Assassination Plots Involving Foreign Leaders,
    94th Congress, 1st Session, November 20, 1975, p. 14. See below,
    n. 11.

8. Weissman, op.cit., pp. 81-83.

9. Memorandum for Mr. Ralph A. Dungan The White House, "Analytical
    Chronology of the Congo Crises", From L. D. Battle, March 9, 1961,
    p. 25, National Security Files, John F. Kennedy Presidential Library
    (NSF-JFK).

10. Ibid.

11. Senate Select Intelligence Committee, Assassination Plots, p. 14.
    Although this report uses a pseudonym for Devlin, and identifies
    him only as a "Station Officer", it is clear, from the context
    that he is the Chief of Station. On Devlin, see Weissman,
    op.cit., pp. 95-96, 97n., 138.

12. Senate Select Intelligence Committee, Assassination Plots,
    pp. 55-58, 15.

13. Ibid., pp. 60, 15.

14. "Analytical Chronology", pp. 26-27.

15. Weissman, op.cit., pp. 88-98.

16. "Analytical Chronology", p. 30.

17. Senate Select Intelligence Committee, Assassination Plots, p. 17.

18. Weissman, op.cit., p. 109.

19. "Analytical Chronology", pp. 46-47, 57-58.

20. Weissman, op.cit. pp. 91-95; "Analytical Chronology", p. 57;
    Memorandum for Mr. Ralph Dugan, The White House, "Supplement:
    January 20 to March 6, 61 to Analytical Chronology of the Congo
    Crises", March 11, 1961, p. 1, NSF-JFK.

21. Senate Select Intelligence Committee, Assassination Plots, p. 18.

22. G. Heinz and H. Donnay, Lumumba: The Last Fifty Days (New York:
    Grove Press, 1969), pp. 23-24, 61-62; see also "Analytical
    Chronology", p. 38 which refers to Gizenga's release by U.N.
    Moroccan troops.

23. Heinz and Donnay, op.cit., pp. 22-23; "Analytical Chronology",
    p. 37; Senate Select Intelligence Committee, Assassination Plots,
    p. 17.

24. Ibid., pp. 48-49; Heinz and Donnay, op.cit., pp. 69-78, 145-46.

25. Senate Select Intelligence Committee, Assassination Plots, p. 49.

26. Ibid., pp. 49, 16-48.

27. Weissman, op.cit., pp. 87-109.

28. CIA Memorandum, "Congo: United States Assistance to Adoula Against
    Gizenga", n.d., pp. 1-3, NSF-JFK. A CIA-Embassy planned "psychological"
    campaign is referred to in Leopoldville to Secretary of State, October2,
    1961, NSF-JFK.

29. Basil Davidson, In the Eye of the Storm: Angola's People (Garden City,
    N.Y.: Anchor, 1973), pp. 239-240.

30. Weissman, op.cit., pp. 109, 208, 210.

31. Ibid., ch. V and pp. 204-07; G. Mennen Williams to George C. McGee,
    "Steps Against Gizenga", December 12, 1961, Williams Papers, National
    Archieves (WP-NA); Leopoldville to Department of State, December 23, 1961
    and January 16, 19, 26, 1962, and Department of State to Leopoldville,
    January 12, 1962.

32. Weissman, op.cit., pp. 226-230; Cyrus Vance to W. Averell Harriman,
    April 20, 1964, National Security Files, Lyndon Baines Johnson Library
    (NSF-LBJ).

33. Memorandum, "A New and Longer Term Approach to the Congo", from G. Mennen Williams to the Secretary, August 7, 1964 (with Addenda August 10, 1964), p. 1, WP-NA.

34. Weissman, op.cit., pp. 239-243; Les Dossiers du C.R.I.S.P., Congo 1967 (Brussels: Centre de Recherche et d'Information Socio-Politiques, C.R.I.S.P., 1969), p. 355; Les Dossiers du C.R.I.S.P., Congo 1965 (Brussels: C.R.I.S.P., 1966), p. 291.

35. Leopoldville to Department of State, January 11, 1965, NSF-LBJ.

36. CRISP, Congo 1965, p. 248; Congo 1966 (Brussels: C.R.I.S.P., 1967), p. 37; Congo 1967, pp.350, 362, 510; New York Times, April 26, 1966, pp. 1, 30.

37. For evidence of increasing Cuban visibility, see Weissman, op.cit., p. 230, n. 47.

38. Ibid., 246-252.

39. C.R.I.S.P., Congo 1967, p. 362.

40. Senate Select Intelligence Committee, Foreign and Military Intelligence, pp. 155-56.

41. New York Times, August 3, 1967, pp. 1-2; Lyndon B. Johnson to Richard B. Russell and J. W. Fulbright, December 16, 1967, White House Central Files, LBJ.

42. Anthony Lake, The "Tar Baby" Option: American Policy Toward Southern Rhodesia (New York: Columbia University Press, 1976), p. 120.

43. Memorandum, "Congo Situation", from G. Mennen Williams to Robert W. Komer, The White House, November 16, 1965, WP-NA; Briefing Memorandum, "Congo Leopoldville's Position on Chinese Communist Admission to the U.N.", from G. Mennen Williams to the Secretary, October 26, 1965, WP-NA; Directorate of Intelligence, Office of Current Intelligence (CIA), Intelligence Memorandum: "The Situation in the Congo", August 26, 1965, NSF-LBJ; C.R.I.S.P., Congo 1965, pp. 388-406.

44. Memorandum for Mr. Walt W. Rostow, The White House, "Reply to Letter from Dr. Close to President Johnson", from John P. Walsh, August 25, 1967, White House Central Files, LBJ.

45. U.S. Congress, Senate, Subcommittee on African Affairs and Subcommittee on Foreign Assistance of the Committee on Foreign Relations, Security Supporting Assistance for Zaire, 94th Congress, 1st Session, October 24, 1975, pp. 3, 32-33.

46. New York Times, September 25, 1975, pp. 1ff; October 16, 1975, p. 2.

47. Ibid., January 4, 1976. IV, p. 2.

48. Leslie Gelb, "Should We Play Dirty Tricks in the World?", _New York Times Magazine_, December 21, 1975, p. 15.

49. Senate African Affairs Subcommittee, _Security Assistance_, p. 3.

50. Figures obtained from the Zaire Desk of the Agency for International Development (U.S.), Washington, D.C., February 1977: see also, Emma Rothschild, "The Politics of Debt", _New York Review of Books_, June 24, 1976.

51. For influence in Angola and especially oil-rich Cabinda Province.

52. On the Mulelists, see Weissman, _op.cit._, pp. 215-17; these tentative judgements about the PRP and ex-soldiers said to be partially "radicalized" by fighting with MPLA in Angola are based on interviews with U.S. diplomats and scholarly observers.

53. Leopoldville to Department of State, October 14, 1961.

54. Victor Marchetti and John D. Marks, _The CIA and the Cult of Intelligence_ (New York: Dell, 1974), p. 139.

55. Lisbon to Secretary of State, July 15, 1961, p. 3, NSF-JFK.

56. _Report of the Chairman of the Task Force on Portuguese Territories in Africa_, July 4, 1961, pp. 1-3, NSF-JFK.

57. Memorandum for Mr. McGeorge Bundy, The White House, "Task Force on Portuguese Africa: Chairman's Report on Actions Taken", From L. D. Battle, July 31, 1961; Lisbon to Secretary of State, July 15, 1961, p. 3; NSF-JFK.

58. "Chairman's Report"; Memorandum for the President, "Portuguese Use of Military Equipment in Angola", From Robert S. McNamara, August 25, 1961; Memorandum for Mr. McGeorge Bundy, "Report on Lincoln University African Student Center at the Conclusion of its First Year", From William H. Brubeck, July 16, 1962; NSF-JFK.

59. G. Mennen Williams to W. Averell Harriman, May 2, 1963, p. 3, WP-NA.

60. Senate African Affairs Subcommittee, _Angola_, p. 8.

61. Lisbon to Secretary of State, May 1, 1961; Department of State to Lisbon and Leopoldville, May 10, 1961; Lisbon to Secretary of State, May 20, 1961; NSF-JFK.

62. Memorandum of Conversation, "Angola", April 3, 1962 (U.S. and Brazilian participants), p. 2, NSF-JFK.

63. G. Mennen Williams to Mr. Rostow, December 13, 1961, pp. 1-2, WP-NA.

64. Williams to Harriman, May 2, 1963, p. 1, WP-NA.

65. Ibid.

66. Holden Roberto to the President, December 19, 1962, NSF-JFK.

67. Stanleyville to Department of State, March 28, 1964, p. 2, NSF-LBJ.

68. G. Mennen Williams to the Secretary, December 18, 1963; John Marcum, "three Revolutions", Africa Report, 12 (November 1967), pp. 9-10.

69. Marcum, The Angolan Revolution, Volume I: The Anatomy of an Explosion (1950-1962), (Cambridge, Mass,: M.I.T. Press, 1969), p. 259.

70. Department of State Circular to All African Posts, July 4, 1963; July 17, 1963, NSF-JFK.

71. Department of State Circular, July 4, 1963, p. 2, NSF-JFK.

72. Leopoldville to Department of State, December 30, 1963, p. 1, NSF-LBJ.

73. Ibid.

74. Ibid.

75. Department of State to Lisbon, January 17, 1964, p. 5, NSF-LBJ.

76. "Portuguese African Territories: Action Memorandum", to the Secretary from G. Mennen Williams, April 29, 1964, p. 1. NSF-LBJ.

77. Ibid., 3-4, 7-8.

78. Marchetti and Marks, op.cit., pp. 155-57.

79. G. Mennen Williams to Mr. Kitchen, September 17, 1965, WP-NA.

80. Lisbon to Secretary of State, July 31, 1964, NSF-LBJ, reveals that the U.S. asked Portugal for "early action" on its request for LORAN-C facilities for Polaris submarine missles. The installation of a Portuguese complex was considered "exceedingly important" for missile accuracy and "redundancy of navigational aids" for Polaris submarines and eventually a multilateral force. The American Ambassador to Lisbon believed that any agreement was "likely to be a straight quid pro quo deal" involving U.S. military equipment for the war in Africa.

81. Marcum, loc. cit., pp. 11, 14, 16; Davidson, op.cit., P. 242.

82. Mohammed A. El-Khawas and Barry Cohen eds., National Security Study Memorandum 39: The Kissinger Study of Southern Africa (Westport, Conn.: Lawrence Hill and Company, 1976), p. 153.

83. Davidson, op.cit., pp. 216-226.

84. El-Khawas and Cohen, op.cit., pp. 105; Memorandum for the President, "Decisions on Southern Africa Policy", from Henry A. Kissinger, January 15, 1970, p. 2.

85. Ibid., p. 3 (Approved by President Nixon); Memorandum for the President, "Policy Issues Regarding South Africa and the Portuguese Territories", from Henry A. Kissinger, January 15, 1970, p. 4.

86. Ibid, pp. 4-5; El-Khawas and Cohen, op.cit., p. 47.

87. Davidson, op.cit., pp. 226-227; John Marcum, "The Anguish of Angola: On Becoming Independent in the Last Quarter of the Twentieth Century", Presidential Address, Eighteenth Annual Meeting African Studies Association, San Francisco, October 29, 1975, p. 17.

88. Senate African Affairs Subcommittee, Angola, pp. 184-185; John Marcum, Lessions of Angola", Foreign Affairs 54 (April 1976), p. 410.

89. Senate African Affairs Subcommittee, Angola,p. 191; Marcum, "Lessons", p. 410.

90. Senate Select Intelligence Committee, Foreign and Military Intelligence, p. 152; "The Pike Papers" (House Intelligence Committee Report), Village Voice Supplement, January 1976, p. 37.

91. Senate African Affairs Subcommittee, Angola, pp. 6-19.

92. Ibid., pp. 46-47; New York Times, September 25, 1975, pp. 1ff; December 21, 1975, IV, p. 1.

93. The quotation is from an interview with an intelligence source. The substance of Colby's disagreement is conveyed in Washington Post, December 19, 1975.

94. Senate African Affairs Subcommittee, Angola, pp. 20, 37, 40.

95. Ibid., p. 15.

96. Senate Select Intelligence Committee, Foreign and Military Intelligence, p. 152.

97. U.S. Congress, Senate, Select Committee to Study Government Operations with Respect to Intelligence Activities, Staff Report, Covert Action in Chile, 94th Congress, 1st Session, December 18, 1975, pp. 28, 37-39.

98. Weissman, op.cit., pp. 257-274; Joseph Sebastien Ramazani, CNL, "La Naissance du Mouvement de Liberation Nationale au Congo-Kinshasa", April 25, 1972, mimeo.

99. Davidson, op. cit., esp. pp. 148-156, 259-260, 303-305; Marcum, "On Becoming Independent", pp. 18, 20; see also Immanuel Wallerstein, "Luanda is Madrid", Nation, January 10, 1976, pp. 12-17.

100. "CBS Reports", April 26, 1962: "The Hot and Cold Wars of Allen Dulles". Transcript obtained from CBS Television, pp. 19-20.

101. Zbigniew Brezezinski, ed., Africa and the Communist World (Stanford, Ca.: Stanford University Press, 1963), p. 178.

102. Graham Hovey, "Fog and Worse on Angola", New York Times, December 30, 1975. According to an informed governmental source, the CIA's Directorate of Intelligence concluded that the Soviets had "no long term interests" in Angola.

103. Senate Subcommittee on African Affairs, Angola, pp. 167-169.

104. Weissman, op.cit., pp. 200-204.

105. Ibid., p. 219, quoting from Verhaegen's study of the Rebellion in Maniema Province.

106. Ibid., p. 217, quoting from Verhaegen's study of the Rebellion in Kwilu.

107. J. Ph. Peemans, "The Social and Economic Development of Zaire Since Independence: An Historical Outline", African Affairs 74 (April 1975), pp. 149-177.

108. Senate Subcommittee on African Affairs, Security Assistance, p. 2; Stephen R. Weissman, "Zaire: Fisticuffs for Mobutu", Nation, November 30, 1974, pp. 558-559, "The Style of Mobutu", Africa Report 20 (March-April 1975), pp. 2-3.

109. Peemans, loc.cit., p. 171.

110. Information obtained from the Zaire desk of the State Department in February 1977.

111. I have benefitted from Herbert Weiss's ongoing study of the single party, the Mouvement Populaire de la Revolution (MPR).

112. As at Lovanium University in 1969 and 1971.

113. New York Times, March 13, 1977, p. 18.

114. C.R.I.S.P., Congo 1966, ch. VII.

115. New York Times, September 2, 1975, p. 21; Manchester Guardian Weekly, July 12, 1975, p. 12.

116. "The Style of Mobutu", loc.cit.; Manchester Guardian Weekly, July 12, 1975, p. 12.

117. Ramazani, "La Naissance", passim.

118. Marcum, "Lessons", p. 410.

119. Davidson, op.cit., p. 216. This charge is also supported by a foreign diplomat with long experience in Zaire.

120. Ibid., pp. 216-232.

121. Ibid., pp. 212-214, 226-227, 242-244; Marcum, "Three Revolutions", pp. 10-12.

122. Davidson, op.cit., p. 241n; Marcum, "Lessons", pp. 410-411.

123. Ibid., pp. 411-412; an American diplomat in Luanda noted the shift of Army veterans to MPLA.

124. See n. 82 above.

125. Marcum, "Three Revolutions", p. 12.

126. Davidson, op.cit., pp. 239-240.

127. Kevin Brown, "A New Angolan Society", The Nation, July 17, 1976, pp. 42-46. New York Times, May 6, 1976, p. 4.

128. Weissman, op.cit., pp. 206, 230-236.

128a. Department of State, Memorandum of Conversation (Congolese and U.S. participants), October 31, 1962, p. 7, NSF-JFK.

129. Washington Post, February 19, 1976.

130. Immanuel Wallerstein, Africa: The Politics of Unity (New York: Vintage, 1967), p. 43.

131. Weissman, op.cit., pp. 244-246, 254.

132. New York Times, January 8, 1976; January 4, 1976, p. 17.

133. Amin refers to the CIA and Lumumba's death in New York Times, February 26, 1977, p. 6.

134. Mozambique Revolution, n.d. available.

135. Senate Select Intelligence Committee, Chile, pp. 44-49.

136. Ibid., pp. 14-23.

137. Ibid., p. 19.

138. Roger Morris, "The Aftermath of Intervention", Society, 12, (March/April 1975), p. 79.

139. Marchetti and Marks, op.cit., refer to the CIA operations in Peru and Boliva, pp. 138-145.

140. Senate Select Intelligence Committee, Foreign and Military Intelligence, p. 156.

141. Washington Post, April 10, 1977.

142. Times of Zambia, March 21, 1977.

CONCLUSION:

THE FUTURE OF THE CARTER POLICY TOWARD SOUTHERN AFRICA

BY EDGAR LOCKWOOD

KENNEDY LIBERAL ERA PARALLELS.

Judging by public tone, style and ideological emphasis alone, the casual observer of U.S. foreign policy is impressed by the novelty of the Carter Administration's approach toward southern Africa. Kissinger had stressed America's tangible interests, sought alliances with ideological "enemies" to advance or at least to protect those interests, and operated a clever, manipulative and secretive diplomacy with calculated ambiguity. The Carter Administration now seems to espouse once more American ideals and principles allegedly in eclipse during the Nixon and Ford years, open diplomacy for announced clearly-stated objectives, and decision-making by consent. But closer examination shows us that what is involved is a reversion to the active use of ideology and salesmanship to defend America's mission, as it sought to justify its economic and political expansion and domination. It is of a piece with "helping our little brown brothers" in Puerto Rico, Cuba and the Philippines, making the world "safe for democracy" and saving Vietnam from Communism.

Although many commentators have compared Carter's moralistic foreign policy to that of Woodrow Wilson, a chief executive also reared in Southern piety, a more immediate and relevant precedent may be the Kennedy-Johnson era. A reading of the recently declassified Africa: Guidelines for United States Policy and Operation (1963) establishes parallels of intention, orientation, objectives and methods which may prove instructive as we try to imagine what the shape of the future American initiative toward southern Africa will be.

Under "Basic Approach" we find the following language:

"1. What we do - or fail to do - in Africa in the next year
will have a profound effect for many years... The United
States, as a country with no colonial heritage in Africa, has
great opportunities... We see Africa as probably the greatest

open field of maneuver in the worldwide competition between
the [Communist]Bloc and the non-Communist world.

3. ...We propose to build up certain areas of strength and
of maximum co-operation which can serve as models to influence
others in constructive directions. [Nigeria and Tunisia were
identified as possible primary moderate 'bellwether' countries
with Tanganyika, Ivory Coast, Sudan and Senegal as second-tier
models.]

4. ... The critical factor in African nation-building is
leadership. In choosing countries for special emphasis, we
propose to make a major effort to help dynamic and progressive
leaders who are reasonably friendly [without neglecting the
unfriendly ones for, in the end] today's opponent may be
tomorrow's friend.

5. Our revolutionary background and democratic aspirations
constitute a basis for sympathy between ourselves and the
Africans."

In the section entitled "Background" the following words
underline the usefulness of ideological commitment and
domestic civil rights:

"the most helpful things we could do to enhance our image and
obtain the friendship of the African peoples are (a) to make
our commitment to freedom in Africa clear without peradven-
ture of doubt in such cases as Angola, Algeria and South Africa;
and (b) to move more quickly to solve our problem of according
dignity and equal opportunity to our own African-descended
population."

Under thirty-three "Objectives" we find:

"15. Gradual emergence or growth of a middle class capable
of creating and managing a private enterprise sector in a
mixed economy.

16. Encouragement, where appropriate, of private enterprise
economies.

23. Gradual and orderly transfer of power to the majority
of the African populations during the next few years, with
the fullest possible protection of minority rights.

33. Denial to the Sino-Soviet Bloc of military bases, and to
the maximum extent practicable, of military influence in any
African country."

These high-sounding peaceful objectives were accompanied by the use of

United Nations forces to secure American goals in the Congo. Furthermore,

CIA covert operations, buying of African "assets", assasination and mercenary

recruitment were not thought inappropriate means to the promotion of leaders
thought to be favorable and popular.

But as the United States was drawn deeper and deeper into the quagmire
of Vietnam, the Johnson Administration lost the missionary zeal of the Kennedy
years; Africa became once again a "neglected" area. As the Kissinger-Nixon
era opened, hostilities between the Arab states and Israel had broken out,
putting two major crisis areas into contention for major effort. Nixon and
Kissinger chose to draw closer to the white regimes because they judged that
guerilla war was futile and a crisis was not immediately in the offing there:
"the whites are here to stay". They therefore chose dialogue over moral
lectures, and protection of investments, trade and strategic interests in the
white areas rather than sacrificing them in order to protect similar interests
in black Africa.

To Kissinger, the Portuguese coup of April 25, 1974, however, demonstrated
that there was indeed a crisis that needed management. When Angolan de-colonization developed into civil war, the National Security Council's covert backing
of FNLA and UNITA was a costly failure, yet also a lesson. Further "Angolas"
must be prevented. Kissinger therefore launched an all-out diplomatic effort,
with the full backing of the Congress, to settle the Rhodesian and Namibian
issues before they developed a momentum that would install radical regimes
threatening to western interests not only in those countries, but, more importantly, in South Africa itself.

THE CARTER THEMES.

This cursory summary of the Republican years is intended to show that
it is the threat to western interests which has now rescued Africa from "neglect".
The pursuit of American idealism, in this context, should, then, be seen not
as an abstract philosophical preference but as an ideological weapon in a very
real conflict in which the United States acts to protect very material benefits.

While it would be foolhardy to predict outcomes at this stage, we would
like to sketch out certain themes which seem to be emerging as characteristic
of the Carter approach. We will see that in many respects they are an
attempt to recapture the Kennedy image of American activism typical of the
initial period of decolonization, in an era when gradualist reform is more
and more being questioned as a viable method.

1. The Promotion of Capitalism and Non-Violence as more Revolutionary
than Revolution and Socialism

The most brilliant political choice of Jimmy Carter's career so far, we
would argue, has been the selection of Andy Young as his Ambassador to the
United Nations. A man of charismatic charm, aptitude and eloquence, Young
is no mere preacher. He is a living advertisement that non-violent political
struggle can advance blacks in America into the political elite.

His main role is a pastoral ministry to developing countries in order to
create trust in American sincerity. Carter put it this way:

> "[Third world nations] now look on the United States as having
> at least one representative ... who understands their problems,
> who speaks their language... I think we have a new sense in
> the mind of those kinds of peoples of caring about them and to
> a major degree it is because of their trust in Andy Young."[1]

The way in which Young goes about the creation of that trust is to use
his own situation as proof that America's recent experiences have equipped
it to lead a struggle for revolutionary ends.

At the United Nations conference on Zimbabwe and Namibia held in Maputo
in mid-May, 1977, Young took the offensive. The United States had a policy
which represented "something of a revolution in the consciousness of the
American people." "We have known those struggles [against racism, colonialism,
and imperialism] ourselves and somehow we have been able to come through them."

In Young's view, the use of boycotts to fight racism ultimately succeeded
because they affected and drew in the multinational corporations. Later, in

Johannesburg, he encouraged South African businessmen to believe in their own
power to overturn apartheid:

> "... when in Atlanta, Georgia, five banks decided that it was
> bad business to have racial turmoil, racial turmoil ceased."

Young's apostleship for capitalism is based on a belief that it is so
fundamental, so irreversible, so pervasive and so powerful that it amounts to
a law of nature, whose inevitablity is also, conveniently, beneficial:

> "... the places where I see the naked being clothed, the places
> where I see the sick being healed are the places where there
> happens to be a free market system."[2]

2. Building a Moderate Zimbabwe and Namibia: Disarming the Militants.

The key problem for the United States is how to promote a gradual transfer of power to African leadership favorable to western economic investment,
development patterns, trade and political needs while at the same time avoiding
the appearance of intervention in revolutionary processes.

The history of the struggle for freedom in the Portuguese colonies suggests
that a prolonged period of guerilla struggle may be necessary to establish a
unified political ideology favorable to socialist development and a common
experience of co-operation capable of overcoming regional, ethnic and personal
divisions. On the other hand, the same history suggests to the western powers
that they must create a quick solution by devising processes that will delay
or shortcircuit the armed struggle, put it at a political disadvantage, or
transform it into processes subject to western management.

Clearly there are limitations on what can be done by the West. The
Congress in the post-Vietnam period has demonstrated that, at this point, it
does not favor the use of U.S. funds for covert military, guerilla or paramilitary activities. Given the degree and nature of legitimacy accorded to
SWAPO and the Patriotic Front, the western powers cannot easily support "internal solutions" such as the Turnhalle Constitution or various Ian Smith
proposals. Such a course would, in effect, be a choice of white rule's

continuation through a palpable sham. Agreeing to a Muzorewa-style referendum
to choose a single leader with whom Smith could negotiate would ignore the
security arrangements under which such an election would be held. The necessity therefore emerges of inserting a "neutral" force capable of claiming a
type of legitimacy and power which would be a substitute for militant white
and guerilla forces.

In regard to Zimbabwe, the Administration has worked with the British
to devise a package complete with ready-made constitution, development fund
and a security arrangement to manage the transition to one-person, one-vote
parliamentary elections by the end of 1978. Where the Kissinger plan called
for the present white regime and the nationalist movement to co-manage the
political transition, the present plan calls for a temporary restoration of
British rule under a retired Field Marshall for that purpose. A United Nations
force composed primarily of Nigerians (and perhaps other British Commonwealth
forces) would be inserted between the opposing armies, whose key units would
be de-mobilized.

In regard to Namibia, the South Africans have shown no disposition to
withdraw their army, police or administrative personnel, so long as there is
a security threat. In the present negotiations the West has proposed a withdrawal of South African forces into key strong points like Grootfontein and
Walvis Bay while United Nations peacekeeping forces are gradually inserted.

In neither instance has a total demobilization or withdrawal of the
colonial settler forces been proposed, although this demand would seem to be
a minimum pre-condition for security under "neutral" auspices.

3. The Protection and Preservation of a Private Enterprise Economy in
order to Expand the Interests of International Capital in Zimbabwe and
Namibia.

The present Zimbabwe economy, partly under the spur of sanctions, has developed into a more diversified economy than existed before UDI. Small

national industries have developed using retained earnings, but growth has

been slow and exports of minerals and tobacco have remained key elements in

what is still largely a dependent peripheral economy.

To capitalize on Rhodesia's growth potential, Britain and the U.S. have

proposed an international fund of $1 - 1.5 billion which would promote heavy

inflows of foreign capital for private investment, retain existing managerial,

technical and other skills and expand African access to "better" jobs and

"better" land. The model of development uses traditional capitalist mechanisms:

--encouragement of "commercial capital flows, especially in
extractive, processing and manufacturing industries, supported
as appropriate by national export credit and investment
insurance agencies."

--balance of payments support

--encouragement of skilled labour and managerial personnel to "contribute to Zimbabwe development" and "effect a smooth transition
to a more balanced pattern of access to ownership of farms, houses
and businesses."[3]

The new Constitution guarantees the right of private property. It

forbids "expropriation except on specified grounds of public interest and even

then only on condition that there is prompt payment of adequate compensation ...

and that compensation may be remitted abroad within a reasonable period."

The purpose of the Fund is not primarily developmental. AID officials have

had to admit that, given Rhodesia's singularly advanced industrialization in

the African context, another explanation needs to be sought. Rather, the Fund

is intended to benefit, directly and indirectly, the interests of international

capitalists who have been largely excluded from Rhodesia's potentially profit-

able economy during the last decade. Giovanni Arrighi points out that it was

this same conflict between international and national capitalists which partly

underlay African decolonization during the 1960's:

"The 'colonial perserves of European imperialism' were opened

up to American capitalism, in which the oligopolistic corporation
plays a more central role than in French or British capitalism.
More important still was the outflow of small-scale, competitive
capital that accompanied independence. In fact, de-colonization
was, among other things, the result of a conflict between the
dynamic elements (the big companies) and the backward elements
(marginal enterprises, small planters, small trading houses,
small semi-artisanal workshops) of colonial capitalism."[4]

The Namibian economy, on the other hand, is not nearly as industrialized

or diversified as that of Rhodesia. It is very largely dependent on the economy

of South Africa. Western mining firms are eager to expand their exploitation

of Namibia's copper, zinc, uranium and other minerals. As yet, however, the

western governments do not seem to have evolved an international plan similar

to the Zimbabwe Development Fund to promote the interests of the multinationals.

However, the reaction of the five western powers to the issue of Walvis Bay

suggests that South Africa's continued domination of the Namibian economy is

not contrary to western interests.

On August 31, South Africa announced by proclamation that it was annexing

Walvis Bay, the only viable deep-water port in Namibia, the center of one of

the most productive fishing industries in the world and a naval and military

base which dominates the Namibian littoral. Despite western deploring of these

actions, informed U.N. sources speculate that the West, for its own reasons,

is not unhappy with South Africa's seizure. A member of the U.S. negotiating

team told an anti-apartheid group recently that eventually Namibia would get

Walvis Bay just as India had got Goa, hardly a relevant comparison.

4. The Use of Carrots instead of Sticks to Build Areas of Support in the
Front-Line States and in South Africa.

A. Throwing money at the Crisis. One time-honored American method of dealing

with a crisis is to create client states whose political inclinations are re-

enforced by dependencies on outside money. During the Kennedy-Johnson years

of 1962-68, for example, the United States put some $350 million of its economic

and military aid into Zaire. When the crisis eased, aid fell to relatively modest levels. But with the Angola war and the Shaba rebellion, and large arrears in Zaire's international debt payments, aid is once more rising.

Similarly, as the crisis mounts in Zimbabwe and Namibia, the United States is planning to spend unprecedented amounts of political money to underwrite the states which border on Zimbabwe, Namibia or South Africa. For the first time, Congress is authorizing large programs of "Security Supporting Assistance" for southern Africa. This huge category of aid is designed to be used at the discretion of the President to "promote economic or political stability," and was first poured into Indochina, then the Middle East. In FY 1978 Congress will probably authorize the following sums[5]:

Botswana	$18 million
Lesotho	20 million
Swaziland	15.5 million
Zambia	30 million
Zaire	10 million
Regional-training, refugee aid and studies	21.5 million
	$115.0 million

At the same time Congress announced its intent to fund the Zimbabwe Development Fund if the progress of negotiations warranted such a step, which would mean another $100 million or so per year for five years. In short, what we may be seeing in the next few years is security aid at a level of $200 - 250 million in order to create or support moderate governments in the six above-mentioned countries during the period of crisis.

B. Encouraging the South African Liberals. In the Kissinger era, very little was done publicly to support the opposition parties in South Africa. Kissinger saw moral lectures as doubly counterproductive. On the one hand, the Nationalists would harden their attitudes, withdraw into their "laager" and be unco-

operative in dealing with American business and political interests. On the
other, the African states would be encouraged to demand sanctions which the
United States would not support.

The Carter Administration's approach has been to revert in a gingerly
but nevertheless visible manner to public posturing against the South African
regime. Carter declared at Notre Dame in May that American was committed to
majority rule in all of southern Africa. At the same time, Mondale was telling
Vorster that while America had no road map or time table, South Africa had
to move away from apartheid or suffer deterioration of its relations with
America. The Administration had said that certain options were being considered:
doing away with tax credits for American businesses, curtailing Ex-Im facilities,
withdrawing intelligence co-operation, military attaches, etc. The issue of
police-state violations of human rights, such as those believed responsible
for Steve Biko's death, will not be ignored: it will be utilized to extract
public political advantage in order to move the Afrikaaners or at least to
encourage the human rights movement in South Africa.

But these gestures remain symbolic, designed to support rather than compel a shift away from overt racism. Furthermore, the Carter Administration
appears, for now, to be shifting back to the Kissinger view that it is unwise
to stir South Africa's internal pot further while seeking a solution in Zimbabwe and Namibia. The U.S. has resumed its unabashed attack on proposals for
sanctions against South Africa. Repeal of the Byrd Amendment in March has not
been followed by any form of pressure on the multinational oil corporations
operating from South Africa or on South Africa itself to close off Rhodesia's
supply of petroleum. Ambassador Young has aggressively defended a posture
against sanctions at U.N. gatherings both in Maputo and Lagos. Even the apparent
U.S. confrontation with South Africa over its nuclear testing in August, 1977,
appears to have served South Africa's interests. Carter publicly accepted

Vorster's assurance that they never intended to explode a nuclear device,
despite U.S. intelligence reports to the contrary. The U.S. then rejected
an African call at the Lagos U.N. meeting for an end to nuclear collaboration
with South Africa, and instead suggested a very limited American approach to
encourage South Africa to accept international inspection but of only its
nuclear power reactors.

C. Building a Black Middle Class. While South Africa and Rhodesia's African
population is more literate, more employed in industry and more highly educated
than has been the case anywhere else on the continent prior to independence,
its native bouregoisie involved in significant business is relatively tiny.
Africans who have advanced degrees have tended to go into teaching, the clergy,
the law and similar non-business careers. Bantu education systems and color
bars have operated to make technical skills inaccessible or, if learned, irrelevant. In Namibia, the general level of education is much lower. Only 1%
of African children reach the first form of secondary school.

As a substitute for a redistribution of the wealth, Ambassador Andy Young
argues, South Africa's business needs to draw blacks into the free market system
by making them consumers:

> "When blacks became a part of the free enterprise system in the
> South ... blacks had very much a stake in it... The tragic irony
> is that nothing was taken from the whites but the income gap be-
> tween whites and blacks actually expanded. But blacks were so much
> better off than they ever thought that they would be."[7]

How this is to be done has not been made clear, but America is using its
own black bourgeoisie to build support for such a strategy. The Urban League,
PUSH, NAACP, OIC and an host of other black organizations are being mobilized
and harnessed to support the program. State's Bureau of Cultural and Educa-
tional Affairs and AID will expand studies and programs that will involve black
Americans as consultants. Budding technicians, community action specialists,
professionals and other aspirants to middle-class status will come to America

from Africa for "enrichment", to make contact with consultants who can help them create programs in southern Africa, or to get education and skills. African American Institute scholarship programs will be greatly expanded. Crossroads Africa is developing a network of contacts for African visitors. A black consulting firm on the West Coast is under contract to AID to develop a "constituency" for Africa.

The most critical competition of all will be that played out for the minds of South Africans of tender years but militant spirit who have emigrated since the Soweto uprising. With Mozambique, Angola and Tanzania pre-occupied with their own internal difficulties, the more capitalist-oriented states such as Nigeria and Ghana enjoy a natural advantage in being able to offer schooling opportunities in formative years.

WILL IT WORK?

History has a way of changing human consciousness. To revert to methods, and objectives and techniques of an earlier day may simply be to ignore what has been learned in the interim. Ending colonialism in southern Africa by re-viving the models of 15 years ago is therefore not a particularly promising approach.

The people of Africa know very well that it was the liberal, morally idealistic Kennedy and Johnson Administrations which intervened massively and with unparalleled violence in Vietnam. A number of the Carter Administration's top policy-executors such as Secretary of State Vance and Defense Secretary Brown filled high posts in the Vietnam years. Those who opposed the war at least in part, such as State Department Policy Planner Anthony Lake, were in-volved in discreet disagreement over details, and criticized "rigidity" in application rather than America's principles. As mentioned above, American promotion of African nationalism in the Congo had its dark manipulative aspect.

Conversely, liberation movements in the Third World have demonstrated

in Indochina and in Africa that they can be a major force in transforming
the world. Their victories show that western technical prowess and power can
be overcome by ideological awakening and the organization of popular, mass-
based resistance. The victories of the liberation movements in Guinea-Bissau,
Angola and Mozambique gave to the people of Zimbabwe, Namibia and South Africa
a great resurgence of hope and hence a willingness to suffer and to sacrifice.

At the same time, in other countries of Africa, the fruits of western-
managed de-colonization have proven to be a hollow form of majority rule. As
Colin Leys has shown us, Kenya, the country which the Carter Administration
holds up as a model for Zimbabweans, continues to suffer from gross inequalities,
dependency on foreign captial and under-development. By 1970, 44 percent of
the Africans who had purchased white lands through a large foreign-financed
settlement scheme were in arrears in paying their debts for acquisition. The
poorest were using 70 percent of their incomes to pay for an unproductive expen-
diture, an asset transfer, which would ultimately go to former European settlers.
At the same time, large-scale farms came into the hands of a wealthy and politically powerful African elite. Payments to Europeans meant an outflow of capital
or re-investment in foreign-controlled enterprises in industry or tourism.[8]

Countries such as Tanzania, which emerged from colonialism without an
armed struggle but with a vision of an African socialism, are leading voices
in a chorus of Third World protests against continued foreign domination over
terms of trade, technology and the right to nationalize or expropriate resources.
It is thus apparent that offers of foreign aid simply do not address issues
that have emerged from post-colonial experience.

Furthermore, when Africans examine the domestic record of the United States,
they must inevitably question Andy Young's advocacy of boycotts, black consum-
erism and non-violence as a sufficient nostrum for the ills of colonialism,
racism and imperialism. Over 14 percent of black Americans looking for work

are unemployed (double the white rate). In the cities, the figures for unemployed black youth average over 40 percent and in some areas, such as New
York City, are more than double that figure. The domestic priorities of the
Administration so far do not reflect the demands of even those blacks who are
alleged to have picked Carter.

If the Carter Administration is aware of these contradictions, it is
showing few signs of candor or determination. On the countrary, its spokesmen
seem curiously indifferent, insensitive, or unwilling to confront the depth and
reality of African determination to use militant methods. A white South African
professional who had heard Ambassador Young's May address in South Africa told
the author: "I couldn't believe it. He was talking about things that were
talked about in the twenties or in the time of Jabavu. Good will. Things
like that."

The forthcoming U.N. General Assembly will furnish a test of whether
Young's very considerable talents in organizing African support for American
efforts to negotiate solutions in southern Africa can succeed.

While the history of the past 15 years outlined above suggest that the
western intiatives for settlements may be rejected, they will not be rejected
out of hand. At no point has the Patriotic Front or SWAPO rejected discussion,
continued negotiation or possible compromise if essential demands are met.
Quite aside from their own goals, they are under tremendous pressure from the
Front-Line states, whose pragmatic interests necessarily are different from
those of liberation movements. Angola would like to be able to concentrate on
UNITA without having to deal with South Africa as well, a possibility that
would be enhanced by even a "moderate" solution in Namibia. Mozambique's
economy is struggling against dependency on South Africa, Rhodesian aggression
and severe organizational and technical problems. Support for the Zimbabwe
struggle is extraordinarily costly in money terms, in personal losses and in

destruction of infrastructure. Zambia has similar problems. Tanzania is
bone poor, dependent on western aid. Botswana is a hostage of the white states.
Under the circumstances, what is surprising is the unity and depth of commitment to liberation among the Front-Line states and not their understandable
prudence.

The foregoing analysis is not meant to support the view that if Zimbabwe
or Namibia were to become free soon, their economies would necessarily be
socialist. On the contrary, it is probably that the new states would retain
may present arrangements while attempting to gain a greater measure of control
over mineral resources, agricultural land and productive facilities. An yet
people, having taken up arms, or even rocks, to risk their own deaths in order
to be free will not meekly surrender the freedom, the camaraderie, the unity
and the vision that comes from persistence in a growing struggle that seeks
profound transformation of an inhuman system.

FOOTNOTES

1. See President Carter's press conference text, The Baltimore Sun, June 14, 1977.

2. U.S. Mission to the United Nations Press Release USUN 30 (77) May 27, 1977, Statement of Ambassador Young to South African businessmen, Johannesburg, South Africa, May 21, 1977.

3. See United Kingdom, Rhodesia, Proposals for a Settlement, with Annexes A, B and C. U.N. Security Council document A/12393, 1 September 1977, pp. 23, 24.

4. See Giovanni Arrighi, "Foreign Investment in Tropical Africa," in African Social Studies: a Radical Reader, edited by P. Gutkind and P. Waterman (N.Y.) 1977, pp. 168-69.

5. See Conference Report to accompany H. R. 6884, International Security Assistance Act of 1977, July 15, 1977. Report 95-503, pp. 23-25.

6. Zaire is also getting $20 million in foreign military credit sales and $2.5 million in military training.

7. See statement of Ambassador Young cited in footnote 2.

8. See Colin Leys, Underdevelopment in Kenya, (Berkeley), 1974, especially pp. 78-79, 83-98.

About the Author

Rene Lemarchand is Professor of Political Science at the University of Florida (Gainesville, Florida)' and a recognized authority on former Belgian Africa. His works include Political Awakening in the Former Belgian Congo: The Politics of Fragmentation (1964), Rwanda and Burundi (1970), and African Kingships in Perspective (Ed.) (1977). His work on Rwanda and Burundi earned him the Herskovits Award in 1971. Professor Lemarchand has contributed articles to American, British, French and Belgian professional journals, and was commissioned by the London-based Minority Rights Group to write a Report on Burundi in 1973. He was a Fellow at the Hoover Institution in 1973, and at the Truman Institute of the Hebrew University (Jerusalem) in 1976. He is currently writing a book on problems of dependency in Sub-Saharan Africa.